ALSO BY MICHAEL SHNAYERSON

The Killers Within:
The Deadly Rise of Drug-Resistant Bacteria
(with Mark Plotkin)

The Car That Could:
The Inside Story of GM's Revolutionary Electric Vehicle

Irwin Shaw: A Biography

COAL
RIVER

COAL RIVER

Michael Shnayerson

Farrar, Straus and Giroux   New York

Farrar, Straus and Giroux
18 West 18th Street, New York 10011

Distributed in Canada by Douglas & McIntyre, Ltd.
Printed in the United States of America
First edition, 2008

A portion of this book originally appeared, in somewhat different form,
in the May 2006 issue of *Vanity Fair*.

Library of Congress Cataloging-in-Publication Data
Shnayerson, Michael.
    Coal river / Michael Shnayerson.
        p.   cm.
    ISBN-13: 978-0-374-12514-1 (hardcover : alk. paper)
    ISBN-10: 0-374-12514-7 (hardcover : alk. paper)
    1. Coal mines and mining—West Virginia.   2. Coal mines and mining—
Environmental aspects—West Virginia.   3. Mountaintop removal mining—
Environmental aspects—West Virginia.   4. Mountaintop removal mining—
Economic aspects—West Virginia.   I. Title.

TN805.W4S56 2008
338.2'72409754—dc22   2007019264

www.fsgbooks.com

1   3   5   7   9   10   8   6   4   2

For Renée

CONTENTS

Prologue: A Valley Under Siege 3
One: The Tip-off from Tony 11
Two: A Brute Force Called Massey 19
Three: Fighting Back 36
Four: A Short-Lived Legal Victory 59
Five: Stacking the State Supreme Court 76
Six: The War with Washington 95
Seven: A School in Massey's Shadow 128
Eight: The Dead Souls of Smithers 146
Nine: Marching in the Valley 164
Ten: Massey's Unwelcome New Friend 183
Eleven: Don's Terrible Year 200
Twelve: Turning a Courtroom Loss Around 210
Thirteen: A Walk Through West Virginia 218
Fourteen: Back in Court Against the Corps 236
Fifteen: Don Goes for It All 261
Sixteen: A Ruling at Last 276
Epilogue: The View from Kayford Mountain 295

Notes 299
Acknowledgments 307
Index 309

COAL
RIVER

A VALLEY UNDER SIEGE

S omething looks very wrong with southern West Virginia.

Seen from a plane, its forested ridges lie below, stretching like waves into the misty distance. But there amid them, like cancerous growths, lie large gray splotches. They might be clearings for new subdivisions, if they weren't so remote. They might be a blight, except that there's nothing for a blight to infect: everything, from trees to grass, is gone. More than anything, they look like crop circles: mysterious signs made to be read from above. But made by whom? And signifying what?

On Interstate 77, running south from Charleston with its gold-domed capitol, the hills on either side of the highway rise and dip with not a tree out of place. No strange clearings here. In ten minutes comes the turnoff for Route 94 east and then, a short way farther, Route 3 south, the two-lane blacktop that snakes through the Coal River valley. No clearings here yet, either.

Soon the hills on either side move in, narrowing the sky to a slit. The road bobs down and up and down again, under canopies of trees and around hairpin curves. Then the trees recede, and the valley widens just enough to hold a scattering of small houses, sunlit at noon but soon shadowed by the steep hillside behind them. The houses are separated from Route 3 by a stream overlaid with wood-plank crossings, like drawbridges over a moat.

This is the heart of the Appalachian coalfields—not fields at all but rugged, forested hills that still hide billions of tons of coal. No shiny new McDonald's restaurants or Burger Kings punctuate Route 3's 56-mile passage from Racine south to Beckley. No hotels or motels; no Home Depots or Targets; no Applebee's restaurants or Olive Gardens or TGI Friday's. The Coal River valley is too steep for the malls and crossroads that could support such establishments. More to the point, it's too poor, and the coal companies own most of the land anyway. The residents of the Coal River valley are safe from the restless spread of franchise businesses of almost every kind. It's about all they *are* safe from.

In some ways, the valley confounds expectations. There are no tarpaper shacks, no miners in overalls with coal-smudged faces, no old jalopies. A few of the roadside houses have porches, but on none of them is an autistic mountain boy playing a banjo. The houses are wood or brick, neatly kept, and the pickup trucks that stop at the gas marts are mostly late-model American brands.

Yet coal's legacy, in the valley that bears its name, is everywhere. Nearly all the hamlets on Route 3 are old coal towns, named after the camps' founders—Edwight, Stickney, Pettus—or, as with Eunice and Dorothy, the founders' daughters. In the 1910s, when train tracks began to stretch like vines through the valley, coal operators put up company towns here almost overnight. That was when miners lived in slapped-together two-family cottages with no electricity or indoor plumbing. Those cottages are long gone, as are the company stores and the company scrip the miners were paid, instead of money, for their long hours underground. But the towns remain, in some semblance or another. Some are mere meadows, with a few remaining foundations turned to mossy mounds. Others are just clusters of houses without a store. A few have gas marts, and fewer still a second or third store that might qualify them as a proper American town.

So close in are the hillsides that a visitor might be forgiven for thinking, as he drives through, that he's seeing all the life there is to see here. Most residents of the valley live up the hollows that go off like ribs from Route 3's curving spine. The roads that wind up those hollows grow narrow and give way to dirt. The houses tucked into the nooks of those hollows are mostly hand-built. Some are cottages, and some are just shacks, and many of the inhabitants of those dwellings do speak in an Appalachian patois that mixes the accents of their

Scotch and Irish and English forebears. Some of them don't come down much, and if they do, they don't go much farther than the nearest town.

On Route 3, the first sign of mining in the valley is typically a coal truck that heaves into view. The road has no shoulder to speak of, and in places an outcropping of rock from the hillside extends just overhead, so that a car has only inches of leeway as the truck hurtles by. Coal-truck drivers are often paid by the haul, not by the hour, and so the faster they arrive at their destination, the sooner they can start their next haul. If they bear full loads and a car appears suddenly in front of them, the trucks can't always stop in time. The local papers announce coal-truck accidents with depressing frequency, usually with fatalities and pictures of a car or pickup crunched to smithereens.

Two miles north of Whitesville—roughly the valley's social midpoint—looms the next indication of mining in the valley. Fences and "Keep Out" signs surround an industrial site of drab, factorylike buildings and conveyor belts. This is a coal-preparation plant, not a mine. Coal from various mines is brought here, by belt and by truck, to be cleaned of debris, crushed into chunks or dust, and loaded onto trains for market. Massey Energy, the large, Virginia-based company that owns this operation, calls it Elk Run, after the elk that used to run here before it was built.

After the small, sleepy coal towns that line much of Route 3's northern stretch, Whitesville comes as a shock. Once it was a thriving town, the hub of commerce between Charleston and Beckley. Now it looks desolate, its storefronts abandoned, its streets and sidewalks still. Hardly a car rolls by or lingers at the curb; even the parking meters are gone. Aside from the gas marts at either end of town, few businesses of any kind remain: two are funeral homes, and two are florists that serve the funeral homes. West Virginia may rank forty-ninth in prosperity among America's fifty states, yielding only to Mississippi, but its citizens feel strongly about funeral flowers. At the valley's largest cemetery, almost every gravestone is decorated with a bouquet.

At Whitesville's south end, Route 3 crosses a set of train tracks. At least once a day, traffic backs up half a mile on each side as a loaded coal train, impossibly long, passes slowly, slowly by. For a moment or two after the train passes, Whitesville seems a boomtown once again, with bustling commerce. But then the road clears, and a silence settles back, sure as coal dust, over Whitesville's desolate Main Street.

For the industry, this *is* a boom. Prices have soared, and demand is keen. Coal trains traverse the valley day and night. Coal trucks race up and down Route 3. Barges piled high with coal go down the broad Kanawha River, to the northwest. Yet little of this wealth has trickled down the hillsides into the Coal River valley, as it did in earlier booms. Whitesville resembles a wartime town pillaged by an advancing army. In a way, that's what it is.

You have to get up to a ridgetop to see that army's path. The view from Larry Gibson's place will do just fine. Gibson lives on the top of Kayford Mountain, just east of Whitesville. His ancestors moved to the valley in the late 1700s and acquired five hundred acres of the mountaintop by wedding dowry in 1886. Twenty years later, a land-company agent from out of state gulled an illiterate forebear into marking his X on a contract that transferred most of the land for "one dollar and considerations." Almost everyone in the Coal River valley has a story like that. The Gibsons, unlike most families, managed to keep fifty acres at the top of the mountain. Gibson lives there still. His mountaintop is a little green island surrounded, as far as the eye can see, by brown, raw, devastated earth.

This is what lies behind the picturesque backdrop of roadside hills in the Coal River valley: mountains reduced to rubble by the practice the industry calls mountaintop mining and its critics call mountaintop removal. The landscape from Gibson's place is so much lower than his mountaintop compound that it's hard to imagine the forested ridges that rose here before. It's like a man-made Grand Canyon, except that the Grand Canyon teems with life, and this panorama has none—none except the men who work the distant dozers and huge-wheeled dump trucks, their motors a constant, hornetlike hum. An underground mine needs hundreds of miners, but a skeleton crew can handle a miles-wide mountaintop site, setting the blasts and operating the heavy machinery to push rubble into valley streams below. That's one reason Whitesville looks as desperate as it does. The coal industry is making a killing. The Coal River valley is just getting killed.

The coal companies have tried hard to buy Gibson out because, he says, Kayford Mountain has more than a dozen seams of coal, worth millions of dollars, directly under his property. Gibson has turned them down. They want him gone, too, because he still bears witness to what they're doing here. That's rare. The coal companies own or lease nearly all the land outside the valley towns—the legacy of similar land grabs one hundred years ago by out-of-state speculators—and for the most part they can gate their operations, keeping people a ridge or two away from their mountaintop sites. Gibson looks out and reports on every new ridgetop and valley destroyed in the Kayford area. His mountain-top compound, with its half-dozen shacks and family cemetery, is a vantage point for anyone from out of the area who wants to see what mountaintop mining is about.

Miners hate that, and they find ways to let Gibson know it. They've shot up his place when he was there; his trailer has the bullet holes to show for it. They've torched one of his cottages. They've shot one of his dogs and tried to hang another. They've driven his pickup off the road, tipping it into a ditch, and paused long enough to laugh at him trying to get out. Gibson keeps a growing list of all the acts of violence and vandalism committed against him and his property. Currently, it totals 118. The stress of these threats—and of making his mountain a cause—led his wife to leave him not long ago. Gibson says she told him that if he stopped fighting for the land, the marriage might survive. But the mountain is his heritage, he says. How can he walk away from that?

Kayford is just one of nearly a dozen large mountaintop-mining sites that ring the Coal River valley like numerals on a watch face. It's one of 229 surface mines in West Virginia, most amid these crenellated ridges of the Allegheny Plateau. Beyond southern West Virginia, the coalfields seep into three other states: eastern Kentucky, eastern Tennessee, and western Virginia. Hundreds of mountains in this region have been destroyed, reduced to half their heights, their ancient forest covers eradicated. The Environmental Protection Agency, even while sanctioning the practice, concluded in 2003 that more than 380,000 acres—all rich and uniquely diverse temperate forest—were destroyed between 1985 and 2001 as a result of mountaintop mining in Appalachia. Another way to put it, the EPA acknowledged, was that 3.4 percent of the land area of southern West Virginia, eastern Kentucky, western Virginia, and eastern Tennessee had been leveled or buried. That figure is probably more than 100,000 acres out of date by now. In those same sixteen years, the EPA estimated, more than 1,200 miles of valley streams were affected by mountaintop-mining waste. Of those, more than 700 miles were buried entirely. That figure is old now, too. Assuming the practice continues, the EPA suggested, more than 1.4 million acres will be destroyed before all the mountaintop coal in Appalachia is mined—in sum, almost as large an area as Delaware.

This would never happen in rural Connecticut, Maine, northern California, or other places where such devastation would stir outcry and people with money and power would stop it. But Appalachia is a land unto itself, cut off by its mountains from the east and Midwest. Its people are for the most part too poor and too cowed after a century of harsh treatment by King Coal to think they can stop their world from being blasted away.

The story of mountaintop mining—why it happens and what its consequences are—is still new to most Americans. They have no idea that their country's physical legacy—the purple mountain majesty that *is* America—is being destroyed at the rate of several ridgetops per week, the result of three million pounds of explosives set off every day. They remain oblivious to the fact that, along with the mountains, a mountain culture is being lost. The valley's Boone County is named for Daniel Boone, who traded ginseng and furs here with the Shawnees and Cherokees. There are Clays from Clay's Branch and Pettrys from Pettry's Bottom. There are Stovers and Cantleys and Jarrells and Webbs and Bonds, all descended from the valley's first pioneer families. Americans outside the Coal River valley move, on average, 11.7 times in their lives, often state to state and coast to coast. Here, nearly everyone traces his lineage in the valley back six or eight generations, some ten or twelve. That lineage is the braid of a mountain culture unique to these towns and hills. The valley has rich traditions of storytelling, quilting and woodcrafts, ramp feasts, home gardening and canning, moonshine stills, bluegrass music, and more. All that, along with the hills, is under siege today.

If Don Blankenship, chairman and CEO of Massey Energy, were asked why he blasts the mountains instead of mining underground, he would likely view the question as naïve. Massey—biggest, most aggressive, and most hated of the coal companies in this southern part of the state—has led the way in mountaintop mining because in the long run it's cheaper, much cheaper, than labor-intensive underground mining in many areas, especially the Coal River valley. Massey must compete with Arch, Peabody, and Consolidated, among other Appalachian coal companies, for its markets. All, in turn, must compete with the big open pits of Wyoming and other western states. And the United States must compete with China, where labor and life are cheap and environmental standards are low. Capitalism is just survival of the fittest, Don likes to say, and in this unforgiving market mountaintop mining is the only way for an Appalachian coal company to survive.

This is a story of great forces in America destroying America itself: the need for cheap fuel, even if it pollutes more than any other kind and puts the planet at risk; the need of the companies that mine coal to make profits, whatever the environmental cost; the brute force of the coal industry that buys political influence with campaign contributions, gets its own lobbyists put in charge of the state and federal agencies assigned to regulate it, and pushes for loopholes in laws it hasn't already broken. And looming over the industry, the greatest force of all: Wall Street.

Yet in the spring of 2004, when I made my own first visit to the Coal River valley, a few stubborn West Virginians were fighting those forces. One was a boyish-looking environmental lawyer from Charleston. Another was a coal miner's daughter and granddaughter, raised in a hollow outside Whitesville. With them were a few dozen locals who felt they had no choice but to fight the coal companies destroying their land and way of life. This ragtag band had none of the money and power of King Coal. But they had won some battles, and, for all the scorn Don Blankenship heaped upon them, they were about to win some more.

ONE

THE TIP-OFF FROM TONY

Night fell on the mountain where Tony Sears lived, but darkness never came.

From the valley below, a yellowish phosphorescent glow lit the hills on either side and beamed up into the southern West Virginia sky, obliterating the stars. On his porch, Tony could hear the trucks returning from the mines and groaning to a stop by the conveyor belt, and then the rumble of raw coal filling the belt's cars, and the grinding of the belt as the cars rode to the preparation plant. He couldn't see the men in the prep plant spray the raw coal with water and chemicals to free it of dirt and debris. He couldn't hear the coal get crushed to chunks or pulverized into dust. But he knew when the cleaned coal was loaded on trains, because the trains lurched off in the night to market, away from the always bright fenced site they called Green Valley.

Tony was used to all this, and there was nothing to be done, but he kept an eye on the growing number of pits where liquid waste from cleaning the coal was put. The pits looked like swimming pools, Tony thought—a lengthening row of swimming pools filled with toxic sludge. Beside them rose the piles of solid waste: the rock and dirt and debris from which the coal had been separated. Those piles rose all the time. So Tony wasn't surprised by the rumor he heard on Thursday, April 1, 2004, that Green Valley was about to start pushing debris into a nearby tributary of Hominy Creek. But he was mad.

Hominy Creek wasn't just any stream winding its way through a wooded Appalachian valley. It was one of the best native-reproducing brown-trout streams in southern West Virginia. Tony Sears loved that stream. At forty-three, he'd fished Hominy Creek his whole life. So had his father and grandfather for theirs. Many of Tony's neighbors in the forested hills and hollows of Nicholas County could trace their families back nine generations. Tony knew only as far back as four, but all four had lived in the family's wood-frame mountaintop house. And all four had fished Hominy Creek. Now, if the rumor was true, Green Valley was about to start burying the creek because the company had run out of storage space on site for its solid debris.

Once before, Tony had gone up against Green Valley. That time, he'd heard the company intended to dispose of some of its liquid waste by injecting it into nearby abandoned underground mines. Together with a few neighbors, he'd raced up to a meeting of the West Virginia Surface Mine Board to explain that those abandoned mines contained the underground stream that nearly one hundred people depended on for drinking water. He'd walked in to see a row of lawyers in suits and ties representing Massey Energy, the huge coal company based in Richmond, Virginia, that owned Green Valley, along with so many subsidiaries in the Appalachian states.

The chairman of the Surface Mine Board asked if both sides were ready to proceed. The Massey lawyers said they were. Tony raised his hand. He didn't have a lawyer. He and his neighbors were representing themselves. "You-all are dealing with lawyers and everything, we're poor people from the community," Tony said. "We've got to do our own legwork. . . . I can't really see how you-all can say that we should be as ready as you-all."

"There's four board members down here," the board chairman retorted, "and . . . about ten other people sitting across the table from you, that have scheduled this for today. Why didn't you tell us earlier that you needed more time?"

Tony began to feel his temper rise. "We have time, too, you know, we're taking out of our time also."

The chairman convened the hearing anyway. Massey's chief lawyer, Bob McLusky, explained that the engineers had done their work well. The slurry would be injected, at five hundred gallons per minute, into an abandoned mine across the valley from the one that had the underground stream Tony and his neighbors relied on for drinking water. So the stream would not be at risk. What was more, the slurry would be injected at an elevation fifty feet below it. The slurry would have to flow uphill and across the ridge to cause any problem. And everyone knew water didn't flow uphill.

"What are the chances," Tony asked, "of those two mines being connected?" The hills were catacombed with mines that might easily connect with one another at points no one now knew about. "I can't see how you can jeopardize all of our water and our livelihood," Tony said, "by relying on a map that's—what—fifty-eight years old."

On it went, sometimes comically: the lawyers cool and controlled, using technical and legal terms, Tony and his neighbors jumping up to say what they knew about their hills and old mines. Usually the Surface Mine Board sided with the coal operators. That was the way things worked in West Virginia. This time, though, it didn't. The board chairman ordered Massey to test the injection system with dye-colored water before putting slurry into it, given the risks that Tony and his neighbors had described. The slurry was designed to come out at two discharge points at the bottom of the hill. "If dye never comes out of those discharge points, then there'll be no slurry injection," the chairman said to the coal-company lawyers, "because it's not working the way you-all thought it was going to."

McLusky, the Massey lawyer, was stunned. "Well, to drill a hole for a five-hundred-gallon-a-minute discharge and a test is big bucks," he said weakly. "And then I find I can't use it, it's a half-million-dollar hit or so. We will have done the whole project and . . ."

Green Valley never did run that dye experiment for half a million dollars. Quietly, it abandoned its slurry-injection plan. A backcountry West Virginian and his neighbors had stood up to Charleston's highest-paid coal-company lawyers—and won.

This time, Tony was better prepared. He knew a lot more about Green Valley than he had before. And he knew a lawyer who could help.

The message light on Joe Lovett's phone was blinking when he reached the two-room office he kept in a small commercial building in Lewisburg, the genteel town of colonial-era brick buildings east of Beckley, where he lived. The Appalachian Center for the Economy and the Environment was, like other nonprofits on the L-shaped second floor, rather less grand than its name. Joe's room had two desks and a futon sofa. The adjacent room had a third desk for a part-time fund-raiser or summer intern. The rent was $250 a month.

Joe's office looked more like a college dormitory room than a lawyer's sanctum. The wood-paneled walls were bare but for posters of Louis Armstrong and Robert Frost. The scuffed wood desks were strewn with papers and topped by computers. On the lumpy futon lay scattered books that Joe might have just brought in from class: a collection of Frost's poems, Saul Bellow's *Herzog*, a book of gardening essays.

At forty-four, Joe still resembled a college student himself, with clean good looks, round, metal-framed glasses, a full head of brown hair cut boyishly short, and a lean, athletic build usually garbed in a denim shirt, chinos, and hiking shoes. He had a student's restlessness—he was always in motion—and yet when he plunged into writing a court motion he stayed grimly focused for hours, lacing his strong, clear sentences with the case histories and regulatory references that gave them legal heft. His one indulgence in the office, if it could be called that, was a straight-backed wooden rocker, like the one President Kennedy had favored in the Oval Office. Rocking as he fielded calls, he took in the news of each coal-company move with the saturnine humor of a battle-tested lieutenant whom the enemy could surprise but no longer astonish.

"Have they done anything yet?" Joe asked when Tony Sears passed on the rumor about Hominy Creek.

No, Tony said, not as far as he could see. As of that afternoon, no debris had been dumped in the stream.

Joe's first call was to the local office of the U.S. Army Corps of Engineers in Huntington. The Corps had no direct authority over mountaintop mining. It was, however, responsible for America's waters. Since mountaintop mining almost inevitably buried valley streams with debris, the Corps, to its deep and eternal regret, had been assigned under the Clean Water Act to be the watchdog for those streams. Specifically, it was charged with granting—or denying—permits to fill in those streams, based on how much environmental damage the projects would do. Army Corps engineers liked building bridges and dams. They liked to reroute water in the Everglades, then route it back again. That was manly work for Army engineers. Looking at plans for yet another mountaintop-mining site in Appalachia was a bore. When the

Clean Water Act had passed in its initial form in 1972, mountaintop mining was a novelty, practiced on a few small-scale sites. The engineers could handle that. Now the practice had exploded—literally—all over the coalfields, with vastly larger sites that often spread one to the next, contiguously, making things easier for the heavy equipment that scraped the mountaintop "overburden" away. More sites meant more streams filled in. That, in turn, meant more permits needed from the Corps. The Army Corps engineers, as far as Joe could tell, did little more than rubber-stamp the projects to get them off their desks.

Joe asked the bureaucrat he reached if the Corps had just granted Green Valley a permit for dumping debris in a tributary of Hominy Creek.

"Yep," came the reply.

The permit, granted ten days before, allowed Green Valley to fill in exactly 431 feet of the tributary with prep-plant waste, rock, and dirt. The debris would obliterate the stream and climb up the sides of the valley through which the tributary ran. The mining industry had a bland, almost soothing term for this procedure: a *valley fill*.

The permit that the Corps had issued Green Valley was called a Nationwide 21. The Corps issued this kind of permit when it found that the prospective fill would cause "minimal adverse" environmental effects. Because the effects were "minimal," no public notice was required.

"I thought Green Valley was going for an IP," Joe said grimly. He meant an individual permit, the kind that involved a lot more scrutiny by the Corps and public review as well. Coal companies hated going for IPs, but when they had big plans, they sometimes had no choice.

"This is for a much smaller area," the bureaucrat informed Joe. "That's why it qualified for a Nationwide 21."

Green Valley had pulled a fast one, Joe realized. Once again, he was surprised but not astonished.

The previous October, Joe had filed suit in a West Virginia federal court to try to stop the Corps from issuing Nationwide 21s at all. Mountaintop removal caused far more than "minimal adverse effects," he declared. So the Corps was violating the Clean Water Act—not to mention the National Environmental Policy Act—by using them to sanction valley fills and the massive destruction they brought.

At the time Joe filed his suit, Green Valley had applied for a Nationwide 21 to do far more than fill a tributary of Hominy Creek. The company proposed to dump twenty million tons of waste over 422 acres. The plan called for a large valley fill, along with an impound-ment. An impoundment was a huge dam, usually built against the crook of two hillsides, for storing liquid waste or slurry from cleaning coal. Some of the slurry sank to the bottom of the impoundment and hardened. The rest stayed on top as a toxic stew. From a low-flying plane, an impoundment looked like an alpine lake, except that lakes in the Alps are blue and the liquid in an impoundment is black. The more slurry was dumped into it, the higher an impoundment had to be built up the hillside, until its walls, made of coal waste themselves, reached the top of the ridge into which they were built. Many im-poundments contained hundreds of millions of gallons of slurry—quite a few contained billions.

When Joe had filed his lawsuit, Green Valley decided that maybe ap-plying for a Nationwide 21 for all that waste might not be prudent. Better to go for an individual permit. An IP might take a year rather than three months, but going that route would mean that the company would re-main unaffected by Joe's lawsuit. It wouldn't be stuck with a Nationwide 21 it couldn't use if Joe won. And even the Corps had to acknowledge that twenty million tons of waste dumped over 422 acres was a big project.

Why then had the Corps granted Green Valley a Nationwide 21 af-ter all? Because, the bureaucrat explained, this new application ap-plied only to the 431 linear feet of streambed that led into Hominy Creek. The Corps, an agency not known for lightning-quick responses, had authorized this work under Nationwide 21 in just eight days. With no public review, Green Valley would have filled in that stream before Joe found out about it—if Tony Sears hadn't lived right next door.

For the hardy few in West Virginia who took on the coal industry, a little paranoia came with the territory. Was it coincidence that a coal truck in one's rearview mirror was tailgating on a winding two-lane road? Was it just nerves to imagine that the long, deep scratch along the side of one's car was the work of a coal-company flunky, not a ran-dom vandal? Certainly it didn't take much paranoia for Joe to wonder if the Corps had colluded with Massey to help it fill a stream with solid waste. But that wasn't a question he could answer. All he could deter-mine was whether or not its action was legal.

That afternoon, Joe went on one of his twenty-five-mile bike rides from his office down the meandering Greenbriar River. It was a beau-tiful ride, past farms to a trail that cut through the woods, and it never failed to loosen the tension that came from being the state's most active environmental lawyer. Joe rode to stay fit—and he was—but he valued even more the chance biking gave him to think how to counter a new coal company threat.

Joe didn't get through to Bob McLusky until Friday morning. The coal company's lawyer had been traveling. He traveled a lot. His firm, JacksonKelly, had grown so wealthy representing Massey Energy and its many subsidiaries that it now kept private planes at the Charleston airport. If Massey's notorious chairman and CEO, Don Blankenship, wanted McLusky at Massey's corporate headquarters in Richmond in an hour, McLusky could get there.

"So, Bob," Joe said coolly, "can't your client wait until our suit is heard before filling in the stream?"

McLusky explained that the waste site was sorely needed. Green Valley had run out of space to store its solid debris. "We're going to start soon," McLusky said.

"Then I'm going to seek an injunction," Joe said. He would ask the judge in the Nationwide 21 suit for a temporary restraining order, or TRO, that would put a stop to the work. Then he added, as an afterthought, "Nothing's going to happen this weekend, right?"

No, McLusky said. Besides, the weather was supposed to be bad.

After Joe hung up, he called the chambers of U.S. District Judge Joseph R. Goodwin in Charleston. Joe spoke to the judge's clerk. "We need a hearing next week," Joe said. "We've got an emergency here."

That weekend in Lewisburg, Joe talked a lot on the phone to Jim Hecker, the Washington, D.C., environmental lawyer he'd worked with since first taking on the coal industry nearly eight years before. A decade older, more brooding and professorial than Joe, Jim had served as a mentor. At Trial Lawyers for Public Justice, where he worked, Jim had brought hundreds of citizens' suits based on the Clean Water Act. He hadn't known a thing about coal-mining law when Joe called him out of the blue in 1997. He'd never seen the coalfields of West Virginia. But he knew about public-interest law. He was also the only lawyer willing to answer Joe's questions and, eventually, to serve as co-counsel. He'd done it ever since.

Over the weekend, Joe studied Green Valley's freshly granted Nationwide 21 permit. Then he compared it to the broader individual permit that Green Valley was still seeking. That's when he saw what the company had done.

Green Valley had simply cut away part of its proposed 422-acre waste site and presented this smaller chunk—about sixty-seven acres— as a separate site, small enough to qualify for a Nationwide 21. The Corps had approved the idea. So had the West Virginia Department of Environmental Protection (DEP), which had to grant a state permit to go along with the federal one. But the Clean Water Act forbade what it called "segmenting": chopping a large proposed permit site into smaller ones so that the smaller ones could all be granted Nationwide 21s without public review.

By Sunday, Joe and Jim had e-mailed drafts of their motion for a TRO back and forth. When he needed a break, Joe went out to his orchard to check his apple trees and see what latest damage the deer had done. The orchard gave him more pleasure than anything except his wife, Gretchen, and his three sons: Ben, eight; David, four; and John, two. In his twenties, he'd spent two years working on an organic farm. Often, when the brutal power of the coal industry in West Virginia began to depress him, he contemplated farming again.

Over in Nicholas County that weekend, an hour's drive from Lewisburg but a world of culture away, Tony Sears edged down the hill behind his family homestead and toward the valley that Green Valley hoped to fill in. He heard the bulldozers before he saw them.

There they were, pushing debris into the streambed to turn this uppermost part of the stream—the headwaters—into a valley fill. Hour after hour, Tony watched the dozer operators work.

First thing Monday morning, Tony called Joe's office again.

"I don't believe it," Joe said. But he did. It wasn't the first time that a Massey operation had acted that way, and it wouldn't be the last. Massey liked to say that its subsidiaries, like Green Valley, were independent. But Don Blankenship had a reputation for signing off on every decision of consequence for the company's nineteen subsidiaries. Don Blankenship *was* Massey.

Joe had thought he'd present his motion for a TRO later in the week. Now there was no time to waste. As soon as he'd printed out a copy of it, he clattered down the long, steep wooden staircase of his office building and jumped into his Subaru station wagon for the ninety-minute drive to Charleston.

TWO

A BRUTE FORCE
CALLED MASSEY

O ther coal bosses lived out of state, Don Blankenship liked to say, in penthouses and horse-country mansions. Don still lived and worked down by the West Virginia/Kentucky border—a son of the coalfields who'd stayed close to home.

In some ways, that was true.

When he was overseeing Massey Energy operations that lay on the Kentucky side, Don worked out of a roadside trailer. Its offices were comfortable, but it was a trailer all the same. It reminded Don of his childhood home. When he left for the day, he drove himself home: just another workingman on the road, looking forward to putting his feet up. Behind the wheel, he looked less like a CEO than a salesman who traveled too much to exercise. His thinning, wispy dark hair framed a soft, doughy face with watery eyes, a meager mustache, and a weak chin. At fifty-four, he still had the flat twang of rural West Virginia, and his voice tended to trail off, as if he were too tired to finish his sentences.

But Don had two houses to choose from, one on each side of the border, and neither was a modest dwelling by Appalachian standards. The one in Kentucky commanded a forested hilltop. It stood alone in a clearing, a large wood construction with odd protrusions, ungainly as an ark marooned by the sudden subsiding of a biblical flood. The house in the hamlet of Sprigg, West Virginia, was architecturally more conventional: a handsome hillside Victorian with a wraparound porch, built for a mine boss almost a century ago and now owned by Massey. It was the grandest house in the valley then, and only grander now. In seeming recognition of his status as the most hated man in the state, Don had put a black wrought-iron fence around the perimeter of the property, its remote-controlled gates monitored by a surveillance camera. A long, straight driveway led up from the gate, passing a cascade of violently landscaped hillocks and little dales, like oversized moguls on a ski trail. As green as this slope appeared, its every grassy sweep and curve immaculately mowed, the house was greener still: lime green, set off by white trim. A visitor, arriving when its host was absent, would be greeted by a pack of sleek and formidable guard dogs, emerging from the house with bared teeth. A sullen groundskeeper would appear at the door of one of the property's other, smaller houses across the driveway. A succession of mine managers was said to live in these other houses, as much to keep Don company as to learn the business. The chairman of Massey didn't have many close friends. According to one political consultant who'd visited him, Don did have a vast collection of rare baseball cards and spent some of his fondest hours at home, alone, sifting through them.

Don liked to say he was probably the only Fortune 1000 chairman who lived in the same place he'd grown up—in the coal country, that is, that his company mined. But on many days, Don boarded a helicopter or plane. He flew to Charleston, where Massey had offices, and to Richmond, where the company kept its corporate headquarters. On Massey's Challenger 601 jet, Don flew to places far from coal country as well: Las Vegas, the Bahamas, Palm Beach, Los Angeles, Bar Harbor. In fine type, Massey's corporate documents noted that the Challenger was available for the chairman's personal use—just one indication of the near-absolute power that Don had come to wield.

Don had risen to that level of eminence not by luck and certainly not by nepotism. He was a micromanager with a brilliant mind for numbers and strategy. He knew the most minute details of every Massey mine, and in his quiet, unassuming way he was a ferocious competitor. During his twelve years as CEO and chairman, he had put Massey on a course of such aggressive growth that its coal reserves had doubled to more than two billion tons, larger than any Appalachian rival's. He had gobbled up small companies and more than doubled Massey's coal production, from twenty to forty million tons a year. When he'd gotten the top job, only 20 percent of Massey's coal came from mountaintop mines, the rest from underground. Now nearly half of it did.

As chairman, president, and CEO of Massey Energy, Don had transformed the company's culture. Once, Massey had been a family-owned coal company like any other. Now it was a harsh enterprise, not just in the way it blew up mountains but also in how it treated its people. It had a personality, and anyone in West Virginia could tick off its traits: ruthless, relentless, and very aggressive. They were the traits of the man who had remade the company in his own image.

Some sense of that company culture could be seen every afternoon outside Massey's fenced and guarded compounds in the Coal River valley. Weary Massey workers stopped on their way home at the local gas marts, loading up on beer and cigarettes. They were easy to recognize in their blue denim coveralls with large iridescent red stripes on each arm. The stripes were a safety measure; they shone in dark tunnels when a light played on them. But they also lent the coveralls a military snap, as if the miners were infantrymen.

A red striper on his own might linger to gossip with an old schoolmate behind the counter, but groups of two or more stood apart, speaking in low voices, if they spoke at all. They'd been taught not to fraternize with civilians, and they knew what would happen if one of them did: the others might report him to the boss, and he could lose his job tomorrow. At work, it was said, the miners were encouraged to be "team players," which meant ratting on anyone who seemed to be slacking off or acting disloyal. Massey men learned to be wary even of what they said to their wives—best just to say they were tired when they got home and to ask what was on TV.

A lot of red stripers now came from out of state, as their license plates indicated, and had long drives home. That was partly because the coal boom had attracted workers from farther away. It was also because a lot of local sons were blackballed: Massey knew which local families were union sympathizers from generations back. More and more of those out-of-state workers wore red safety helmets indicating that they were novices who had to be supervised by more experienced men. The more red hats there were on a job site, the greater chance there was of something going very wrong.

At some Massey subsidiaries, the men worked eight-hour shifts. But at some, they put in twelve-hour shifts. That way, the company could keep its mines going twenty-four hours a day but pay health benefits to only two shifts of men, not three. How long they worked was up to their boss, though, and sometimes he surprised them. He might say, "I need you to work more," and when he did, the workers he'd asked had to stay. One local man said that his son worked at Massey sometimes sixteen to eighteen hours before he was allowed home. You worked that next shift, he said, because if you didn't there was no need to show up the next day: you were out of a job. Sometimes, the father said, his son worked seven days per week: "You don't have no life. All you got's a job." Managers often had it worse than the men under them. A former Massey man said he'd seen managers work twenty-four hours at a stretch. Almost everyone, it seemed, had a story of someone who'd fallen asleep at the wheel on his way home from a Massey mine and driven into an outcropping of rock on Route 3, or worse.

All these were clues to be gleaned from watching and listening outside the mine-site gates. An inside look at Massey was harder to come by. The company rarely let outsiders onto its job sites, and few miners who still worked for Massey would talk. Occasionally, though, an injured miner would sue Massey for workman's compensation benefits he felt the company had wrongly denied him. Men who did that tended to have a strong sense of right and wrong. They weren't easily intimidated. And when they brought their cases to court, they no longer had anything to lose by speaking out. So it was with Jerry Shelton and Rick Wagner, two miners who'd sued the company and forced it to settle. Both had seen firsthand what happened to working conditions when Massey took over a site. And both had seen Don Blankenship up close, managing his men with all the traits for which his company had come to be known. Their stories had to be taken as what they were: accounts of two men angry enough at the company to sue it. But both were willing to speak on the record about everything they said had happened to them.

Jerry Shelton was forty-four and married, with children in high school and college, when Massey bought Montcoal, a mine complex just south of Whitesville, from Peabody Coal in early 1993. Montcoal was a union operation. Ordinarily, Don Blankenship would have shut it down for a year, let the union contract expire, then reopened the mines as nonunion. At Montcoal, most of the miners were initially let go, and most production stopped. But in a concession to the United Mine Workers of America, Massey agreed that as it ramped up new mines on the site, renamed Performance, two of every three men it hired back would be ex-union members. Theoretically, that would give the union a silent two-thirds majority. Whenever a majority of mine workers called for an election to decide if a mine should join the UMWA, their company was bound by law to hold it. At Performance, the UMWA thought it had the votes to win that prospective election. Don Blankenship had his own ideas.

Jerry was one of the Peabody workers kept on in a skeleton crew. For six months, he helped finish an underground mine that was nearly cleaned out. Then he started in on the first new mine. Massey called it Upper Big Branch.

The new mine was just a pristine stretch of hillside when the first fifteen men began to work it on a cold November day: ten union men, including Jerry, and five nonunion Massey men from other sites. A Massey manager addressed the men like he was a drill sergeant. "This is a Massey mine," he declared. "So forget everything you ever knew about coal mining. Massey does it different."

Jerry was intrigued. He thought, *Lord, how can they do this different? I've done it for twenty-five years.* Soon enough, he saw that Massey's method wasn't any different. What was different was the pressure put on the men. It was *more, more, faster, faster.* The miners were bullied by their managers, and the managers were bullied by higher-ups, and the higher-ups were bullied by the CEO.

Jerry's first boss broke down by Christmas. The men had bought him a little Christmas gift, but he never came back to receive it. A new boss came from somewhere else, and the men, including Jerry, worked harder still. More than once after that, Jerry saw a manager off on his own, apparently wrestling with his thoughts, holding back tears.

Upper Big Branch was what the industry called a longwall mine. It was the modern version of an underground mine. Instead of men with pickaxes, powerful machines called "continuous miners" chewed into the hill's coal seam with large churning blades, creating thousand-foot-wide tunnels. The men then excavated the long wall of coal between the tunnels, using a metal-toothed machine that looked like a giant armadillo. At this early stage, as they dug the first tunnels, the men hauled the coal out themselves. By spring, they had punched four or five parallel tunnels, or "rooms," into the hill. One hundred feet in, they cut a crosswise tunnel so the rooms were linked and the network could be ventilated. With that, belt lines were laid down, and a steady flow of coal began emerging from the hill.

Now the work became more mechanized. With great relief, Jerry became a shuttle-car operator. Then one day a notice was posted: the workforce was being realigned. Massey men would now operate the machines. The union men—most, like Jerry, in their forties or older—were put on what Massey called the construction crew. This was hard, dirty manual work, installing new belt lines in tunnels filled knee-high with water. Worse, it was nonunion. If Jerry took his new assignment, he'd lose his union card and half his union pension. If he refused, he'd have no job at all. He had three days to make his choice—too little time to get the union to help. Grimly, he and the other men on the list took the jobs. They could still vote union, they reasoned, when an election was held.

One by one, the men on Upper Big Branch's construction crew collapsed. They didn't die, but their health broke, and they had to quit. Jerry was one of the few to avoid that fate. He did it by learning how to operate a new, computer-driven belt line that was too complex for the Massey men to master. The first time the belt malfunctioned, bringing the mine to a halt, Jerry was the one who fixed it. With that, he was yanked from the construction crew and put in charge of the belt-drive system. It was a critical job, because thousands of dollars would be lost every minute the belt line was down. Suddenly, Jerry found himself well treated, not just by Massey's managers but by Don Blankenship himself.

Two years after Massey's takeover, about ninety men were working Upper Big Branch. That was when a majority of them—the two thirds whom everyone knew were former union members—called for an election. The outcome seemed inevitable, but not to Don Blankenship. He decided to make the election a personal crusade. In the fall of 1995, he began flying in by helicopter to preside at closed-door meetings. There were meetings for nonunion Massey workers to be sure they all still knew how much better off they'd be without a union. There were meetings, too, for the stubborn union majority, to try to change a few minds. Because of his new job, Jerry found himself sorted into the nonunion Massey group. At the first meeting, Don Blankenship showed graphs of how much more money the men would make as nonunion Massey miners, including bonuses. Politely, Jerry raised his hand. "You've been promising these bonuses since we started," he said. "But we've never received but one, for forty dollars. How do you explain that?"

Don glowered at him, then looked hard at the managers beside him. How had they allowed this union man in? Then he tried to explain that the more the men worked, the more money they'd make. "So your message is the more hours you put in, the more you make," Jerry said. "Well, anyone knows that."

Don went on to talk up Massey's retirement benefits. Once again, Jerry spoke up. "I can't think of a man on the Coal River who's retired from Massey," he said. "I don't see any old men." There were, to be sure, a few miners who'd retired from Massey to claim those benefits. But most older miners that Jerry knew had been fired on a pretext when their strength began to fade. And why, Jerry asked, should he vote nonunion when Massey provided no retirement health benefits? Don looked right at him and said, "Jerry, if you save your money the way I do, you can buy your own health insurance."

Jerry was amazed. "Don, what kind of world are you living in?" he asked. "If we had three million salary a year like you do, we could buy our own health insurance, absolutely. But everyone I know in coal mining, it's payday to payday just to survive."

After that, Jerry was kept out of the meetings for Massey men. He'd thought he'd had his last conversation with Don Blankenship. But he was wrong. When the votes from the December 1995 election were tallied, the result, remarkably, was a tie: 46–46. A year passed, and then a second election was scheduled, for May 15, 1997. Now the full-court press began.

One day, the mine's top manager told Jerry that Mr. Blankenship was flying in and wanted to stop by Jerry's workstation for a lunchtime chat. "Well, I'm not hard to find," Jerry replied.

"Be sure you address him as Mr. Blankenship," the manager warned.

"If he calls me Mr. Shelton, I'll call him Mr. Blankenship," Jerry said.

Lunchtime was just a figure of speech at Massey: the men were expected to eat while working. So Jerry decided to have a little fun. At the appointed hour, he got down from his belt-line station, unwrapped his sandwich, and began to eat in a leisurely fashion. He hadn't taken more than a few bites when a phalanx of Massey managers, in bright new red-striped coveralls, appeared beside him, poised protectively around Massey's chairman. "Mr. Blankenship would like to talk with you," the top manager said.

"Hiya, Redwing," Don said. "How are you?"

"I'm doing pretty good, Don, how are you doing?"

"Redwing" was Jerry's CB-radio handle. Someone had passed this information on to the chairman, along with the fact that Jerry's son was quarterback of the local high school football team. Don asked after the boy, talking football with a frozen smile. Jerry had never in his life seen a boss so uncomfortable with his employees. Not long after, Jerry received a Christmas card personally inscribed by Don. "Dear Redwing," the card read, "have a happy holiday. We're glad you're working with us!"

The union vote was five months away.

Jerry was a miner who'd bootstrapped up to a managerial job. Rick Wagner, who also fixed computerized systems at Upper Big Branch, was a full-fledged manager. He was paid a salary, not an hourly wage. The two men couldn't have been more different. Jerry, like many valley folk, was friendly but reserved at first and deeply religious, though he didn't advertise his faith or proselytize. Rick, a decade younger, was brash and gregarious, almost certainly a class clown in high school— he'd gone to Marsh Fork High School, in Whitesville, and grown up in the nearby town of Arnett—and even now quick with a grin and a quip. Perhaps the swagger was compensation for his modest height, but it was also the sign of a man who knew he was smarter than most of his peers. Hiring him would come to seem a serious mistake to Massey, for Rick wasn't easily cowed.

Soon after he joined Massey at another work site, Rick's boss ushered him into his office and closed the door. "Is Grover putting out
enough?" the boss asked Rick of one of his coworkers.

"What do you mean?"

"I mean, is he sandbagging me?"

Rick put his hands up in bafflement. "I think you need to talk to
him yourself."

The boss scowled. "I don't think you're a team player, Wagner," he
said. "I'm going to be watching you."

Rick was transferred to Upper Big Branch after the first union
vote, and at first he felt pretty pleased. His work wasn't physically
stressful, and Massey seemed remarkably generous. Rick got Christmas presents and bonuses, expensive jackets and work gloves. Not
only that: the company put everyone on buses to Nashville for an all-
expenses-paid vacation to hear country-music stars. And then another
trip to Dollywood in Pigeon Forge, Tennessee. And then a *third* trip to
the Busch Gardens adventure park in Williamsburg, Virginia. Don
Blankenship flew in for each gathering to give a speech about how well
Massey took care of its own.

Jerry Shelton was no longer invited to the pep meetings of Massey
managers for Upper Big Branch, but Rick Wagner was. And there, presiding at most of those meetings, was Don Blankenship. He advised the
managers not to tell the men the mine would shut down if they voted to
go union. But the managers *could* say, "We'll have to make cuts." Separately, Don met with the managers' wives and told them how much better off they'd be if their husbands voted for Massey in May.

Jerry Shelton observed that a number of men who seemed on the
fence about how to vote began coming to work in new cars and began
building new homes. Massey recruited some ex-union members to
make videos urging a vote against the union. Jerry noticed that those
men began driving new cars, too. When he confronted one of them,
the man looked away. "I have to take care of my family," he said.

The second election went just as Massey hoped: the company won
by eleven votes. Upper Big Branch was now a nonunion Massey subsidiary. And that was when everything changed.

Rick, for one, saw his bonuses cut in half, even though production
was stepped up by 70 percent, and, like his coworkers, he was forced

to start working much longer hours. When he asked his boss about time off, his boss replied, "When you need a day off, I'll let you know." If he'd gotten overtime, Rick might not have minded the killing hours, at least for a while. But he didn't, because Massey withheld it. At a production meeting, Rick asked how bonuses could be cut when production was up. The reason, he was told, was that "the more coal you carry, the more they reject."

"Wait a minute," Rick said. "That doesn't seem right. The same *percentage* of coal is going to be rejected whether it's a little coal or a lot, right? And here we are, mining one and a half tons of coal each month." Massey had a different logic.

Don didn't come to the mine for monthly meetings anymore, but his presence was keenly felt. In the Upper Big Branch office, there was a special red phone on the desk. It was the hotline to the boss, who'd let it be known he liked to be called "Mr. B." Frequently and without fail, the manager on duty had to fax a production update to Massey's chairman. If the report was late, or the numbers weren't good, or the mine was shut down for any reason, the red phone would ring. The terrified manager would pick it up to hear Mr. B himself demanding to know why the numbers weren't right.

One night, Rick was in the office when the red phone rang. A buddy of his named Greg was the new office manager for the midnight shift. Eyes wide, Greg looked at the phone as it rang. "You better answer it," Rick said. Greg answered it.

Mr. B was on the line, annoyed it had taken Greg more than one ring to answer. He asked who Greg was and how long he'd been on the job. From his questions, Greg got the sense Don was trying to determine if Greg had voted for the union. In fact, he had. Finally, Don said, "No matter what happens, don't hang up on me."

There was a click on the line, and Don vanished. Greg held the phone until he heard loud beeps and then a recording: "If you'd like to make a call . . ."

Greg turned to Rick. "What should I do?"

"Well, you better hang up," Rick said, "because that's the only way he can call you back."

Greg hung up.

One minute later, the red phone rang again. Greg answered it. Rick watched his friend's face turn white.

"What did he say?" Rick asked when Greg had gingerly cradled the phone.

"He said the only way he could call was because I hung up," Greg croaked. "So I was doing exactly what he'd said not to do."

Greg was fired eventually, though not before a number of other men known to have cast their votes for the union in the second election. As the union men got pushed out, contract miners—temps—took their jobs. All too often, their inexperience led to trouble. One night on the evening shift, part of a mine wall fell, killing a man. Word was relayed to the office, where Rick was sitting with Greg. Greg shut down the belt line, which was standard procedure: production was halted, and all the men on shift came out in deference to the dead man being taken away. Traditionally, the men also donated their shift pay to the dead miner's family, and the company matched it. But that didn't happen this time at Upper Big Branch. Into the office, Rick recalled, stormed the mine's managers to chew Greg out. "He was just a contract worker," one manager bellowed. "You don't need to shut the belts off. If you do that again, you'll be fired." At the mine mouth, where the men had gathered, the manager declared, "I can understand you being concerned about a man being killed. But he was a contractor, he had nothing to do with coal production, so let's go back to work."

That fall, Rick was hurt in a mining accident. Five of his spinal discs were herniated, and he broke a hand. He knew exactly what to expect: Don Blankenship had made that clear in one of the closed-door meetings before the vote. Massey's chairman had stressed to the managers that he didn't want workers taking time off for injuries because the company's premiums for workman's compensation insurance would go up. Injured workers were to come in to work and sit in the bathhouse until they recovered. Injuries were the bane of the business, Don went on, and the older a worker got, the more of an injury risk he was. That was why he wanted the managers to hire and train all the younger workers they could. Rick remembered Don saying his goal was to get the average age of Massey's workers down to twenty-five by 2004. There was a saying around Massey: "A man is like a tool. If it's bent or broke, get rid of it, and get you a new one."

At first, Rick tried to tough it out. When his back pain persisted, he went for free treatment to a doctor recommended by Massey. The doctor was a busy man, overworked. He diagnosed Rick's ailment as a herniated disc before thinking to ask where Rick worked. When Rick told him, the doctor went off to make a phone call. "The company will take care of you," he said upon his return. Back at Upper Big Branch, Rick's boss didn't let him sit out one day. He had to get right back to work.

Right after Thanksgiving, one of the managers at Upper Big Branch announced a big production push for the Christmas season. "It would not please Don Blankenship more than to give each man one thousand dollars at Christmas for breaking the world record on longwall mining," the manager said. The men gave a cheer and proceeded to do just that, working like dogs, day after day. When they gathered for the company Christmas party, though, no bonuses materialized. An angry muttering rose, until some of the men confronted the manager. "What about the thousand dollars we were promised?"

"No one made that statement," the manager shot back.

"Yes, you did," Rick said.

"No—I said, 'It would not please Don Blankenship more than to give each man one thousand dollars for breaking the world record.' It would *please* Don Blankenship to do that. But I didn't say you were getting the money."

Jerry Shelton didn't make it to that Christmas party. In November, a big spool of cable had fallen on him, and he'd started months of surgery to try to regain the use of his arms. When he recovered enough to return for light work, he was told he could no longer perform his duty, and so he was fired. That was when he sought out a labor lawyer and eventually forced Massey to settle.

Rick Wagner lasted nearly two years longer. When a second injury left him with three herniated discs in his neck, he kept working but applied for disability. One of his bosses took note of that. "You'll be sitting pretty good if you get total disability," the manager said. "You'll get half your salary for the rest of your life."

Not long after, Rick was fired. One of Don Blankenship's new young managerial recruits, barely twenty-one years old, called Rick in to explain the reason: he'd missed three days of work. Rick pointed out that those were his days off. "But we needed you," the young manager said, "and we couldn't find you." Rick pointed out that he had a landline phone, a cell phone, a fax machine, and an e-mail account. He hadn't heard from anyone at work. The managers were insistent: Rick had missed work.

Rick, too, sought out a labor lawyer and brought his case to the state labor board. He said that, at the least, he should get the overtime pay that was due him, along with severance pay. Massey's lawyers delayed the case with motion after motion, until the judge grew furious and refused to grant another postponement. After damning testimony that left little doubt Rick would win, Massey's lawyers made amiable conversation with Rick's lawyer during a break. "We're not mad," one of them told her. "This is just what we have to do. There are fifty or sixty other cases where we do win, and that's what we go through this for."

Rick won his overtime and severance and went to work as the manager of a Cracker Barrel restaurant. Some time later, he got a call from the personnel director of Massey's Marfork subsidiary, not far from Upper Big Branch in the Coal River valley. The personnel director said that Marfork was putting in a new longwall mine, and he'd heard that Rick was a good computer technician. Would he like to come in for a job interview?

Rick called his lawyer. "What should I do?" he asked.

"You'd better go in," the lawyer advised him. "It could be a trick."

So Rick went in to see the personnel director and, after some talk about the job opening, mentioned that the director might not want to hire him. "Why's that?" the director asked, perplexed. Rick pointed out that he'd worked at Upper Big Branch. The director turned to his computer and punched in Rick's name. "Oh . . ." he said. "You're *that* Rick Wagner."

Behind his desk, Don Blankenship kept an old Zenith television, circa 1984, with a bullet hole in its screen. It was a trophy of sorts, from the union battle that had made his reputation and shaped his attitude toward the United Mine Workers of America. Before that battle, Blankenship had been a young middle manager at A. T. Massey who, with his soft features and coalfield twang, had made a poor first impression. After that battle, he was E. Morgan Massey's heir apparent, on his way to being the state's most powerful coal baron. He was admired by some as a maverick, feared and hated by most as a man who, in the words of UMWA president Cecil Roberts, caused more suffering to more people in the Appalachian region than any human being Roberts could think of.

Massey had first taken on the union in 1981, a year before Don became an accountant at a subsidiary called Rawl Sales, down by the West Virginia/Kentucky border, close to the house in Sprigg where he was to live one day. The company was still A. T. Massey & Co. then, owned by the Fluor Corporation. Don's prospective bosses decided a new Massey operation in the Coal River valley at Sylvester, just north of Whitesville, would be nonunion—and that was that.

Massey knew it was asking for trouble, and so it situated the Elk Run site accordingly. Like a castle protected by a moat, the new plant hugged the west side of the valley, with the Coal River between it and Route 3. A guarded bridge provided the only access. Set into the bluff on Massey's side of the bridge was a concrete bunker. Later, union protesters at the site swore that three machine guns had been installed in the bunker and aimed at them. Later, locals also swore that Massey men with submachine guns were camped on the opposite hillside, and that a bulletproof truck with a machine gun inside it was used to escort the managers to and from the plant.

Whatever the truth of those stories, the union staged angry protests outside the gates. Union members hurled insults at the nonunion workers driving in. At some point, shots were fired, and a Massey worker was killed. With that, a judge slapped the UMWA with an injunction. If union protesters assembled again within a certain distance of the Elk Run plant, the UMWA would face a five-million-dollar fine. The battle of Elk Run was over, and Massey had secured the first of its many union-free mining operations in the Coal River valley.

Three years later, Massey went further. It told the UMWA that its various mine operations were all separate companies; the union would have to negotiate with each one individually. The Massey Doctrine, as it was called, was clearly meant to neuter the union, since the parent company could simply shut down one of its many subsidiaries, let the clock run out on its union contract, and start it up again as a nonunion shop. And if different subsidiaries won different terms, as they almost certainly would, workers at one would resent workers at another and start to resent the UMWA.

The man behind the doctrine was E. Morgan Massey, whose father, Antonio, had founded A. T. Massey in 1920 as a coal brokerage—a middleman between the mostly small operations that produced coal in those days and the big-city markets. E. Morgan Massey was a patrician figure, with silver hair, a kindly face, and very proper manners, but he was tougher than he looked. It was he who had decided to challenge the union at Elk Run—"it happened on my watch," as he put it proudly, years later—and it was he who had seen the usefulness of the Massey Doctrine. By establishing subsidiaries, Massey could keep the thickest, easiest-to-mine coal seams for itself and transfer the leftovers to nominally outside contractors. The contractors were often underfunded and inexperienced. That led to accidents and spills and an ever-lengthening record of violations. But Massey could wash its hands of those accidents and violations and also claim that it owed no payments to the state workers' compensation fund. The subsidiaries were responsible for the payments, Massey said. That the subsidiaries often neglected to make those payments was nothing the parent company could help—even though, as the company declared, Massey wholly owned those subsidiaries.

To the UMWA, the Massey Doctrine was a declaration of war. The union miners staged angry, ongoing protests. One of their targets was Elk Run. Another was Rawl Sales in Mingo County, the Massey subsidiary then presided over by thirty-four-year-old Don Blankenship.

Rawl Sales lay on the Tug Fork of the Big Sandy River. Just down the road was Matewan, where on May 19, 1920, a local police chief had sided with miners in a standoff that led to ten deaths, mostly of private security guards hired by the coal companies. The violence led to the Battle of Blair Mountain, where ten thousand men marched on a stronghold of guards, firing thousands of shots before President Harding sent in federal troops and military planes to drop bombs. The miners lost that fight but made the nation aware of their brutal working conditions. That led President Roosevelt, more than a decade later, to legalize union organizing.

Don had grown up just down the road from Matewan, but he was fuzzy on union history. As an accountant he was better—much better—with numbers. He saw the union the way E. Morgan Massey saw it: as a drag on profitability. When the strike began in the fall of 1984, he posted hundreds of private security guards at all of Rawl's mines. According to a version of events put forth years later in a class-action lawsuit brought by a disgruntled shareholder, the guards acted as provocateurs, harassing the miners until they retaliated. The guards filmed the ensuing violence and passed the footage on to local television stations. When Don kept Rawl going with nonunion workers from Kentucky, the union miners, he later recounted, tried to kill him. Shots, he said, were fired at his armored car, more than once while he was in it. Over the fifteen months of the strike, three of the cars were destroyed. Striking miners wielded baseball bats at the company gates; they formed blockades to keep nonunion drivers from making deliveries; a few took to the trees as snipers, killing one driver and wounding others. As a precaution, Don never slept in the same bed more than two nights in a row. One day, he said later, eleven shots were fired into his office while he was in it. That was when the television sustained its hit. Don dove to the floor and was fine. Finally, in December 1985, the union leaders caved. After decades of union rule in the valley, the coal bosses were in charge again.

Don had proved his mettle during the union siege, and as E. Morgan Massey noted approvingly, the young manager had a mind for the business. Don became president, then chairman in 1992. He seemed to take a grim satisfaction, through the 1990s, in buying up union mines and taking them nonunion. Massey swelled until it was the fourth-largest coal company in the country. As it did, it operated more and more mountaintop mines.

Other coal companies did mountaintop mining, too: Consol for one, Peabody for another, Arch for a third. But no one did it as aggressively as Massey or as recklessly. West Virginia's DEP, a timid watchdog at best, still managed to issue more than seven hundred violations per year, on average, to Massey's operations. Arch Coal averaged about 120 violations per year by comparison, while Peabody averaged about sixty. Far more serious was a pattern of three violations over time for the same problem. Then the DEP might summon the offender to a show-cause hearing—to show cause why it shouldn't have its permit revoked. Massey averaged about twenty show-cause hearings per year, compared to three for Arch and none for Peabody.

As public outcry about Massey operations grew, Don seemed to enjoy his growing notoriety. Yet beneath the swagger, he had reason to worry. Massey might be the largest coal company in Appalachia, but it wasn't the most profitable, not by a long shot. Somehow, the anticipated economies of scale hadn't yielded many profits. Nor had Fluor's decision in 2000 to spin off A. T. Massey as a separate company, the publicly traded Massey Energy. The company had lost $30 million in 2002 and $40.2 million in 2003, even as Don earned at least $10 million each year in salary, stock, and perks. Now that the latest coal boom had taken off in earnest, Don could report that Massey had earned money at last: $12.6 million in the second quarter of 2004. But that was Massey's first profitable quarter since 2001. If Don wanted Massey to be viewed as a darling on Wall Street—and he did—the price of coal would have to keep going up, and Massey would have to blast a lot more mountains to feed that hungry market.

THREE

FIGHTING BACK

Judy Bonds had just managed to annoy Don Blankenship again. The two had never met, but Judy was definitely an irritant. From a corner storefront in Whitesville, she railed against Massey's chairman and the mountaintop mining his company did—and got heard around the state. She had none of Don's money or political clout, yet she bulled her way into the governor's office and made him listen to her latest complaints. The scrappy band of locals she led, called Coal River Mountain Watch, was no match for Appalachia's largest coal company. Yet their grass roots were strong—less like grass than like the ironweed that served as a symbol for Appalachian women because it grew almost anywhere along the road, all but indestructible, with roots deep in the soil.

Local roots were exactly what Joe Lovett had needed for his Nationwide 21 suit. A lawyer couldn't bring a suit without a client. He needed plaintiffs with standing: locals who could demonstrate to a court that the mountaintop mining sanctioned by the U.S. Army Corps of Engineers was ruining the land they looked out on and experienced as their own. He'd called Judy, and now CRMW was a plaintiff in the case. Judy needed Joe as much as he needed her: to get anywhere, sooner or later grassroots activists had to take their fights to court. Now, with Joe's latest suit about to be heard, he and Judy had their best chance yet to stop new mountaintop mining, on all the latest sites sanctioned by Nationwide 21 permits.

Short and solid in her early fifties, Judy bristled with passion. At her house overlooking Marsh Fork Creek up the valley, she could be warm, even tender. She had a round face that lit up when she smiled, and teasing, shoe-button eyes. But when she took on state officials or spineless politicians, those dark eyes snapped with rage, and her West Virginia twang turned hard and biting. She had some Cherokee in her blood—a lot of valley dwellers whose heritage traced to colonial times did—and when she was mad, she was a warrior. The joke at Massey was that Judy needed "anger management." Perhaps sometimes she went too far. But being nice to coal companies as they blasted your mountains, Judy felt, wasn't apt to get you anywhere at all.

Judy in action was a sight to behold. One day in the summer of 2004, she and a carload of activists from CRMW drove down to confront the good gentlemen and ladies of the West Virginia legislature. West Virginia's lawmakers met at the gold-domed capitol building in Charleston just sixty days per year, starting in January and ending in April. To help keep the state's business on track the rest of the year, they met monthly in summer, rubbing shoulders, when they did, with lobbyists who gently pointed out what industry's latest needs were. In deference to summer, the venue was a landscaped conference center an hour's drive south of Charleston, where the lawmakers could end their deliberations with a round of golf or shooting clays.

Amid the lawmakers and lobbyists in suits and ties that day, Judy and her companions stood out: they wore jeans and short-sleeved shirts. Unabashed, they filed into a meeting on flood control and sat quietly at the back of the large room. Floods, as one agency official after another confirmed to the lawmakers, were a huge and growing problem in the southern part of West Virginia. On a summer Sunday in 2001, the worst flood in memory had wiped out 3,500 homes and killed two people in the coalfields. Now every time it rained, it was said, children slept fully clothed, terrified their homes would be swept away. More than four thousand residents in various counties and watersheds had joined in filing a veritable flood of lawsuits, claiming that mountaintop mining led to unnatural rainfall surges, which deluged the valleys. Like so many lawsuits filed against King Coal, these would eventually be quashed on the usual grounds: not enough proof that the coal companies were to blame.

The officials, two of whom were from the Army Corps, suggested one reason the flooding had worsened was that residents threw trash in the streams, everything from tires to refrigerators. When it rained, the streams overflowed. Timbering was another reason. When ridgetops and mountainsides were clear-cut, rains swept soil into the streams below, and the streambeds rose with silt until they had to be dredged at great cost to the state and federal government.

At no point did any of the officials mention that another cause of flooding might be mountaintop coal mining.

Finally, the moderator opened the floor to questions. Judy stood up. "My name," she said in a clear, ringing voice, "is Judy Bonds, and I represent Coal River Mountain Watch."

The officials grimaced and exchanged looks.

"Flooding is happening more and more in the coalfields," Judy declared. "There's more rain in the eastern part of the state than here, and yet the flooding is here. Why? Because you have allowed the coal industry to create flood zones. YOU. Surface mining causes them, you know that as well as we do. Over five hundred thousand acres have been destroyed by mountaintop removal, and the valleys below those mines are where the flooding is. The citizens of the poorest county in the poorest state in the richest country need your help."

As soon as Judy sat down, one of her companions stood up, a young mother with long dark hair. "My name is Maria Gunnoe," she said. "I've been flooded seven times in the last three years. My property has been devastated so much it's just a rubble of rocks. We all know the flooding is caused by mountaintop removal. The water rolls right off those hills. How many scientists do you need to show you that?"

A third member of the group followed her. He was a man in his fifties with the bearing of a former Marine. He had a striking tattoo of an Appalachian mountain landscape that ran nearly the length of his arm. "My name is Bo Webb," the man declared. "I'm from Coal River Mountain Watch, too. And I'm totally amazed by what I've heard here today. You're only concerned about the developed areas. We don't seem to be your concern at all. Why isn't Massey Energy responsible for this damage?"

Outside, after the meetings, a genial, gray-bearded legislator approached the activists with a look of concern. "Look," he said, "I'm against Massey, too. I've had my run-ins with Don Blankenship. I wish he was gone. But you're alienating people—even people like me."

"You've got the power to do something about this," Bo Webb said. "Why don't you introduce a bill to make coal companies liable for flooding?"

The bearded lawmaker shook his head. "You've got to talk to the chairman of my committee," he said. "I don't set the agenda. All I am is someone to press a red or green button on issues."

"Coal whores," Judy muttered after she and the other activists had piled into cars for the drive home. "Every last one of 'em."

Almost every day, Judy ran up against someone who wanted her to cool down or shut up. Her angriest critics were neighbors who worked for Massey or had a relative who did. Red stripers and their families despised her and weren't shy about telling her so. Mine-truck drivers still made obscene gestures as they rumbled by CRMW's Whitesville storefront or pulled their Jake Brakes and blared their horns as a show of scorn. But subtly, over time, opinions were starting to turn.

In the mountains around Whitesville, residents saw signs every day of a new boom, one larger and more profitable than any before. In the old booms, everyone who wanted to work had worked. The bold and ambitious had started their own mines, mom-and-pop operations that sometimes yielded overnight fortunes. All that had occurred with underground mines. This boom was different. Most of the mines in the valley now were mountaintop operations. Not only was the machinery efficient enough to be operated by a handful of men, it was too expensive for small entrepreneurs to enter the game. Of the few jobs mountaintop mining did generate, nearly all were nonunion. Wages were lower, and so were benefits. More and more of the jobs went to poor out-of-staters willing to work long hours for less pay. They were the ones whose cars were parked on Main Street. Their owners lay within the tiny JKLM Inn, also known as the Alphabet Inn, sleeping between shifts in small, low-ceilinged rooms. The union men were ghosts, scraping by, if they were old enough and lucky enough, on Social Security and union pensions. As one mountain after another around them succumbed to blasting, and the valley streams got buried or poisoned, more and more residents had come to see CRMW as their only hope to save what remained of their natural world.

Like many of her neighbors, Judy Bonds could close her eyes and still see Whitesville in its former glory, when underground mining made it the social and commercial hub of the Coal River valley. CRMW's storefront was the former post office. The Big Star supermarket had thrived just up the street, along with the Dixie furniture store, Branham and Britts Hardware and Electrical, the Boone movie theater, the Whitesville Hotel, Sylvia's drugstore and soda fountain, the Queen Bee restaurant with its famous fruit pies, six churches, and a bowling alley. Now nearly all those buildings sat empty.

Whitesville had taken its name from an early settler, B. W. White, though even earlier it had been known as Jarrold's Valley and Pritchard City. It lay midway between Charleston to the north and Beckley to the south. But it would have arisen here even without those larger settlements, for under its green valleys and hills was one of the world's richest troves of coal.

For that, the miners could thank geological events of some three hundred million years ago. In the Pennsylvanian Period, the seas had receded a final time from Appalachia, but much of what was to become West Virginia remained a nutrient-rich swamp. In that climate, innumerable generations of plants and animals enriched the accumulating mulch, often forming carbon-rich peat bogs that hardened over time. As the land was pushed upon itself, those carbon deposits became buried under sediment. Plants and trees grew in the sediment, over the thick, black carbon deposits that came to be known as coal.

The coal in the Coal River valley was of the hardest and most valuable grade: bituminous coal that burned more intensely than softer grades. Because the coal had formed in a freshwater climate, it contained less sulfur than saltwater coal and burned with so little sulfurous smoke that the miners called it smokeless coal. In 1742, an explorer named John Peter Salley crossed the Allegheny Mountains and noted an outcropping of smokeless coal in a riverbank—reason enough to name the pristine tributary the Coal River. By the 1820s, settlers were using coal from the valley to heat their homes, and geologists began crisscrossing the area to see where the richest deposits lay. Commercial coal operators reached some parts of Appalachia by the 1840s, taking coal out by the cartload as factory fuel. But the steep, relentless ridges of West Virginia's southern coalfields kept most speculators at bay until 1904, when the Chesapeake and Ohio railway extended a line into Raleigh County.

Judy's forebears, like those of her neighbors, had come to the valley long before anyone appreciated the value of the coal that lay below. They came, mostly, from England and Scotland and Ireland in the eighteenth century, seeking to escape religious strictures and persecution. To their great dismay, they found more of the same when they reached New England, so they headed west, into the endless hills of the new frontier. Many saw no reason to go farther than the Allegheny and Cumberland plateaus. The forest of this folded landscape was rich with game. So many kinds of trees grew here that settlers could choose one for each need: chestnuts for fence rails, yellow locusts for posts, hickory for axes and broom handles. Most forests are dominated by two or three species of trees. This one had eighty. It was one of the oldest and richest temperate-zone hardwood forests in the world—the only forest in America not obliterated by glaciers in the Pleistocene Age. Ecologists came to refer to it as America's mother forest. Its seeds, they theorized, had traveled on the wind to grow as the virgin trees of every other forest in the land.

In those frontier times, settlers let their hogs and other livestock roam the forest as pastureland. They went rooting for ginseng and other medicinal plants and herbs. They gathered mountain greens, among them ramps, the mountain green considered a cross between a wild leek and onion, but also poke, dock, Shawnee lettuce, lamb's tongue, woolen britches, and creasies. The woods beyond their homesteads were anyone's to hunt and fish and hike in—a commons, as it was called, rooted in English tradition that the settlers had brought from their motherland, along with a hodgepodge of English and Scottish and Irish dialects. In the early twenty-first century, the dialects remained, but the commons was gone, bought up by the land and coal companies from out of state.

By the 1920s, when Judy's grandfather began working the valley mines, coal companies were importing immigrant workers by the trainload. Most were Welsh, English, Irish, and Scots, but as labor needs kept growing, waves of Italians, Poles, and other Europeans arrived, too.

Southern blacks, many the children and grandchildren of former slaves, flocked to the minefields as well, only to be segregated as completely as their forebears. The black miners were put in the least desirable part of a camp, usually by the prep plant, and given the least desirable jobs. Just up the valley from Whitesville, in the hollow known as Shumate's Branch, a camp of black workers lived in Honey Bottom, a wry reference to the human sewage from settlements up the hollow that the blacks had to bury there.

In that first boom, the sidewalks of Whitesville were so crowded on Friday nights that miners and their wives spilled into the streets, before turning into one or another of the town's nineteen beer joints to drink the workweek cares away. One night in 1926, so many people crowded onto a suspension bridge to see a carnival performer set himself on fire before plunging into the Coal River that a calamity occurred. "Death Stalks in Whitesville" was one newspaper's headline. "While the Fire Devil performs, Death Leaps to its Chance; a cable snaps; a mass of humanity crashes to rocks below; lives are snuffed out, and bodies are torn, bruised and mangled." The death toll was twenty-four.

Judy—her given name was Julia—was born in 1952, just south of Whitesville up Marfork Hollow. Coal's second big boom, led by World War II, was coming to an end. As a little girl, she remembered coal camps up and down the valley closing one by one. Train spurs from their mines fell into disuse, to be covered over with weeds. By 1959, the local paper ran a sad front-page headline: "The Story of Whitesville: Boom to Ghost Town." The latest waves of immigrant miners who had come to the coalfields during the war were cast aside. Most found no other kind of work in the hills of southern West Virginia. The coal industry's promise of easy riches had proved, for most, an illusion. Like any boom-and-bust economy, it left little more in its wake than poverty and despair.

Yet compared to what it would become, Whitesville still seemed robust. No storefront stood vacant. A child could still linger, as Judy did, at the malt shop reading the latest comic books and leafing through *Life* magazine. She could still get her clothes and school supplies down the street and go to the movies on Saturday night. Down in Marfork Hollow, Judy's family was one of about fifty scratching out a living, enough to support a post office and general store. While many of the immigrants had left as the boom died, most of the local men still worked in the mines. Judy's father was a miner, like her grandfather and great-grandfather before him. He worked an eight-hour shift, starting from when he was fourteen until his early sixties, when he retired, just months before his death. Sometimes the mines were tall enough to stand in. Sometimes they weren't, and so the miners spent their days on their knees, digging by the light of their helmet lanterns. A few of the tunnels were no more than thirty-six inches high. Then the men lay flat on four-wheeled boards, digging inch by inch into the mountain darkness. "Low coal," the men called it. It wasn't work for the claustrophobic. When Judy's father came home, his face was black with coal dust, but Judy's mother would have water heating on the potbellied woodstove, ready to fill the washtub so he could bathe. Judy or one of her four siblings would help clean his clothes and the rest of the family's laundry by soaping them on a scrub board in the creek.

Judy's father, like all the miners in the valley by that time, was a union man, and union jobs paid well. Still, the family kept chickens and a hog and cultivated a garden to put food on the table. In early spring, Judy's father and grandfather plowed the garden with their mules, often by moonlight. From their mountain foraging, Judy and her mother brought home armloads of ramps, fried them in bacon grease, then added pinto beans and served them over fried potatoes with cornbread on the side. In summer, her mother fried up green tomatoes and canned them in relish. She put hot banana peppers in relish, too, and stored jars of sauerkraut. The greens and canned goods were stored in a hillside cellar lined with rocks.

Killing the chicken was one of Judy's chores. She'd wring its neck, pour boiling water over its carcass, and pluck its feathers. To supplement the larder, Judy's father hunted groundhogs, raccoons, deer, and squirrels. But like their neighbors, Judy's family relied on the yearly pig for most of their meat. Nurtured through spring and fattened through summer, it was killed, without much sentiment, in late fall. Judy's father shot it neatly with a .22, then cut its throat to drain the blood. Ham and bacon were smoked in the family smokehouse and cured to provide food for the family all winter. The rest of the hog was used, too. The feet were pickled for a winter treat. So were the ears. Even the hog's head was used to provide a dubious delicacy called souse. Judy's mother boiled the meat off it and skimmed off the gelatin, adding pimentos and green peppers for flavoring. By the time Judy was a grownup, most of these culinary customs were vanishing from the valley.

A golden era was ending, though no one sensed it at the time. Mining was changing, too. By the time Judy reached high school, stripmining was all too common in the valley. The coal operators tore off wide swaths of hillside, often all the way around the mountain, like a key opening a can of sardines. Without ground cover to absorb the rains that pelted the valley each year, flooding worsened dramatically, and houses—sometimes whole hollows—got washed away. But the mountaintops remained intact as yet, and most coal still came from underground mines.

Life in the valley was good—in hindsight, very, very good. But it did move fast. By the time Judy graduated from Marsh Fork High School in 1971, she was married and had a daughter. She worked as a manager at a Pizza Hut in Beckley and sometimes at Branham and Britts Hardware in Whitesville. A new, short coal boom was beginning as spiking Arab oil prices drove more and more U.S. power plants to switch to coal, but only men worked in the mines. Eventually, Judy got divorced, then married and divorced twice more. By then, the coal boom of the 1970s had turned into the bust that was to last from the 1980s through the 1990s. Even then, life in the valley was good. Friends and relatives that Judy had grown up with still lived in the hollow. The woods were still rich with game and medicinal plants and herbs, and the stream that ran down Marfork Hollow was clean and filled with fish. From her porch at dusk, Judy could look up at the mountain and see the lineaments of her late father's face in the way the mountain, the shrubs, and the trees came together. Then Peabody sold Montcoal, its mostly underground mine operation, to A. T. Massey. That was when life as Judy and her neighbors had known it came to an end.

The first thing Massey did was shut down the underground mines and let Montcoal's union contract run out. The UMWA managed to negotiate the deal that forced Massey to rehire two union men for every nonunion man—the deal by which Jerry Shelton, among others, kept his job—but a large and growing number of union miners were put out of work. A broad, historical change was at work, one that

Massey readily exploited. Not only had coal prices slumped, but half the state's coal now came from surface mines (strip mines and, increasingly, mountaintop removal) that required far fewer men than underground mining did to produce more coal. In the 1940s, West Virginia coal operators had employed 130,000 miners. Half a century later, that number had dropped to 15,000 even as production soared. Most working-age men simply left for the cities, hoping to find factory work. The few who remained were too desperate for jobs to give the union any clout. Massey could do as it pleased, and under Don Blankenship it did just that, breaking the union at mine after mine as efficiently as it blasted the mountains.

With nonunion workers, Massey's newest subsidiary, Marfork Coal, opened for business in 1994, at the top of the hollow where Judy Bonds lived. For two years or more, she and her neighbors had no idea the company was readying to strip-mine the mountain. They found out when a steady succession of coal trucks began roaring up and down the hollow's road, scattering coal dust as they made their turns, and blasts shook the hollow. Again and again, neighbors found the stream chocolate brown—blackwater spills, they were called. Many were releases of wastewater from the new impoundment above, often done during a hard rain in hopes of disguising the source of the blackwater. In a day, the stream would regain some of its clarity, but its aquatic life—minnows, crawfish, various panfish—would be dead. Other spills were from the sprawling prep plant built beside the impoundment.

Was it the blackwater spills that led children to start complaining of headaches, stomach pains, and diarrhea? And did the coal dust from the mining and the trucks induce asthma in one after another of the students at the Pettus Grade School? Or were these just coincidences? All Judy knew was that her nine-year-old grandson woke up curled in pain more often than she felt any child should, and that on the days he got to school he needed an inhaler. Many of his friends did, too.

By 2000, Marfork Coal had strip-mined hundreds of acres in every direction. As it did, its impoundment of toxic slurry grew larger and larger, the earthen sides built higher and higher up the crook of two mountains, like a giant wasp's nest. The impoundment was named after the stream it had buried: Brushy Fork, a tributary of the Marsh Fork. Soon it would be the largest by far of three impoundments in the

Coal River valley, all three built by Massey. In fact, it would be the largest of Appalachia's 110 impoundments, the majority of which were clustered in the coalfields of southern West Virginia. With a capacity of eight billion gallons of sludge and rising to 920 feet, Brushy Fork would soon be the biggest impoundment in America.

As the mining expanded, it reached one of the family cemeteries that dotted the hills of the Coal River valley. For Massey, these sites were always a hindrance. With underground mining, the company could tunnel beneath them, though occasionally a coffin would fall through the roof and land at a startled miner's feet; one miner had reportedly quit his job on the spot when that happened. Now, as it did whenever a cemetery got in the way of its mountaintop plans, Massey just left it intact and stripped around it, leaving the worn and tilted stones surrounded by acres of raw earth. From then on, family members who wanted to visit the deceased at the Montcoal cemetery had to sign in at a Massey security checkpoint, get hazard training, and don a hard hat and goggles. A guard then escorted them to the cemetery. They needed the guard because the mountain had changed so much that they would get lost if they tried to find the cemetery on their own. The guard also stayed by the cemetery fence as the family members, in their hard hats and goggles, paid their respects—a security precaution, the company explained.

Fed up, some residents of Judy's hollow asked Marfork Coal to buy their houses, and in some cases Marfork agreed. It started by buying houses near the top of the hollow in Packsville, a small community that stood in the way of its mountaintop plans. As part of those deals, it made sellers agree in writing not to divulge what they'd been paid or discuss with anyone the effects of the mining that had forced them to sell. The agreements also obligated the sellers to move a certain distance from the hollow.

By 2000, most of the residents of Marfork all the way down to Route 3 had moved, too, selling out to Massey for "fair market" value— "fair market" being what the houses were worth now that a huge mining operation was situated above them. One by one, Massey demolished the houses it bought. It put up a Marfork Coal sign near the site of the demolished post office and the general store. It placed a guard shack beside the sign, with an armed guard on duty in it day and night. No longer could the last residents of the hollow go hunting and fishing and rooting in the hills. The hills up the hollow were now private property. No trespassing.

Strangely enough, the animals began coming down to the people. Agitated, their habitat vanishing acre by acre, foxes and skunks and coyotes began foraging down by the foot of the hollow. Growing up, Judy had never seen a bear at Marfork, nor had anyone she knew. Now she had to put her garbage on the roof to keep the bears from rummaging through it.

Soon enough, Judy's was one of two houses left for the bears to try. The rest were bought and demolished. Massey had nearly erased the town of Marfork. Together with her daughter and grandson, Judy lived in a state of siege. She couldn't fish in the stream because the fish were dead. She couldn't trust her well because the water smelled bad. She couldn't drive up the hollow to go rooting for ramps. She couldn't even visit her family cemetery without a guard to accompany her. Still, she couldn't imagine leaving the house where she'd lived most of her life, especially knowing that Massey would raze it as soon as she did.

Like most houses in the valley, Judy's was owned in heirship. Often as many as eight or ten heirs owned a single Appalachian home. Some coal companies had perfected the game of seeking out heirs who'd moved away—distant cousins who might not even know who in their family back in the hollow was alive, much less what those relatives' wishes were in regard to the family house—and buying out their shares. When the coal companies accumulated a majority share, their lawyers went to court. Under the law, a judge usually felt he had no choice but to force a sale, even though the law had been written to deal with warring relatives, not relatives and a rapacious coal company. Inevitably, the company would outbid the remaining family members at auction, take control of the house, and demolish it.

At least Judy's fellow heirs were all immediate family. But some were for selling. Stubborn as she was, Judy might have fought her siblings to the bitter end, if not for her grandson's worsening health and the growing anxieties she felt about the Brushy Fork impoundment at the top of the hollow. Instead, she sold. With the proceeds, Judy was

able to buy a small house some nine miles south along Route 3 in a settlement called Rock Creek, on Mountain View Hill. The house was
right on the road, but it had a nice piece of land that dipped toward
Marsh Fork Creek. Judy figured the move bought her six or eight years.
Massey was moving south in the valley, too, blasting the ridges on either side. Eventually, it would reach Mountain View Hill. By the time
that happened, with any luck, Judy's grandson would be out of high
school and could find a place on his own. Then Judy would make her
last stand.

But Judy wasn't going to wait until then to take on Massey Energy.
She'd been educating herself about mountaintop removal. Along the
way, she'd heard about Coal River Mountain Watch. Most of her
neighbors couldn't imagine challenging King Coal, but Judy could. She
was, as she put it, a very no-nonsense person.

A hardy band of two had started Coal River Mountain Watch and
rented the storefront in Whitesville a few years before Judy walked in
one day to help. Freda Williams was a white-thatched widow, gracious
and petite but hard as slate. Like Judy, she was a daughter and granddaughter of union miners. Her whole life, she'd done what she could
about injustice in the coalfields wherever she saw it. She was seeing a
lot of it now. Randy Sprouse, CRMW's cofounder, was an ex-union
miner whose role in the angry UMWA demonstration against Elk Run
in 1981 had led the industry to blackball him. He'd had a lot of time
since then to think. Freda and Randy had started Coal River Mountain
Watch in 1996 and held a first rally. It was less about mountaintop removal than about neighbors losing homes and jobs. Strictly by word of
mouth, the rally drew five hundred people. Despite that support, most
residents resented the new grassroots group. They worried that Massey
would retaliate by firing relatives and friends of anyone who'd come to
the rally. Many felt no one should tell anyone else what to do; they had
a libertarian attitude instilled in them by their pioneering ancestors.
After a century in which coal companies had mined the valley just as
they pleased and with almost absolute power, most residents were also
deeply doubtful that anything would come of the effort. Mostly, they
were afraid.

Freda and Randy had started CRMW after working for another

group, the West Virginia Organizing Project, to do something about blasting. The first indication residents had of the upcoming damage was when the surveyors came, leaving stakes with fluttering bits of red tape. The second was when a freelance timber cutter began clear-cutting a stretch of woods the residents had known their whole lives. The cutter wouldn't say who had hired him. He just went and cut the trees.

Then, without any public meeting, the blasting began. Every day, blasts as large or larger than the one that had devastated Oklahoma City were set off routinely in the mountains. Rick Eades, a hydrologist who did studies for the Ohio Valley Environmental Coalition (OVEC), a grassroots organization, determined that 314,000 tons of explosives were being set off in West Virginia each year. Most of those blasts occurred in the coalfields. That, he concluded, added up to one thousand Oklahoma City–sized blasts per southern county per year. The coal companies could set those blasts as close to homes as they liked, damaging foundations and walls, ruining wells. No law governed them in that regard.

Along with a number of other residents and activists, Freda and Randy began lobbying the state legislature to pass such a law. The lobbying went on for three years. All the residents asked was that blasts be set no closer than one mile from homes. In the final bill, that distance was shaved to seven tenths of a mile. It was a victory, but a modest one. The blasts, after all, could be heard across the valley, and the rock dust traveled for miles.

The most urgent concern of Freda and Randy, as cofounders of CRMW, was the Brushy Fork impoundment atop Marfork Hollow. Freda worried that the impoundment's wall would break, and billions of gallons of slurry would come cascading into the valley below. She began asking questions of the West Virginia DEP up in Nitro, just west of Charleston. The officials told her the impoundment would be expanded over time to hold eight billion gallons. It would grow in phases, nearly a dozen in all, each time adding a thick new layer of sludge. As for how likely the impoundment was to break, no one in the DEP could say. But the impoundment was well designed, so no one at the DEP thought there was any reason to fear.

That changed with the Martin County spill on October 11, 2000— the worst environmental disaster in America east of the Mississippi, though it earned only a fraction of the coverage of the *Exxon Valdez* oil spill in 1989. On that day, 300 million gallons of slurry spilled out of Massey's Big Branch impoundment in Martin County, Kentucky, near the West Virginia line. Massey initially called the spill "an act of God." The only evidence of God's hand was the lack of casualties: no one was killed or injured. That truly was a miracle. In 1972, a smaller spill at Buffalo Creek, West Virginia, had killed 125 people. Big Branch had been built over long-abandoned underground mines that likely collapsed under the pressure of all that sludge. Freda suspected that Brushy Fork, too, was built over abandoned mines, because her father and grandfather had worked in some of them.

Freda could do her CRMW work on a modest pension from her late husband's years as a union miner. Randy had no such stipend. To make ends meet, he bought an old tavern in Sundial, just south of Whitesville. Every weekend night, locals bellied up to the bar in a haze of cigarette smoke to trade stories over the blare of country-and-western songs and the *pock-pock* of balls colliding on the pool table. With Randy presiding, more and more of the stories were angry ones about Massey. Historically, in the valley, unions had started in bars. To Massey, then, loose talk was a threat to be squelched. In the spring of 2001, Massey offered to buy Randy out. One story had it that he needed the money, another that his wife was tired of living in the valley as an activist's wife. Randy signed a sales contract that stipulated he move more than one hundred miles from Sundial and never say anything bad about Massey again. The ink on the contract was barely dry when Massey tore down the tavern. Three years later, the site sat empty and forlorn, a reminder to residents who drove by every day of what came from stirring up the ire of King Coal.

Judy arrived at Coal River Mountain Watch about the time Randy left. She sat at an old computer that someone had donated and started figuring out how to get information on new mountaintop-mining sites from the Internet. There wasn't much yet on the state's DEP Web site, or on that of any other agency. But she kept trying. Freda and Randy had learned to watch the local newspapers for announcements that a coal company had filed for a permit to blast another ridge or build another valley fill. The state required these modest disclosures, but the ads were small and offered only the sketchiest details. Most residents had never noticed them. As part of the state disclosure process, the DEP was obligated to hold a public meeting about the prospective work, but only if some member of the public noticed the small ads in the paper and asked for one to be held. Judy started asking, and when the meetings were held, she started attending them.

The meetings, usually held in a school gym, were very strange. One DEP official, smartly dressed in the agency's park-ranger-green uniform, would describe the latest plan to a smattering of residents. Any resident could then address the moderator and the four or five other uniformed DEP officials who sat in a row beside him at folding tables. The officials, however, could not respond. They sat in stony silence, moving only to check the large reel-to-reel tape recorder that sat in front of them. Judy could lash out at the DEP officials as bitterly she liked. The officials would just sit there, staring impassively at her as the spools turned. The tape was supposed to be handed over to the head of the DEP, who would listen to the residents' complaints in his office at Nitro. The head of the DEP never came down to attend a meeting himself, and no one could ever confirm if he listened to the tape. No one could remember a time when the DEP had withheld a permit, either.

Still, Judy went to the meetings, and as she did she started to realize that she was good at speaking out. She got fired up, and the words started coming like punches, one after another. "These mountains don't belong to anyone but God," she would say. "In my heart, I can feel God's anger. I can just imagine tears running down His face at what He sees happening to His creation."

The meetings were useless: Massey continued to get every permit it sought. But a new, high-ranking arrival at the DEP was listening, and if he couldn't stop Massey from getting its permits, he did have the power to issue violations when coal companies broke the law. To the companies' astonishment—and to Judy's—he even had the power to shut them down.

Matt Crum came to his job at the DEP in the spring of 2001 with a mission that would have seemed modest in any other state: to enforce the law. Crum had a couple of greenish credentials on his résumé. He'd worked as an environmental lawyer in Charleston, then as an environmental prosecutor with the U.S. Department of Justice. But he had no particular objection to coal mining, and he knew almost nothing about mountaintop mining when he took a call from a fellow prosecutor named Michael Callaghan.

Callaghan had just been named the new head of West Virginia's DEP by a new governor, Bob Wise, who said he wanted to make a difference. Callaghan was young, smart, and ambitious; he wanted to make a difference, too. When he asked Crum to think about how he might fit at the agency, Crum had just one question. "What's your biggest challenge?" he asked.

"Coal enforcement," Callaghan said.

"Okay," Crum said. "I'll do that."

As the DEP's new head of enforcement for mining and reclamation, Crum inherited a small army of inspectors. When news came in his first week that a Massey subsidiary had just had a sizable spill, he hurried down to see how his inspector would handle it. The inspector was amazed. Mining directors rarely did that.

At the site of the spill, Crum and the inspector watched coal fines—powder and small particles—pour into the stream at their feet. "What are you doing to do?" Crum asked, ready to learn.

The inspector gave him a look. "Well," he said slowly, "I could do nothing. Or I could write up a notice of violation." A notice of violation was just that: a notice that the coal company had done something wrong and needed to correct it. The fine involved was usually a few thousand dollars, perhaps just a few hundred—chump change to a coal company. "Or I could issue a C&D—cease and desist," the inspector said. That required a coal operator to shut down immediately until the problem was fixed. "For a C&D," the inspector added, "you need imminent harm to the environment."

"Doesn't this constitute imminent harm?" Crum said.

"Oh, yes," the inspector nodded.

"So, what are you going to do?"

The inspector hesitated. "What do *you* want me to do?"

"Write a C&D, don't you think?"

"What's going to happen to me if I do?" the inspector said, his bitterness showing through. "Am I going to have a job next week?"

"Absolutely," Crum said.

The inspector got quiet for a minute, then wrote up the C&D. Back in his office, Crum learned that the inspector had been penalized before for writing C&Ds on other Massey operations; he had been removed from oversight of those sites by his superiors.

Early on, Callaghan and Crum asked the state's major coal operators to come in for individual meetings. They wanted to make a good-faith effort to understand each operator's situation. One of the first to come in was Don Blankenship. Somewhat disconcertingly, the Massey head came dressed entirely in black: black suit, black shirt, black tie.

Both Crum and Callaghan quickly realized that Don was very smart. Later, Callaghan said that Don was in fact the smartest person he'd ever met. In a soft drawl, the Massey CEO rattled off numbers for his various subsidiaries—costs, production, taxes, workforce numbers—like a human computer.

It was clear, too, that Don wasn't just a well-prepped CEO. He cared passionately about his company and gave up no ground in its defense. According to Don, inspectors who wrote up violations on Massey mines were "in the hands of the union." The reason they wrote so many more violations against Massey than other coal operators was that Massey had more operations than other companies. But the inspectors also held Massey to a higher standard. For that matter, the whole DEP was biased against Massey. Just look, Don said, at how long the agency took to grant Massey its permits.

If Don had thought his bluster would make the new boys back off, he was wrong. Crum soon realized that the DEP's record of enforcement with Massey was, in fact, shockingly lax. He decided to change that. Three Massey subsidiaries were dragged before a DEP panel to show cause why they shouldn't be shut down for chronic violations—mostly blackwater spills. After hearing both sides, Crum slapped Massey with various suspensions. The one that stung most was at Marfork. Crum ordered Marfork to shut down for thirteen days. Massey appealed to the Surface Mine Board, the same state body that Tony Sears had appealed to in order to stop Massey from injecting coal slurry into abandoned mines at Green Valley. The board upheld Crum's ruling, but reduced the suspension to nine days. Furious, Massey took the matter to court—first a lower court, then a higher court, then a lower court again. Was a nine-day suspension really worth all this legal defense? To Don Blankenship, it was. Four years later, Massey lawyer Bob McLusky was still filing motions to get it struck down, like a lawyer out of *Jarndyce and Jarndyce* in Charles Dickens's *Bleak House*.

As word went out in the valley that the new guy at the DEP was standing up to Massey, Crum began to get more calls from residents reporting blackwater spills and other violations. One came from a pair of feisty ladies who lived in Sylvester, a once postcard-pretty town just north of Whitesville on Route 3. Mary Miller and Pauline Canterberry had watched their town turn black from coal dust after Massey's Elk Run operation built a prep plant right above it. At Crum's suggestion, the "Dustbusters," as they came to be known, started wiping the sides of several coal-dusted houses every day with paper towels, putting the towels in plastic bags, and dating them while a video camera filmed them doing it. When the Dustbusters and nearly 150 neighbors decided to sue Massey for ruining their town, Joe Lovett took the case. Eventually, he handed it over to a bold young Charleston lawyer named Brian Glasser, who represented them on contingency: he would get no money unless they won in court. With the unassailable proof of those dust-blacken paper towels in Baggies, they did win: $473,000, to be divided among 151 plaintiffs, plus about that much more in legal costs to Glasser's firm. Uncharacteristically, Massey chose to pay up, not appeal. Brian Glasser thought he knew why. In the trial, the judge had accepted Massey's claim that Elk Run was an independent subsidiary. That had limited damages. In judging an appeal, the state supreme court might strike down that claim, opening Massey to far greater punitive damages.

For a while, the Dustbusters allowed themselves to feel they'd won. Massey had put a white nylon dome over its prep plant, before the trial, to contain the coal dust; in accordance with the ruling, it drastically reduced coal-truck traffic through the town and paid for a street-sweeping truck to clean coal dust from Route 3 each week. Yet three years later, the Dustbusters were again wiping down their houses with paper towels. And Matt Crum was gone.

In early 2003, Michael Callaghan announced he was resigning as secretary of the DEP to be chairman of West Virginia's Democratic party. Crum had hoped at one point to succeed him, but Callaghan gave the nod to Stephanie Timmermeyer, another high-ranking DEP official. Not long before this, the white nylon dome at Elk Run had collapsed. Timmermeyer, in charge of air-quality enforcement, had allowed Elk Run to keep operating while the dome was patched and reinstalled. Crum had felt that was rewarding Massey for its own mishap.

Timmermeyer was confirmed as acting head of the DEP in April and took over in June. Crum couldn't help noticing that Timmermeyer began presiding over regular meetings with Massey Energy to review the status of the company's pending permits on new mines. No other coal company enjoyed such preferential treatment. For that matter, Crum couldn't recall a time when the director of the agency had become personally involved in any coal company's permit applications. Crum was invited to the meetings, but always on short notice and at times when he was already busy.

One day in August, Crum walked into his office to find Timmermeyer and the DEP's general counsel waiting for him. He was being fired.

Crum announced publicly that he was resigning. In the coalfields, the news was met with indignation. No one thought Crum had made the decision on his own. Within a day, Judy Bonds drove to the DEP's headquarters with two dozen protesters from CRMW and OVEC. The protesters brought placards and marched in a circle on the sidewalk, calling for a meeting with Timmermeyer. The new head of the DEP stayed inside. "It's over," she said later to a reporter. "It's a done deal. I'm moving on."

But why had Crum been fired, the reporter persisted? No reason had been given. "It's a will and pleasure appointment," Timmermeyer said. "I don't have to have any reasons."

Coal River Mountain Watch and its newest firebrand, Judy Bonds, had come a long way in the two years that Matt Crum had held his job. Just knowing that the DEP could be willing to enforce the law—and stand up to Massey—gave the beleaguered residents of the Coal River valley enormous hope. They hadn't yet blocked a new Massey permit for mountaintop mining, but now, when a blackwater spill came down the hollow or blasting started up too close to homes, they had the satisfaction of knowing that DEP inspectors would actually follow up on their complaints.

In that time, Judy had made a name for herself. Her pithy quotes peppered stories in the Charleston *Gazette* and *Daily Mail*. TV news shows beamed her face into homes around the state. In April 2003, she was named the North American winner of the international Goldman Environmental Prize, which annually gave $125,000 to each of six environmental heroes, one on each continent. Judy had been earning $12,000 per year for working more than full-time at CRMW. That year, the group's entire annual budget was $43,800. The Goldman award was huge. After paying $30,000 in taxes, Judy wiped out the mortgage on her Rock Creek house with $40,000. She spent $3,500 on her grandson's braces and gave her daughter $3,000. The remaining $48,500, Judy gave to CRMW.

Along with the prize came more publicity. Perhaps inevitably, the relationship between Judy and Freda cooled. One day at the storefront, a routine disagreement boiled over, and then Freda was gone. She would keep lobbying against the ever-expanding Brushy Fork impoundment, but on her own. In her place, the ex-Marine with the tattoo of mountains on his right arm, Bo Webb, began working as Judy's full-time partner, helped by a half-dozen passionate volunteers. "The fight," Judy declared to the Charleston *Gazette*, "is just starting."

But to what end? "Your golden era is over," a coal-company spokesman gloated to Judy in the wake of Matt Crum's departure. Even if the DEP was somehow inspired to keep up Crum's standard of enforcement—a dubious prospect—it was still giving more and more permits to mine. Whitesville was nearly ringed now by mountaintop-mining operations. Day and night, bulldozers pushed debris into valley fills, and blasts rocked the valley. Now, at least, CRMW knew how to track each new permit application. But aside from raging at public meetings, about all the activists seemed able to do was join Joe Lovett's lawsuit.

"We're a colony here, and the coal companies rule," Judy told a visitor bitterly one day in the summer of 2004. "We can complain all we want, but those complaints are just swept aside in the name of progress and jobs. It's like we're selling our children's feet to buy shoes. And it's not just here, this corruption. It's from cradle to grave. The cradle is the mine, from which the coal comes forth in corruption and evil and sorrow and death. The grave is when the coal is gone and they dispose of the waste, which affects us all in acid rain. The industry is literally twisting the law of the land.

"The way they've done it is by dehumanizing us, so that the rest of America doesn't care about us. That's how they got away with slavery for so long. When they say, 'Don't go to West Virginia or Kentucky, those people are ignorant and inbred,' then who cares if my grandson is sleeping nights in his clothes because he's worried there'll be a flood or mudslide?

"And for us now there's no place to move. We can't get any money for our houses, and everywhere else is more expensive. No one on the Coal River can get off the river. There's no place on the river where you can get away from mining."

What Judy needed, she realized, was a focal point, one Massey operation so appalling that valley residents would rally against it, so illegal that judges would rule against it. That focal point lay just seven miles down Route 3 from Whitesville. Set back behind a wide lawn, against a curve of Marsh Fork Creek, was the little Marsh Fork Elementary School, a one-story brick building that drew 241 students from nearby towns. Behind it, just across Marsh Fork Creek, rose a prep plant called Goals Coal, one of Massey's subsidiaries. And behind the plant, lodged in the former Shumate's Branch, was an impoundment that contained two hundred million gallons of coal waste, rock, and water. Over its lifetime, it was designed to absorb 2.8 billion gallons in all. So nestled was the impoundment in the hillside that it was invisible from Route 3. Most of the school's parents and teachers had had no idea it was there until they were shown aerial pictures of it. The parents had become concerned the year before, when Massey built a 110-foot silo less than three hundred feet from the school. More and more coal was being mined from mountaintop sites just over the ridge, and Massey needed the silo to store that coal before loading it on trains. A number of children had subsequently reported chronic symptoms: headaches, respiratory problems, stomachaches, and diarrhea. So far, the reports were just anecdotal, unconfirmed as a pattern by any

school nurse or state agency. But a growing number of parents had begun to wonder if Goals was making their children sick. And what
would happen, they asked, if the impoundment at Goals happened to
rupture?

In fighting a force as large and implacable as the coal industry,
Judy knew she had to pick her battles. The school at Marsh Fork was
the one to pick.

FOUR

A SHORT-LIVED
LEGAL VICTORY

Sometimes it seemed to Joe that every bridge, highway, and build-ing in West Virginia was named after Robert C. Byrd, the ban-tamweight senior senator who for more than half a century had wrested West Virginia's share of federal-government pork—and then some—for all the projects that bore his name. There were Robert C. Byrd highways, schools, and science centers, a prison, a library—more than twenty public-works projects in all, handed down by the former chairman and now ranking Democratic member of the Senate appro-priations committee. West Virginia was Byrd's fiefdom, and he was a benevolent king, especially to the coal industry.

Judge Joseph R. Goodwin's chambers were in Charleston's new Robert C. Byrd Federal Courthouse, an impressively massive, block-size building with three-story-high stained-glass windows and a central rotunda. It was into those chambers after his tense drive up from Lewisburg on Monday, April 5, 2004, that Joe burst, out of breath, his legal papers in hand, to plead for the temporary restraining order that would stop Green Valley from filling in the tributary at Hominy Creek.

Because Judge Goodwin had convened the TRO hearing in a con-ference room of those chambers, he had dispensed with his black robes in favor of a dark suit. Except for his air of quiet authority, he looked as much a lawyer as everyone else in the room. Already seated was Massey lawyer Bob McLusky. Rounding out the group was an assistant U.S. attorney representing the West Virginia DEP. The DEP had lent its own stamp of approval to the Nationwide 21 permit granted by the Army Corps to Green Valley—the permit that was now part of Joe's larger suit arguing that Nationwide 21s were, on their face, illegal. In the middle of the table was a speakerphone, patching in two lawyers from the U.S. Department of Justice, representing the Army Corps.

"I talked to Mr. McLusky, who represents Green Valley, on Friday," Joe began, "and he told me he didn't know what was going to happen at the site but as long as the weather was bad nothing would be happening. This afternoon, he informed me that Green Valley had started filling the stream."

McLusky acknowledged that yes, Green Valley had begun filling in the stream after all. Though neither he nor Joe said as much, both men knew that if the company ruined enough of that 431-foot stretch of stream, Joe's argument would be moot, and Judge Goodwin would have no cause to prevent Green Valley from ruining the rest.

The judge knew that, too. "Mr. Lovett," Goodwin said, "what would you say to the idea that it's a fait accompli?"

A wry, scholarly man in his late fifties, Goodwin was a federal judge, insulated in his lifetime appointment from the pressures that came from standing for election every few years, as state judges did. In a state dominated by the coal industry, Joe saw no point in bringing cases before local judges. It was just a waste of time. Goodwin was also, presumably, a Democrat, since one of his two brothers—lawyers both—had run one of Senator Byrd's many reelection campaigns. But in the state where coal was king, party affiliation meant almost nothing. In one way or another, virtually everybody in West Virginia was beholden to coal.

As a federal judge, Goodwin offered Joe the best chance he could get. Even so, Joe only bothered to try a certain kind of case. He didn't fight a coal company that blew up mountaintops too close to people's homes or sent a ceaseless parade of coal trucks down their Main Street day and night or flushed black sludge down their mountain streams and covered their houses with coal dust. He knew lawyers who did that, and he was grateful they did, and when desperate residents called him with those stories, as the Dustbusters of Sylvester had done, Joe put them on to the lawyers he knew. But as a rule, he didn't go after coal companies at all. That was the kind of case where you ended up arguing matters of degree. How close *was* the blasting? How black *did* the streams get? Exactly how endangered *were* the aquatic insects? Then it was their experts against his, and the coal companies always had more money to hire more experts.

Joe set his sights higher than that. He looked for ways in which the whole industry was blatantly breaking the law, aided and abetted by the state and federal agencies assigned to oversee it. Those ways were easy to find. So lax were the overseers and so powerful the industry that laws were broken in plain sight. All Joe had to do was point out the glaring illegalities, conducted so routinely over so many years that no one even thought to cover them up anymore. Joe's briefs had a lovely simplicity to them: Here is what the Clean Water Act says the Army Corps of Engineers must do; this is what the Corps is doing instead. As Joe's fellow lawyer Brian Glasser put it, the beauty of what Joe did was that he merely asked agencies to read their own rules. The law was the law, and flagrant disregard for it was hard for any judge to ignore, even a conservative one.

When Joe won a case like that, his victory did more than stop a particular coal company from polluting a particular town. It produced what lawyers called a programmatic ruling. Something about the way mountaintop removal was permitted or carried out was found to violate the law. For a while, at least, such rulings stopped the industry in its tracks. The Nationwide 21 case was just that sort of suit. Soon, Joe would argue it in Judge Goodwin's court. Today, he simply needed a TRO for Hominy Creek's headwaters.

Based on what Tony Sears had told him, Joe said the fill job appeared about one-third complete. "I think it's only 130 feet of rock." Rocks had been put in as a bed for the mining waste that would follow. "Bad as it is, it isn't nearly as harmful as the refuse that will follow, or filling in the remainder of the stream, because only 30 percent of the stream has been filled so far, and the rest is important to protect."

"I have a map here if it would help at all," McLusky said.

"It probably would," Goodwin said.

Together, the lawyers pored over a four-color map of the Green Valley site. Joe had explained in his motion for a TRO that the small

area granted a Nationwide 21 was part of a much larger area that required an individual permit. The larger area was known as IBR Number 9. Goodwin asked McLusky, "How is it that you've taken a chunk
right out of the middle of IBR Number 9 and made it subject to an application for and apparently the receipt of a Nationwide permit?"

"The company is out of room for refuse disposal," McLusky replied. "Without being able to expand in this area, the company will shut
down its refuse disposal area, its preparation plant, and two deep mines
very soon, and that would result in layoffs of somewhere between 100
and 150 people."

Goodwin thought about that. "So as you understand it, the reason
they pulled this piece out was a matter of necessity to keep mining."

"Absolutely," McLusky said. "And it's the smallest segment they
could possibly—"

Sternly, the judge cut him off. How, he asked, did that justify
bending the law? "The fact that somebody waits until they're in ex-
tremis to do something is no reason, in my view, to shortcut what is
otherwise proper procedure."

McLusky had no answer for that. He'd walked into a trap, and he
knew it.

This was a complex issue, Goodwin declared, and he wanted to
understand it better in a more formal hearing—one with expert testimony on either side. Meanwhile, he would grant Joe's TRO for an obvious reason. "I think that the balance of harms here are decidedly in
favor of the plaintiff," the judge said. "The stream cannot be repaired
once it's filled in."

The TRO would stop the dumping at Green Valley for just ten
days. Joe could get an extension for another ten days, but to make the
injunction stick beyond that, he'd have to win in a hearing with witnesses. And that was just for Green Valley. The broader case against
Nationwide 21 would have to be heard in a separate trial. Still, for the
first time in hours, Joe felt his shoulders relax.

As he drove back south on I-64/77 from Charleston, Joe could look
to forested mountains on either side, not one of them less than pristine. The mountains were like a screen, hiding great blotches on the
landscape behind them in either direction. Many of those blotches

were hundreds of acres wide. A few were five or more square miles. Close up, an active mountaintop-mining site looked like a broad, barren plateau plunked down from some desolate part of the American West. At least one side of each plateau had a zigzagging, stair-step appearance, the raw, rocky earth packed and graded in steplike levels, the way a child might fashion the side of a sandcastle.

Once upon a time, in the 1970s, mountaintop mining had been done on a modest scale in the coalfields. Then, in the 1980s, operators imported methods and new machines from the open-pit mines of the West. Sites grew suddenly from hundreds of acres to thousands. On some of the largest sites, one of the biggest machines on the planet pitched in. A dragline was like a steam shovel as high as a twenty-story apartment building. Built on-site, it scooped up 100,000 pounds of debris at a time: the equivalent of forty standard-sized cars.

Eventually, the blasting and scraping away uncovered the prize: a layer of coal, dusty black and veined with gray shale. Bulldozers pried the coal loose and loaded up long semidetached trucks. Some sites had conveyor belts that came all the way up from the prep plant, over the next ridge or beyond. Then the coal was loaded right into the belt's cars, and the belt would run all day and night, its safety lights after dark giving it the cheery look of a roller-coaster crisscrossing the hills. Blast by blast, seam by seam, a mountain was reduced by as much as six hundred feet before the miners moved on. The valley below was filled in with the overburden—buried, along with any stream that coursed within it.

King Coal's lobbyists, starting with Bill Raney of the West Virginia Coal Association, took issue with those who found the results displeasing. The industry's top flack was a bantam figure with a small dark mustache who took pride in the ever-expanding mountaintop operations. The son of a coal-camp bookkeeper, he'd gotten his early education in a three-room school, gone on to college, and traveled all over the state as a surface-mine inspector before jumping over to the industry side. Pointing to a framed picture of a large mountaintop site on his wall, he told anyone who asked that the leveled mountain to him looked "pretty." Besides, Raney observed, the site would soon be reclaimed: "If you came back and took a picture of that site in five years, you wouldn't even know it had been mined."

There was some truth in that, assuming that that observer knew

little or nothing about West Virginia's mountains and wildlife. Most reclaimed mountain sites were grassy meadows with bushes and perhaps
a pond. They might support one or two kinds of fish, a few turkeys, or a
herd of deer. Gone, though, was the unique midtemperate Appalachian
forest—the eighty kinds of trees the early settlers had prized—and the
complex ecosystem of indigenous flora and fauna the forest had supported. Gone, too, was the top third of the mountain.

Lobbyists such as Raney were quick to invoke the other kind of
reclamation that occurred on some mountaintop sites. In a state that
had so little flat land for commercial development, a leveled ridgetop
presented, in theory at least, an economic opportunity. Charleston's
airport had been built on a mountaintop site. So had the Mount Olive
Correctional Facility, a short drive south from Charleston along the
Kanawha River. Farther south, in Mingo County, a mountaintop site
had been transformed into the eighteen-hole Twisted Gun golf course.
Eastern Kentucky had a new Wal-Mart on a mountaintop site and an
industrial park on another, as well as its own mountaintop airport and
prison. Raney neglected to mention, however, that of the hundreds of
leveled ridgetops created by mountaintop mining in the southern coalfields, only a handful had been so transformed.

Nor were even those transformations all they were said to be. One
problem was that the coal operators weren't required to see the development plans through, only to suggest them on their permit applications. It was a field-of-dreams approach: if they leveled the land,
someone would surely figure out how to use it. Occasionally, lawmakers did pitch in to help make the dream real. But that could get expensive. The Big Sandy federal penitentiary, built on mountaintop land in
eastern Kentucky, had been dubbed Sink Sink when the blast-softened
land beneath it kept subsiding during construction. Big Sandy ended
up costing $60 million more than its planned $140 million cost, making it the most expensive U.S. prison ever built. By comparison, the
Twisted Gun golf course had been a bargain at $5.4 million, though
the blast-softened land had inflated the cost of its construction, too.
Worse, the course was in Mingo, one of the poorest counties in America. Golf, it turned out, wasn't a high priority for most residents.
Twisted Gun's clientele was almost all in Charleston, ninety minutes
north. Not too many lawyers and doctors wanted to make that drive, at

least not more than once. Those who did found the course attractive but a little strange. Playing at an 1,800-foot elevation felt like playing on some other planet. Coal operators had actually paid for this reclamation vision themselves, but with the expectation of handing it over to the state as an addition to West Virginia's park system. The state, to their surprise, had declined their kind offer. Much as the lawmakers wanted to oblige King Coal, they felt Twisted Gun was doomed to be a money loser.

Both Mount Olive and Twisted Gun were situated on older mountaintop sites. Those sites were small compared to recent ones. The footprint of an average site had grown from about a hundred acres to a thousand acres or more. Worse, these sites were often adjacent to others just as large; a typical complex of sites might actually measure many square miles in all. The larger the sites, the more challenging and expensive any commercial reclamation project would be: more ground to cover. Generally, too, these large new sites were in backcountry areas, in the midst of vast tracts of land owned by the coal operators. Who wanted to live or work or shop there? None of these sites had groundwater—a huge problem. Just getting power and basic services up to a remote mountaintop was a daunting prospect, let alone getting people to follow.

As Joe drove south down the interstate toward Beckley, mined coal on either side of him was making its way to market—every hour, day and night. Trains wound slowly, funereally, out from prep plants in the Coal River valley to the world beyond. Some in the summer of 2004 numbered as many as 150 open-topped cars, each filled high. A sudden wind could scatter coal dust from the train cars like a great black cape across the nearest hills and houses and cars. At other prep plants, coal was loaded onto idling semis, open topped like the trains, that barreled up two-lane roads through Raleigh, Boone, Logan, and Mingo counties, sometimes by the dozen each hour. At riverside prep plants, coal was loaded onto barges for the slower, more dignified trip down river. In that part of the state, "down river" meant north, as the rivers flowed into the Ohio River. To most people outside Appalachia, the sight of all this coal on the move might seem both odd and quaint. Most Americans in the opening years of the twenty-first century had never seen a lump of coal, much less a trainload of it. Who even used coal anymore for fuel?

The fact was that for decades, coal *had* been on the wane: the last fuel of choice, visibly dirty and messy, its blackening smoke an urban blight. Coal in fireplaces sent soot up chimneys that coated the lungs of city dwellers and brought on respiratory disease as it blanketed buildings and monuments. Burning coal released sulfur dioxide and nitrogen oxides, pollutants known to form acid rain that left leaves riddled with holes and killed downwind lakes and ponds. It also generated carbon dioxide, one of the greenhouse gases most responsible for global warming. Coal's fellow fossil fuels, natural gas and oil, generated carbon dioxide as well, but in smaller amounts. As homes and buildings once heated by coal were converted to gas and oil, scientists predicted that coal would soon be a fuel of the past, as outdated as the lump that naughty Victorian children found in their Christmas stockings.

Unfortunately, half of the country's electric plants were still powered by coal, and power companies balked at the cost of abandoning it. When pressure from the states or federal government grew, the power companies grudgingly put expensive filters called scrubbers on their smokestacks that trapped some of coal's soot and greenhouse gases. But they did as little as they could get away with, and they kept burning coal as they pondered how to avoid replacing their aging plants with cleaner—but very expensive—new ones.

Once, not long ago, natural gas had seemed the fuel to replace coal: less polluting and almost as cheap. But by the spring of 2004, the price of natural gas had skyrocketed, a result of declining supply and increasing demand. Oil prices had shot up, too, in part because of market tensions caused by the war in Iraq. As oil rose to $60 or more per barrel, coal looked better and better—even at $50 per ton, up from just $20 when the boom began. In Appalachia, that meant blowing up more and more mountains to get to the coal seams that rested like layers of icing within.

As the industry saw it, there was simply no choice. Coal cost less to produce from mountaintop removal than it did from underground mining. Partly that was because draglines could scrape up 100 percent of an exposed coal seam, whereas underground miners could extract only 70 percent: some coal had to be left there in the shape of pillars or the tunnels would collapse. As a practical matter, mountaintop mining could get at much narrower seams of coal than underground mining could. The seam for an underground mine had to be high enough for miners to dig a tunnel into it—if not on their feet, then on their knees. In more than a century of Appalachian mining, a lot of those had been mined out.

As it happened, a lot of the thinner seams in southern West Virginia also yielded low-sulfur coal. Less sulfur meant less air pollution when the coal was burned, which made the coal much more valuable. But there was a cruel irony in this. When the Clean Air Act was amended in 1990, Congress had forced power plants to choose between burning lower-sulfur coal and installing hugely expensive scrubbers to take some of the sulfur out of high-sulfur coal as its smoke went up the stack. Most power plants took the easy course: burning low-sulfur coal. They knew just where to find it. E. Morgan Massey had been among the first to start buying up low-sulfur coal reserves in anticipation of that Clean Air Act amendment. Don Blankenship had followed his course.

This new incentive appeared nearly a decade before the George W. Bush administration. Coal operators blasted mountaintops with abandon through both terms of the Clinton administration, in a state whose two U.S. senators, Robert Byrd and Jay Rockefeller, were both Democrats. Coal never much cared which political party was in power. But the presidential campaign of 2000 had presented the industry with an unusually stark choice: Democrat Al Gore, card-carrying environmentalist, who talked bluntly of coal's contribution to acid rain and global warming, versus business-friendly Republican George W. Bush. The industry knew which one to back. Almost as soon as Bush took office, key restrictions on mountaintop removal were eased, loopholes were widened, oversight was softened, and a flood of Nationwide 21 authorizations were approved, to the celebratory sounds of blasting in the mountains. So bold and aggressive would the industry get over the next three years that it would stop tucking its latest sites behind the screen of mountains flanking I-64/77. Already, as he drove on toward Beckley, Joe could see the first of them: rude and startling interruptions in the flow of green.

———

In the seven years that he'd brought suits to stop or at least limit mountaintop mining, Joe had achieved landmark victories, followed in most
cases by stinging defeats. After each defeat, he took a fresh tack. But all
his suits were essentially the same. They said that federal and state agencies were violating the Surface Mining Act or the Clean Water Act, in
one way or another, every time they sanctioned a new mountaintop-
mining site.

When he'd decided that the Nationwide 21 permit was his best
next target, Joe had found plaintiffs easily enough. Along with Coal
River Mountain Watch, the Ohio Valley Environmental Coalition had
joined the suit. It, too, was based in West Virginia. Eventually, the Natural Resources Defense Council joined as a third plaintiff.

Figuring out which coal operators had applied for Nationwide 21
permits was harder. Joe couldn't just call the Corps and inquire, because the Corps wouldn't tell him. The Corps was a public agency in a
democratic government, but the records, for reasons never explained,
were said to be private. And the Corps could grant these permits without even a public hearing, since they were, by definition, granted for
work that had "minimal adverse environmental effects."

The only way to find out anything about Nationwide 21 authorizations was by filing a Freedom of Information Act request. This dreary
but critical task fell to Joe's tireless legal researcher, Margaret Janes.
Each time she filed a request, the Corps took the longest time under
the law that it could to comply—twenty days—and even then supplied
as little information as it could.

Despite that, Joe and Margaret had managed to compile spread-
sheets of all the Nationwide 21s sought by all the coal companies in
the southwestern part of the state. Then they determined which were
ripe to be stopped by a lawsuit. If a permit had been applied for but not
yet granted, a court would say the permit might still be denied, so the
court was wasting its time debating the issue. It wasn't yet ripe. If the
permit *had* been granted, but the company had gotten too far along in
its work, then the case was overripe.

Eventually, Joe and Margaret came up with a list of eleven
mountaintop-mining operations whose owners had either received, or
were about to receive, a Nationwide 21 authorization but had not yet
done the work the permit allowed. To be eligible for the suit, each one

of those had to lie in the vicinity of one or more of Joe's potential plaintiffs, who could testify that the blasting about to occur would, in fact, dramatically disturb his or her immediate environment.

In all, Joe and Margaret determined, those eleven sites were about to sprout thirty-six valley fills and two huge slurry impoundments that would destroy more than twenty-six miles of streams in southern West Virginia. On the ridgetops above those fills, fourteen square miles of land would be clear-cut and destroyed. Yet this damage would be, according to the Corps, insignificant. "If these activities taken together are insignificant," Joe wrote in his initial complaint, "what would be significant?"

Now Green Valley had lent the case new urgency and put it on Judge Goodwin's docket sooner than expected. No one doubted Judge Goodwin would grant Joe a ten-day extension on the TRO. The judge had already made clear that Green Valley deserved a more formal hearing. The question was whether that formal hearing would take only Green Valley into account, or if Goodwin would go right to trial on the bigger issue of whether the Corps should issue Nationwide 21s at all. Goodwin chose the latter. There would be no jury, just a hearing with expert witnesses on either side.

Judge Goodwin convened this more formal hearing in his courtroom. Jim Hecker had come down from Washington to be co-counsel with Joe, who began by pointing out that Nationwide 21 was different in a fundamental way from all the other "nationwides" that the Corps had been granting since 1977—the year the 1972 Clean Water Act was amended—for various kinds of projects affecting waterways of the United States. As a category, nationwides were fast-track permits sanctioned by Congress so that the Corps didn't have to send engineers out to inspect the site of every homeowner who wanted to put a pond on his property or build a little wood-plank bridge over his stream. If the project in question was a "minor" activity unlikely to cause controversy or cause more than "minimal adverse" damage to the environment, the Corps could permit it with a nationwide. There were about forty numbered nationwides in all, from mooring buoys (number 10) to marina modifications (number 28). With one exception, nationwides could be

used only when the project in question affected no more than 300 linear feet.

That exception was Nationwide 21.

As Joe pointed out, one of the eleven mine sites he'd put on his list
was seeking a Nationwide 21 to dump mountaintop fill into 18,394 linear feet of perennial streams. If "minimal adverse" damage was defined
in the other nationwides as 300 linear feet, he asked, how could it be
defined as sixty-one times more than that in Nationwide 21?

Joe didn't need to answer that question. Everyone in the courtroom knew why. What the coal industry in West Virginia wanted, it got,
even from—often especially from—the federal government.

Every five years, Joe observed to Judge Goodwin, the Corps was
bound to subject each kind of nationwide to careful environmental
study, to see if the activity was still having a "minimal adverse" impact
on the environment, not only on a case-by-case basis but cumulatively.
Whenever Nationwide 21 came up for renewal—it had last in March
2002—the Corps simply declared that mountaintop mining had no
significant impact. "It is difficult," Joe declared, "to imagine how any
agency, no matter how delusional, could construe the complete destruction of more than one thousand miles of streams and hundreds of
thousands of acres to have minimal effect."

At least when a coal company applied for a Nationwide 21, Joe acknowledged, staffers from the Army Corps came out to look at the site
in question. When they did, though, they studied only the prospective
effect of mountaintop mining on the *aquatic* environment. That was
like bending over a stream with blinders on, ignoring the effects of
mountaintop blasting and dumping on the mountain itself, the valleys
on either side, the forest, the animals, and the people who lived nearby.

The Corps did have a way to rationalize how obliterating streams
caused minimal damage to the environment, Joe explained to Judge
Goodwin. A coal company could "mitigate" the damage by reconstruct-
ing the buried stream somewhere else. When a plan for such mitigation was submitted, the Corps revised downward its estimate of the
damage about to be done. Unfortunately, as Joe pointed out, the miles
of obliterated mountaintop and stream were still obliterated. And so
far, there was almost no evidence that a stream *could* be created somewhere else—by engineers or anyone else—any more than a mountain

could be built back up to look as it had before. The whole concept of mitigation was unproven at best, and the Corps knew it as well as the coal companies did.

If the Corps did little or nothing to measure the impact of each plan submitted for a Nationwide 21, it did even less after that, Joe argued. The Corps never went back to a site to see if the damage had been more than minimal, or if the mitigation had worked. "So glaring are these failures that the court would be fully within its powers to order the Corps to stop using Nationwide 21 anywhere that mountaintop mining is done," Joe said, and then he paused. "But we aren't asking the court to do that."

Joe knew from bitter experience that asking for an across-the-board ban was a mistake. A federal judge might grant it, but looming above was the Fourth Circuit Court of Appeals, the most conservative court in the land. Twice before, Joe had learned just how conservative the Fourth Circuit could be.

"All we ask," Joe said, "is that the court enjoin the Corps from issuing Nationwide 21s to the eleven mines attached to our suit, and that it cease from using Nationwide 21s in the Southern District of West Virginia."

A juryless trial was, by definition, anticlimactic. The judge merely called an end to the proceedings and went off to ponder his verdict. Goodwin had seemed sympathetic to the arguments against Nationwide 21, but Joe slogged through the next weeks assuming the worst. He always did. He was the most negative person he knew. He was the most negative person any of his friends knew. This was partly due to the way he prepared for a case. He liked to plot the other side's case as thoroughly as he did his own, so that he could play against it that much more effectively. By the time he finished the plotting, he usually thought the other side had the stronger case. The pessimism was also self-protective: if he expected to lose, he couldn't be disappointed. Then, perhaps, he could summon the will to go on to the next case. For Joe, pessimism wasn't just a strategy. He really did think he'd lose every case he brought. Yet somehow, his indignation always got the better of his despair.

Joe was in his office on July 8 when he heard that Judge Goodwin had handed down his ruling. A colleague read him the key sentences over the phone: "The court . . . finds that Nationwide Permit 21 does not comply with the plain language, structure, and legislative history of the Clean Water Act." Joe felt exhilarated as the words tumbled through his mind.

The ruling was better than he could ever have hoped. Goodwin had zeroed in on two facts that seemed, to him, unassailable. Congress had indeed sanctioned Nationwide 21 for projects that would cause minimal adverse impact, and the projects proposed for those eleven mines were anything but minimal. Moreover, mitigation rang hollow to Goodwin for a quite specific reason. The judge didn't venture an opinion on whether re-creating a buried stream somewhere else might work or not. He noted merely that the Corps did nothing to test the impact of a plan before it granted a permit. It accepted the word of the coal company that the impact would be what the coal company said it would be, offset by the mitigation that the coal company said would occur. That was a clear failure of the Corps' oversight duty.

There was no doubt, Goodwin wrote, that Nationwide 21 was unlawful. The question was what to do about it. Goodwin cited a U.S. Supreme Court precedent that if a law was found to be illegal as applied in one case, the court could strike the law altogether. Goodwin might have done that, but he, like Joe, was mindful of a ruling by the Fourth Circuit Court of Appeals in Joe's last big case. The Fourth Circuit had declared that no federal judge in its purview had the power to grant circuit-wide programmatic relief, only relief within that judge's district.

Goodwin thus declared he was granting exactly what the plaintiffs had asked. As of that day, the Corps could no longer use Nationwide 21 in the Southern District of West Virginia. For the eleven mines Joe had focused on, the Corps was ordered to suspend the permits for work that had not yet started. Instead, the mine owners would have to apply for the far more stringent individual permits that they hated.

The coal industry was furious. Bill Raney held forth to anyone who would listen on how wrongheaded the ruling was. As it was, he said, a coal operator had to invest at least ten million dollars to open even a small mine and then grapple with no fewer than 105 agencies that had oversight authority on his business. Now Goodwin's ruling had introduced yet another hurdle. How could the coal operator know he'd even be able to get a return on his investment?

Allowing for considerable exaggeration—the number of permitting agencies, state and federal, was a small fraction of 105—Raney was still expressing a powerful industry's frustrations. Those frustrations grew with the news, barely a month after the ruling, that Joe had asked Judge Goodwin to intervene at six *more* mines.

Through early summer, Margaret Janes had kept filing Freedom of Information Act requests with the Army Corps concerning Nation-wide 21s. Some of those FOIA requests had taken the Corps longer to respond to than others. By early August, Margaret realized that six more stealth applications for Nationwide 21s had been filed since the start of the case the previous fall. The companies clearly hoped that even if Judge Goodwin struck down the eleven applications that Joe had cited in his suit, they could still sneak these six by.

"I've already done this!" Judge Goodwin declared when Joe submit-ted a motion to stop the Corps from issuing more Nationwide 21s in southern West Virginia. Grimly, he read through the motion and real-ized what had happened. He was reluctant to revisit his order, he de-clared, since it granted the plaintiffs the relief they'd sought. But he was not inclined, he wrote, to allow discharges into waters of the United States by unlawful permits merely because they weren't known to the plaintiffs when the suit was filed. Rather than risk a repeat of this annoyance, Goodwin flatly ordered the Corps to suspend *all* exist-ing Nationwide 21 authorizations in the Southern District of West Vir-ginia on which work had not started as of July 8, 2004—period.

Howls went up around the coalfields. The second Goodwin deci-sion, coal operators moaned, was worse than the first one. As many as fifty permit applications might now be stalled.

Perhaps Joe should have known not to push Goodwin further than that. But the stories he began to hear were maddening. At many of the eleven sites originally enjoined, bulldozers were said to be clear-cutting trees—the first step in readying a site for mountaintop removal. In the valleys below, sediment ponds were being built. Sediment ponds were put at the foot of an impoundment and filled with chemicals. When slurry was released a bit at a time from the impoundment down into the pond, the chemicals were supposed to pull the slurry's toxins to the bottom. The remaining water was then clean enough—supposedly—to be dumped into the nearest stream.

Both of these were baby steps, taken well in advance of blasting a mountain and creating the actual valley fill. But Goodwin had been clear: on any of those sites where work had not yet started on a valley fill, nothing further was to be done—at least, until the coal operators received individual permits. The coal operators seemed to be willfully ignoring what a federal judge had ordered them to do.

The tip-off had come from Don Blankenship himself. Massey owned subsidiaries that had applied for five of the eleven permits on Joe's list. In a conference call with analysts in late July, Don complained about Judge Goodwin's ruling but said he didn't expect it to halt work at any of those five sites. "While what constitutes the commencing of construction has not yet been specifically defined," Don declared, "Massey [had] started some construction on all five permits by the date of the ruling." When an analyst asked him what exactly Massey was doing at those sites, Don said, "It varies a little bit, but in all cases we are, at a minimum, building ponds and in some cases, we are dumping material into the fills."

When Joe saw Don's comments in the Charleston *Gazette*, he got right on the phone with Bob McLusky. "What's going on here, Bob?" Joe demanded. "You can't start work if you don't have valley fills, you know that."

"I think it's okay if you have sediment ponds," McLusky said.

"No it's not," Joe said.

"Let me get back to you."

McLusky called back later that day. "It's our position," he said, "that it's okay if you've started cutting trees out there."

"Bullshit it is."

Joe called the Corps to ask that it enforce Judge Goodwin's ruling. The Corps declined to help. He called the DEP. It declined to help, too. "We prefer not to be caught in the middle," one DEP lawyer explained. Finally, Joe wrote a motion for Judge Goodwin, asking him to clarify what did and did not constitute the commencement of work on a Nationwide 21. "Although plaintiffs see no ambiguity in the Order," Joe wrote, "some coal operators are apparently interpreting the Order in a way that contradicts the Order's plain language." The refusal of agencies to help, he wrote, had created a "vacuum of authority that allows operators to fill streams with impunity."

Judge Goodwin declined to clarify his ruling. "I trust that the Corps will enforce my unambiguous orders," he ruled. Perhaps, Joe thought glumly, the judge was limiting his order with an eye on the Fourth Circuit Court of Appeals, mindful that the more action he took, the more likely the Fourth would reverse him. Goodwin did emphasize—for the third time, he noted—that Nationwide 21 was "unlawful." All coal companies now had to pursue individual permits. But as to what defined the start of work on a valley fill, he said, no further clarification was needed.

The next day—September 2, 2004, two months before the presidential election—President Bush's senior environmental policy advisor, James Connaughton of the White House Council on Environmental Quality, traveled to the historic Greenbrier resort in White Sulphur Springs, West Virginia, to tell a group of coal operators exactly what they wanted to hear. Judge Goodwin's ruling, he said, put a "halt to the work that West Virginia miners do for their communities and their families." And so the Bush administration, on behalf of the U.S. Army Corps of Engineers, would appeal the Nationwide 21 case to the Fourth Circuit. Connaughton didn't need to say what the barons were thinking. The Fourth Circuit would squash those puny environmentalists as surely as it had done two times before.

In his two-room office in Lewisburg, Joe read the news with grim humor. Once again, he expected to lose. But perhaps the Fourth Circuit would find the law as clear on Nationwide 21 as Judge Goodwin had. Perhaps, if it did, it would uphold Goodwin's ruling. Perhaps if that happened, Joe could at least slow the steady destruction of mountaintops in southern West Virginia.

Perhaps.

FIVE

STACKING THE
STATE SUPREME COURT

Every summer, Don Blankenship presided over a company picnic attended by Massey's five thousand employees and their families, along with thousands of other company friends. Every guest was given a xeroxed ticket that entitled him or her to one club sandwich or one peanut-butter-and-jelly sandwich, but not both. A well-known country-and-western band usually performed, and Don himself took the microphone to address the grateful crowd. This summer, he sounded more political than he had in the past. "If you are against coal, you are against West Virginia and America," Don declared. "There's more global warming caused by the hot air coming out of the mouths of environmental extremists than there is from burning American coal. . . . Rich nations like ours have the luxury of acting to preserve the environment. But the desperately poor nations struggle only to meet today's needs. China is the greatest polluter in the world, and yet we help them expand their coal production while we try to suppress our own."

The picnickers applauded, though more out of duty than passion. Not many in the audience cared about China.

"Some express concern about coal mine safety," Don went on. "Well, we will be close to having one thousand American soldiers killed in Iraq before the end of this year. That's more than have been killed in coal mines in the last twenty years. . . . Coal mining in America is safer than war in Iraq. In fact it's safer than dairy farming. . . . Besides, coal mining keeps getting safer."

At this, the applause was a little more scattered. Most in the audience knew someone who had been injured or had died in a mining accident. They were happy to have jobs, but not many would have called coal mining safe. Most also knew someone in the military serving in Iraq and still strongly supported the war. Don's mention of the death toll sounded vaguely unpatriotic.

"Your taxes are being used to create improved life in China, Iraq, Afghanistan, and elsewhere throughout the world," Don thundered. "At home your taxes are being used to fund agencies like EPA and U.S. Fish and Wildlife. These agencies paid for by your taxes want to destroy your job, your company, and your vehicle." Now Don hit his main point. "Don't vote for judges or representatives who put Massey and your job at risk," he cried. "Fight back and vote."

Don wanted his audience to think hard about two justices on the West Virginia Supreme Court of Appeals. "You've probably heard of Justice Warren McGraw in particular. He and Larry Starcher are responsible for many of the court's most disturbing decisions. The type of decisions that allow uninjured and healthy individuals to receive workers' compensation benefits. We've all seen the fake injury claims. It's McGraw and judges like him that make such behavior profitable."

This was a lot more politics than the picnickers wanted to hear. Their applause, when he finished, was more out of relief than anything else. Don's delivery as a public speaker was wooden: his arms stayed at his sides, and his eyes never seemed to connect with any of his listeners. But he liked what he had to say, and he was going to say more of it in the months to come. What he said and did would make him more than a coal boss. Soon he would be the most powerful political force in the state.

"Think bigger" was Don's new mantra to the bullied and morose executives who worked for him. "Think bigger!" It was time, he decided, to take his own advice. He was tired of the abuse that Massey took in simply trying to do its business. Tired of DEP inspectors who wrote up violations every time one of his operations had a blackwater spill or ventilation problem. Tired of the circuit judges who let nuisance cases against Massey Energy be heard. Tired, above all, of the West Virginia Supreme Court of Appeals, to which those cases inevitably ascended, and where, to Don's profound annoyance, three of the five justices seemed to go out of their way to find against Massey Energy.

One of those five justices, as it happened, was up for reelection in November. Warren McGraw wasn't the most liberal of the lot. In truth, he was the court's swing vote. But while he often swung to the conservative side in law-and-order cases, he did tend to sympathize with coal miners who claimed they'd been cheated out of disability pay for work injuries. Don hated that. He thought McGraw was a bleeding-heart, antibusiness blowhard, and it bothered him that the term of office for a West Virginia state supreme court justice was twelve years. That was a long time. Massey had a few serious cases pending with the state supreme court that would come up sometime in those next twelve years, no matter how much stalling the company's lawyers did, and Don felt he knew just how McGraw would vote on every one of them. On August 7, 2004, Don wrote a letter to a select list of West Virginia businessmen, urging them to help defeat McGraw by supporting the justice's all-but-unknown Republican challenger. In the letter, he didn't say just how far he was willing to go, personally, to get McGraw out. For the next two months, almost no one would know that Don had decided to embark on the most blatantly bare-knuckled political campaign in the entire United States that year.

McGraw, a sandy-haired, sixty-five-year-old lawyer with a southern West Virginian twang and a jovial manner that didn't always mask his flinty pride and quick temper, had survived a surprisingly strong challenge in the Democratic primary from a Greenbrier County circuit judge named Jim Rowe. A lot of the trial lawyers who were supporting McGraw felt he'd now coast through the general election. He was a well-known figure in the state, and, of course, he was the incumbent. But McGraw's campaign manager, Andy Gallagher, wasn't so sure. He'd seen how much support Rowe had received from the state's Chamber of Commerce, and he knew just what that meant. The chamber was no longer a little office on Main Street with boosters who talked up local restaurants and inns to visiting tourists. Over the last few years, the national network of chambers of commerce had become a potent political force. Behind them were big businesses ranging from insurance giants such as the American International Group (AIG) to Home Depot and DaimlerChrysler, as well as the national Republican party. All were allied in an effort to unseat mostly Democratic judges around the country whose rulings suggested an antibusiness, pro-union, pro-plaintiff tilt. Between 2000 and the start of 2004, the national Chamber of Commerce had spent one hundred million dollars on twenty-four judicial elections in eight states. Its candidates had won in twenty-one of those elections. It was poised to spend another fifty million dollars just in 2004. Near the top of its target list for 2004 was Warren McGraw.

The Republican-dominated Chamber of Commerce had backed Rowe, a Democrat, because it felt he had the best chance of knocking off McGraw. After all, a large majority of West Virginians still voted Democratic in local races. But with Rowe's loss, the chamber gamely shifted its backing to the Republican primary winner, a forty-six-year-old Charleston lawyer and political question mark named Brent Benjamin.

In person, Benjamin was as genial as he was rotund: a boyish Humpty Dumpty of a figure who liked to stress his courtroom experience but who had served neither as a litigator nor a lower-court judge. In fact, Benjamin had spent most of his time as a lawyer in the Charleston offices of Robinson & McElwee, a firm with strong ties to the energy industry, working for corporate clients.

Benjamin had decided to run, he said, because of what he called a fundamental fairness issue. He knew litigants, he said, who didn't even bother going to court—corporate clients, that is, who had been sued by employees and felt the court was too biased to make the legal fight worthwhile. They would simply write checks to the workers, because that was the less expensive way to go. Warren McGraw, Benjamin declared in his campaign appearances, seemed to give workers more than the benefit of the doubt—he seemed to side with them all the time.

There was some truth to this. In five years of workman's comp cases, McGraw had favored workers 88 percent of the time, *Forbes* magazine discovered. But these were all cases in which a lower-court judge or jury had sided with the workers already, after hearing the best arguments of both sides. The only reason these cases were being brought to the state supreme court was that the companies found guilty were trying to get those verdicts overturned.

Andy Gallagher saw his fears confirmed in late August as the Benjamin campaign launched television commercials that branded McGraw as an "extreme" and "activist" judge who put "the interests of criminals before the rights of law-abiding citizens." One commercial featured silhouettes of children as a stern voice addressed Benjamin's opponent directly: "Judge Warren McGraw, the facts in the case are a matter of public record. The children in this case will never be the same." Another commercial declared, "Letting a child rapist go free to work in schools—that's radical Supreme Court Justice Warren McGraw."

The case in question, which McGraw's primary challenger had invoked as well, concerned a twenty-three-year-old man named Tony Dean Arbaugh Jr.; the court had issued a ruling on the case in February 2004. As a teenager, Tony had sexually molested several younger siblings, peers, and relatives. In exchange for a single guilty plea of first-degree sexual assault, the state had dropped several other sexual-assault charges, and a judge had placed Tony in a treatment center with a suspended jail sentence of fifteen to thirty-five years. Tony had bounced from one facility to the next but regained his freedom at eighteen, on strict terms of probation: no alcohol, no drugs, a commitment to counseling, and a monthly probationary fee. Shortly after, he had violated all those terms, and the state revoked his probation. A circuit judge declared he had no choice but to hit Arbaugh with his full suspended sentence. That was the ruling that Arbaugh had appealed to the state supreme court. He wanted one more chance.

McGraw had joined two other justices in a 3–2 decision to give Arbaugh that chance. In an unsigned draft opinion, the majority noted that Arbaugh had endured a long history of sexual assault himself, beginning when he was seven or eight years old. Two adult family members had routinely sodomized and otherwise abused him for years. So had one of his teachers. (Arbaugh would soon receive a settlement of five hundred thousand dollars from the state Board of Education as the result of a civil suit against the teacher.) The assaults he'd then engaged in himself were reprehensible but psychologically understandable and short-lived. The draft opinion noted there was no evidence, nine years after those incidents, that Arbaugh was any longer a threat to anyone. "A decent society," the opinion declared, "is [one] where a child who has been sexually victimized for years, and who becomes seriously disordered, but who does work in structured situations to improve, gets our help, not a thirty-five year prison sentence."

Moreover, the state would not be paying a cent for Arbaugh's last stab at rehabilitation. A social-work volunteer with the Marist Brothers, a Roman Catholic group, had vouched for Arbaugh and offered to enroll him in a program called Youth Systems Services, which would pay for his stay. The volunteer, Paul Flanagan, believed that Arbaugh could be saved and "brought around to a pro-social life." Flanagan explained that Arbaugh would start living in another part of the state, to remove him from peers who had influenced him negatively. He would live in a community apartment and have access to Youth Systems staff twenty-four hours a day. To get him acclimated to work, he would be employed as a janitor at a local Catholic high school.

First Rowe and now Benjamin had seized on that last detail and waved it at McGraw like a matador's red flag before a bull. And yet, in fact, Arbaugh hadn't worked at the school after all. And the draft opinion in which that damaging directive was found did not remain the last word on the case. The three justices in the majority rejected it and instead endorsed a concurring opinion by one of the justices that reached the same conclusions but with no mention of prospective employment at a school. Strangely, the first, unsigned opinion for the majority was written by Justice Robin Davis, who then wrote the blistering *dissent* from that opinion that campaign ads for Rowe and Benjamin gleefully quoted. That was because the appeal was assigned to her, and by court tradition she was obligated to write the majority opinion even if she wasn't in the majority herself. McGraw among others wondered if Davis had set up the majority with the coming campaign in mind— a charge she vigorously denied. But to McGraw's opponents, these were mere nuances.

"What are you going to do with this?" Gallagher demanded of his candidate as the Arbaugh commercials saturated the airwaves.

"Well, for God's sakes," McGraw thundered. "We wouldn't have ever let that kid work at a school!" McGraw said he hadn't even known the directive about Arbaugh working in a school was *in* that first, un-signed opinion that Robin Davis had written. "The second opinion's the legal one," he said. "Not the first one."

"Yeah, I know," Gallagher said with a sigh. "But it's the first one the public is focused on."

Over the Labor Day weekend, the whole state seemed to bristle with politics. Both members of the just-nominated Democratic presi-dential ticket, John Kerry and John Edwards, made appearances, stress-ing that they, not George W. Bush, would help working West Virginians. The notorious "Swift Boat" campaign had lambasted Kerry in commer-cials around the country, and the candidate was still struggling over how to respond to the charges. In West Virginia, a probusiness group with ties to the state Republican party was running commercials against him, too, claiming he supported a ban on mountaintop coal mining. Kerry had said nothing about mountaintop mining, but Republicans knew Democrats were divided over it. Both of the state's Democratic senators, Robert C. Byrd and Jay Rockefeller, were mountaintop-mining supporters—in a state dominated by the mining industry, they had to be—and Kerry would annoy them if he knocked the practice to please more liberal voters. Yet by saying he *didn't* oppose a ban on mountaintop mining, he risked alienating the liberals. The commercials were dishonest but clever. That weekend, Bush joined the fray with an address to party faithful in Wheeling. And then, on Labor Day itself, Warren McGraw let loose a rant in Racine.

McGraw was seething from the Arbaugh commercials, which had begun running the week before. At a rally where Kerry spoke as well, the crusty judge got a lot angrier when he caught sight of a camera-man unobtrusively videotaping the event. The cameraman was Chris Hamilton of the West Virginia Coal Association. McGraw confronted Hamilton, who said he was working that day for the state Republican party. A furious McGraw took to the stage and seized the micro-phone. "They follow us everywhere we go," he shouted to the crowd. "They followed us to Marmet today. They followed us to Hinton. They follow us *looking for ugly* . . . trying to take ugly pictures to do ugly things with." McGraw's voice rose as he spoke. "Ugliness! To re-port lies. Things that are untrue." His voice rose again. "Who do they think elected me?"

Many in the crowd cheered McGraw on, just as many in an Iowa convention room the previous winter had cheered on Democratic hopeful Howard Dean when he shouted out the names of states whose primaries he hoped to win. But McGraw, like Dean, seemed over-wrought and somewhat alarming on videotape after his speech. He looked like a man out of control.

The next day, a veteran Republican strategist named Gary Aber-nathy heard a playback of the speech and started laughing. He started jotting down bemused remarks to interject at certain points in the rant. Within a couple days, his spliced version of the "Rant at Racine," com-plete with interjections, was playing all over the state. McGraw was in trouble, and he didn't even know yet that Don Blankenship had de-cided to spend millions of dollars setting up a 527 political-action group to blow him away.

Brent Benjamin didn't know that, either, or so he said. Soon after Labor Day, he later recounted, he was driving down a Charleston street when he saw something that nearly made him drive onto the curb. There on a billboard in huge letters was the question, "Who is Brent Benjamin?" Benjamin was astonished, he said. He got out of his car and walked over to see who had paid for the ad. In small type in one corner, he read that the ad had been sponsored by a group called "And for the Sake of the Kids." On his cell phone, Benjamin punched in the number for his campaign manager, Rob Capehart. "Rob, what's 'And for the Sake of the Kids'?" Capehart didn't know, either. Benjamin's first thought was that the McGraw camp had done it. But why mount a campaign that gave name recognition to his little-known opponent? It didn't make sense.

And for the Sake of the Kids, it turned out, was a newly formed 527 political-action group that listed one Dan McGraw, a doctor from Parkersburg, as its only member. (The doctor was no relation to the jus-tice the 527 was trying to unseat.) The McCain-Feingold Bipartisan Campaign Reform Act of 2002 had closed some fund-raising loopholes but opened this new one: anyone could form a 527 and donate any amount of tax-exempt money to it. The 527, in turn, could promote any cause or candidate it liked. It just couldn't have any link to the candidate or political party it was pushing. No communication at all was allowed. And for the Sake of the Kids was in business, it now seemed, to further the candidacy of Brent Benjamin. But according to Benjamin, neither he nor anyone in his camp knew who was behind it.

Within days, the state was blanketed with billboards and TV commercials that didn't just ask who Brent Benjamin was. They declared McGraw was soft on crime. It was a charge belied by his record: a study of eight hundred cases that McGraw had participated in during his years on the court showed that the court had refused to consider nearly 84 percent of appeals filed by convicted criminals; McGraw had disagreed with just 3 percent of those rulings. Worse, the ads hammered on the Arbaugh case, skewing details and all but declaring McGraw an advocate of child molestation. The campaign reportedly included push polls, in which ostensibly neutral telephone pollsters couched slanderous charges in their questions. It used robocalls: recorded announcements sliming McGraw, often with a sideswipe at his brother, Darrell, the state's attorney general, who was also up for reelection. One series of calls told listeners to tune in to a local TV station that night. When they did, they saw a purported documentary on Warren McGraw, complete with his rant in Racine. The calls were so pervasive that Andy Gallagher began getting three or four of them per day at McGraw's own campaign headquarters.

From the start, Gallagher had a hunch that the shadow behind And for the Sake of the Kids was Don Blankenship. He even said as much to local reporters and urged them to print his suspicion. "Just run it, and let's see if Don denies it." But without any evidence to support the claim, the reporters refused. Gallagher felt he was in campaign-manager hell. Not only did he lack the funds to respond to this anonymous onslaught, but he had a candidate who refused to discuss the Arbaugh case with the press—refused, for that matter, to do interviews at all. McGraw was sour, as Gallagher put it, because he felt whatever he said was used against him. Certainly many of the newspapers were owned by businesses more apt to side with the Chamber of Commerce than Warren McGraw—that was a reality of political life in West Virginia. And several of the TV stations were owned by a Benjamin supporter, Bray Cary. But there was more to it than that. McGraw was a proud man and very, very angry. He could see how he was being gamed, and as September unfolded he could see the game was working. But he simply refused to get down in the gutter with his antagonists, whoever they were. He was *Warren McGraw*—a figure of rectitude who'd dedicated his life to furthering justice wherever he could. Surely the voters knew that and would vote accordingly.

The voters both did and didn't. Most West Virginians who knew Warren McGraw personally were fond and respectful of him. But to many more voters, he was merely a name, easily tainted by suggestion. And hardly any voters saw this race for what it really was: a struggle between integrity and raw power in West Virginia, between a man who'd stood up to the coal industry, again and again, and the industry's self-appointed king, Don Blankenship, who would use his money and power to push aside anyone who stood in his way. In court, the two had already butted up against each other for several years. Of all the coal companies in West Virginia, Massey Energy was among the most delinquent in its payment of premiums to the West Virginia Workers' Compensation Fund. The suits provoked by that failure were just a few of those involving Massey that had reached the state supreme court during McGraw's term—cases often decided against Massey. But most voters were unaware of that, too.

Don stayed behind the curtain as his 527 group pummeled McGraw through September and early October. By then, the campaign had become, in the estimation of the New York University School of Law's Brennan Center for Justice, which tracked political races, the nastiest in the nation. Like all 527s, however, And for the Sake of the Kids was obligated by law at a certain point to disclose the names of its contributors. For the group now known as AFSK, the disclosure date was October 15. Don Blankenship, the group duly divulged that day, had given $1.7 million, making him the 527's largest contributor by far. It was money he could easily afford: the Massey chairman had earned $6,105,714 in 2003, making him the highest-paid CEO of a publicly traded company in the state. That didn't include the enormous windfall he was about to receive by selling company stock: $17.6 million. The stock sale in itself was more than the $13.9 million Massey would make in profit for 2004.

Outed at last, Massey's chairman seemed to enjoy the spotlight. "Over the years," he declared in a written statement to the press, "I and the companies for which I worked have donated millions to WV charities. However, I decided this summer that the most productive donation

I could make to my fellow West Virginians was to help defeat Warren McGraw." That, he said, was because "Warren votes almost every time for plaintiffs and against job providers—unless the Charleston *Gazette* is the defendant."

Don was a bit more partial to the Charleston *Daily Mail,* which he considered more sympathetic to business—despite the fact that the newspapers had a joint operating agreement—and so he granted the *Daily Mail* an interview to explain himself further. "It will be worthwhile win or lose for me personally," he declared. "I wanted the satisfaction of knowing I had done the right thing, which is what I always try to do."

Don was asked if the name of his 527 indicated some intent on his part to help children. Don said it did. After the election, he said, he would start a foundation to "provide needed clothing and other necessities to the most needy children of West Virginia." Over the next few years, he said, he would help the foundation raise an amount of money similar to what he'd spent on the campaign to date for these children and their needs. A year later, asked how the foundation was doing, Don allowed that it hadn't started up quite yet. But it would start up eventually.

The news that Don Blankenship was the driving force behind AFSK angered Warren McGraw, and it depressed Andy Gallagher, but it had a much more chilling effect on a well-bred West Virginian ex-coal operator named Hugh Caperton. He thought he knew exactly why Don was spending so much money to oust Warren McGraw. A jury settlement of more than fifty million dollars hung in the balance.

The endless parade of workman's comp cases was reason enough for Don to want to put a thumb on the scales of the West Virginia Supreme Court of Appeals. Even more compelling were the Matt Crum cases—the ones in which the DEP was actually insisting that one Massey subsidiary or another be shut for some days as punishment for chronic violations. But *Harman Mining and Hugh Caperton v. Massey Energy* was in a class by itself.

Hugh Caperton was a tall, handsome scion of old coal money whose cousin, Gaston Caperton III, had served two successful, scandal-free terms as governor of West Virginia, from 1988 to 1996. The Capertons had started in coal in 1907, a little more than a decade before the Masseys, as soon as the railroad tracks reached Beckley. Hugh's great-grandfather had opened several mines around Slab Fork—a once-thriving coal town not far from Beckley. In its heyday, Slab Fork had produced a million tons annually of high-grade metallurgical coal—the kind used not to heat homes or run power plants but to make steel. The business had passed down through two generations to Hugh's father, then closed in the bust years of the early 1980s. Hugh had loved growing up in Slab Fork and always felt that a powerful sense of community knit the town together. The workers were union, but they felt equally loyal to Hugh's father because he treated them with respect. Occasionally they struck on behalf of the UMWA, but when the strike was over, everyone went back to work with relief. More than anything, Hugh longed for a chance to start his own version of Slab Fork. When the chance came along in 1993 with Harman Mining, he seized it.

Harman lay just south of the state border in Grundy, Virginia, though still within the heart of the southern coalfields. Like Slab Fork, Grundy was a company town that had come into being only because of high-grade metallurgical coal. And like Slab Fork, Harman had died in the 1980s. Hugh was able to start it back up by winning concessions from the UMWA in return for creating 150 jobs. Then he managed to sign up one large customer. United Coal, just down the road from Harman, had a long-term contract to supply high-grade metallurgical coal to LTV Steel. It was delighted to take all such coal that Harman could send its way. Hugh didn't even need to use Harman's antiquated, labor-intensive prep plant. He just shipped raw coal to United, which washed it at its own prep plant and sent it on to LTV. Everyone was happy, and Hugh fully expected to stay happy for at least ten years. That was the length of his contract with United. Unfortunately, Don Blankenship had a different plan.

Rumors that Massey might be buying United Coal came true in July 1997. Initially, Hugh felt fine about that. After all, he had his ten-year contract. Legally, Massey would have to honor it. Then came a letter on August 5 informing Hugh that Massey might use force majeure to break the contract.

"Force majeure," Hugh knew, was a term of art in contracts that meant a change forced by some major, unforeseen event that no one could predict or control—essentially, an act of God. In the coal business, a train derailment that prevented a shipment from reaching its market was force majeure. A flood that inundated a mine, or a major mine collapse, was force majeure. Massey, its lawyers informed Hugh, was contemplating economic force majeure. It didn't like United's contract terms with Harman: it paid $33.50 per ton. Massey didn't want to pay that much. That was its force majeure.

Hugh wasn't sure that Massey wanted to deal with Harman on any terms. Harman, after all, was a union operation, and everyone in the coal business knew how Don Blankenship felt about the UMWA. But perhaps, Hugh thought, this was just a negotiating ploy to lower the price a bit. Hugh sent the president of his mine to talk to the new president of United. "Yeah, well, if you lower your prices enough, we might be able to talk," the new Massey man said, according to Hugh. But no price seemed low enough. Finally, Hugh called Don directly to suggest they meet and work things out.

The week before Thanksgiving, Don walked into Hugh's modest offices in Beckley, a block or so from the town's historic square, across the street from a Subway sandwich shop. With him was his president of mining operations. Hugh had never met Don before. He was struck by how socially awkward the Massey chairman seemed. Don didn't smile, and he didn't make small talk. He just sat down and got right to business.

Was this, in fact, force majeure? Don asked rhetorically. Hugh said it wasn't. Don said it was. Hugh noticed that as he spoke, Don used a particular phrase as a refrain. "You don't understand," the Massey chairman told him. He used it to show who was in charge and what was going to happen. "You just don't understand."

Don made clear what was in store for Hugh if he contested Massey's claim. "There was the intimidation factor," Hugh recalled later. "'You don't want to take us to court over this. For every expert you hire to say it's not force majeure, we'll hire three that say it is. We spend one million dollars a month on attorneys, and we'll tie you up for years.'"

Hugh had never even seen the inside of a courtroom. The prospect of endless legal expenses was not only daunting but depressing as well.

"Look," he said to Don, "why don't you just buy my company? Then it's your coal, and you can do what you want with it. Let's just come up with a plan."

Don nodded slowly. He seemed to like the idea. "That's something we'd consider," he said, as Hugh recalled. "Why don't you put some numbers together, just let me know what you want, and we'll take it from there."

The meeting, to Hugh's surprise, ended very cordially.

Three days later, Hugh got another letter from Massey. Harman's contract was formally canceled on grounds of force majeure.

"What the hell is this?" Hugh asked Don when he got him on the phone. "I thought we were talking about a deal."

Don apologized. Someone, he said, must have sent that letter out without his knowledge. Hugh had trouble believing that. Nothing, he knew, happened at Massey Energy without Don's express approval. Hugh had heard a story from a friend who went to work for Massey. One day, the friend told his immediate boss he needed an oil change for his company car. "All that has to come through Richmond," the boss had replied. The friend duly requested an oil change in writing. Back came the okay: a scrawled marginal note on his request from Don Blankenship himself.

Don told Hugh to submit a purchase proposal, and Hugh did. But when Hugh suggested a price of about seventeen million dollars for Harman's sizable coal reserves, Don just laughed. That, Hugh later recalled Don saying, was far, far more than Massey was willing to pay.

Hugh knew he was in a poor position to negotiate. After all, he had no customers for his coal, and no one else had expressed interest in buying him out. By now, he'd also heard that Massey intended to shut down United altogether. If so, then the negotiations with Harman to buy its coal at a lower price were suspect, to say the least. All along, Hugh suspected, Don's plan may have been to get United's lucrative LTV contract and transfer it to his nonunion operations in West Virginia. Since he could get coal far more cheaply from those mines than from Hugh, he'd make more money that way, even if it meant closing United. He'd also have the satisfaction, in quashing Harman, of delivering another kick in the shins to the UMWA. But how astonishing, Hugh thought, to go to all this trouble—and cause all this misery—for the million or so tons of coal per year that were at stake in the deal. Compared to the forty million tons Massey produced overall each year, it was a pittance.

Over the next weeks, Hugh submitted new proposals to Massey, each price lower than the last. Don or his lieutenants would make a show of studying each of them, only to reject it. Meanwhile, Hugh kept his workers mining coal. But with no customers to sell it to, the piles of coal just grew and grew, along with Hugh's debts. As bankruptcy loomed, more and more miners claimed workplace injuries and filed for workman's compensation pay.

Later, when he filed his suit and the details of his plight became known in the industry, Hugh heard from other operators who'd been squeezed by Don Blankenship in just the same way. Don, they told him, was adept at identifying companies in financial hardship, then offering to bail them out. He loved to play the "settlement game," as one put it. Having dangled the prospect of a lifesaving deal to his victim, Don would then back off. The victim would take Don's word that a deal was imminent and make business decisions based on that— decisions that made him more vulnerable over time. Eventually, Don would buy the helpless company at a bargain-basement price.

In January 1998, Hugh lowered his price to about five million dollars—basically giving his company away for the cost of its debts. Papers were drawn up, but just as Hugh was preparing to go to Richmond to sign them in March, a call came from Massey's lawyers. There was a problem with the deal. Hugh didn't own the Harman land; it was only leased. Massey's lawyers knew that already, Hugh countered. Yes, they said, but they didn't like the wording on the contract for how Massey would assume the lease. "Fine," Hugh cried in exasperation, "so change it."

But Massey's lawyers never did change it. The closing date slipped away, and so did the rest of the winter. Hugh had to declare bankruptcy. Furious now, he filed a breach-of-contract suit in November 1998 and steeled himself to confront Massey's legal team. On the advice of the Philadelphia lawyer who took on his case, Hugh filed a second suit, this one for tortious interference, which meant not just breach of contract but *intent* to breach contract, with actual damage. Don's game of cat and mouse had cost Hugh much more than a contract, Hugh felt. It had cost him his business, his capital, and, he feared, his reputation.

Sometime before the first of those cases went to trial—early 1999—Hugh got a call from Don Blankenship. Don said he wanted to meet one more time, to see if they could reach an agreement. Don wanted to talk to Hugh alone, he said, without any lawyers present.

"If you want to meet me, you come to Beckley," Hugh said between clenched teeth. "I'm not meeting you on anyone's turf but my own."

The meeting was stranger than Hugh could have imagined.

Don flew to Beckley in his corporate helicopter and was driven to Hugh's office. While his driver waited out front, Don came up alone to the office. Hugh took Don's hand warily, then sat back down to listen. Don started talking, only he didn't talk business. He asked after Hugh's brother, who was battling cancer at the time. Don recalled that Hugh's brother had worked for Massey at one point and said what a good man he was. Then he lapsed into silence for a moment. Out of nowhere, he said, "You know, I don't understand it, but people don't like me anymore."

"What do you mean, Don?" Hugh asked.

"When I was in high school and college, I had lots of friends," Don said. "I played sports, we palled around. But it just seems like now, people don't like me. I don't have any close friends."

It was as if Don were talking to his therapist, not the man he'd just put out of business.

Maybe Don had a girlfriend, Hugh ventured. A lot of men were closer to the women in their lives than to other men, when you got right down to it. Don shrugged. He was dating a girl, he said, and he'd built her a house. But he'd been down that road before, and it had cost him a fortune. So he'd built his girlfriend a house, but if the relationship ended he'd just take the house back.

With that, Don got up. The meeting was over, it seemed. Or maybe it wasn't. At the door, he turned and said, "By the way, I think what we could maybe offer is five hundred thousand dollars. My lawyers have told me that the way it works, we have a say in how that money gets split, so maybe you'd get half of it and the company would get half."

Hugh could hardly believe his ears. It was like offering him fifty bucks. "Don," he said evenly, "it's way too late for that kind of a deal."

And that was the last Hugh saw of him, until Don testified in the second of two trials that Harman brought against Massey.

The breach-of-contract case was argued in front of a Virginia judge after numerous delaying maneuvers by Massey's lawyers. Hugh's lawyer, Dave Fawcett, made the case that Harman should be compensated for the seven years remaining on its ten-year contract with United. Massey's lawyers observed that the contract had a one-year out clause: United could have terminated the contract with one year's notice. Thus, Massey should have to pay only one year's damages. The judge agreed, but one year's damages still came to the respectable figure of six million dollars, which only rose with interest as Massey fought the decision to the Virginia state supreme court. Finally, in November 2002, Massey had to write Hugh a check for $7.2 million.

Both sides knew the stakes in the "tortious interference" case would be much higher. Hugh had filed the suit in Boone County, West Virginia, because his case alleged personal distress, and that was where he lived. Massey tried every legal gambit it could to get it moved to Charleston, fearing that the company's poor reputation in Boone—the heart of the Coal River valley—would adversely influence jurors. For nearly two years, the case bounced from one court to another. Finally a trial date was set in Boone for June 2002. Just before the trial started, each side had to provide the other with all documents it intended to use. Hugh was sorting through the pile from Massey's legal team when he came upon photographs of his house. Massey had sent private investigators to the gated community where Hugh and his family lived. The investigators had trespassed onto the Capertons' property to take photographs that would help Massey's lawyers make the case Hugh was too affluent to deserve punitive damages. Hugh was stunned. His wife, he later said, was devastated by the maneuver.

At this second trial, Don took the witness stand to explain that everything Massey had done in its dealings with Harman was just a matter of cost-benefit analysis. There wasn't anything personal about it. It was all business. After a trial of eight weeks, the jury needed only six or seven hours to find Massey guilty. The various damages totaled fifty million dollars.

Massey filed the inevitable posttrial motions, all to no avail. Judge Jay Hoke grew irate enough to declare the jury had "had sufficient evidence before it to conclude that Massey's conduct was reprehensible" and that Massey "stood to profit substantially from their wrongful conduct." Now Massey had one last resort: to appeal the verdict to the West Virginia state supreme court.

No one could predict how a state supreme court justice would vote, but three of the presiding five had often sided against coal companies in the past. Now that balance was about to change.

In the final days of the presidential campaign of 2004, West Virginia voters could hardly turn on their televisions without seeing a political commercial for Bush or Kerry. The state's five electoral votes were very much up for grabs, and for all anyone knew they might help decide a tight race, as they had four years before. As in 2000, West Virginia's traditionally Democratic voters in the southwestern coalfields worried that their candidate might be too much of an environmentalist. Bush was clearly willing to do almost anything to help the coal industry. Here, as in other swing states, Republican operatives did all they could to sway voters with fearmongering talk of Kerry's alleged positions on cultural issues. One mailing accused him of wanting to ban the Bible. Flyers distributed in churches said he favored "anti-Christian, anti-God, antifamily" judges, along with same-sex marriage and abortion. The National Rifle Association painted Kerry as an elitist liberal who wanted to take away voters' hunting rifles. On election night, Bush took the state with ease.

That evening, Andy Gallagher sat at the bar of the Marriott Hotel in Charleston, glumly watching one county after another go for Brent Benjamin. For the first hour or so of returns, Warren McGraw's campaign manager could kid himself: McGraw was strongest in counties yet to be counted. But Benjamin's lead held steady all night. In the other most closely watched race in the state, Warren's brother, Darrell, won reelection as attorney general, but by a mere 0.4 percent of the vote. AFSK had come that close to knocking him off, too. Only later did Andy learn that both McGraws were in the same hotel, watching the results from rooms of their own. Warren had not bothered to tell his campaign manager where he'd be for election night, and Andy hadn't bothered to ask. It wasn't the first time that a losing candidate and his campaign manager watched the results in separate rooms.

Brent Benjamin was watching the results nearby at the Capitol Roasters, his favorite Charleston coffee bar. After a victory speech, he declared he would be a fair judge who followed the law. "I can tell you I am not bought by anybody," he said. But when asked if he would recuse himself from cases involving Massey Energy and its subsidiaries, Benjamin declined to say.

Don Blankenship was also nearby, celebrating in a hotel bar with a group that included state supreme court justice "Spike" Maynard, one of the two dissenting justices in the Arbaugh case. Asked if he'd just bought a court seat, Don said he'd spent his money to beat McGraw. "I think any time you have to deal with the kind of evil the McGraws represent, you have to do what the law allows you to do," he said. "I think he will be more fair," he added, "simply because I don't think anyone [could] be less fair."

Soon enough, that prediction would be put to the test.

SIX

THE WAR WITH WASHINGTON

Judge Goodwin's ruling of July 8, 2004, should have halted every new large mountaintop-mining site in the Southern District of West Virginia, or at least all those proposing to operate under the Army Corps' woefully inadequate Nationwide 21 permit—which was to say, nearly all of them.

It hadn't.

First, the judge had declined to clarify his order after hearing reports that coal companies were ignoring it. Then, when the Corps reported back to him on seventy-three mining sites that might be subject to the ruling, he seemed to shrug at their verdict that work had begun at twenty-three of those sites. The Corps appeared to agree with Don Blankenship about the definition of "work": anything from creating a sediment pond to building a road to relocating a stream seemed to count—and exempted the sites from Goodwin's ruling, though much of that work could have been done a week or month after the ruling and reported as having been done before it.

Appalled, Joe Lovett and Jim Hecker dashed off a motion asking Judge Goodwin to hold the Corps in contempt. After all, the judge's own ruling had said work should stop at any new Nationwide 21 site where a valley fill hadn't yet been built. On December 10, Judge Goodwin declined to do so, and he seemed annoyed by Joe and Jim's continuing motions.

By then, George W. Bush had defeated John Kerry to win a second term in office: four more years to pursue a whole array of policies, from the Iraq war to tax cuts, that happened to include a commitment to doing everything possible to encourage mountaintop coal mining.

From his two-room office in Lewisburg, Joe looked out at redbrick walls that seemed to suggest what he was up against and tried not to let his frustrations stop him from accomplishing anything at all. He knew exactly what Bush's reelection meant for the fight against mountaintop removal. For four years, the Bush administration had done all it could to help the mining industry thwart the lawsuits brought by him and Jim Hecker. It had gone so far as to rewrite laws expressly to stop their legal advances.

Like a colonel outflanked on the field of battle, Joe had fallen back each time to regroup and try a new line of attack. But now the enemy had all the power it needed to squash him: the power of four more years. Even as he filed a new, identical Nationwide 21 suit against the Corps for a valley fill in eastern Kentucky, Joe talked privately about changing his practice, maybe working on political issues for future candidates. With Bush in power for another term, fighting the Corps over coal no longer made sense.

How drastically the world had changed since Joe had graduated from law school less than a decade before. A late bloomer at thirty-six, he had found himself, much to his surprise, taking on the coal industry on his very first day of work as a lawyer. He knew the industry fought every suit as long as it could, usually exhausting the opposition. "I don't want to get stuck in coal for the rest of my life," Joe had exclaimed to a friend later that day. But he'd let an angry West Virginian tell his story, and he'd been hooked. That was in 1997, before anyone imagined George W. Bush would be president of the United States for two terms.

People age fast in Appalachia—hard work, bad diet, and poverty will do that—and so to Joe the figure who walked into his office that early autumn day seemed an old man. White-haired and in failing health, Jim Weekley did look older than his fifty-seven years, but he had plenty of fight left.

"See that?" Weekley asked. He opened the issue of *U.S. News & World Report* that he'd brought rolled up in his fist and showed Joe a photo of visual devastation.

"Good God," Joe said. He'd never seen anything like it: a panoramic landscape of leveled ridgetops, the contour of the hills gone, the forest cover yanked away like a rug to show raw, blasted earth. He had to read the caption to see that the picture had been taken in West Virginia.

"That's across the road from where I live," Jim Weekley said. "Now they want to come across the road and blast my hollow, too. My family's lived in that hollow more than two hundred years. I've lived there my whole life. They want to destroy it. And apparently, you're my only chance of stopping them."

Jim Weekley said this last with grim mirth. Utterly green about coal-mining law, Joe Lovett seemed a less-than-ideal candidate to take on the seasoned, high-paid Charleston lawyers of Arch Coal, the company whose Hobet Mining subsidiary had already chewed up seven square miles of mountains across from Weekley's Pigeonroost Hollow. Would they even respond to a notice of intent to sue from this recent law-school graduate, who worked at a nonprofit firm called Mountain State Justice?

The article in *U.S. News & World Report,* entitled "Shear Madness" and dated August 11, 1997, marked the first time a national publication had shown photographs of mountaintop removal in Appalachia. Written by senior investigative reporter Penny Loeb, the story came as a shock to almost everyone outside the coalfields. It was southern West Virginia's dirty secret, unknown even to residents of Charleston, a mere hour's drive away.

Like most West Virginians, Joe had never seen a mountaintop-removal site. For that matter, he'd never seen the inside of an underground coal mine. He thought coal mining was winding down in the state. Sometimes when he was hiking, he ran across an abandoned strip mine, the hill rock still bare and exposed. That was about all mining meant to him. Mountain State Justice just happened to have the word "mountain" in its name. Started by a public-interest lawyer named Dan Hedges, it had taken on everything from poverty cases to state education policies—no coal, though.

"As bad as it looks in these pictures," Jim Weekley said, "it's worse when you see it up close." A day or two later, at Weekley's invitation, Joe drove down Route 119 until he reached Logan County, then took small, windy roads until he reached Pigeonroost Hollow. Jim and Sibby Weekley lived just up from the mouth of the hollow in an old wooden house with a nice front porch. Once, Sibby Weekley said, she'd enjoyed sitting on that porch with her morning coffee. But since 1992, when blasting had begun over the ridge at the site that Hobet Mining called Dal-Tex, she couldn't do that, or "swing of a summer," as she put it, on her rope-hung porch bench, without wiping the coal dust off every piece of furniture every morning. She couldn't sleep at night with her bedroom window open anymore, either, because of the dust and noise. One by one, all her friends and neighbors had moved away. In Pigeonroost Hollow, the Weekleys were the only ones left. Weekley told Joe that he and his wife had been promised $40,000 by Arch to move away, then $50,000, then finally as much as $150,000. They'd turned down all offers.

Weekley took Joe on his four-wheeler up to the ridgetop to see just how close the devastation had come. One minute they were riding up amid thickset trees. The next, they were looking out on a wide-open landscape of utter destruction. In the distance, a dinosaurlike dragline swept up 100,000 pounds of dirt with each scoop from a freshly blasted ridgetop. Soon it would devour the other side of Pigeonroost as part of a new, six-square-mile mine site. The new mine would destroy hundreds of vertical feet from several mountains and destroy the forest cover, so that Arch could extract up to eighty million tons of coal. Left behind would be one billion cubic yards of waste material, a portion of which would be dumped into ten miles of streams, filling them up to three hundred feet high. The destruction would come right up to this ridgetop. The Weekleys' side wouldn't be clear-cut and blasted. But a sediment pond would be placed on their side near the ridgetop, and a valley fill in the stream below that. The valley fill would destroy Pigeonroost Branch, a stream where trout and creek chubs still swam amid crawdads, toads, snakes, lizards, and salamanders. It would make the hollow all but unrecognizable to its residents, were they stubborn enough to stay and endure the onslaught. Joe looked out at Dal-Tex and then behind him, down into the Weekleys' tree-canopied hollow. "This is horrible," he said.

A week later, Joe drove back to Pigeonroost. Arch Coal was holding a public meeting in the nearby town of Blair to explain its plans.
This was a new approach: in 1992, when Arch had embarked on the
operations it now hoped to expand, it had started blasting and earthmoving with no warning to residents. The idea was to make the area
unlivable, so that residents would sell their homes to Arch at "fair market value." Softened up by the blasting, by the coal trucks and coal
dust and blackwater spills that followed, residents would be willing to
sign sales contracts that forced them to move a significant distance
away and forbade them to protest the mine. The whole valley, as a result, would be depopulated. "Our philosophy is not to impact people,"
an Arch vice president explained, "and if there are no people to impact,
that is consistent with our philosophy."

Over the next several years, the number of houses in Blair had
dropped from three hundred to about sixty. Many of those bought by
Arch were mysteriously torched. Jim and Sibby Weekley were among
the holdouts who came to a meeting to hear a company lawyer named
Blair Gardner explain why more of this would be a good thing.

Before Gardner could get very far, Weekley stood up to object. He
didn't look like an old man that day. He yelled and kept yelling. Joe
thought there might be a fight. Nervously, the company lawyer kept
fiddling with his hair. In his double-breasted suit, he looked as out
of place as a game-show host at a funeral. "Mr. Weekley," Gardner
said at last, "I'll come to your house and show you exactly what we're
going to do."

Gardner drove up Pigeonroost Hollow a few days later to find that
Joe Lovett had made his first decision as a lawyer: he'd called the media. Charleston *Gazette* reporter Ken Ward Jr. was there. Soon he
would write a prizewinning series on mountaintop removal, and his
ongoing stories would serve as a unique chronicle of Appalachian
destruction. A team from National Public Radio was there, too, waiting on the Weekleys' porch for Gardner, who arrived true to type in a
double-breasted suit and expensive shoes. "We have a permit," Gardner said as he cautiously picked his way up the dirt trail from the Weekleys' house up Pigeonroost Hollow, the reporters behind him, "and we
intend to use it. We have a resource that is valuable and that the market wants. That is coal."

Arch did have a Nationwide 21 permit to fill in the streams of a new, six-mile-square tract of forested hills it was calling Spruce Mine No. 1. But a small grace period remained while the EPA weighed whether to allow the Corps to grant that permit. Technically, the Clean Water Act called for EPA to oversee the Corps' granting of its permits in every case. Most times, the EPA seemed oblivious to the task. But since Spruce No. 1 would constitute the largest mountaintop operation ever commenced in West Virginia, the EPA had decided to ponder it. And until the EPA gave its blessing, Arch couldn't get the state permit it needed, either. Joe still had a chance.

Back in the Charleston offices of Mountain State Justice, Joe began calling environmental groups for legal and financial help. To his shock, each group he called had an excuse. The coalfields were out of one's jurisdiction; another had never taken on coal-mining issues. He did find a law professor named Pat McGinley from Morgantown to help at the start. And through a random call of desperation to Trial Lawyers for Public Justice in Washington, D.C., he reached Jim Hecker.

Jim knew nothing more about coal-mining law than Joe did, but he'd done enough public-interest cases to offer some career-changing advice. "Don't go after Arch," he said. "Then you're just fighting one company. Go after the government. See if the Army Corps permit violates the Clean Air Act—or the Clean Water Act. Then maybe you can stop the whole thing." Unfortunately, Jim added, he strongly doubted that his colleagues at Trial Lawyers for Public Justice would see that as a case Joe could win. So they would not want TLPJ to get involved.

At the time, Joe was living in Charleston with his wife, Gretchen, a clinical child psychologist, and their first son, Ben, age two. When his eyes were bleary from reading environmental law at the office, he would go to the cozy cottage he and Gretchen had found to rent on a private estate in the woods, take a break for dinner, then resume in his home office. There, at least, he could listen to his records.

Perhaps surprisingly for the well-bred son of a lawyer who'd settled his family in the leafy affluence of a Charleston suburb, far from any hub of live music, Joe Lovett was a jazz fanatic—a jazz *record* fanatic. He had thousands of scratchy recordings by Charlie Parker, Thelonious Monk, Duke Ellington, and others. His Miles Davis collection alone encompassed more than 150 records. Whenever he traveled to Philadelphia or New York, he sought out the used-record shops and, to his wife's exasperation, came back laden down with more vinyl treasures. He felt no less obsessive about the stereo equipment on which those records turned. After much shifting of components and poring through stereo magazines, Joe had settled on a Bryston amplifier, a Basis turntable, BBC monitors, and Harbeth speakers. These purchases had provoked a little tension on the home front, and there were times when Gretchen thought she recognized in her husband some of the obsessive symptoms of her juvenile patients. But as vices went, it was, ultimately, a forgivable one.

Along with his four thousand jazz recordings, Joe had three thousand classical-music recordings, and in these more of a family heritage was apparent. Joe's father, Chester, had grown up in Charleston playing violin well enough to join the Charleston Symphony Orchestra and to consider becoming a professional musician. In 1938, he'd nearly gone to study at a German conservatory. Fortunately, he'd thought better of that idea, for Chester was Jewish. Instead, he'd gone to Europe as a mortar gunner in World War II and participated in the liberation of France, surviving dozens of firefights as his 222nd Infantry pushed into Germany to take Würzburg, Schweinfurt, Fürth, Nuremberg, and Munich, eventually freeing the skeletal prisoners of Dachau. After the war, he became a general-practice lawyer and a partner of a Charleston firm. Seared by his wartime experiences and imbued with a deep aversion to social injustice, he dedicated much of his time to the civil rights movement. It was a passion his son inherited, along with a love of music.

A jazz record was playing softly one evening, long after Gretchen and Ben had gone to bed, when Joe began reading Section 404 of the Clean Water Act. At one paragraph, he stopped and sat up straight. "Oh, my God," he said. "That's it!"

Most of the Clean Water Act described standards to keep the waters of the United States clean. But appended to the act were hundreds of pages of rules of a more pragmatic nature. They recognized that industry could not avoid affecting U.S. waters altogether, and so they sought to regulate those effects. Under Section 404, a permit might be granted to place "fill material" in U.S. waters. The rule Joe had just read listed the sorts of fill that might qualify for a 404 permit.

A farmer might apply for a permit under 404 to place fill in a stream for some agricultural purpose: to create a stock pond or drainage ditch or temporary road. A contractor who wanted to build a structure on wetlands might apply for a permit to dredge and fill them. But neither the farmer nor contractor could put just anything he liked in the water and call it "fill." Specifically, the government was prohibited from sanctioning the discharge of materials that would have "an unacceptable adverse effect on municipal water supplies, shellfish beds and fishery areas (including spawning and breeding areas), wildlife, or recreational areas." Put another way, fill had to have a beneficial *purpose*.

Reading those words was a revelation. For as Joe knew by now, the mining industry had been dumping mountaintop waste into streams and calling it fill ever since the Clean Water Act became law. And the Corps had gone along with it, rubber-stamping permit after permit on the rationale that coal waste was fill under Section 404. But if coal waste didn't qualify as "fill," then the Corps was breaking the law every time it granted a permit for valley fills under Section 404. The coal industry was breaking the law with every stream it filled.

Within days, Joe had found other laws the state and federal government were violating every time they granted permits for another mountaintop-mining operation. One was the National Environmental Policy Act (NEPA) of 1969, which required federal agencies to compile an Environmental Impact Statement, or EIS—a thorough, multi-agency study—before sanctioning a project that would significantly despoil U.S. waters and their outlying environment. An EIS was intended to ponder not just ecological effects but aesthetic, cultural, historic, and social ones, too. The Corps had never done an EIS on *any* mountaintop-mining application. Nor, therefore, had it ever explored feasible alternatives to the work in question, which an EIS was also required to do. The Surface Mining Control and Reclamation Act (SMCRA) of 1977 called for mountaintop sites to be restored to their "approximate original contour," or AOC. That never happened, because putting a mountain back together again was hard, if not impossible, and the industry couldn't be bothered to investigate how or if it might be done. Instead, the industry routinely sought AOC variances with the promise to transform their mined-out mountaintop sites into "fish and wildlife habitats," a creative solution nowhere sanctioned by

SMCRA and in practice a euphemism at best. The Corps and the state approved those variances time after time. Another SMCRA rule prohibited mining activity within a hundred-foot buffer zone of a perennial or intermittent stream unless serious study was done to be sure that the stream and its aquatic life could survive the experience. The industry simply asked for variances to that rule, too, and always got them.

Joe passed on his findings to Jim Hecker, who began to get excited. Perhaps Trial Lawyers for Public Justice might be talked into underwriting a suit after all. That was welcome news to Joe, since there was no way Mountain State Justice could foot the bill on a case against the U.S. government, which might drag on for months. Eventually, TLPJ did indeed pay for the case—nearly $400,000—and went on to support Joe in almost every mining case he brought after he started the Appalachian Center for the Economy and the Environment. None of that money would go to Joe directly: it was for legal researchers and expert witnesses and all the other expenses of bringing a suit. Joe's salary would be drawn from the Appalachian Center's shoestring budget— about $300,000 a year raised from private contributors, which had to cover a lot of expenses. Joe's own take was less than six figures, modest indeed for a very good lawyer in any state, even West Virginia.

Joe needed, in addition to money, more plaintiffs like Jim and Sibby Weekley—local residents whose lives would be directly impacted by Spruce No. 1. An obvious choice was Cindy Rank, one of the few West Virginians who'd already spoken out against mountaintop removal. Rank's grassroots group, the West Virginia Highlands Conservancy, had battled the industry in court for years. Rank herself had become an expert in the mind-numbing details of industry mine permits and had mapped the location of every mountaintop removal mine and valley fill in three counties—not an easy task when the authorities often seemed as reluctant as the coal companies to divulge any information at all. A petite figure in round glasses with a soft, deliberate manner, she seemed more like a college professor than an activist. But with quiet persistence, she got a lot done.

Another obvious plaintiff was Patricia Bragg, a mother and housewife from Pie, whose community had lost thirty-seven wells as a result of blasting from mountaintop operations. Bragg had been knocking on doors for some time now, exhorting neighbors to fight for their rights. Because her last name came first alphabetically in the list of plaintiffs, hers was one of two names which identified the case. The other name was that of the first defendant, Colonel Dana Robertson, local district engineer for the U.S. Army Corps of Engineers.

Bragg v. Robertson, the case that became a landmark of coal-mining law, began with a letter of intent from Joe and Jim in the spring of 1998. It listed all the ways the DEP and the Corps had failed to uphold the law in issuing mountaintop-removal permits, and it gave the prospective defendants sixty days to redress those failings or be hit with a suit. To the coal industry, lawsuits were as common and inconsequential as mosquito bites in the West Virginia summer. But this newest filing caused some unrest. Most suits were filed against a particular coal company for its local misdeeds, not against the state and federal government for illegal permitting. Most were the work of a single lawyer angling for a quick settlement, not a consortium of lawyers backed by a Washington nonprofit that couldn't be bought off. Of some concern, too, was that every charge in the letter was true.

The DEP and the Corps remained predictably mum during the sixty-day grace period. They stayed mum as the suit's filing duly followed. But in late fall, after the federal government's motion to have the case dismissed was struck down, Joe took a call from an assistant attorney general in the U.S. Department of Justice named Lois Schiffer. In his suit against the Corps, Joe had made some fair points, Schiffer said briskly. They should talk.

To Joe's amazement, the talks led to a settlement. In December 1998, the U.S. government agreed to conduct an EIS on the effects of mountaintop removal, cumulatively, on the multistate area of the coalfields. During the two years the EIS was projected to take, the Corps would not use Nationwide 21 to approve any new surface-mine operations involving valley fills of more than 250 acres. For Joe and his legal team, it was a signal victory. It essentially put a two-year moratorium on new, large-scale operations, especially the kind that relied on draglines. A coal company could still apply for an individual permit, but that involved so much more scrutiny that even the cavalier Corps would have trouble concluding that the environmental effects of the larger sites were minimal.

Not all the concessions were on the government's side. Schiffer insisted that Hobet's Spruce No. 1 be allowed to proceed. Joe could still go to court to try to stop the mine when final permissions were granted. If he did, though, he couldn't sue the Corps on the basis of Section 404 and its definition of fill—the point on which the government clearly felt most vulnerable.

Jim and Sibby Weekley were angered by the compromise and argued against it. Stopping Spruce No. 1 was why they'd joined the suit in the first place. Adamant, Joe brought them around. He would still sue to stop Spruce No. 1, he assured them. There was no shortage of illegalities to invoke. In fact, the settlement would only strengthen his case. From a legal perspective, he reasoned, the government had just made a huge blunder. It had admitted that each of these mountaintop sites had a significant impact that required an EIS. How could it then argue that Spruce No. 1, the biggest mountaintop operation in the history of the state, should be exempt?

The Justice Department had promised to give Joe forty-eight hours' notice when work on Spruce No. 1 was about to begin, and so it did. First, in early January 1999, it notified Joe that the EPA had withdrawn its objections to the proposed mine. The EPA concluded its effects had been "minimized to the extent possible while maintaining a viable project"—an extraordinary admission, Joe thought, because economic concerns were not supposed to play any part in the agency's reviews. With that, the Corps granted its Nationwide 21, and the DEP issued a state permit. Any day now, the first ridgetops would be clear-cut, and blasting would begin.

With no time to lose, Joe sent his request for a temporary restraining order over to the offices of Judge Charles H. Haden II, chief of the U.S. district court in Charleston, also known as the Southern District of West Virginia. The judge agreed to hold a TRO hearing at 4:00 p.m. on February 3, 1999—the day before work on the mine was to commence.

Joe knew enough about Judge Haden to wonder if the hearing was just a waste of time. For a time after law school, he'd clerked for Haden and found him a conservative Republican on most social issues. In more than two decades on the federal bench, the judge had displayed a stern reluctance to expand upon the law in civil rights cases, along with a certain provincialism: at sixty-one, he was proud to say he'd never lived outside of West Virginia. Also, as it happened, the judge's brother and father had both been coal operators. But Haden was very smart and widely respected—he'd been named a federal judge at thirty-eight—and consistently demonstrated a deep reverence for history and law. Joe had to hope his thirty-seven-page brief appealed to that reverence.

Precisely at the appointed time, a black-robed Judge Haden convened the hearing Joe had requested. At one table sat a phalanx of dark-suited lawyers representing the West Virginia DEP, the U.S. Department of Justice, Arch Coal's Hobet Mining, and the coal industry. At the other table, in less well-fitting suits, sat Joe Lovett and Jim Hecker, along with Patrick McGinley, the law professor, and McGinley's wife, Suzanne M. Weise, a lawyer in her own right. Joe had decided not to tell his co-counsel and his plaintiffs a somewhat embarrassing and terrifying secret: it was his first day in court as a lawyer.

If Judge Haden recognized Joe, he gave no sign of it. It was just as well, for Joe's clerkship was hardly a plus: Haden was known to be especially tough on former clerks who appeared before him. If anything, Haden seemed to look benignly at the lawyers on the other side, as if to say, How amusing that we grown-ups have been brought together by those children across the way. Or was that Joe's imagination?

As he listened to Haden convene the hearing, Joe felt a stab of doubt. Could he do this? Could he be even half the lawyer his father had been, holding a courtroom in the palm of his hand with the calm, all-knowing voice of reason? Everyone had known Chester Lovett; he was a pillar of the community, beyond reproach. Joe wanted more than anything to measure up, and yet the challenge had rattled him and made him rebel. After college he'd startled his parents by working for an organic farm. One grandfather had run a farm in a rural area near Charleston—with forebears who had been subsistence farmers for two hundred years—and Joe had always enjoyed working with him. But farmwork was a step backward in his family, he knew. He'd gone on to graduate school in philosophy, another rebellion of sorts, at the University of Virginia. There he met Gretchen, who was doing graduate work in psychology. Joe's mother had been a psychologist, too; perhaps in choosing Gretchen as a partner, Joe was taking a first step toward becoming his father's son. At thirty-two, he enrolled in law school at last, but with a caveat that seemed like a final little rebellion: instead of practicing criminal and business law like his father, Joe would take up environmental law.

Judge Haden startled the lawyers on both sides with his opening words. If he granted the TRO that day, he said briskly, he wanted to go right on to the hearing for preliminary injunction, or PI—the more binding injunction that, if granted, would stop all work until a full-blown trial. The PI hearing would involve expert witnesses and might take days. Joe and Jim had assumed they'd have at least a week to prepare for it. Judge Haden said no. "I might put you to your proof as early as tomorrow," he declared. How did the defense feel about that, the judge asked? One of the expensively suited lawyers on the industry side stood to say the sooner the better. The judge then turned to Joe.

"We would be ready as well," Joe said, ignoring the look he knew Jim was giving him. He had no idea how they'd be ready.

The TRO hearing began in earnest. Judge Haden hadn't completed reading the "small pile of papers," as he put it wryly, that both sides had submitted, so he asked each side to present its arguments in brief. Joe went first. With a clarity and calmness that gave no hint he was trying his first case, he launched into the reasons the state had acted unlawfully in granting permits for the mine, from its failure to recognize that the mountains in question couldn't be restored to their "approximate original contour," to its flouting of the buffer-zone rule.

Jim Hecker then stood up to take on the Corps. The federal agency responsible for guarding America's waters had just granted a Nationwide 21 permit to Hobet for what would be the largest and most destructive surface mine in West Virginia's history. Yet in its settlement, the government had just acknowledged that an EIS must be completed before major mining operations could be permitted. How could the government now claim Spruce No. 1 should be excluded from that review? Hobet claimed it would "mitigate" the damage of Spruce No. 1

by "compensatory" land improvements somewhere else, but the plan was so vague that the U.S. Fish and Wildlife Service had rejected it. The Corps had granted its permit all the same.

One after another of the defense lawyers stood to counter those and other charges in language that seemed deliberately obtuse, as if by jumbling the facts enough they might just wear the judge down. One of their arguments, untangled from legalese, was that the Corps had decided Spruce No. 1 would have "minimal adverse environmental effects" on streams in its area, and so the Corps must be right. The EPA had agreed, and so it must be right, too. One lawyer actually suggested the TRO be denied because the mine wouldn't cause irreparable harm in the ten days the TRO covered. Another observed that the harm would be negligible in any event because the streams to be buried or affected had virtually no aquatic life, and certainly no fish.

Joe listened to these arguments with growing despair. Absurd as they seemed to him, he worried that Judge Haden would be swayed by the lawyers' tone of authority. They were, after all, speaking for the federal government. But then another government lawyer stood up and made a fatal mistake.

All these issues, lawyer Roger Wolfe declared, were better adjudicated by the state Surface Mine Board than a federal court. "It can enter stays," Wolfe noted of the Surface Mine Board. "It has people that hear these cases all the time. And with all due respect to the Court," Wolfe added, "we don't need to explain what on-bench sediment control or excess spoil means with that board. They are well equipped, they are very familiar with mining, and that's where this case ought to be heard."

The condescension of those remarks, though surely not intended, seemed to strike Judge Haden like a slap. "We all understand, despite our levels of sophistication or lack of sophistication," Judge Haden said acidly in summing up, "that in environmental areas where streams are diverted, trees are cut, aquatic life is disturbed, human and animal residence of the area are involved, that this is an area where you cannot unring the bell." With that, he granted the TRO.

"That's my ruling," Haden concluded. "I will see you at nine o'clock in the morning."

That evening after dinner, Joe's team met at the Charleston offices of Mountain State Justice. Joe put it succinctly. "We're screwed," he said. In twelve hours, they would have to call their first witness to the stand for the more formal hearing. Joe had never examined a witness. Nor, as it turned out, had Jim Hecker: all his public-interest cases had been conducted on paper. Pat McGinley was a professor; Suzanne Weise had no more experience in this kind of case than the others.

Joe started writing up questions for one of the experts they planned to call, then another. At 4:00 a.m., he was still writing. He liked pulling all-nighters—he did his best work when everyone else was asleep. Finally, he put down his legal pad and looked at a very bleary Jim Hecker. "Can we win this thing?" he asked.

Jim shrugged. "I never told you this," he said, "but in my first five years as a lawyer, I lost every case I tried."

Jim and Sibby Weekley opened the hearing the next morning with simple, strong testimony about Pigeonroost Hollow: what they'd lost already and what they hoped to save. Independent experts followed, assessing the potential damage with dizzyingly technical terms. But it was the government officials, dragged against their will to the stand by Jim and Joe as adversary witnesses, who made the strongest impressions. Again and again, they had to admit under oath that they'd failed to force coal companies to follow the law. Larry Alt, the DEP manager in charge of mountaintop-removal permitting, described how he judged whether a coal operator had returned a site to approximate original contour. He used his hand as a mountain, he said, and held up a closed fist, "these being the peaks," he said, pointing to his knuckles, "and then this"—he opened his fist and indicated the back of his hand—"would be flat with an AOC variance."

Still, Judge Haden seemed to keep an open mind—until the "motion to view."

The idea, oddly enough, came from the coal side of the courtroom. The industry lawyers wanted Haden to see how well Hobet Mining had reclaimed portions of the sprawling Dal-Tex operation. The mountaintops might be gone, but the lawyers felt sure Judge Haden would agree that the reclaimed land—grassy and open like an African savanna—was postcard-pretty. The lawyers looked smugly over at Joe and Jim, expecting them to object. "That sounds fine to us," Joe said. "As long as the judge gets flown over the *whole* of Dal-Tex and also visits Pigeonroost Hollow."

There were two trips. First, the judge was driven from Charleston to Dal-Tex and Pigeonroost Hollow in a van rented by the coal industry. A second van was needed for all the lawyers and expert witnesses from both sides who wanted to be there. Each van bore an "I Love Coal" bumper sticker. The judge was quiet when he arrived at a trimly landscaped company village at a reclaimed part of Dal-Tex. After touring the village and taking in the savannalike view, the judge asked to be taken to a ridgetop from which he could see active mining. For safety reasons, his hosts explained, they had to decline. The judge just shrugged.

Then, as Joe had requested, the group drove over to Pigeonroost Hollow. A biologist hired by the coal company started guiding the judge to the mouth of Pigeonroost Branch, the stream that came out of the hollow. That, she said, was all the judge needed to see to confirm the stream had no aquatic life that an upstream valley fill would imperil.

"Actually, no, we want to go up the watershed."

The judge turned to see who had spoken. John Morgan was a British-born engineer whose Kentucky-based consulting firm had designed various kinds of mines all over the world. Though he worked for the industry, he had deep qualms about mountaintop removal and had agreed to be one of Joe and Jim's expert witnesses. The biologist started to object, but the judge cut her off. "I'd like to go up the watershed," he declared.

Six of them squeezed into John Morgan's Land Rover. When they'd gone as far up Pigeonroost Hollow as they could drive, they got out and tramped over to the stream. Ben Stout, the biologist for the plaintiffs, noticed that the coal-company representatives had worn ordinary shoes. Judge Haden had his L.L. Bean duck boots on. They looked well-worn.

Roger Wolfe, the coal-industry lawyer, observed that an old refrigerator had been dumped near the stream. How, he chortled, could anyone think this was a high-quality stream? The coal-company biologist pointed to where the stream had undercut the bank. "There, you see?" she said. "That's erosion. This watershed has already been destroyed."

"No, it hasn't," Stout countered. "That's just part of the natural stream process."

The biologist pointed up. "Look," she said. "This is an open canopy forest. The forest cover is gone."

The group looked up to where she pointed. It was late February. The trees had no leaves. But their branches extended high overhead, crossing over the stream. There was no need, Stout saw, to bother contradicting her. The judge could see she was wrong.

The coal-company biologist pointed into the stream. "No fish," she said. "And no shredders."

Stout knew all about shredders: little aquatic bugs that inhabit clumps of fallen leaves in water, shredding them for food. When Stout reached into the stream and came up with a leaf clump, half a dozen different shredders wriggled out. The judge recognized several of them. Stout identified the others. "I'm a fisherman," the judge explained when Stout asked. "When this is all done, I'd love to go fishing with you and learn more about aquatic insects."

As they made their way back to the Land Rover and down the hollow, the coal-company biologist was silent.

The entourage was smaller for the flight over Dal-Tex and Hobet 21, a huge, active mountaintop-mining site nearby. The judge sat up front with the helicopter pilot; two of his law clerks sat behind. No lawyers came along. For the defense, perhaps, that was a mistake. Instead of just flying over Dal-Tex and Hobet 21, the pilot headed southeast from Charleston, making a three-hour loop over most of southern West Virginia. The helicopter's roar drowned out any possible conversation, but sometimes as the chopper passed over a particularly large mountaintop site, the judge would turn around and share a look of horror with his clerks. Astonishingly, the chopper was almost never out of sight of a mountaintop-mining operation. For two hours, the party looked down at one scene after another of devastation. When the judge disembarked at last and settled into a car with his clerks, he shook his head. "That was horrible," he said. "The dead places are so . . . vast."

Back in his courtroom, Judge Haden called for summations. Joe went first.

"Hobet can mine Spruce when it presents a complete permit application which conforms with the law," he said. "It didn't do that." Why? Because it owned a dragline currently operating on the Dal-Tex

site, and downtime was expensive. So it had cut corners. But economic
need wasn't a valid reason to do that. "Hobet, DEP, and the Corps of
Engineers must not be allowed to twist the law to accommodate the
coal industry's move to larger machines and larger mines with deeper
cuts," Joe declared. "Rather, the industry must be required to make its
technology conform to the law."

Like barristers out of a Gilbert and Sullivan operetta, the defense
lawyers stood, one after another, to respond in such legal mumbo
jumbo that even they seemed to have no idea what they were saying.
They left it to Roger Wolfe to offer the defense's final words in plain
English—a calamitous decision.

"We all know what the standard is," Wolfe harrumphed. "We have
talked about it enough. . . . Balance the harms, consider the merits,
and consider the public interest. We submit, Your Honor, in this case
we need go no further than the inquiry with respect to the balancing of
harms."

Any laws broken in the process of granting Hobet its permits for
Spruce No. 1, in other words, had no bearing. All that mattered was
who would be harmed more, the plaintiffs or Hobet. Wolfe had no
doubt about that. "An unfavorable ruling on some of these legal rulings
will be a mortal blow to coal production in this state," he declared. Layoffs would soon follow; tens of millions of dollars would be lost. "Love
it or hate it, coal is West Virginia in many ways. Wipe it out, and we
better be prepared to face the consequences."

This, Joe thought, was always what it came down to: laws be
damned. The industry, like a dark god, must be appeased, or it would
get very angry, and everyone would be punished with layoffs and lower
tax revenues. In a way, Joe admired Wolfe. He was giving the bald,
blunt industry rap without any embellishment. Joe tuned in again as he
heard Wolfe say, "on the other hand, plaintiffs have offered no evidence of specific harm."

No evidence?

"It can't be the law that any environmental harm trumps all other
harm of all other kinds in all other circumstances," Wolfe intoned.
"When a tree is cut, there is a change to the physical environment.
Now, if you want to call that harm. . . ."

Judge Haden seemed to wince. "I agree with you that if you take the environmental argument to the extreme, if one tree is cut, that is environmental harm," he interjected. "But from the standpoint of scale that we are talking here, many square miles of complete—a rather complete change of the water, the topography, the wildlife, we aren't talking about the same thing as losing a particular tree."

"Additionally on the issue of harm, Your Honor, heaven knows, as well as the rest of us, that Pigeonroost is not a pristine stream," Wolfe said. Joe saw the other defense lawyers looking at one another with concern. "I didn't see any eighteen-inch trout floating around the stream," Wolfe blundered on, "when Mr. Stout was vainly looking for his bug as the rest of us stood by that rusty refrigerator!"

"He found his bug," Judge Haden said quietly.

"Did he find his bug?" Wolfe echoed.

"Indeed."

"I don't believe he did," Wolfe insisted. "Not the one bug he was looking for."

Joe kept his poker face, but it was a challenge. If he'd written them himself, he couldn't have put more inane words into Roger Wolfe's mouth.

In his ruling, issued less than a week later on March 3, 1999, the Republican judge wrote eloquently about what he'd seen on his flyover. "On February 26, the ground was covered with light snow, and mined sites were visible from miles away. The sites stood out among the natural wooded ridges as huge white plateaus, and the valley fills appeared as massive, artificially landscaped stair steps. Some mine sites were twenty years old, yet tree growth was stunted or non-existent. Compared to the thick hardwoods of surrounding undisturbed hills, the mine sites appeared stark and barren and enormously different from the original topography.

"If the forest canopy of Pigeonroot Hollow is leveled," the judge continued, "exposing the stream to extreme temperatures, and aquatic life is destroyed, these harms cannot be undone. If the forest wildlife are driven away by the blasting, the noise, and the lack of safe nesting and eating areas, they cannot be coaxed back. If the mountaintop is removed, even Hobet's engineers will affirm that it cannot be reclaimed to its exact original contour. Destruction of the unique topography cannot be regarded as anything but permanent and irreversible."

Strict constructionist though he might have been, political conservative though he most certainly was, Judge Haden was also an out-
doorsman who loved the hollows and hills of his native state. On the
day of that flyover, he had made up his mind. Mountaintop removal
was an abomination. And the permits that allowed it in this case violated the law. Among other reasons, Arch had illegally segmented the
vast project into smaller pieces and applied for Nationwide 21s for
each of those: the same maneuver that Massey had used to wangle per-
mission for burying Tony Sears's beloved Hominy Creek. The preliminary injunction Judge Haden granted that day would put Spruce No. 1
on hold until a full-blown trial.

Outside the courtroom, Arch knew how to retaliate: by laying off three
hundred union miners who had been hired to start Spruce No. 1 and
by telling them that the environmental lawyers, their plaintiffs, and the
judge were to blame. In Pigeonroost Hollow, laid-off miners burned
Jim Weekley in effigy and drove up nightly to yell obscenities at him.
On the steps of the capitol in Charleston, hundreds of miners gathered
to protest.

Yet as such scenes unfurled, cooler minds began meeting. The industry could see where this was going. So could the Clinton administration. If the permits were illegal for Spruce No. 1, they were illegal for
every other mountaintop-removal operation in Appalachia. Joe and Jim
would sue for programmatic relief, and in Judge Haden's courtroom, at
least, they would probably get it. All over the coalfields, mountaintop-
removal operations would grind to a halt. To avoid that, industry and
government would have to bend.

That spring, as part of the Clinton settlement of the preceding
December, lawyers from both camps sat down with Joe and Jim to embark on a series of secret negotiations. Point by point, they went down
Joe and Jim's list of sixteen ways in which mountaintop removal was illegal. One after another was resolved pretty much as the environmental lawyers wanted. Perhaps most significantly, the rules for restoring a
mountaintop-mine site to AOC were tightened. No more would an inspector's knuckles define how a mountain should look after mining.
No more could plateaus be left as they were, garnished with a little

grass seed. More mining spoil would have to be stacked back up on the plateau to give it a semblance of the mountain it had been. Or, if the coal operators preferred, they could plant trees—carefully, as prescribed by a local forestry expert—on a gentler slope or plateau. The operators could still get a variance for AOC to accommodate a shopping mall, say, or a new correctional facility on a postmining site. But they would have to plan for it from the start, keeping the soil compact instead of blasting away willy-nilly, and taking into account the roads, power, water, and other basic services a commercial project required. They couldn't just write "prison" on the AOC variance form and hope that a prison materialized on their site some day.

Two weeks before the July trial date Judge Haden had set, the U.S. Army Corps of Engineers made a shocking admission. It couldn't justify its Nationwide 21 permit for Spruce No. 1, not under the scrutiny to which it had been exposed. Hobet Mining could go ahead and apply for an individual permit, but Hobet's parent company, Arch, knew how futile an exercise that would be. Spruce No. 1 was just too big. In desperation, Arch flew its executives to Washington to plead with West Virginia's congressmen and senators to quash Judge Haden's decision by an act of Congress. Senator Robert Byrd had been a coal-industry booster for nearly fifty years, but even he begged off from what he knew was a fool's errand. Arch's request, he declared, was "illegal and unethical." Furious, Arch then sued the Corps, claiming the agency *had* to grant it a Nationwide 21. But on the eve of trial, the company withdrew its suit.

The blocking of Spruce No. 1 was a huge win for Joe and Jim and all who stood behind them. But Arch wasn't about to walk away from the largest and richest coal reserves in the state. It had one last card it could play. It could ask the government to conduct the EIS that Joe and Jim had said from the start was required. Under the Clinton administration, such a thoroughgoing study would likely conclude that Spruce No. 1 would have a devastating and unacceptable impact on the environs of Pigeonroost Hollow. Under a new president, though, Arch could hope that an EIS might be conducted with more sympathy for the coal company's needs.

Still, in that summer of 1999, Joe dared to think he might get all he'd pursued in court: not a complete halt to mountaintop removal but a new era of strict, enforced rules that limited the practice to a scattering of small sites and fills. Agreement was reached on fifteen of the sixteen contested points. Both the federal government and the state of West Virginia signed consent decrees in regard to those points and filed them in Judge Haden's court. Only one point remained in dispute: the buffer-zone rule.

Joe saw no reason to retreat from the rule, which dictated that mountaintop spoil be kept one hundred feet from either side of any perennial or seasonal stream below the site, in order to protect not only that stretch of stream but water quality and aquatic life downstream. The rule had emerged from the Surface Mining Control and Reclamation Act (SMCRA) and been on the books ever since, but coal operators had ignored it: in truth, they couldn't follow it and still do mountaintop removal—not economically, at least. Dumping "overburden" down a mountainside—the easy, economical way to deal with it—inevitably buried the stream below. The only way to comply with the rule was to transport overburden down the mountain by truck and stack it neatly somewhere away from the stream, perhaps even in the next valley. The industry felt that could be done only at exorbitant expense, if at all, so it saw no way to compromise with Joe. The rule simply had to be ignored or struck down.

When Joe realized the industry wouldn't budge on the buffer-zone rule, he appealed to Judge Haden's court for programmatic relief on it. This was, in fact, a continuation of the suit he'd filed almost exactly a year before—Haden 1, as it came to be known—with this one last point at stake. The federal government was no longer a defendant because of its settlement. The suit now was aimed exclusively at the DEP for the state's own violation of the buffer-zone rule. In retrospect, that would seem a mistake.

In his ruling of October 20, 1999, Judge Haden wryly dismissed the industry's claim that the buffer zone applied only to waters downstream of a valley fill. That, he wrote, would lead to the "*reductio ad absurdum* that miles of streams could be filled and deeply covered with rock and dirt, but if some stretch or water downstream of the fill remains undiminished and unsullied, the stream has been protected."

Then came the bombshell.

Not only must the buffer-zone rule be upheld as written, the judge decreed, but valley fills by definition violated it. In a landmark ruling, the judge issued a permanent injunction enjoining the DEP from approving *any* further surface-mining permits that would authorize placement of spoil in any permanent or intermittent valley streams. This time, the cries of protest weren't from just one coal company. They rose up from the whole industry. Haden had just banned all mining waste from all streams in West Virginia! In so many words, he'd just outlawed mountaintop mining. The industry would come to a halt. Or so it declared.

In fact, the judge hadn't prohibited all mining waste from all streams, only from permanent and seasonal ones, just as the buffer-zone rule held. There were still plenty of drier valleys that had what were known as ephemeral streams. But in the firestorm of protest, as Judge Haden put it nine days later when he agreed to suspend his decision pending appeal, few made that distinction. Senator Robert Byrd held a rally with hundreds of miners at the Capitol in Washington. Arch Coal might have been "illegal and unethical," as he'd put it, to ask Congress to overturn a court decision, but now Byrd proposed an amendment to do just that. "Fie on this judge!" he railed in an hour-long rant against Haden on the floor of the Senate.

Furious, the coal industry joined the state in appealing Haden 1 to the Fourth Circuit Court of Appeals. An unlikely ally was the United Mine Workers of America, incensed by the loss of jobs the ruling appeared to herald. But in April 2000, another potential party to the suit dropped out. After initially criticizing Haden 1, the Clinton administration declared the judge right after all: the buffer-zone rule had to be followed. Moreover, Section 404 of the Clean Water Act had to be clarified so that the Corps couldn't keep sanctioning the placement of mining waste as "fill" in valley streams. The word "fill" itself would have to be better defined—no small job of lawyerly hairsplitting.

At first, Joe was thrilled to have the federal government on his side. Then he began to get nervous. Lois Schiffer, the Justice Department assistant attorney general, seemed to want to loosen the definition of "fill," not tighten it. Though when Joe pointed this out to her, she did agree to tighten the buffer-zone rule as a quid pro quo. With that informal agreement struck, Schiffer's lawyers finished clarifying the meaning of "fill" but put it aside and turned to the buffer-zone rule.

Unfortunately, they were forced to leave the work undone. For on November 7, 2000, George W. Bush was elected president—sort of—

and for any Americans who cared at all for the environment, the world soon became a much darker place.

All through the presidential campaign, the coal industry had stumped hard—very hard—for George W. Bush. Al Gore was, after all, an *environmentalist*. If he won, he'd surely sign the Kyoto Protocol imposing new limits on greenhouse gases. He'd push through the dreaded New Source Review, under which coal-fired power plants had grudgingly agreed to pay billions of dollars for new smokestack scrubbers that would trap much of the sulfur released when coal was burned. Bush, by contrast, was all business. Eagerly, the coal industry contributed $3.8 million nationally for the 1999–2000 period, nearly all of it to Republicans, most of it to Bush or his surrogates. That was four times what the industry had given in the previous presidential campaign.

On one of his many campaign trips to West Virginia, Bush found himself on the tarmac of Charleston's modest airport with a pair of unlikely lobbying partners: Bill Raney, head of the West Virginia Coal Association, and Dick Kimbler, director of a local UMWA chapter. The mining industry, they told Bush, was being killed by Judge Haden's rulings. New mountaintop sites had been put on hold, and miners were out of work as a result. Bush asked what he could do as president if he won. Simplify the permit process, the two men said. Then lawyers and judges wouldn't be able to screw things up on technicalities. Bush said he'd do what he could. Gratified, Raney and Kimbler went on to raise $275,000 for Bush from West Virginia coal-mine operators and workers alike, five times what Al Gore managed to collect in the state.

Bush won office for any number of reasons that fall, from the serendipity of having his brother as governor of Florida to the U.S. Supreme Court's decision to stop the postelection counting of Florida ballots. But without West Virginia's five electoral votes, none of the overtime dramas would have occurred. While that might have been said of almost any state, swing states were the ones that mattered. And of those, West Virginia was perhaps the unlikeliest to go to Bush. It had nearly twice as many registered Democrats as it did Republicans. Since 1928, only four Republican presidential candidates had won its electoral votes, three of them incumbents who won in landslides (Eisenhower, Nixon, and Reagan). Yet by flooding the airwaves with fearmongering commercials saying that Gore was anticoal, Bush beat the odds and prevailed. He knew exactly what the coal industry wanted of him for his "coal-fired victory," as one aide put it, and he intended fully to comply.

In his first months in office, the new president refused to sign the Kyoto Protocol and all but killed it, since the United States was the world's largest contributor of greenhouse gases. He had his new administrator of the Environmental Protection Agency, Christine Todd Whitman, signal to the coal industry that New Source Review was dead. Sulfur emissions from power plants would still be limited, but on a far more forgiving schedule. Carbon dioxide, another greenhouse gas produced in greater quantities by coal-fired electrical plants than by any other source, wouldn't be capped at all, Bush declared, reversing a campaign pledge. Meanwhile, Vice President Dick Cheney held a series of closed-door meetings with energy-industry leaders to ask them what they wanted. Not surprisingly, they wanted more coal-fired electrical plants. Over the next three years, more than one hundred gargantuan plants would be proposed in thirty-six states, potentially increasing greenhouse gases by staggering amounts.

Bush also agreed to let the coal industry name its government overseer. Many government officials helped regulate the coal industry, both at the state and federal levels. But at the top of the pile in the new Bush administration would be the deputy secretary of the Interior Department: the right hand to newly appointed Secretary Gale Norton, whose own job would be perceived as somewhat ceremonial. The industry knew just whom to suggest for this power-behind-the-throne position: one of its favorite and most effective lobbyists, J. Steven Griles. His was a name Joe Lovett would come to know well.

At the time, Joe was distracted by the Fourth Circuit's imminent ruling on the appeal of Judge Haden's buffer-zone decision. A random selection system had chosen three of the court's most conservative members to hear it: Paul V. Niemeyer, J. Michael Luttig, and Karen J. Williams. Lawyers for the coal industry and the state had avoided confronting Haden's ruling on the merits. Instead, they argued that the case shouldn't have been heard in federal court at all, since it no longer involved a federal defendant: only the West Virginia DEP remained. Haden had reasoned that the case did belong in his federal court because the state's buffer-zone rule had begun as a federal law and, though it had then been handed down to the states, remained subject to federal oversight. On April 24, 2001, the Fourth Circuit overturned Haden 1 on jurisdictional grounds: the judges agreed that the state must be sued in a state court, not a federal one. Joe and Jim would have to start all over again with a state judge—who would be subject to reelection pressures in the state that coal controlled.

Less than a month after that blow, Steve Griles, fifty-three, all but sailed through his Senate confirmation hearing. He described himself as a man who understood the value of natural resources and said that as a rising bureaucrat in President Reagan's Interior Department, he'd devoted himself to upholding coal-mining regulations. Democrat Ron Wyden of Oregon was the only one at the hearing to challenge this view. Wyden's own sources suggested that at the Interior Department's Office of Surface Mining, Griles had tried to gut SMCRA, which he was duty bound to uphold, and discouraged government inspectors from writing up violations against coal companies. One inspector who worked under him at the time, Jack Spadaro, felt that Griles had also done more than anyone in the Reagan administration to loosen the rules that governed the new practice of mountaintop mining, be-fore spending the 1990s as a lobbyist, mostly for the coal industry. Wyden felt that Griles, like many of George W. Bush's nominees for high positions, appeared to be a fox assigned to guard a henhouse. A big, broad-shouldered Virginian who could charm listeners one mo-ment only to turn wrathful the next, Griles kept his cool under Wy-den's questioning and was easily confirmed.

Griles took up residence in July 2001 in a big corner office of the vast Interior building on C Street. He placed a full-grown, stuffed Alaskan grizzly bear outside his door, upright, with its long teeth bared and front claws extended, ready to pounce. He had heard that it was gathering dust in a state historical-society basement and ordered it brought up. "Children love him," Griles would say, when visitors asked.

No sooner had Griles put silver-framed, Reagan-era photos on the walls of his new office than he gave a speech to the West Virginia Coal Association. The message was blunt. "We will fix the federal rules very soon on water and spoil placement," he proclaimed in his deep, bass voice. On August 16, he met with one of his former lobbying clients,

Hal Quinn, senior vice president of the National Mining Association. Later, Griles characterized the meeting as a brown-bag lunch on the balcony of his office with an old friend—an important distinction, because the new deputy secretary had signed a recusal agreement that barred him from discussing "particular matters" with former clients, of whom Quinn was one.

Quinn's National Mining Association certainly did have a particular matter of concern to raise with others in the new administration, if not with Griles. The Fourth Circuit ruling on Haden 1 had solved the buffer-zone problem, at least for a while. But the industry knew it was still vulnerable on the issue of fill. The NMA wanted the new administration to finish the task the Clintonites had begun: clarifying the definition of fill. The industry lobbyists, however, didn't have quite the same definition in mind as the Clintonites.

The other housekeeping item on the industry's list was the EIS, which had also been left unfinished when the Clinton administration left office. In a memo of October 5, 2001, to all agencies involved, Griles seemed to set the EIS on a whole new track. Instead of focusing exclusively on the adverse environmental impacts of mountaintop removal, he declared the EIS should focus at least as much "on centralizing and streamlining coal mine permitting"—the very promise George W. Bush had given on the tarmac of Charleston's airport.

Separately, an EIS was now assigned for Arch's Spruce No. 1 mine. The administration issued a first draft with standards so low and tests so lax that Arch's permit would simply sail through. Jim Hecker, working with Joe, submitted blistering written comments in response, pointing out the draft's many glaring flaws. With some embarrassment, the EPA withdrew it for review. More field tests, it vowed, would be done at the site. Once again, Joe and Jim had bought time—perhaps another year, perhaps two. But Joe knew better than to expect the next draft would be much tougher than the last.

Joe had vowed he wouldn't get stuck in coal. But now he felt he couldn't walk away. He could see not only that the coal industry was breaking state and federal laws on a daily basis but that its very existence posed a global threat. And once again, the Army Corps was sanctioning large-scale valley fills for vast new mountaintop operations. Under the Bush administration, the federal agreement to suspend large valley fills until the EIS was done had simply been abandoned.

In September 2001, Joe and Jim filed a new lawsuit in Judge Haden's court. This time, their only target was the U.S. Army Corps of Engineers. If the Fourth Circuit said they could sue only a federal agency in federal court, then fine—they would do that. With an environmental group called Kentuckians for the Commonwealth as their plaintiff, they focused on the Corps' issuance of a permit for a valley fill at a surface mine in eastern Kentucky.

Now that Joe and Jim were bringing suit only against the Corps, the Bush administration sensed real danger. In private, the government lawyers felt they had a loser in what was now being called Haden 2. They simply had no answers to Joe and Jim's airtight legal points. And Judge Haden had already shown where his sympathies lay. There was only one card the administration could play. If it could change the definition of "fill" before the judge had a chance to rule, the suit would be mooted.

Much more than a single dictionary definition was involved. Pages of legal language had to be parsed, each word and phrase weighed with Talmudic care. On May 3, 2002, the new definition was finished and made public. Fill, the administration declared, need not be defined as having a primary purpose of filling a streambed or wetlands for construction. Almost anything that had that *effect* was fill. With this seemingly minor change, the whole law was turned on its head. Mining waste, after all, had the effect of filling a streambed for what could be construction, even though construction wasn't its purpose. Joe had expected this. What he didn't anticipate was that Judge Haden would react with such fury.

At the start of Haden 2, Joe had asked the judge to strike the Corps' permit in Kentucky based on the old definition of fill. Legally, he felt, that would put the ruling on safer ground with the Fourth Circuit Court of Appeals. Haden plainly disagreed. If fill was the issue, then the government's new definition of it was relevant to the case. "Congress never permitted . . . fills . . . to be permitted solely to dispose of waste," Haden railed in his ruling of May 8, 2002, while the ink was still wet on the government's new definition of the word. "To read the [Clean Water] Act otherwise presumes Congress intended the Clean Water Act to protect the nation's waterways and the integrity of its waters with one major exception: the Army Corps was to be given authority to allow the waters of the United States to be filled with pollutants and thus destroyed, even if the sole purpose were disposal of waste."

Joe knew he should have been thrilled to see those telltale words: "Plaintiff's motion is granted." But he wasn't. He felt sick to his stomach. He knew Haden had gone too far. The Fourth Circuit would crucify the judge for striking down a government rule he hadn't been asked to consider—a new rule that hadn't even been formally adopted.

Once again, uproar followed a Haden ruling. Bill Raney spoke for the whole coal industry when he declared the ruling a "devastating" exercise in "judge-made law." Government lawyers rushed into Haden's courtroom to ask that he suspend his ruling pending an appeal on those grounds. This time, the judge rejected the appeal. He need look no further, he said, than the Kentucky coal company that had been the suit's original target. The company had just acknowledged that it could mine its reserves without creating the twenty-seven valleys fills it had planned—without dumping any waste into waters at all.

With new mountaintop projects brought to a virtual halt, the government filed its appeal to the Fourth Circuit. On December 4, 2002, Joe and Jim went back to Richmond to appear before a three-judge panel that included two of the three judges they'd drawn for Haden 1: the ultraconservative J. Michael Luttig and Paul V. Niemeyer. What were the odds, Joe wondered, of a random process twice producing the same two judges from more than a dozen? It was like a slot machine coming up with two cherries twice in a row—an unlikely coincidence, as any gambler would attest.

Just as Joe feared, the panel found Haden's ruling "overbroad." Anyway, the court ruled, the Corps had authority to grant permits as it did simply because it had been doing so in a consistent manner for years in conjunction with the EPA. The court, stressed Niemeyer in his written opinion, did not consider "the question of whether mountaintop coal mining is useful, desirable, or wise." The ruling considered only whether the government could define fill as it liked and issue permits accordingly. It could.

If Joe had held out any hope that the long-awaited EIS on mountaintop mining might limit the practice in ways he'd argued for in court, those hopes were dashed in May 2003, when a draft was made public. The emphasis was now entirely on "streamlining" the permitting process. "All we have proposed," rued one government scientist in an e-mail to another upon reading the draft, "is alternative locations to house the rubber stamp that issues the permits."

Anyone with eyesight good enough to read the tiny type at the back of the EIS, where the scientific studies had been relegated, could see a story very different from what the rest of the document presented. Between 1985 and 2001, some 6,700 valley fills had been approved in West Virginia, western Virginia, eastern Kentucky, and eastern Tennessee. Together, those fills covered nearly 84,000 acres. In West Virginia, the fills had buried more than 25,000 acres. All told, the fills had buried 724 miles of perennial or intermittent streams. At the rate it was going, mountaintop removal would destroy another thousand miles of streams in the next decade. Overall, the practice had probably destroyed 3.4 percent of the forest cover in the study area: about 380,547 acres. At that rate, it would eradicate or severely affect 1,408,372 acres, or 11.5 percent of the study area, before the region's mineable coal was gone. The final EIS, issued in October 2005 after eighty-five thousand public comments of concern and dismay, bore exactly the same recommendations as the draft.

By then, Steve Griles was gone. He'd been an industry hero, bending public policy to coal's desires at every turn, but he'd left himself open to withering criticism for dozens of meetings held with former clients in possible violation of his recusal agreement. Those meetings had provoked a formal eighteen-month investigation by the inspector general of the Interior Department. Griles had been cleared of violating any laws or federal ethics rules, but the inspector general had voiced concerns nonetheless about some of those meetings. It was time for Griles to leave. On December 7, 2004, he bid a final goodbye to the bear outside his corner office and once again passed through the revolving door from government to business. This time, he helped start a new lobbying firm, Lundquist, Nethercutt & Griles, which advertised that its partners had "longstanding relationships with senior officials in the Bush administration." Soon, one political relationship would come back to haunt him: the one with disgraced lobbyist Jack Abramoff. Under oath, Griles would declare that relationship insignificant. An ensuing investigation would make clear that this wasn't true. In the summer of 2007, a red-faced Griles would plead guilty to perjury and be led off in tears to a ten-month jail term.

A whole network of Bush officials had blocked Joe's greatest legal victory by redefining fill. They'd kept the EIS from doing any harm to mountain-top mining. There was just one more legal dangler to deal with.

When the judges of the Fourth Circuit Court of Appeals had re-versed Haden 1, they hadn't ruled on its merits. Sooner or later, Joe and Jim might go, as directed, to a state court to challenge the DEP on the legality of issuing permits for mountaintop mining in violation of the buffer-zone rule. Even West Virginia's version of that rule, after all, was crystal clear: no mining activity within one hundred feet of a perennial or intermittent stream was allowed without serious study.

The solution, as with fill, was a little change in wording. In January 2004, the Office of Surface Mining proposed a "clarification" of the buffer-zone rule. The revised rule would allow operators to obtain vari-ances if they simply *tried* to avoid mining within one hundred feet of streams "to the extent possible, using the best technology currently available."

This time, more citizens seemed to understand how much was at stake with a minor "clarification." Angry crowds gathered at public meetings obligatorily held by OSM. Astonishingly, in June 2005, OSM pledged to conduct a formal EIS on the buffer-zone rule and only then decide if and how the rule should be clarified. Joe was certain the EIS would be as useless as the one for mountaintop mining.

This was hardly the sign of an administration that had awakened to environmental concerns. In the same four years that Joe had battled Bush and his operatives on mountaintop removal, the administration had bashed the environment in literally hundreds of ways. With an enthusiasm for Orwellian language that meant the opposite of what it said, the administration had wheeled out a Clear Skies initiative that would loosen, not tighten, future air-quality standards. It had proposed another called Healthy Forests that gave loggers nearly free rein to cut timber in national forests under the guise of clearing underbrush to help prevent forest fires. It had slashed the Superfund for toxic cleanups and let polluters off the hook for their costs: from now on, taxpayers would foot the bills. It had proposed vastly increased drilling and mining on federal lands and also suggested selling off sizable chunks of federal land to help make up budget shortfalls caused by tax breaks and the war in Iraq. It had abandoned the first President Bush's pledge of "no net loss" for wetlands. It had moved to kill the Endangered Species Act and pushed hard to open the Arctic National Wildlife Refuge to oil drilling at last. Most important, it had ignored global warming and gone so far as to rewrite a federal agency report that said global warming was a real, imminent, and man-made threat. One could say this, at least, about Bush and the environment: so egregious had his policies been at every turn, damaging public water, air, lands, and human health in order to benefit corporate political contributors, that he'd managed to make mountaintop removal seem modest by comparison. What, after all, were a few thousand mountains in Appalachia compared to the fate of the world?

Such, in the winter of 2005, was the gallows humor that kept Joe Lovett from simply giving up as he contemplated the effects of four more years of George W. Bush on the mountains that he had tried so hard to save. He still hoped that when his Nationwide 21 suit reached the Fourth Circuit, the notoriously conservative judges would agree with Judge Goodwin: the Corps was clearly, fundamentally violating the Clean Water Act by issuing those authorizations for vast mountaintop sites. Joe and Jim might prevail with their new, nearly identical Nationwide 21 suit against the Corps in Kentucky. If they won at the federal district level there, the suit would move up to a different circuit court of appeals—the Sixth—which had a reputation for more centrist opinions. Sometimes Joe would dare to imagine this scenario: he'd lose in the Fourth, but win in the Sixth, which would provoke a "circuit split"—two federal courts of appeal reaching opposite decisions on the same issue. The U.S. Supreme Court might then decide to hear the case, and Joe would get to argue his first case there. The justices would see how plainly the law was being broken and a thundering verdict would stop the Appalachian coalfields from being destroyed.

But then his thoughts would drift back to earth. The reality Joe was facing now was four more years of Bush. Joe had lost on coal, that was all there was to it. Bush, Griles, and the collective clout of a coal-fueled administration had won.

A casualty of that conflict—symbolically, at least—was Judge Charles H. Haden II, dead of cancer on March 20, 2004. His legacy was one he never would have predicted or imagined: a pair of brave decisions on mountaintop mining batted down by the Fourth Circuit Court of Appeals. The reversals could not have helped his health, for Haden had come to believe that every time a mountain was blasted for coal a grave illegality was being committed in the state he loved. The Fourth Circuit's back of the hand to his decisions must have stung him deeply. While the law he'd made was unmade, however, something remained: a line of legal reasoning that another court might take up, sooner or later, in another case against King Coal.

Months passed before anything roused Joe from his funk. But then, in the early summer of 2005, Don Blankenship started pushing to build a coal silo in the shadow of the Marsh Fork Elementary School, the very school that Judy Bonds had realized was the cause to focus on. When Judy called to ask for Joe's help, Joe would realize he wasn't unstuck from coal after all.

SEVEN

A SCHOOL
IN MASSEY'S SHADOW

O ne by one, schools were closing in the Coal River valley. Families were moving out, giving up under the onslaught of coal trucks and blasting and blackwater spills, heading to Ohio or Illinois. As they did, class rolls dwindled, until the county faced the inevitable and shifted the children of one faltering school up or down the valley to another. By state recommendation, though not by law, children were to travel no more than thirty minutes to school, but in some cases they did. Before dawn on winter mornings now, many children in the valley waited in the dark for their buses and rode an hour or more on winding Route 3 to their new schools, looking out on the dark and desolate building that had been their school the year before.

Whitesville's junior high was one of the abandoned ones. So was Marsh Fork High, a white granite hulk of a school that now stood silent a few miles south of Whitesville. A short drive farther south lay a more modest but cheerful-looking redbrick bunker of a school, set back from the road by a wide, fenced-in front lawn. This was Marsh Fork Elementary, alongside a stretch of the Coal River also known as Marsh Fork Creek. The school's survival, when so many other schools in the valley had expired, was impressive in itself, but all the more so because of the towering coal plant that loomed right behind it.

Some 240 children attended Marsh Fork Elementary, filling classrooms that had the usual displays of student art and work projects on the walls. Most days, the students milled outside for recess on the wide front lawn, and their happy cries could be heard even over the drone of traffic on Route 3. To them, the Massey-owned prep plant across the creek was just part of the scenery, barely noticeable in spring and fall through the foliage on either bank. But the plant was closer than it seemed. There were rumors that children grew sick after drinking at the school water fountains and that the fountains were covered in plastic on certain days, particularly when it rained. The front lawn had coal dust on it, it was said, enough to darken children's sneakers when they played there. The creek itself was visibly polluted, its once-clear waters muddy brown. Not long ago, children had gone swimming and fishing there. Now, almost none did. One child who was foolish enough to wade into a tributary of the creek came out with a persistent headache, a rash on his face and chest, a stomachache, and diarrhea for days. He also reported that he'd gone fishing and reeled in a ghastly catch: a fish with its head half eaten away, as if by acid.

So far, the reports of chronically sick students at Marsh Fork were just anecdotal. But there were quite a few of them. Herb Elkins's granddaughter, age seven, had a runny nose and cough and earaches all through the school year. Two weeks into summer vacation, away from the school, the symptoms disappeared. Bob Cole's son Davy came home routinely with stomachaches. If a stomach bug was what he had, his parents never seemed to catch it. Davy told his parents he wasn't the only one. Often, he said, several kids in his class would experience diarrhea and vomiting at the same time, sometimes even throwing up in class. Carolyn Beckner's daughter, Brittany, had such bad stomachaches that she asked her mother nightly to pray for her stomach to feel better. Kenny Pettry's nine-year-old son, Jacob, complained of chronic upper-respiratory symptoms; he, too, felt better as soon as he got out of school at the start of summer. And Sherry Pettry—no relation to Kenny—had to keep her sons Tyler and Corey home on account of headaches and stomach pains so often that she'd run through every kind of antibiotic the doctor had to offer.

When chronically sick children from Marsh Fork Elementary graduated to middle school up the valley, their symptoms seemed to vanish altogether. So it was with Justin Cantley's stomachaches and allergies; he was thirteen and healthy now. Gina Jarrell's son Josh had missed fifty days of school per year with asthma at Marsh Fork Elementary; now that he'd graduated, his symptoms too, had subsided.

The Massey subsidiary behind Marsh Fork Elementary was called Goals, for the production goals its workers were supposed to reach. It wasn't the only subsidiary to which Massey had given an inspirational name: Performance was another, Independence a third. Like Elk Run and Montcoal, Goals had a prep plant that served as a hub for coal brought from mines all around it. And like both of those other operations, it had a huge impoundment: on the hillside directly above the school. The Martin County disaster of 2000 had led parents to wonder how likely this one might be to rupture as well, sending a high flood of toxic slurry across the creek and over the school. Officially, the county had an evacuation plan for the children that involved an alarm sounded "personally or by bullhorn." When it sounded, the children were to be driven to schools down the valley. Unofficially, as far as the parents could tell, the children would be buried.

From the roadside, Goals's dreary, industrial buildings almost obscured the hollow behind them. But a local who knew these hills could spot the small cemetery that remained halfway up the hillside. Half a century ago, the cemetery had served black miners in the hollow when it had been called Shumate's Branch. Their bones lay underground still, their eternal peace disturbed on a daily basis by blasting over the ridge. In all, more than five hundred people, most of them white, had lived in Shumate's Branch, cultivating their hillside gardens and gathering at a cheerful shack of a restaurant called the Coffeepot. Now all their houses were gone, along with the gardens. All that was left of Shumate's Branch was a moonscape of slate and coal and slurry and blasted rock.

The story of Shumate's Branch, from its first settlement to the school that now lay at its foot, was in a sense the story of the whole Coal River valley. "It goes back to old man Absalom Petre, he was the owner of all this land," Sylvia Bradford liked to recount. Sylvia was a lifelong, eighty-seven-year-old resident of Edwight, the community right next to Shumate's. She would tell the story on the porch of the humble wood house she'd lived in with her husband and son since 1946. The rooms inside had sagging beds, bare lightbulbs dangling from perilously low ceilings, and stacks of old newspapers, but not much else. In one corner, three rifles, dark with rust, stood set against one another—probably Civil War relics. The kitchen was filled with skillets and crockery that looked at least one hundred years old.

"He was an old hillbilly, he had no education," Sylvia said of Absalom. "When he and his brother Burwell needed money, they had a habit of selling off a piece of their property. Then they'd try to retrieve it from whoever they'd sold it to, by buying it back. But when they sold it to the Rowland Land Company, they didn't retrieve it. Oh, no."

Sometime in the 1890s, four families from out of state came on a speculative trip to the valley, directed by Samuel C. Rowland, a Baltimore lumber merchant who had expanded into banking, railroads, and then coal. (Rowland was said to be "a man of strongly marked social nature" who found "recreation in the rearing and training of horses, motoring, and shooting."). They started by buying timber rights from landowning locals. Then they came back with a geologist. Apparently, the geologist discovered that Shumate's Branch contained a motherlode of coal. So the speculators fanned out to all the landowning families of the hollow, justices of the peace in tow, and got them to sign their Xs before any of them realized the leverage they'd have by holding out. "These old people knew absolutely nothing about the minerals," Sylvia said. "They didn't even know the timber was valuable." One local widow on nearby Sturgeon Fork sold her mineral rights for a hog and some pigs. "Pigs and cows is what counted to these mountain people. They'd make their mark, those Xs, on the contracts, and that would be that," said Sylvia. The key parcel was 120 acres at the mouth of the hollow: land owned by Absalom and Burwell Petre. Unfortunately, Burwell and his two sons chose that inopportune time to shoot two of their cousins to death.

"No one knew for sure why," Sylvia said. "One story was the cousins were selling chickens they'd stolen from Burwell. Another was they were throwing rocks in Burwell's gristmill and tying up the grinding wheel. Still another was they let cattle into Burwell's garden. But nobody knows for sure. One person said of those cousins, 'They just had too much nerve.'"

So now Burwell needed money to hire a lawyer, and that meant selling some land. The Pennsylvania speculators were all too happy to oblige. On June 29, 1903, the Petre parcel was added to the others, and the whole patchwork of acquired properties, covering Shumate's Branch and beyond, was reconstituted as the Rowland Land Company.

Nearly a century later, Rowland still owned Shumate's Branch and a lot of other land in the valley, too, with an office in Charleston to administer it. It leased that land to various coal companies. By 1985, decades of underground mining had diminished the thickest and purest seams. The coal being mined now needed more washing to separate it from the various kinds of rock and dirt that clung to it. So Peabody, the company working Shumate's at the time, built a first, modest impoundment in the crook of the valley. A few locals still lived on that side of the hollow, so Peabody bought them out for good money and put them in houses and trailers at rents of as little as five dollars per month. Peabody had started some mountaintop mining, too, but on a scale too modest for anyone to mind. Besides, Peabody was a union operation.

Then, in December 1994, Massey took over the lease, and as at Elk Run and at Montcoal it turned the locals' world upside down. The last residents of the hollow were soon dispatched. Then came the gates and guards and no more access to land up the hollow. The guards assumed police powers, dressed up like sheriffs with guns and walkie-talkies and high-tech surveillance tools; several residents brought a suit alleging that Massey security guards pulled handguns on them, beat them, and transported them against their will. When the blasting started, Sylvia Bradford was astonished to see the hollow's entire animal population come foraging right by her house in the valley: bobcats and bears, squirrels and possums. When she fed them, they hung around for more, pets whether she wanted them or not.

Month by month, Massey expanded its mountaintop operations just over the ridge from Shumate's Branch. Locals could walk up the valley side of a nearby hill and still be surrounded by trees. When they got to the top, they found themselves looking down at bowls of blasted land. In the distance, tiny figures would plant neat rows of explosives, like crops, in already flattened hilltops. When they'd finished, the tiny figures would drive off a distance in their trucks—huge trucks with giant wheels that still looked ant-sized at a distance—and wait for a minute or two of eerie silence. Then the blast would come, sending spumes of dirt hundreds of feet in the air, where for a gravity-defying moment they lingered, strangely beautiful, before drifting back down to earth. The coal exposed by the blast would be loaded by bulldozers onto the trucks or onto conveyor belts that moved solemnly over the ridge, into the hollow once known as Shumate's Branch, to be washed at the prep plant now called Goals beside Marsh Fork Elementary School.

Children at the school had reported chronic symptoms almost since Massey's arrival at Shumate's. But the reports multiplied beginning in 2003, the year Goals built the silo to store all the coal it was taking down from the mountaintops. From there, the coal was loaded directly onto train cars that passed under the silo itself. The best place to situate the silo, it turned out, was near the creekside edge of the prep-plant property, fewer than three hundred feet from the school. SMCRA prohibited coal companies from building that close to a school, but Massey said that the prep plant had been operating since 1975, so it was exempt from the law, which had passed in 1977.

The silo was just a storage facility for already-washed coal: no health risk in that, Massey said. Indeed, the whole point of the silo was to store the coal in a closed container, not in open stockpiles, and so keep the dust from blowing around. But one local who'd helped construct the silo and seen it in operation felt it wasn't an improvement at all. When an empty coal car passed under the silo to be loaded, he explained, a thick spray came on to coat the coal. The idea was to keep coal dust from blowing as the coal was loaded. A huge fan was set up to disperse the spray. That fan, the local said, could blow spray through the opening between the coal car and silo. The spray settled in the hair of the workers in the silo, leaving it thick and greasy. It settled on the ground in an oil-like slick, where the men hosed it away. Anyone could see, the local said, that the spray worked into the ground, disturbingly close to Marsh Fork Creek.

In the late summer of 2004, a local man named Ed Wiley had begun asking why Massey refused to disclose what chemicals it used at the plant beside the school. Wiley had a granddaughter who attended Marsh Fork Elementary and reported her share of chronic symptoms. He wondered why state agencies seemed to take no interest in testing the water and air around the plant. He also wondered why the school made no effort to get answers from Massey and why the county, after all the children's complaints and the threat of the looming impoundment, made no effort to relocate the school.

Wiley was a young grandfather at forty-seven, tall and broad-shouldered, a standout athlete in high school who still radiated a commanding strength despite the toll that cigarettes and hard living had taken, and he had his reputation still as one of the valley's best turkey shots. When no one gave him answers, Wiley joined up with Coal River Mountain Watch and began learning how to lobby state lawmakers. His fight for the children had just begun.

Theresa Lewis, principal that summer of Marsh Fork Elementary, found Wiley's alarm somewhat baffling. Wiley had shown no previous interest in his granddaughter at the school. Lewis had to wonder if he'd been directed by Coal River Mountain Watch to stir things up. The parents' complaints, she felt, were overblown. One child had complained of bellyaches, and then another had joined in. But that was it. Some students were chronically absent, she allowed, but that was usually the fault of parents too lazy to get them to school each day.

Water at the school was tested each month, Lewis observed. It was fine. The air was fine, too. As for the prep plant, the principal put her trust in the DEP, whose inspectors, she understood, visited the site several days each week. She had no communication with them or with anyone at Massey or Goals. No one, she said, issued reports. But the wife of a Massey superintendent at the plant worked at the school and said everything was fine. No one liked having the impoundment up there, and if it burst, Lewis acknowledged, it would take out the whole valley right up to Whitesville. But she trusted that the people who were running it were doing what they should be doing.

Anyway, Lewis said, the only alternative would be closing the school. There was nowhere for it to relocate. So the students and teachers would just sit tight, Lewis said, and hope for the best.

Despite Ed Wiley's protests, classes convened as usual in the fall of 2004 at Marsh Fork Elementary, and, aside from more stories of chronically sick children, no mishaps occurred that school year. As the spring term was tapering to an end, however, teachers and students looked out one day to a spectacle without precedent in the Coal River valley. A motley band of protesters, seventy-five or so strung out in a line along the side of Route 3, were beating drums and waving placards that read "Stop Poisoning Kids." Ed Wiley and Judy Bonds were at the head of the march, but many of the rest were young and scruffily dressed, with scraggly long hair. The first Mountain Justice Summer had come to Coal River.

With Matt Crum gone from the DEP and the golden era over, Judy had decided she had nothing to lose by pushing Coal River Mountain Watch to a new level of confrontation with Massey Energy. Bo Webb, her tattooed coleader at CRMW, was all for that. A Marine corporal in Vietnam from January 1968 to March 1969, he'd spent most of those months a few miles from the North Vietnamese border and Khe Sanh, manning a gun on truck convoys as they made supply runs. His convoys had been hit a lot with artillery, rockets, and mortars, and twice they had encountered ambushes. If there was one thing he knew, it was how to return fire. That winter, he and Judy and the half-dozen others who came faithfully each day now to CRMW's storefront in Whitesville had decided to reach beyond the valley for reinforcements. They'd hooked up online with a wide array of environmental groups, including groups focused on mountaintop removal in other Appalachian states. Judy herself had gone on the road to give talks and show a video of mountaintop devastation done by Massey and its subsidiaries. She'd called for volunteers to engage in what she called Mountain Justice Summer, modeled after the California protests to save old-growth redwoods from being clear-cut. In May 2005, to Judy and Bo's private amazement, nearly fifty young protesters had shown up in the valley for a training workshop.

The protesters were nearly all college age, from all over the country, with political philosophies to match their long hair, elaborate tattoos, various body piercings, and tribal earlobe extensions. Some called themselves anarchists. Many allied themselves with Earth First!, the radical environmental group that advocated extreme action: putting sand in the gas tanks of earthmoving machines, for example, that were due to destroy precious land. A lot of the new arrivals went by first names only. Squirrel and Elliot were two young women in handmade clothes who rolled their cigarettes and talked of having made a promise to the mountains. They had hitchhiked from North Carolina and said they would stay until they stopped the mountains from being blasted. Brian, of the tribal earlobes, said he'd given up his house and job in South Carolina to hitchhike to the valley; all he owned now were his clothes and backpack. A young woman who called herself America had come from Athens, Ohio, where she'd worked as an activist since she was sixteen.

Judy was a bit taken aback by her new foot soldiers. She was a daughter and granddaughter of coal miners. She'd never seen anyone quite like Squirrel and Elliot, Brian and America. But she was pleased to have them. At that first protest in May, Judy, Ed Wiley, and Bo Webb led them in chants outside Marsh Fork Elementary, then marched down to the gates of the Goals prep plant. When Judy and Bo tried to walk across the bridge that led over Marsh Fork Creek to Goals's property, they were arrested, briefly, by nervous police, who'd never seen a protest in the valley before.

A week later, the ragtag army of Mountain Justice Summer was back. It had swelled to 150 with the aid of local environmental groups and a few residents angry enough to stand up publicly to Massey Energy. One of the locals was an eighty-year-old woman who could barely walk. Another was Sylvia Bradford's son, Rick, sixty-one, a retired teacher who'd lived with his parents his whole life in their backwoods house at Edwight. The Dustbusters of Sylvester, Mary Miller and Pauline Canterberry, were there. So were a few mothers whose children attended Marsh Fork Elementary and were often sick. This time the marchers sang "Amazing Grace" and "Which Side Are You On?" while state police guarded the bridge and Goals employees looked on. When a pair of grandmothers and a retired teacher walked to the bridge with a list of demands, sixteen protesters were arrested and handcuffed. Among them was Larry Gibson, the lone holdout on Kayford Mountain. This time they were taken to a nearby police station. There they were given citations for disturbing the peace and released.

And there, despite high hopes and earnest vows, Mountain Justice Summer might have peaked, if not for a development that none of the marchers, even Judy, could ever have anticipated. Don Blankenship had decided that the Goals operation needed a *second* silo to house all the coal coming from mountaintop mining over the ridge. The second silo would be placed even closer than the first one to Marsh Fork Elementary. Massey had applied for a permit to build the silo, a process it assumed would be routine. But its application was to lead to a drama in which Don, Judy Bonds, Joe Lovett, and Joe Manchin, the new governor of West Virginia, were all involved.

Ever since his success in toppling Warren McGraw from the state supreme court, Don Blankenship had made clear he regarded West Virginia politics as his new arena. In speeches he began giving around the state, he stressed that he had no interest in running for office himself. He merely wanted to make himself heard on issues that mattered to working men and women whose interests had been ignored in the state for too long. He felt they'd been shortchanged by both parties. He called himself a populist and a radical. "What is a radical?" he'd ask his audiences rhetorically. "I looked up the word to be sure. A radical is someone who insists on change. And so that's what I am." Perhaps one reason for Don's new, public profile was a private sense that his days at Massey might be numbered. Subservient as his board of directors was, that spring it had chosen to renew Don's contract for merely the remaining eight months of 2005. Even if the directors had wanted to, they couldn't slip Don another contract like his last one, for three years with a string of perks attached no matter how the company fared. Massey Energy was attracting too much attention, from media and shareholders alike.

The elections of 2004 had brought the state a new governor, and almost immediately Don had seen fit to challenge him on an initiative he felt would ill serve the working-class voters he'd chosen to defend. Joe Manchin III was a Democrat, though it was, perhaps, more relevant to say that he was a former coal operator, if perhaps a well-intentioned one. Telegenic, with a full head of dark hair and a strong jaw, he had already shown a Clintonesque talent for speaking in whole paragraphs, not just preprogrammed sound bites, and for identifying emotionally with a wide range of voters. Behind the warmth, he had a reputation for micromanaging, not unlike the coal baron he was about to take on.

Just days into his term, the new governor proposed a bond issue to shore up pension funds for state workers. The bond would raise $5.5 billion. The state would then take that money, Manchin explained, and put it into the stock market where, he predicted, it would earn more than the 4.5 percent interest to be paid to the bondholders. The difference would go to the state workers' pension fund.

Don Blankenship saw that as a dangerous gamble. He may have been right. In a good or even sluggish market, steady returns of 6 percent or more seemed a reasonable expectation. But when the market stayed flat or lost money for a decade or more—as it had done in the 1970s—6 percent looked pretty rosy. "I grew up sleeping on a dirt floor," Don told one local reporter. "And no matter what kind of successes I have, I haven't forgotten what the average citizen lives like. And the average citizen doesn't need the state out there gambling with $5.5 billion of their tax dollars."

That spring, as the governor took to his bully pulpit to urge voters to approve the bond issue in a special June election, Don spent hundreds of thousands of dollars on a slick multimedia campaign to disparage the idea. The governor began to complain that some of the ads misrepresented his plan. Don scoffed that the governor was turning the bond battle into a personal feud. Manchin responded through a spokesperson that the feud wasn't personal at all. But then he questioned whether Don had a right to weigh in on West Virginia politics. Wasn't the coal baron's primary residence in Kentucky? Wasn't that where he voted? At the least, the governor suggested, Don would have to expect that with his greater involvement in state politics would come greater scrutiny of his business. Don countered that he'd lived in Sprigg, West Virginia, for twenty-one of the last twenty-three years. His recent residency in Kentucky was a two-year aberration, concluded now that he was again a resident of Sprigg. And the governor's remark about greater scrutiny sounded a lot to him like a not-so-veiled threat. Still, if it was, Don ignored it, pouring more money into his campaign in the critical days before the vote. Once again, he carried the day. The bond issue was handily defeated.

Was the governor, as a result, a bit more receptive than he might have been to angry cries from Coal River residents about a second silo at Goals? Or was he just doing his job to hear them out at a meeting two days after the vote? Probably the latter, since the governor's staff had called Coal River Mountain Watch right after the first rally at Goals to set up the meeting that Ed Wiley and others had been trying to get for more than a year. Still, to Don Blankenship if no one else, the timing looked suspect.

With the bond-issue defeat stinging, Manchin met at the capitol with Judy, Bo, Ed, and a dozen or so other valley residents, most of them members of CRMW. For more than an hour, he listened to their concerns about the children at Marsh Fork Elementary and the proposed second silo. Massey's permit for the silo was pending with the DEP. Any day now, a ruling would be rendered.

Manchin made no promises, though he did say he'd speak with Stephanie Timmermeyer about the permit. For almost two years now, Timmermeyer had headed the DEP. The Coal River residents had had no faith in her from the day she pushed out Matt Crum. All she'd done since, as far as they could see, was speed up the rate at which permits were granted for mountaintop mining. She'd even said as much. A backlog of sixty pending permits, she'd proudly declared, had been all but eliminated. Still, the residents felt cheered by the governor's evident concern. They felt even better when they gathered in the ornately paneled office of Bob Kiss, West Virginia Speaker of the House, who'd sat in on the meeting with Manchin. "I think you made an initial case with the governor this morning," Kiss said approvingly. "And I think he's going to have a much more detailed conversation with Stephanie."

"Stephanie has never once talked to us," Bo Webb said bitterly.

"Matt Crum came to us," Judy added, "and not just to our community but others as well, and sat down and explained what he was doing."

Kiss nodded. "Well, one thing I asked her, 'Have you taken time to talk to these people?' And she indicated to me it was part of the permit process."

Timmermeyer just meant that she would listen to the tape from those DEP meetings where uniformed officials listened, stone-faced, while residents railed on. "I said, 'That's not what I'm talking about,'" Kiss said he'd told her. "'You've got concerned citizens that want to meet one on one.'"

Kiss said he hoped Timmermeyer would do that at last. He said the governor was serious about seeing the issue through. "I'm confident you'll hear from him or from one of his staff people in the next eight to ten days," he said. He pledged that the governor would call for a thorough study of conditions at Marsh Fork Elementary. "We need to study the soil and air and water around that school, send it to a qualified lab and see what the results are."

Three days later, the DEP announced its decision on the Massey permit application for a second silo. The application was approved. Massey could now build a 168-foot-tall coal silo 260 feet from Marsh Fork Elementary. Just for good measure, the DEP also approved a permit for Goals to extend its impoundment farther up Shumate's Branch. The impoundment would now be 385 feet high.

At the corner storefront in Whitesville, Judy heard the news first with astonishment, then fury. For once, she'd allowed herself to hope that a state politician might actually do something to help the Coal River valley. Now the governor had confirmed all her worst suspicions about him. He was even worse, she decided, than his predecessors, whose sympathy with the industry was clear for all to see. Machin's slick charm and silver tongue made him appear a man you could trust. That, she saw now, was what made him so dangerous.

Ed Wiley felt all of that and more: he felt personally betrayed by the news. Like a lot of mountain men from southern West Virginia, Wiley had no hesitation about saying whatever he felt to whomever he felt should hear it. That week, he got in his pickup truck and drove to Charleston to give the governor a piece of his mind.

The governor, as it turned out, had too busy a schedule to speak with Ed again. That was fine, Ed told the staff person who gave him this news. He could wait.

Ed went out to the steps of the capitol and began to wait. After a few hours, reporters and television crews, alerted to his vigil, came over to hear him out. "I want the governor to explain to me why Massey Energy's profits are more important than these kids' health and safety," Ed told them. "Where is the governor's heart? Where is his loyalty?

"I've been in the governor's office," he added. "That didn't help. I want him to come out here and explain how he's going to fix this problem that could have been prevented with a phone call."

Minutes after Ed appeared on the six o'clock news, the governor's staff person came out to see him. "The governor will see you now," the staff person said.

Ed followed him into the building and through the rotunda, past the life-sized statue of Senator Robert C. Byrd. When Ed was ushered into the governor's office, Manchin hurried out from behind his desk to greet him. Once again, he was genial and gracious, not a dark hair out of place. But this time, Ed was less impressed.

"Sir," Ed said, "how could you let the DEP issue those permits to Goals just days after you promised us you'd do something to help?"

The governor tried to explain that the DEP had its own process for reviewing permit applications. Once the governor had assured himself that that process was being followed—and he had, he told Ed—there wasn't any more he could do. "I'll not second-guess the decisions of the DEP," he said.

"Sir, my issue is the children," Ed said bluntly. "That's why I got involved with this at the start. What if that impoundment breaks, the way the one in Martin County did?"

The governor started explaining how the state was working to see that impoundments were safe. To his astonishment, Ed got up and started walking out. "Hey," said the governor, "where're you going?"

"I'm going back out there to sit down," Ed said, pointing in the general direction of the capitol steps.

"Don't go, Ed," the governor said hastily. "I really want to hear you out."

Ed sat back down. He looked at the governor a moment, then shook his head. "You mind if I call you Joe?" he said.

"That's fine, Ed," the governor said. "That's fine."

The men kept talking. More than once, Ed gaveled his fist onto the governor's desk to make a point. Twice more, he got up and started to walk out. Each time, the governor urged him to stay. Finally, the governor got on his speakerphone and started talking to various officials. He said he wanted a multiagency team to go down to Marsh Fork Elementary that week—the next day, if possible—to check out the citizens' complaints and run tests on water and air on the premises.

The two men stood up and shook hands. As Ed left, a staffer looked after him warily to see if he'd head back out to the steps. He didn't. Instead, he went out to his pickup and headed south on the hour's drive home. He was behind on his truck payments, he thought, as he joined the flow of evening traffic leaving the city. If he didn't start earning some regular money, his truck was going to be repossessed.

Within forty-eight hours of Ed Wiley's sit-down on the capitol steps, the governor's inspection team arrived at Marsh Fork Elementary. The inspectors, most from the state Department of Education, walked into the empty classrooms. They examined the filters in the air-conditioning system. They did no testing for coal dust or any toxic chemicals in the air, however. One of the inspectors said he would have no idea how to do that. "Which chemicals do you look for?" he wondered out loud. "There's a bazillion of them." They did do a visual search for coal dust and found none. No students were tested, in part because they were on summer vacation, in part because the education-department representatives had no idea how to test them.

The inspectors would release their findings before the summer was out, they promised. They muttered to one another that the school seemed just fine.

Along with the school inspection, the governor had promised Ed a meeting with Stephanie Timmermeyer and other top officials of his administration. The officials would listen to the residents before sending more inspectors to test the impoundment and prep plant at Goals. Ed Wiley walked into this meeting, two days after the school inspection, with Judy, Bo, other members of CRMW, and a somber, bearded fellow in his early sixties named Jack Spadaro.

Spadaro was a former federal mining inspector who'd tangled with Steve Griles during the Reagan administration and later participated in a government investigation of the Martin County disaster—an investigation he felt that the Bush administration had squelched. After speaking out about what he perceived as the loosening of mine-safety policies in the Bush administration, Spadaro had been hounded into early retirement. Now he was a freelance Cassandra, telling whomever would listen how unsafe he felt impoundments were. As Timmermeyer and the others listened impassively, he explained why he thought the Goals impoundment presented a serious threat to the students of Marsh Fork Elementary. The design of Goals' impoundment, he said, was all too similar to that of the one at Buffalo Creek that had ruptured in 1972, killing 125 people. "Over time," he said, "as you increase the height of the dam and the weight of the slurry behind it, you could indeed approach a critical point in the structure of the dam and the people there might be in danger."

Timmermeyer and the others heard Spadaro out but said almost nothing. They would send their inspectors; the inspectors would tell them if they had a problem.

So intent was Don Blankenship on doing exactly what he wanted, when he wanted, that he hadn't even waited for approval of the new silo permit for Goals before ordering work started on the site. Massey contractors, it turned out, had begun the second silo's foundation back in April. By the time the permit was issued in late June, the foundation was done. A spokesperson for the DEP, confronted by this apparent flouting of the law, said the foundation "was just pouring concrete in the ground."

Over at the Charleston *Gazette,* Ken Ward Jr. had reported each day's developments on the silo story, assuming it would turn out like most of the stories that he wrote about Massey and mountaintop mining: the company would get its way. Like Joe Lovett, he'd lost his capacity for astonishment with the industry. Anyway, he would say wryly, what would he do if the industry reformed? He'd be out of a job. Still, he took a grim satisfaction in exposing the industry's hardball tactics. A lot of his stories came from hanging around the DEP's new headquarters, a big box of a building on the shabby side of Charleston's Kanawha River adjacent to a shopping mall and an Applebee's restaurant. The new headquarters had narrow white corridors with bare walls that seemed to stretch forever, as in a bad dream. But it also had sources behind its office doors, permit applications to study, and maps. One July day, Joe Lovett got a call from a sympathetic government official. "You ought to check out Goals Coal's maps," the source said. "Not just the latest one—all of them." Joe passed the tip on to Ward, who drove right over to the DEP.

Together with a reporter from his sister paper, the Charleston *Daily Mail,* Ward began poring over the survey map that Massey had submitted with its application for the second silo. Nothing seemed amiss. There were the two silos, both on the Goals side of the prep-plant boundary line, 220 feet from the school. Then the two reporters started looking at earlier maps of the site, submitted for past permits. "Wait a minute," Ward said. "Look at *that.*"

Put in chronological order, the maps showed something very curious. The boundary line between Goals and the school had clearly migrated westward, toward the school. It appeared to have moved to accommodate the first silo, built in 2003. On the latest map, it had moved again, closer to the school, to accommodate the second silo. There was no record in Massey's file to show the company had requested an expansion of its property. Massey's engineers appeared to have just drawn the new lines and submitted them without any indication that they were different from the original boundary.

When the reporters showed the migrating boundary to DEP officials, the officials were stunned. Randy Huffman, who now held Matt Crum's old job as director of mining and reclamation, said he'd had no clue about the boundary adjustment. Clearly, he admitted, the DEP had made a mistake in not scrutinizing Massey's maps. And since the latest map was clearly inaccurate, the DEP had made a mistake in granting Goals its new permit. After tense meetings with Stephanie Timmermeyer and other DEP officials, Huffman issued a formal order. Work on the second silo was to stop immediately, pending a full investigation of the migrating boundary line.

For the DEP, this was radical action. No one could recall the agency ever doing anything like it before. Yet neither Huffman nor any of his colleagues wanted to confront the most uncomfortable truth of the story. The first silo was on land outside the original boundary line, too.

Even as Ward went to press with the news, Joe Lovett drafted a letter to Timmermeyer. This was just the kind of case he tried not to take on: a specific instance of coal-company malfeasance. The precious time and money it would take would do nothing, even if he prevailed, to stop mountaintop mining in Appalachia. It would just be one silo, next to one school, in one town of the Coal River valley. But every rule had its exceptions. Judy Bonds and the volunteers at CRMW needed his help. Joe advised Timmermeyer that not only must the permit for the second silo be formally rescinded, but the first silo must be demolished as well. Otherwise, he advised Timmermeyer, he would sue.

Don Blankenship was furious. The DEP's order to halt work at

Goals seemed a personal affront—the latest and most outrageous example of agency bias toward Massey Energy. "It's a technicality much like being a mile over a speed limit," he declared publicly of the apparent boundary discrepancy. "They could apply this to every coal company in West Virginia and probably shut them all down. If all of us are going fifty-six miles per hour and I'm the only one getting a ticket, I have to be concerned about that."

Don thought he knew who was behind the DEP's unprecedented action: his new nemesis, Governor Joe Manchin III. Clearly, this was Manchin's revenge on Don's campaign against the pension bond issue. Hadn't Manchin publicly said that Don's greater involvement in public issues would earn him greater scrutiny? And what was it that Don had been doing in that campaign? Exercising his right of free speech.

By that logic, Don felt, the governor had deliberately repressed his—Don's—First Amendment right. Now he had no choice, he declared. On the very same day in July that the DEP formally rescinded its permit for the second silo at Goals, Don sued Governor Manchin. He and Manchin, he declared, were like soldiers shooting each other at close range: "He shut my silo down, and I shot him with this lawsuit."

For the unconscionable repression of his First Amendment right and the terrible injury dealt him by it, Don asked for $300 million in damages.

EIGHT

THE DEAD SOULS
OF SMITHERS

If Don felt his right of free speech had been trampled by the governor of West Virginia, about 230 miners in the nearby town of Smithers felt that some First Amendment rights of their own had been quashed by Don Blankenship—namely, the right to assemble and the right to express grievances. Unlike Don, they had no legal recourse, because they had no jobs and no money. Massey had bought the company they worked for, kept it shuttered for a few months, then started it up as a nonunion operation. The 230 miners were union men, so they were out. Worse, the health insurance they'd been promised their whole working lives was gone, whisked away by a bankruptcy judge. Even in a state long accustomed to the callousness of coal companies, the Horizon Natural Resources deal and its aftermath came as a shock. It also revealed a lot about Don Blankenship.

Horizon's Cannelton was one of West Virginia's oldest coal-mine sites, dating to the mid-nineteenth century, decades before train tracks reached the Coal River valley. It owed its history to its location: not in the valley itself, but over the valley's eastern mountain ridge, on the banks of the broad Kanawha River. There, coal could be loaded onto barges for the twenty-five-mile trip north to Charleston, then to the broader Ohio River for Cincinnati and points beyond. Cannelton's location was even more valuable now, for environmental regulations all but prohibited new riverfront operations. That was one reason Don wanted the Cannelton mine complex. The other was that cannel coal, from which the mine took its name, was rare and highly prized. Once known as candle coal for the clean, bright flame it gave off in fireplaces, it brought a premium now at power plants for its high energy, or BTUs.

Cannelton's woes had started some years before, with the arrival of the dubious Addington brothers, a Kentucky clan of four who had a history of abandoning surface mine sites without doing any reclamation on them. The Addingtons had bought the West Virginia mine while on a four-state spending spree in the late 1990s, aiming for the same economies of scale that Don was attempting with his own acquisitions. Unfortunately, along with forty-two mines the Addingtons acquired $1.2 billion of debt. In March 2002, their company, AEI Resources, filed for bankruptcy. Larry Addington, eldest and most visible of the brothers, wrote off his 97 percent interest in the company, but retained enough money to spend forty million dollars building a golf and tennis resort on Caye Chapel, a Belizean island he'd bought years before. That spring, the mines of AEI Resources—twenty-seven surface, fifteen underground—emerged from bankruptcy as Horizon Natural Resources, oddly enough with the same business address as AEI Resources. Six months later, Horizon was bankrupt, too.

How could a coal company go bankrupt twice at the start of a coal boom? Stories swirled of how Horizon had forced its individual mines to buy supplies at inflated prices from Horizon-owned suppliers. It was a way, suggested a lawyer from the United Mine Workers of America who looked into the situation, for Horizon to suck cash from its holdings, then cut and run. Another owner might have tried to make even more money by running the mines well and selling coal in a boom market. But there was a likely reason, the lawyer observed, why the Addingtons may have preferred to take short-term profits from Cannelton, then let it go. Cannelton's workers, like those of many Appalachian coal mines, were aging. Most of the miners were in their early fifties, two or three years from the age, fifty-five, at which the company would be obligated to pay them health benefits for life.

As the company foundered in bankruptcy through the spring of 2004, continuing to operate twenty-one of its mines—the rest had been sold off piecemeal—but looking for a buyer, a New York billionaire named Wilbur Ross began circling. Ross, a perennially tanned, professorial man with wire-rimmed glasses, was one of the country's most successful bottom-feeders. He'd spent twenty-five years at New York's Rothschild firm, buying bankrupt companies on the cheap and restructuring them. In his early sixties, he'd gone off on his own, raising $450 million in 2000 to buy a string of Rust Belt steel companies. To make them economically viable, he talked the United Steelworkers union into cutting workers' benefit and pension packages. Since the steel mills were shut down and the men were out of work and no one else was stepping up to buy their mills, the union had felt it had no choice.

With that strategy, Ross had accumulated a whole new fortune— breaking into the Forbes 400 list of wealthiest Americans—along with a very social new wife, Hilary Geary, whom he squired to New York's fanciest charity benefits. Now he had turned his gimlet eye to coal. That spring, he and a consortium of partners offered to buy Horizon's remaining mines for $786 million. There was, however, a catch. Ross wanted the bankruptcy judge overseeing the mess to strip all health benefits from Horizon's 4,800 workers. Only then, he felt, would the company be worth buying. Ross declared that he hoped to keep most of Horizon's mines open—the nonunion ones, at least. He had no interest, however, in retaining the company's six union mines, including Cannelton and a Kentucky operation called Starfire. Ross could have shut them down and reopened them later as nonunion operations, but it was "a bit of a mantra," as he put it in his professorial way, for his company not to do that. He preferred to parcel out Horizon's union mines to other investors who would do it for him.

In early August 2004, Judge William S. Howard of Lexington, Kentucky, issued his ruling: health benefits for Horizon's workers could be eliminated. The company, he said in so many words, could not otherwise be sold for a high enough price to get it out of Chapter 11. With that settled, the judge went on to declare Wilbur Ross and his unnamed investors the new owners of Horizon Natural Resources. Out from the shadows, in the days after this ruling, emerged the Cannelton miners' worst nightmare: Don Blankenship. He announced that Massey Energy, a silent partner in the deal, would soon be the new owner of

Cannelton and Starfire for a reported pittance of five million dollars and assumed liabilities.

On September 27, 2004, Cannelton was shut down, its 230 miners put out of work. Massey announced that Cannelton would be renamed Mammoth Coal and would start operating with one shift early in the new year. A company spokeswoman, Katharine Kenny, said it would be hard to find qualified men in what was a very tight labor market. Massey began advertising jobs at Mammoth on highway billboards and at job fairs. It even hired an airplane to fly up and down Myrtle Beach in South Carolina, where many West Virginians vacationed, trailing a banner that advertised jobs.

Heartened, a lot of the longtime union men from Cannelton applied for those jobs. But none were hired. Despite their experience of decades per man, they were of no interest to Massey Energy. As far as Don Blankenship was concerned, they were dead.

For Mike Lambert, the mine's closing came just eight months before his fifty-fifth birthday. A genial, heavyset man with shaggy hair, Mike had worked in the mine off and on, mostly doing belt maintenance, since his tour of duty as a Marine in Vietnam. Unfortunately, he'd taken one long break from the mines, beginning in the early 1980s when the coal bust shut it down; otherwise he would have put in his twenty years by now. If a miner had twenty years in, he got his health benefits for life from the company even if he hadn't reached fifty-five.

The reason Mike had extended his break through the 1980s and into the 1990s was that he'd started a bar, Big Dog's, in Smithers, the riverfront town that had grown up because of the mine. Smithers still had nineteenth-century redbrick buildings, though its best days were behind it. Now it lay scrunched between the Kanawha River and Route 60, an elevated state highway that shadowed the town and vibrated with the traffic of coal trucks day and night. Mike had opened Big Dog's in one of those redbrick buildings. He made a great bartender, jovial and generous. He also sponsored a Big Dog's baseball team, served as its coach, and spent more than twenty-five thousand dollars on uniforms and equipment and travel expenses. Nearly all the players were over forty, and yet they won a state championship.

The shelves behind the bar were filled with trophies. Mike kept Big Dog's going until faltering business forced him to sell it in 1997. Only then did he return to the mines. By then, he was in his late forties. He knew he probably wouldn't reach his twenty-year mark now, but he allowed himself to hope, as this latest coal boom came on, that he might work until he turned fifty-five. Now that the mine was shut down, Mike had neither benefits nor pay. He could draw down a pension from the union, but it would be a fraction of what he'd get if he waited until he turned fifty-five—as little as ten thousand dollars per year—so he didn't want to do that. Meanwhile, he had no idea how he'd be able to make rent and put food on the table for himself and his seventeen-year-old daughter, Alison.

The week after the mine closed, a public meeting of support for the miners in Smithers drew hundreds of neighbors and merchants. Every business in town pledged to help. The Kroger supermarket was especially helpful: its managers invited the unemployed miners of Cannelton to start taking day-old breads and pastries down to the union hall.

Some mornings, Mike Lambert went with the local union president, Bolts Willis, to pick up the baked goods and distribute them to the men at the wood-framed union hall. Later, he walked from his yellow house on the hill to Smithers's Main Street and sat on the corner across from the building where he'd had Big Dog's. His friend Dave Crawford would join him, and the two men would talk about what they were going to do. Often, their talk lapsed into silence. They had no idea what they would do.

At least now Mike could be home when Alison got out of school. Alison's mother lived in the area, but Alison didn't see her that much. She lived with her dad, and the two were close. Almost every evening, she and Mike went out to Pizza Hut for dinner or ordered a pizza to go from Frank's. They ate a lot of pizza. And they talked. Mostly they talked about Alison's boyfriend, Brian, whom Alison had dated since she was fourteen. Recently, Alison had quit school, taken a job for a while, then quit that and divided her time between her dad's house and Brian's. She and Brian were thinking about getting married, she told her dad. Mike sighed. He knew she was too young to get married, but he'd always indulged her, and he couldn't imagine trying to stop her.

As winter came on, Mammoth reopened with a first shift of fifty nonunion miners, many of them from out of state. Now Mike often drove over to put in a shift at one of the picket shacks he'd helped build at each of Mammoth's gates. The shacks were just that: small, square plywood shelters, with plank benches on each wall inside so that the men had a place to sit. At least two men worked each eight-hour shift.

On cold days, the men sat outside around wood fires burning in fifty-five-gallon drums. Cecil Roberts, the UMWA's president, had promised picket lines if Massey tried to move any coal out of the Cannelton mining complex, and at first, when the mines reopened, a line of sorts had formed. But soon it was down to just these two or three men at each shack, shouting at the nonunion trucks that drove in and out and hoping that the UMWA presence at the gates meant something. Privately, the men weren't sure it did.

As he warmed his hands at the fire, Mike listened to a lot of men in the same fix he was in. Like him, they'd lost their health benefits. The UMWA had stepped in to cover those men and their families for six months, not just at Cannelton but at the other union mines once part of Horizon Natural Resources. That gesture would cost the union between twelve and sixteen million dollars. But come late March 2005, the extension would end, and the men would have to fend for themselves. For a lot of them, the prospects were dire. More than a few had wives with expensive medical conditions or conditions of their own.

That January, Alison got engaged and moved in with Brian and his family. She was still just seventeen. Mike was torn about that. He missed her fiercely—his little yellow house on the hill seemed huge and empty with her gone—but he knew that Brian's family could better afford to feed her than he could. She and Brian had a wedding date: July 2. Mike wanted to give her one thousand dollars as a dowry, though he wasn't sure how he'd pull that together. He was already falling behind on his rent.

By a strange quirk of fate, Don Blankenship and Mike Lambert had been born within three months of each other, about fifty miles apart. Both had been born to poor working families. Both had stayed, as grown men, close to home. And both had made their livings from coal. Of course when Don turned fifty-five on March 4, 2005, he wouldn't have to worry about health benefits or pensions, because as chairman of Massey Energy he had them guaranteed, along with annual compensation that had risen now well beyond ten million dollars per year. He had millions more due him in stock options and more millions after that in severance money, should his handpicked board of directors choose not to retain his services.

According to his own public statements, Don keenly recalled his childhood hardships. How, then, could he have so little sympathy—none, really—for the 230 out-of-work miners at Cannelton who, like Mike Lambert, were now struggling just to survive? His showdown with the union as a young Massey manager had hardened him, to be sure. But the heads of rival coal companies—Arch, Consol, Peabody—had fought the union, too. Somehow, they'd emerged from those fights without the deep personal animus, the cold fury that Don showed in all his union dealings now. The truth was that Don's harshness went back further than that. It was rooted in the stern moral convictions of his mother.

Like a lot of Appalachians who lived close to the border of West Virginia and Kentucky, Don's mother had descended from one of the region's famously warring clans, the Hatfields and the McCoys. Nancy was a McCoy. Like most in the region, she was poor. And like most, she married young—to a Blankenship, another of the region's oldest families, of German and English descent but present in the Tug Fork valley ten generations or more. By the late 1940s, Nancy was a mother of three in the blink-and-miss-it border town of Stopover, Kentucky, with a husband in the military. By one of the few newspaper accounts of Don's early life, Nancy grew lonely when her husband was sent to Korea, so she took up with another man and became pregnant by him. Perhaps the affair started sooner than that version suggested, since Don was born on March 4, 1950, and the first U.S. troops were sent to Korea that July. But the child, indisputably, was Don. For Nancy, Don's arrival meant the end of one life and the start of another.

In the fairly amicable divorce that ensued, Nancy boarded a bus with the infant Don and five-year-old George, while Beulah, eight, and Anthony, ten, stayed with their father in Stopover. Don's natural father played no further role in the story. Neither Don nor any of his siblings ever knew who he was until the day Nancy pointed out an obituary in the local paper to Don, by then a grown-up. "This was your dad," she said. Nancy told Don to keep the obituary, and so he did, storing it in a dresser drawer in one of his houses.

Within a year, Nancy had moved to Delorme, a railroad-depot town in West Virginia right on the Kentucky line. Stopover was a short drive away, so the older two children, Beulah and Anthony, moved in with their mother, and a semblance of family life resumed. Nancy's ex-husband drove over to Delorme often, genially making household repairs. On his visits, he treated Don no differently than the older children. But when Beulah, Anthony, and George went to visit their father, Don watched his siblings board the bus while he stayed home. One childhood friend recalled speculation around town about Don's paternity, but no one knew for sure.

The town Nancy had chosen was perfect for a woman who sometimes felt too much alone. The Kentucky side of the Tug Fork was dry, so thirsty miners flocked over the bridge to the seven beer joints that lined Delorme's half crescent of a Main Street—its only street—between the bridge and the railroad tracks beyond. People came to Delorme to raise Cain, as one of Don's childhood friends put it. A man could hardly drive through town without running into a fight. A lot of revelers managed to get into a fight without driving at all: they rode their horses to the taverns, hitched them up, and went in to get drunk, like cowboys in the Wild West. From down the street, Don's friend Eddie Croaff would see them stagger out a few hours later and whip their horses, a horrifying sight.

Don had the better view: his mother's trailer was directly across the street from one of the rowdiest taverns. The trailer had two bedrooms, so Nancy slept in one, and the two oldest children shared the other. Don and George slept in the living room. Don could watch the tavern fights from the living-room window. If a really good one broke out across the street, he would scurry over to a nearby barbershop and climb up on its roof for a better view. Out back of the trailer was a nightly drama nearly as wondrous: the clattering trains of the Norfolk and Western Railroad. They were close enough that Don felt he could reach out and touch them.

Delorme was more depot than town, its very name bestowed by
the Norfolk and Western. Perhaps there was a certain corporate arro-
gance in that, since the town already had a name—Edgarton—that occasionally showed up on maps. Or perhaps the distinction of living by
a depot of the N&W seemed greater, to the residents of Delorme, than
occupying a town so modest that it had no post office, merely a post-
man who sorted the mail in his living room. In any event the trains
were ubiquitous, bearing either freight or coal across the road where it
curved northward out of town. A lot of the men worked with the railroad. But there was also a mining company on the Kentucky side, with
large underground mines.

Across the street from the Blankenship trailer was a gas station
with two pumps out front and a little market within. As far back as Don
could remember, it was his mother's store, purchased with her divorce
settlement. She worked there all day and evening, until the children's
bedtime and sometimes beyond. Don and his older siblings worked
there, too, as soon as they were able. Both to please their mother and
customers in a hurry, the Blankenship children learned early how to
tote up purchases. Nancy didn't have an adding machine, though later
she did have an old manual cash register. Until then, Nancy did numbers on the back of a matchbook. The children did them in their heads.
All three boys went on to become accountants. Years later, E. Morgan
Massey was amazed by Don's mastery of Massey's finances: it was not
just the numbers he knew, but every aspect of the coal business. He
knew almost intuitively when one number or another was off.

The store was as much a home as was the trailer across the street.
Most nights, Nancy cooked dinner for the children on the stove in
back. She fixed meals in one kettle: green beans and new potatoes or
sauerkraut and potatoes. The children would get behind the counter
to sit and eat. They pretty much lived in the store, even after Nancy
was able to trade up from the trailer to an A-frame house of unpainted
cinder blocks. Don and his friend Eddie Croaff would sit on the wide
windowsills of the store, and when a car drove up Don would have to
go pump the gas.

To Eddie and the other kids who hung around the store, Nancy
Blankenship was a stern presence. Mostly she was quiet, but if the
children were doing something she didn't approve of, she would say

exactly what she thought. Years later, Don recalled that his mother wasn't very strict. But somehow, he said, she instilled "accountability" in all four children. That was an achievement in a town where, as Eddie Croaff put it, most kids didn't turn out too well. But there was more to it than that. Nancy Blankenship had a work ethic that wouldn't slow down. She worked sixteen hours a day, six days a week. The store was open until 10:00 p.m. Don later said that his mother was his greatest influence. From her, Don learned that he would have to work for everything he wanted and work very, very hard.

There was a dark side to this lesson, however. Don's mother would point out the town drunk to her children or criticize a customer's sloppy dress after he left the store. Anyone who didn't meet Nancy's high moral standards deserved to be scorned. Anyone who didn't work as hard as she did deserved to fail. Sympathy appeared to play no part in her reckonings. People got the lot they deserved, and that was that. Survival of the fittest was Nancy's credo, and extending a hand to someone in need was as inappropriate as one species helping keep another from extinction. Nature took its course.

Until high school, Delorme was Don's entire world—so much so, he later admitted in newspaper interviews, that Matewan, just ten miles up the road, seemed a city by comparison. He didn't seem to be daunted, though, either by Matewan, where he ranked second in his high school class, or by Marshall University, in the humble but legitimate city of Huntington. There he took accounting courses and graduated in just three years—taking, he proudly noted later, more credit hours than anybody ever had at Marshall. Between his second and third years, he worked for college money as a union coal miner in Pittston, Pennsylvania, a brief employment that left him with no great love for the industry.

With his mother's stern admonitions echoing in his head, Don cast about for a company large enough to let him rise. Almost any kind of company, it seemed, would do, in almost any locale. He answered a newspaper ad for an accounting job at Keebler, the cookie and cracker company. He started in Macon, Georgia, accepted transfers to Chicago and Denver, and got married along the way. The job ended in 1977. Somehow, Massey Energy heard about the former local boy who'd become a crack accountant and made him an offer. But Don had no desire to get into the coal business. Instead he went back to Georgia to work for another bakery, Flower Industries, until 1982, when that job ended, too. This time when Massey called with an offer to join Rawl Sales, Don accepted. Later, he said that it was almost like predestination. He had been out of a job twice, and Massey had called both times.

And so began his rise, with a backward look every so often to see if his mother, still tending the store in Delorme, felt that he'd met her stern standards at last. Along the way, he and his wife had a son and daughter, John and Jennifer, then filed for divorce in 1992. Nancy kept the gas mart going until the early 1990s, when her health began to fail and she handed the business to her oldest son, Anthony, and his wife. The other two older Blankenship children stayed in the area, too— George as an accountant, Beulah as the wife of a mine electrician.

Don's success, of course, was on a different scale. And so it fell to the son born out of wedlock, the one who'd stayed home when the others visited their father, to pay for full-time care for Nancy in her final years. "I was with her when she died," he told a newspaper reporter. Then he added, "I was the one she wanted to be there when she died."

Whether they knew it or not, a lot of Massey miners had had their lives shaped by the cold moral lessons of Nancy Blankenship. "It doesn't matter whether you're hated or not," Don liked to say, "all that matters is that you do the right thing."

That philosophy justified leveling the mountains and the towns in the Coal River valley's hollows because mining coal the Massey way was, to Don, the right thing to do. Just as troubling, it seemed to justify an indifference to Massey's own miners. In public, Don praised Massey men. But in practice, he seemed to regard them as cannon fodder in the war for profits.

The federal Mine Safety and Health Administration (MSHA) is the agency that records serious injuries and deaths at all underground and surface-mining sites in the United States. By 2006, its enforcement powers were being reined in by an administration that clearly sided with the country's coal operators. Even so, MSHA inspectors kept writing up their notices and issuing violations, where appropriate, for illegal conditions that had precipitated the deaths and injuries they investigated. From 1995 through 2005, the MSHA reported a total of twenty-one deaths at Massey mines in West Virginia. Consol, Massey's largest rival in Appalachia, had fourteen deaths for that same period in the state. For that same period, Massey had 3,719 injuries in West Virginia; Consol had fewer than half as many: 1,796.

The numbers spoke for themselves. But they were silent on the human suffering a decade of accidents at Massey mines had caused.

In the file cabinets of half a dozen southern West Virginia county courthouses were personal-injury suits filed by disabled Massey miners or the estates of the deceased. In Boone County alone, where far more coal was produced than in any other county in the state, there were scores of these suits. Some, perhaps, were exaggerated, possibly the pure fabrications of miners looking for easy money. Yet one suit after another going back to the early 1990s was settled out of court—an indication that the stories were too strong to be knocked down in a trial. Others had gone to trial, only to end with six- or even seven-figure jury awards.

The suits were a catalog of gothic horrors. An electrician unhooking a tester from a mining cable had received a shock so strong it caused brain damage. An experienced supervisor had been on his regular rounds when a roof rib fell on him, forcing surgeons to amputate his leg above the knee. One worker had slipped beside a conveyor belt in muddy conditions and had his arm pulled into the belt's roller. A shuttle-car operator had been trying to fix a trimming feeder when it jumped sideways, pinning him against a coal rib and crushing him. A miner had been pulled toward an electric magnet by the metal objects in his pocket and seriously burned.

In a disturbing number of those suits, a supervisor's negligence was alleged to be the cause. A miner had been directed to unhook a water line feeding a pump assembly. Unknown to him—but known to the supervisor, the plaintiff alleged—the pump assembly was broken and had heated water to boiling. As a result, the plaintiff sustained third-degree burns on his legs, arms, hands, abdomen, buttocks, and genitalia. A "red hat" miner with fewer than ninety days' experience was sent unaccompanied into a mine shaft—legally, he had to be accompanied at all times by an experienced "black hat" miner—and walked into extended roof bolts, which caused permanent injuries. His mine managers never filed an accident report for him. A worker alleged that at his mine he had received no safety training; while installing a "man-door," he had fallen and been rendered a paraplegic. A miner manning a continuous-miner drill had suggested to his supervisor that the bit on the drill be changed because it kept flying off. The supervisor told him no. The bit had then flown off into the miner's eye. A bulldozer operator had hit underground gas pipes with his front loader and was thrown to serious injury; he claimed that his supervisors knew about the pipes. A miner had been pinned between two shuttle cars because, he alleged, the canopies on the cars had been lowered, reducing visibility. A miner alleged that his managers had failed to secure safety belts and lines and had not turned the conveyor belt off when maintenance was needed; he had fallen thirty-five feet as a result. A shuttle-car operator had sustained crushing and permanently disabling injuries when a large rock fell from the roof of a mine; only nine hours before, his supervisor had signed a citation for that problem from an inspector from West Virginia Health Safety and Training. Due to the failure of one worker's managers to weld a mine-shaft cover on an abandoned mine, the shaft had been improperly vented, and an explosion of methane gas had burned 40 percent of his body.

The worst stories ended in death. Some of the deaths were electrocutions when a cable shorted in wet conditions. Most were from roof falls in the underground mines. Sometimes the roof falls were just bad luck. Sometimes they seemed to come as a result of negligence. After one man was killed in a roof fall at Massey's Independence operation, his estate charged that managers altered the accident site to make the dead man appear responsible for his fate. That one was settled out of court for one million dollars.

On the pages of their lawsuits, the plaintiffs were just names. But at their homes in hollows of the Coal River valley and elsewhere, the disabled plaintiffs suffered with their injuries for life. One was Jackie Browning, a bulldozer operator with twenty-eight years' experience when he started feeling sick from working a mountaintop site for Goals. Jackie's job was to shape the valley fill. As more and more coal waste was dumped into the valley, Jackie drove over it, compressing it and molding the switchbacks that enabled trucks to drive up the side of the mountain and be loaded up with fresh coal. One summer day he noticed that his mouth felt frozen. So did his nostrils and his throat. Even his stomach and bowels were cold. The bulldozer's air-conditioning system had a leak: freon was coming directly into the cab where Jackie sat.

Jackie said he wasn't sure which was more to blame, the freon or the chemicals at the prep plant where he began to work as an alternative to driving the dozer. Goals had begun using stronger chemicals at its prep plant to recover more of the coal particles from the mountaintop coal it was washing. The chemicals adhered to the fines, as the particles were called, so that they could be skimmed off the top of the bath in which they were floating and packed together as a salable form of coal. Working around those chemicals, Jackie felt his mouth, throat, and lungs burning, as if he'd swallowed acid. Soon his tongue was white with red bumps, his eyes were bloodshot, and his face was covered with acne. He tingled from his groin to his feet all the time, and he staggered when he walked. He felt heart palpitations, and couldn't sleep, and had severe and chronic diarrhea. When Jackie applied to Massey for workman's compensation, he made a mistake by reporting both sets of symptoms on the same form; the Massey lawyers, he says, were able to show that the statement was technically inaccurate, and his application was denied.

Now Jackie spent most of his days on the porch of his hillside house. His mother's and father's forebears had lived in the valley for generations, coal miners on both sides. Jackie's father had been disabled at fifty, but those were different times. Montcoal, the operation he'd worked at in the golden days before Massey owned it, had paid him disability ever since, and so had the union. Jackie's father was eighty-two now. Jackie was in his early fifties but looked a decade older. His symptoms still bothered him. Sometimes they were pretty bad. He had very little expectation of reaching his father's age.

And yet Jackie's sons both worked for Massey. To stay in the valley and earn a good living, they felt they had no choice. Jackie's son Daniel, twenty-eight, woke up at 4:00 a.m. to get to the mine site by 5:00 for his twelve-hour shift. Scott, thirty-three, worked the corresponding twelve-hour evening shift. Massey would get fifteen or twenty years out of his sons, Jackie felt. Then they'd be cast out on a pretext—broken tools, as Massey put it, to be replaced by fresh ones.

Sometimes Jackie tried to talk to his sons about the future—they ought to be aware, at least, of how expendable they were. But the company, he said, had his sons too scared to question anything. It controlled them by fear. "There's nothing," he'd say of Massey, "that they won't do to you."

That, Jackie felt, was pure Don Blankenship. But perhaps it would have been more accurate to say it was pure Nancy Blankenship: survival of the fittest. By those terms, Don was among the fittest. Mike Lambert, unfortunately, was less so.

For a while in the winter and spring of 2005, Mike and his friend Dave Crawford got work that made them feel things might be looking up. The UMWA hired them to drive around the countryside and try to recruit new members. They got paid eighty-eight dollars per day each—not mining money, but good enough. Driving for hours at a stretch, they talked about everything, and the humor that Mike had once been known for came back in flashes and streaks. Once, Dave got out of the car to knock on a cabin door while Mike stayed at the wheel. Suddenly from around the side of the cabin came a very large snarling dog. Dave ran back to the car with the dog at his heels—only to discover that Mike had locked the doors and was heaving with laughter. The joke might not have been so funny if the dog had bitten Dave's leg. But the dog just barked, and Mike unlocked the doors at last. Dave had to admit he would have laughed, too, if he'd been the one at the wheel.

One evening not long after that, Mike was lying alone on his sofa when he felt a sharp pain in his chest. Mike lay there a long time until the pain finally eased. He knew it might be more than indigestion. But he'd never been one for doctors, and besides, he had no health insurance: the UMWA's six-month extension period had just run out.

That June, Mike was on his couch again when he felt a second jolt of pain and pressure on his chest, this one worse than the first. It was late afternoon, and Mike's brother-in-law was home, just down the way. Mike managed to call him, and he ran right over. As soon as he saw Mike, he tried to persuade him to go to a hospital. Mike shook his head. "Can't afford it," he said. Mike's sister, Bonnie, a nurse's assistant, soon arrived. His pulse seemed all right, Bonnie thought, but his skin was clammy, and when she held up his arm and asked him to keep it up, it fell right down. "That's it," she said firmly. "You're going to the hospital."

The hospital was in Montgomery, only a few minutes' drive away. Mike's daughter, Alison, rode with him, holding his hand tightly. As soon as the nurse at the emergency desk saw Mike, she called for a doctor. The doctor came right out, took one look at him, and turned to the nurse. "This man's having a heart attack," he said. "We need a helicopter." The doctor explained that Montgomery wasn't well equipped for coronaries, but Charleston Area Medical Center had one of the best heart centers in the country. Mike, still conscious, tried to tell the doctor not to call for the helicopter. How would he ever pay for that? His sister shushed him. "Mike, we'll worry about it later." The helicopter would cost nearly nine thousand dollars. For Mike Lambert, it might as well have been nine million.

Mike was still conscious at the Charleston hospital when doctors gave him an EKG and looked at the screen. "My God," one doctor said. "He's got a hundred percent blockage of his main artery. How's he still walking and talking?"

"Got me," Mike said.

The doctors wheeled Mike right into an operating room. Over the next hours, they put two stents in his aorta. As they did, he flatlined on them. Frantically, the doctors shocked him back to life and put him on a ventilator.

Bonnie knew just how slim Mike's chances were at that point. When she asked, the doctors nodded. They were surprised he'd come back to life at all. They felt sure that when they took him off the ventilator, he'd die within minutes. His heart had sustained too much damage. It couldn't keep him alive.

By now, legally, Bonnie was making the decisions. "Okay," she said. "Let's take him off the ventilator and see what happens."

The doctors removed the ventilator. Mike blinked and gave them a weak smile. "I'm starving," he said. "What do you have to eat around here?"

Over the next several days, Mike was often too drugged to respond. But when he was conscious, he joked with the nurses, with Bonnie, and with his daughter. Alison spent every night in the waiting room, sleeping on hard chairs. During visiting hours, the room was filled with friends and relatives, going in one at a time to say hello. Mike Lambert was an out-of-work miner with almost no money at all. But there were a lot of people in Smithers who loved him.

When it was Alison's turn by his bedside, she'd ask her father if he was all right. "Quit asking me that!" he'd say. Then he'd ask her, "Have you gotten married yet?"

"You still have a week," Alison would say. "You better get well fast."

When his sister came in, Mike would ask how he was going to pay for all this. Bonnie told him, reluctantly, that she'd gotten him a Medicaid card. It had come through because Mike had no assets—no car, no house. He was months behind on the rent now. When he heard about the Medicaid, Bonnie saw Mike seem to lose hope. He was a proud man. Being on Medicaid was an admission that he would never be better than poor again.

At a little after midnight on July 1, Mike died in his hospital bed. He had $186 in cash and a debt of one thousand dollars owed him by Alison's mother, with whom relations had been rocky for a long time. He'd told Bonnie he wanted Alison's mother to give Alison that money as his wedding present—that and the $186. The next day, at Alison's wedding, her mother honored that wish.

There was a lot of talk, on that Friday, July 1, 2005, about canceling Saturday's wedding. But then everyone agreed that Mike wouldn't have wanted that. So they didn't. At a nearby church, Alison wore a white wedding dress and lit a candle at the start of the ceremony for her father. On the program, her new father-in-law had written, "We dedicate this day to Mike Lambert, who cannot be with us in body but is here in spirit. We love you." When they read that, the nearly seventy guests began to cry.

Two days later, all those guests and nearly three hundred more gathered for Mike Lambert's funeral. In all, 367 signed the funeral register. Some of his closest friends spoke about Mike's sense of humor, his love of his family, particularly his love for his daughter, and also what made him mad. What he hated above all, his friend Dave Crawford said, was being led to believe that if he just kept working, the coal company would take care of him. Instead, that trust had been broken.

In one sense, at least, Don hadn't forgotten the 230 miners of Cannelton. Two weeks after Mike Lambert's death, in addition to his lawsuit against the governor of West Virginia, he directed Massey to file a three-hundred-million-dollar lawsuit against the Charleston *Gazette*. Don said the paper had accused Massey of putting Cannelton's 230 miners out of work when it knew that wasn't true. The truth was that the bankruptcy judge in Kentucky had made the decision that those miners could be terminated and their health benefits cut off on August 9, 2004. Only then had Wilbur Ross purchased the twenty-one mines of Horizon Natural Resources, and not until October 1 had Massey officially purchased Cannelton and Starfire from Ross. So clearly, Don's lawsuit concluded, Massey Energy had had nothing to do with terminating those workers.

Mammoth Coal, the former Cannelton mine, was ramping up now, but Massey was still having the hardest time finding workers to fill its shifts. A spokesperson for the company said Massey had to hire twice as many workers as it needed because the turnover was so significant: most were inexperienced red hats who found they couldn't do the rough work. In desperation, the company was now advertising nationwide for miners in *USA Today*, as well as in the local papers of Atlanta and Charlotte, two areas where a number of Appalachian miners had relocated during the last industry slump. Company representatives even contacted high school principals and coaches, urging them to talk up Massey as a good employer for graduates.

Many of the 230 seasoned miners who'd lost their jobs when Cannelton shut down stood ready to work now at Mammoth Coal. Desperate to feed their families, they were willing to work nonunion, to accept the permanent loss of their health benefits and union pensions in order to make a living wage. Still, they got nowhere with Mammoth. The company wouldn't give them their jobs back, not now or ever, if Don Blankenship could help it. But Don wanted to be clear: he hadn't taken those jobs away.

NINE

MARCHING IN THE VALLEY

In the unlikely drama of a silo by a school in the heart of the Coal River valley, an eerie lull descended in the midsummer of 2005.

Joe Lovett had warned the DEP's Stephanie Timmermeyer that he would sue the state if Massey wasn't forced to tear down its first silo as well as abandon its second. Timmermeyer had yet to respond. Don Blankenship had sued Governor Joe Manchin because he felt the governor had urged the DEP to nix the second silo as an act of revenge. The governor's lawyers had yet to respond. Ed Wiley had pushed the governor into having inspectors pay a visit to Marsh Fork Elementary. The inspectors had yet to report on what they had found. In that sultry July, the only characters in the drama who were moving were the marchers of Mountain Justice Summer and Coal River Mountain Watch. They seemed to be marching all the time.

The extraordinary news that Massey's permit for a new silo had been rescinded had had a galvanizing effect on marchers young and old. They felt their protests of May had made a real difference. From their storefront in Whitesville, Judy Bonds and Bo Webb chose dates for more marches. Then they passed on the word, both to a growing number of neighbors willing to join in and to the young volunteers of Mountain Justice Summer, encamped in a house down Route 3, in the town of Naoma. The den mother of the house and leader of the volunteers was a thirty-two-year-old woman who had spent nearly half her life as an environmental activist, carrying out "direct actions." With her arrival, the protest against Massey and mountaintop mining rose to a new level.

Tall and lean, with sinewy muscles from clambering up endangered redwoods and the hulls of contraband-carrying ships, Hillary Hosta was a veteran of Greenpeace, the group best known for doing battle in motorized Zodiacs with whale-hunting Japanese trawlers. She'd joined the group as a teenager in Los Angeles, after a childhood of divorce and confusion. Much as a lost eighteen-year-old might join the army, she joined Greenpeace to lend a purpose to her life. Since then, Hillary had become an expert in civil disobedience. In British Columbia, she had rappelled herself to the top of a hundred-foot tree and stayed aloft in it for five days, helping pressure Canadian timber companies into preserving a swath of old-growth forest. In Miami, Hillary and another Greenpeace activist had braved ten-foot waves in an inflatable raft to reach a boat bringing illegal mahogany from Brazil, then slung ropes over the lowest deck railing and shimmied up like pirates. They were stopped before they could unfurl a banner that read "President Bush Stop Illegal Logging," but their subsequent arrest—and indictment on outlandish charges by U.S. Attorney General John Ashcroft—made headlines around the world.

Early that summer, rumors spread up and down the valley that the young volunteers of Mountain Justice Summer were planning violent acts. Where exactly these rumors started was hard to tell, but at one point the wives of some Massey employees made calls to neighbors, asking them which side they were on. Another rumor had it that anyone on disability from Massey could lose his checks if he joined in the marches. No one needed to warn neighbors that if they did join in with the young volunteers, Massey's institutional memory was long. Yet the only acts of violence that summer were committed against the marchers. One night at the Naoma house, Hillary awoke to the sound of a windshield being smashed. She went out front to see one of the marchers' pickup trucks vandalized and, in the distance, red taillights vanishing around a curve. During one of the roadside marches, a car swerved toward Bo Webb, coming within inches of him before screeching away. A thousand feet down the road, the driver and passenger got out of the car, tore off the rear license plate, got back in, and

sped off. That was the only violence in the valley during Mountain Justice Summer, but feelings ran high on both sides when the protesters
embarked on three days of marches in mid-July.

Since May, the young volunteers had done no marching at all. Instead, they worked on what Hillary called the listening project. Most
evenings, they fanned out to the neighboring towns and up the hollows, knocking on doors like traveling salesmen. They had clipboards
with interview forms attached, and if doors weren't shut right away in
their faces, they eased into their questions. Hillary taught them not to
engage in debates: if someone grew angry or agitated, she told them,
back off and move on. The goal was to test the level of support already
out there, not to make converts. It was hard work: at the end of an
evening, six volunteers might have knocked on fifty doors each. They'd
straggle back to the house in Naoma with six or seven completed interviews among them. But some of those interviewed might be willing to
come to Coal River Mountain Watch and help, and some might join a
march.

At the same time, other volunteers sought out the parents of
Marsh Fork Elementary's students for a survey of their children's
health. Of the 60 participating households, 53 reported health problems among their children. Of those 53 households, 48 had children
with respiratory problems such as asthma and chronic bronchitis. Of
those 48 households, in turn, 43 had children who also reported having headaches or nausea while at school. And of the 53 households
that had frequently sick children, 22 reported hearing their children
complain of coal dust or strange smells at the school or of blasting
noises from the Goals site, while 18 households had students with
learning difficulties. Later, when state epidemiologist Loretta Haddy
was asked to respond to the survey, she wrote that because of the way
it was conducted, she could make no conclusions from it. There was,
for example, no comparative study to determine whether the rates of
symptoms among students at the school exceeded those of students in
a school not exposed to the prep plant. All she could say with any certainty was that the health risks for Marsh Fork students remained
unknown.

Almost anywhere else, the three days of marches would have been
meaningless: a wavy, narrow line of seventy-five or one hundred people

upset about something, forgotten as soon as they passed out of sight. Here the marchers were news. Primed by the first two marches in May, every news channel in West Virginia sent camera crews to film the curious sight of young hippies allied with valley residents too mad and old to care about the consequences of joining in. The volunteers had been given drums to beat and rattles to shake. They looked like a Native American funeral procession.

On the first of those three days, an angry contingent of pro-Massey teachers and mothers waited in front of Marsh Fork Elementary to shout their own chants in response. The counterprotesters were furious. Who were these out-of-staters to come tell them what to do? Around the valley now it was a joke that the protesters looked and smelled unwashed. What they needed was soap and a shower. As for the stories the outsiders were spreading about sick students, they were just that: stories. If it weren't for confidentiality laws, one teacher declared bitterly, she could tick off the names of all those "sick" children: they were the ones whose parents were about to go to jail because they didn't send their kids to school. Marsh Fork had test scores that put it among the top five elementary schools in the state, another teacher declared. The school was well run and clean. If anything, the silo had made the area cleaner than it was before. The silo *contained* the coal, after all; that was better than storing it in an open stockpile. As for the impoundment, it had been sitting right there in Shumate's Branch for twenty-five years, built to withstand thousands of tons of pressure. It was fine.

The teachers were mad their school was being impugned, but they were worried, too. If all this protesting shut anything down, it would be the school, not the prep plant. Then the students would be bused halfway up or down the valley, and the teachers might lose their jobs.

The next day, the marchers started in Whitesville, walking north to Sylvester. The weather was hot and muggy, and as the marchers headed up the shoulder of Route 3, heat radiated off the black-tar road. Most of the cars and trucks sped up as they passed by, their drivers jeering or just looking at the protest in stupefaction. But occasionally a driver honked in support, and the weary marchers waved. When they got to Sylvester, they stopped at "Dustbuster" Pauline Canterberry's house for cool drinks and snacks. Then they fell back into line, trudging on to the Elk Run plant. There for the first time they were outnumbered by angry counterprotesters. As state police enforced a distance between the two sides, Judy Bonds grew red-faced with anger. "Coal whores!" she screamed at them."Why aren't you off shopping with your husbands' coal money?"

Perhaps, Judy conceded later, she'd overreacted. On the final day, when the marchers returned to Elk Run, they left their drums and rattles behind and chanted nothing. When the counterprotesters greeted their approach with pro-Massey slogans, they were met with silence. Finally, at Bo Webb's signal, the marchers got on their knees and sang "Amazing Grace." The counterprotesters were duly confused. What else the march accomplished was harder to tell. At least, Judy mused as she walked back along the road, anyone watching the TV reports that evening would see how hateful the Massey side was. And the protests, she felt, had put Massey on notice that residents of the Coal River valley were no longer afraid to speak out.

Up close, the three-day standoff had been more complex. At Marsh Fork Elementary, teachers and parents were now divided. The pro-Massey voices were nearly all those of women whose husbands worked at one Massey site or another. Now, for the first time, they had stood off against parents who felt just as strongly that Massey was to blame for their children's ill health. The marches had made neighbors take sides, and no one would soon forget whose side each neighbor was on. That was true up the road at the Elk Run prep plant in Sylvester, too. One protester had glared over at the jeering Massey employees on the Elk Run bridge and seen her cousin glaring back. Rick Bradford, the gentle retired teacher who'd lived his whole life at his parents' hillside house in Edwight, put it best that week. "Massey has come down here and divided the place," he said, "brother against brother."

Just how safe *was* the Goals prep plant and its impoundment? In the eleven years that Massey had owned the site, Goals had been written up often for various violations, many of them minor but some quite significant, by inspectors from the MSHA. When Dan Heyman, a reporter for West Virginia Public Radio, asked the MSHA for more details on the violations, he was forced to file a Freedom of Information Act request, and even then he received only heavily edited reports. Heyman learned that the MSHA had been far more forthcoming before the Bush administration. In fact, an environmental group had made the same request in early 2001 and been given the reports unedited.

The comparison of Heyman's edited reports to the earlier, unedited ones was chilling. The MSHA had deleted concerns voiced by one of its inspectors in 1998 and 1999 about the way Goals was forming the outer wall of its impoundment. The wall was composed, as impoundment walls typically were, of solid coal waste. Trucks built up the wall by dumping waste on it, then drove across the waste repeatedly to compact it. MSHA rules called for the trucks to compact the waste with each next foot of accumulation. But Goals, to the inspector's alarm in 1998, had let ten feet of waste build up along the wall before compacting it. That meant those ten feet of new wall were soft and spongy and might easily blow out from the pressure of liquid waste rising behind it. "If the dam failed," the inspector wrote, "fatalities would be expected to occur. It's reasonably likely an accident would occur if the condition continued to exist."

That judgment was redacted from the report that Heyman received from the Bush administration's MSHA.

Usually, Massey ignored press reports, but not this time. A company spokesman issued a blistering response on Don Blankenship's behalf, accusing Heyman of fearmongering; oddly, Heyman was let go shortly after, though his employers claimed his termination was unrelated to the Goals Coal story. The flack noted that the MSHA had found "no safety concern at this time at this site," and that the West Virginia DEP had given the dam a clean bill of health. "The sole person to disagree with MSHA, DEP, our consultant engineers and company engineers is Davitt McAteer," the spokesman wrote. "The Shumate impoundment was continually inspected by MSHA when McAteer led the MSHA and he did not find reason to be concerned."

This was a fair point. McAteer, a West Virginia native whose Irish Catholic forebears had come to the state in 1847 and worked in the mines, had just the sort of résumé that Don despised—and just enough clout to be a nuisance. He had worked in the sixties as a Nader's Raider for the consumer advocate and gone on to be a health and safety lawyer for the UMWA. His expertise in mining safety issues had won him a post in the Clinton administration as assistant secretary of enforcement for the MSHA, and he hadn't appeared to worry then about the Goals impoundment. But in the wake of the 2000 Martin County spill, McAteer, back from Washington, had headed up a three-million-dollar study of Appalachian impoundments for Senator Robert Byrd. He knew a lot more about impoundments now, and what he'd learned was not reassuring. There were 110 impoundments in West Virginia, more than in any other state. There had been fifty-five serious spills at those impoundments. About half of those involved Massey operations, including Martin County. The fact that so many belonged to one company, McAteer felt, suggested that that company was ignoring its problems. Perhaps the Goals impoundment now was safer than before. Perhaps the small seepages noted in some of those MSHA violations were little more than ones meant to occur as part of the dam's design. Still, as McAteer said to any reporters who asked, why should even the world's safest impoundment be set above a school? While Don Blankenship could rail all he liked, for McAteer that was the bottom line.

In a conference call with industry stock analysts, Don Blankenship waved off the silo drama as a mere distraction that had little effect on his Goals operation. "It's primarily a quality control and cost issue as opposed to a production issue," he said. "It's not overly significant." What he meant was that coal would flow at the same rate down from the mountaintops around the Goals plant, second silo or no second silo.

Privately, Don was seething. The DEP had gone so far as to demand that he rip up the foundation he had had laid down for the silo. Bob McLusky, Massey's hardest-working lawyer, observed in consternation that the company had already spent $400,000 on silo construction. How could the DEP ask Massey to ruin this business investment? After some deliberation, the DEP agreed to let the foundation stay until Massey appealed its ruling to the Surface Mine Board. Massey wanted a hearing right away, McLusky said. Goals had hoped to have its silo built and in use by mid-August.

Normally, the Surface Mine Board seemed to favor the mining industry, so Massey's eagerness for a hearing was understandable. But the seven-member board wasn't quite as monolithic as, say, the West Virginia legislature. By law, seven fields of expertise had to be represented on it, one by each member: coal mining, agriculture, forestry, civil engineering, water pollution, public interest, and environmental advocacy. Generally, the civil engineer was a reliable vote for the mining industry. That made two votes for mining, with four in the less predictable ground between them and the environmentalist on the other side. As it happened, the environmentalist was the board's longtime director, Tom Michael, a lawyer who could debate the minutiae of coal mining with any industry expert or lawyer and sometimes sway his fellow members.

The board, as a result, could deal the industry an occasionally nasty surprise. Once, when the DEP's Matt Crum was bringing cases against Massey, the board had declared that Massey had the worst pattern of corporate behavior it had seen in thirty-five years of hearing cases. Nor was Tom Michael shy about saying that, in his opinion, Crum was the best cop on the beat the DEP had ever had, and that Michael had a pretty good sense Crum had been the victim of industry pressure. And so when Joe Lovett asked the board to let Coal River Mountain Watch intervene in the silo-case appeal because it represented local citizens whose children attended the Marsh Fork Elementary School, Tom Michael had little trouble getting his fellow board members to agree to the request.

The irony of the situation, Michael mused, was that neither the first nor second silo was actually required by law. As far as he could see, the only reason Massey wanted the silos was to control the dispersal of coal dust. The worst offender in the industry, then, was fighting in this case to *improve* its emissions. Privately, Michael wondered why Massey didn't simply abandon the effort and keep piling coal in open stockpiles. Perhaps the site was generating so much coal dust that even Goals's managers worried it might pose a serious threat to the children—one that might shut the prep plant down. Or perhaps Don Blankenship was just so annoyed at being told he couldn't do what he wanted to do that he was willing to spend any money it took to have his way.

Joe Lovett, too, wanted the Surface Mine Board to meet as soon as possible. He'd studied Massey's survey maps of Goals with grim delight: the case of the migrating boundary line was clear for all to see. Both silos were over the original line. Joe, unlike Tom Michael, also felt that open stockpiles so close to the school would be just as illegal, especially given the greater amount of coal Massey hoped to store there. But the case slid off the board's docket for August, and it slid through September and October as well. The reason was that Bob McLusky, acting on his boss's suspicions, had put forth a request of his own. He wanted any and all communications between the DEP and Governor Manchin in regard to the silo permit to be made part of the hearing. The governor's lawyers countered that such communications, if there *were* any, must remain privileged. This was a somewhat shaky defense. Florida, for one, allowed the public to access nearly all government communications, and somehow its government had not ground to a halt. Other states granted access to varying degrees. Why would the governor not want his official correspondence with the DEP made public?

As lawyers for Massey and the governor wrangled, the citizens most directly affected by the silo controversy went back to school. Inspectors from the state's Department of Education had declared in August that Marsh Fork Elementary should open as planned. The inspectors were not aware, as they put it in their formal finding, "of any compromise to the indoor environment at Marsh Fork Elementary that [might] affect the health or safety of children." The wording betrayed a lawyer's care. The school might have problems, but the inspectors were unaware of them. The air outside the school might be compromised, but the inspectors hadn't considered it.

Judy Bonds and Bo Webb declared the tests a sham, but they could do nothing more. Summer was over, and with it the tatterdemalion parades of Mountain Justice Summer. Away went its earnest young marchers—Squirrel and Elliot and America and the rest—to wherever tumbleweed idealists went in the fall of 2005. Only Hillary Hosta, the hardworking den mother, remained in the house at Naoma. Her family and friends had pleaded with her to come home at summer's end, but Hillary was resolute: she would stay, she said, until the blasting stopped.

To Ed Wiley, the summer's marches and meetings had ended in failure: the students of Marsh Fork Elementary were back in class as of Labor Day. Yet when the schoolchildren looked up from their games at recess to what lay across Marsh Fork Creek, they at least saw nothing new. The towering silo was still there, but unaccompanied by a second one. It wasn't enough, but it was a start.

Joe Lovett felt pretty sure he could keep that second silo from ever being built. It was one of the few hopes he dared to entertain as this summer of protests and passions came to an end. All in all, the year had been wretched.

Just as Joe feared, President Bush had brandished his slim victory in November 2004 as a mandate to do even more harm to the environment than he had in his first term—all to benefit big contributors in the extractive industries of oil and gas, timber, and, of course, coal. By now, Bush had dismayed even a broad cross-section of Republicans with his environmental policies. Red-state hunters and fishermen were aghast at his efforts to open fifty-eight million acres of roadless forests to the timber industry and to stop protecting 20 percent of the nation's wetlands so that builders could fill them in. Republicans for Environmental Protection, a national group, declared that "over the last four years, the Bush administration has compiled a deliberately anti-environmental, anti-conservation record that will result in lasting damage to public health and to America's natural heritage." The mostly Republican National Parks Conservation Association gave Bush an overall D– for his stewardship of the national parks, along with grades that ranged from C+ for park funding to an F for preserving park resources and an F for park-system expansion. Theodore Roosevelt IV, great-grandson of America's most conservation-minded Republican president, declared, "Moderate Republicans, and I am one, are distressed that an administration that strenuously claims to be conservative is instead intent on maintaining undisciplined and wasteful consumption."

In the first months of Bush's second term, the coal industry benefited from many of his most destructive environmental policies. And with every rollback of standards, every "streamlining" of rules, Joe's field of legal options narrowed. It was a war by the administration on environmental standards at every stage of coal's passage—from extraction to where it was burned to how its emissions were judged.

The first stage of that passage, the granting of permits, was about to get easier. The Environmental Impact Statement on mountaintop mining that Joe had fought for in Haden 1 was wending its way toward formal issuance in October 2005. It was now a document that simply streamlined the permitting process.

Stage two—blasting the mountaintops and dumping the debris into valley streams—was being made easier, too. The new wording of the buffer-zone rule that allowed coal operators to make their "best effort" not to destroy streams was not yet official, but Joe had no doubt it soon would be.

The third stage was the burning of coal at power plants. The administration had hoped to persuade Congress to pass its misleadingly named Clear Skies policy, under which power plants would get far more lenient schedules for trapping toxic emissions over the next decade than allowed under current regulations. At that stage, at least, not all had gone as planned. One moderate Republican senator, Lincoln Chafee of Rhode Island, had kept Clear Skies trapped in committee by refusing to vote as the White House wanted. As a result, every time the bill was considered, the vote on it was 9–9. But Bush was still pushing it.

Finally there was stage four: dealing with a pollutant from burning coal that posed a more direct threat to human health than perhaps any of the sixty other toxins that coal-fired power plants emitted. For that, the administration had just pushed through a new rule that affected the health of at least one of every six American women of childbearing age. The toxin in question was mercury. Released by the burning of coal, it floated down into lakes and rivers and streams. There it was consumed by fish and passed up the food chain to humans, who risked brain damage by consuming it. Pregnant mothers especially were at risk.

In December 2000, while President Clinton was still in office, the EPA had declared that mercury emissions from power plants were a threat to public health and that they must be limited as drastically and as quickly as possible. Specifically, it proposed such emissions be cut 90 percent by 2008. Meanwhile, no fewer than forty-four states issued stern warnings to residents not to eat certain fish from local waters. One of the strictest advisories was for West Virginia: a report published in September 2004 had concluded that every lake, river, and stream in the state was likely contaminated with mercury. Every sample taken from one thousand fish in seventy different lakes and rivers was found to contain mercury, often at levels deemed dangerous to women of childbearing age.

Under the Clean Air Act, the EPA had to follow through with a formal standard for a toxin it had declared a threat to public health. Yet hardly had Bush taken his second oath of office than the EPA came out with a standard so low it made a mockery of the agency's Clinton-era warning. The new system would be based on a concept called "cap and trade." New standards would be adopted, but plants that had trouble meeting them could simply buy pollution credits from other plants. Theoretically, the plants selling credits would be cleaner than required, and so balance out the high polluters. But that would be cold comfort to pregnant mothers who lived near those high-polluting plants, which could trade for the right to put five times as much mercury into the air as proposed by the EPA in 2000. Worse, the whole jury-rigged system would not be put in place until 2018. The new rule was written, it turned out, by industry lobbyists.

The attorneys general of nine states, from Maine to California, responded by filing suit against the EPA, charging that the new rule violated the Clean Air Act by exempting power plants from the best available technology for cutting pollutants. In the U.S. Senate, moderate Republicans began rallying with Democrats against it. These new rules—the most egregious yet from an administration with an environmental record now blacker by far than any other in U.S. history—were a reminder to Joe of what he was up against. He was fighting an industry that finally had the power it had always wanted: the power to set its own rules and govern itself, given to it by an administration that simply wanted money in exchange.

The silo drama, small as the stakes were, might have raised Joe's spirits somewhat more if the summer hadn't brought a stinging personal loss. At eighty-two, Joe's father had weathered two heart-bypass operations, and for a few weeks he seemed likely to survive the third one as well. Then, as happened so often now to frail older patients in hospitals, Joe's father developed a drug-resistant infection. With that, Joe began visiting every day.

Sitting in that hospital room as his father passed in and out of sleep, Joe remembered the indignation he'd felt when his father urged him to be a lawyer—a *tax* lawyer, no less: good pay, steady work, not much pressure. So much better than trial work, his father had added, with all those briefs to write and those courtroom risks. Also, a tax lawyer was, by definition, an insider, privy to the records of his corporate clients. Joe's father, as a Jew in postwar West Virginia, had always felt like an outsider. Joe hadn't known whether to feel insulted or amused by his father's hopes for him; perhaps he'd felt a bit of both. Now he realized his father had said that only because he wanted his son to be happy.

The irony was that his father loved the law in a way that Joe never had. To Joe, the law was just a tool to effect change. He had no intrinsic interest in it; given a choice, he'd read almost anything other than a legal document. His father loved the majesty and logic of the law. He loved the Constitution. As a Jew in World War II liberating a concentration camp, he had nurtured a special appreciation for America's freedoms. Practicing law was Joe's father's way of reaffirming those rights. Joe had a different life and different ambitions. But sitting by his father's bedside, Joe realized that they were, in one sense, the same: neither father nor son had practiced law for the money. They'd done it to do what was right.

Joe's father died on August 14. By then, Joe knew he had a date with the Fourth Circuit Court of Appeals in Richmond on September 19: the court had scheduled thirty minutes to hear both sides of the Nationwide 21 case. All the work that Joe had done with Jim Hecker the previous year hung in the balance. But in the weeks leading up to that date, Joe found he could hardly think, much less work. His father's death had left him stunned.

Fortunately, Joe could turn to his friend and co-counsel. Usually, they'd shouldered equal loads. This time, Joe said, Jim would have to prepare for the appeal on his own.

The hearing was scheduled for 9:30 a.m., but Joe and Jim were at the courthouse nearly an hour ahead of time. With its arcade of ornate arches on Main Street and high arched windows above, the block-size Italianate building of marble and granite had an almost festive air about it. Its history was more somber: Jefferson Davis had used its original central rooms as his headquarters of the Confederacy during the Civil War. By now, the two lawyers knew the drill all too well. Silently, they headed up to the third floor to check the silver-framed signpost that announced which judges had been chosen to hear the day's various appeals. The Fourth Circuit had fifteen seats, though one was vacant at the moment. Not all the judges were as conservative as the court's reputation: President Clinton had nominated a few. In theory, then, the computer might randomly spit out the names of two or even three moderate judges. That hadn't happened in Haden 1 and 2.

His mouth dry, hands clammy, Joe looked for the case as it was titled: *Ohio Valley Environmental Coalition et al. v. William Bulen, U.S. Army Corps of Engineers et al.* He couldn't believe it. There they were—again! For the third time, two of the three judges hearing the appeal were Paul V. Niemeyer and J. Michael Luttig.

Both appointed by the first President Bush, Niemeyer and Luttig were renowned as first-rate intellects. They were also judicial activists of a deeply conservative stripe. Of the two, Luttig was probably the more extreme. He had clerked for Chief Justice Warren Burger but also for Antonin Scalia when Scalia was an appeals-court judge. He had helped guide Clarence Thomas to confirmation on the U.S. Supreme Court. Now he was mentioned often as a prospective Supreme Court justice himself—first to replace Chief Justice William Rehnquist and, now that John Roberts had been nominated to Rehnquist's seat, as a short-list choice to replace Sandra Day O'Connor. In their rulings, Niemeyer and Luttig often seemed eager not just to affirm the law but to extend it, pushing for states' rights over the federal government's, ending court-ordered busing, narrowing abortion rights, prohibiting the Food and Drug Administration from regulating nicotine as a drug, and more. Their rulings were sometimes batted down by the U.S. Supreme Court, but more often the two courts appeared to be partners in refashioning the laws of the land. Rounding out the three-judge panel for *OVEC v. Bulen* was Robert J. Conrad Jr., recently appointed to the court by President George W. Bush.

Though half an hour remained before the judges would appear, a hush pervaded Courtroom 4 on the historic building's second floor. A scrum of U.S. government lawyers occupied one table. With quick nods of greeting, Joe and Jim took the other table. Five or six other lawyers sat along one of the two polished wooden benches behind the rail. They represented various coal interests, including Massey Energy, and were earning hourly fees just to listen and observe. At the front of the long, wood-paneled room, three green leather judges' chairs rose behind the bench in silent majesty, seeming to cast judgment by their very presence. Between the bench and the lawyers' tables stood a rostrum. Here each side would take turns presenting its arguments, and the judges would listen—or, more likely, interrupt with piercing queries. In this court proceeding there was no jury. The hearing was more like an oral exam conducted by very stern teachers, and the lawyers, seasoned as they might be, often felt like underprepared students. Many would still be quaking from the inquisition when the Fourth Circuit judges, by Southern tradition, stepped down after the hearing to shake each lawyer's hand with a decorous greeting.

At 9:30 a.m., the three black-robed judges swept in, and the lawyers hastily rose. Conrad was tall, bald, and owl-like. Niemeyer, in the middle, was short, with salt-and-pepper-hair and a quizzical look. Luttig, also short, bristled with restless intellect: even by his opening remarks, he made clear he was not a man to suffer fools or even very smart lawyers saying foolish things.

First up to the rostrum was Elizabeth Kessler, one of the lawyers representing the U.S. Army Corps of Engineers. "This is the third time in five years," she said peevishly, "that the Corps has been asked to review—"

"Of course that fact doesn't get you very far," Niemeyer cut in. "You're not just saying that the court was wrong because it reviewed this three times, are you?"

Kessler looked startled. "No, no," she said hastily.

Kessler plunged on with her main argument: that the Corps *had* conducted an environmental analysis of mountaintop mining, and valley fills in particular, as part of its Nationwide 21 permit process. The term "environmental assessment" had a very specific connotation. It meant a single, across-the-board review that the Corps had conducted in 2002 before it reauthorized Nationwide 21 as a permit process for individual cases. An "EA" wasn't as thoroughgoing as the Environmental Impact Statement that the Clean Water Act asked the

Corps to do at that juncture. It was sort of EIS lite. But that was what the Corps had chosen to do. Not surprisingly, the onetime EA had determined that mountaintop mining caused no more than minimal adverse effects. To the Corps, that meant no EAs—let alone EISes—then had to be done for individual authorizations, no matter how many thousands of acres the mining companies proposed to blast and fill. In those individual cases, Kessler added, the Corps could and did inspect valley fills after they were built to be sure they did have only minimal effects.

Both Niemeyer and Luttig pounced on that. The Clean Water Act, they pointed out, said Nationwide 21 could only be used to sanction activities *if* those activities had been found to have minimal environmental impacts. "I suggest to you that 'if' is a word that means conditional," Niemeyer said. "You're relying on what happens after."

Kessler stood in silence, groping for logic. "It's a combination of both," she said finally.

But, Niemeyer observed, the only time that "minimal impact" could be determined on a permit-by-permit basis was *before* the authorization was issued, and the Corps seemed to do nothing to determine if the impact *would* be minimal. "So how do you satisfy the government's interpretation that minimal effect be determined before?"

Again, Kessler struggled for words. This time, Luttig cut her off.

"It makes no sense what you're saying," he said. "You say, 'We determine minimal impact because we know that no one will act in violation.' That's empirically wrong.

"History doesn't support you," he added, "because people operate outside the law all the time. Even by Washington standards, that's pretty incredible."

As Kessler's shoulders sagged, Joe and Jim exchanged a quick look. All three judges appeared to see exactly why Judge Goodwin had nixed Nationwide 21. As Goodwin had observed, the Corps couldn't just issue these permits without first determining if the valley fills they sanctioned would have minimal environmental impacts. Of the many ways in which Nationwide 21 violated the Clean Water Act, Goodwin had thought that one seemed the most obvious and flagrant.

Now it was Jim's turn at the rostrum. From behind, he seemed to shake a bit in his dark suit. So much was at stake. Section 404 of the Clean Water Act was very clear, he began, somewhat hesitantly. The

Corps could only issue Nationwide 21 authorizations *if* the environmental effects were minimal. "And the only way to satisfy the statute's
requirement for cumulative impact is before the permit is issued."

"Why?" asked Niemeyer.

Jim was stunned. Niemeyer had just argued that effects had to be
judged beforehand. Or had he?

"This is your whole case," Luttig chimed in. "Why does this require
a determination *before* the permit?"

Luttig had just switched sides, too.

"Let's say the Corps felt it could do a better job of satisfying '21' *after* the permit was issued," Niemeyer echoed. "Is your only argument
that it should do the assessment before?"

"But . . . that's not the case," Jim said weakly. The individual cases
where Nationwide 21s were granted could *only* be judged on their environmental effects before the authorizations were granted.

"But you already conceded that the statute only calls for categorical assessment," Luttig countered. He meant the 2002 EA, when Nationwide 21 as a *category* of permit had been reauthorized.

But, Jim said, where was the chance for the public to participate in
permit applications, as the Clean Water Act intended?

"You want public participation in the individual cases," Luttig said.
"You *have* it in the categorical." Strictly speaking, the public had had a
chance to comment in 2002. By law, Luttig was saying, that was
enough. "All the Corps had to do was determine that the category of
activities would have less than minimal impact, not the activity of an
individual mine."

"But even then," Jim pleaded, "the Corps only studied the aquatic
environment, not the whole environment."

Jim's time was up, and the judges had heard enough. Visibly de-
jected, he shuffled back to the table and sat down, shrugging off Joe's
look of sympathy.

The government's lawyer was summoned up again, and again
Niemeyer and Luttig appeared to switch sides. By now, though, neither Joe nor Jim drew any hope from those words. This was the game
the judges played, baiting one side, then the other, looking for holes in
each side's argument and then retiring, ostensibly, to ponder which
holes were bigger.

The judges stepped down for their customary greeting—the hearing had lasted ninety minutes, an hour more than scheduled—and then the parties dispersed. Joe and Jim were left in the hallway to do a postmortem.

"I was awful," Jim said sadly. "I don't know what happened."

"I don't think anything you said would have made a difference," Joe said. "I think they were looking for reasons to rule against us."

Not for the first time, Joe's pessimism was borne out. The judges issued their ruling the day before Thanksgiving. Judge Goodwin's ruling was overturned on all counts. With stinging succinctness, the judges concluded that Goodwin had "erred" in assuming the Corps had to measure whether individual cases would have more than minimal environmental effects. The Corps had done due diligence with mountaintop mining as a "category" of activities when it reauthorized Nationwide 21 in 2002, and any further inspection of sites could be done as and when the Corps' district engineer pleased.

It was a complete rout.

Resolutely, Joe filed a motion with the Fourth Circuit for an en banc hearing. On rare occasions, a circuit's full field of judges might decide to reconsider a ruling made by one of its three-judge panels. At least, Joe reasoned, the motion would make the circuit's other judges more aware of the issues at stake. In mid-February, by a 5–3 vote, the Fourth Circuit decided not to reconsider. But in issuing that decision, the court made a startling acknowledgment: five of its fourteen judges had recused themselves from hearing the appeal in September. The reason, the court explained, was that all five had a financial interest in mining. Very likely, those five had recused themselves from hearing Haden 1 and Haden 2 as well. So the odds had not been so high, after all, against Niemeyer and Luttig ending up on all three panels.

In the en banc ruling, the dissent filed by Judge Robert B. King, a Clinton appointee, was revealing. The crisp certainty the conservative judges had shown in batting down Goodwin's ruling was not, as it turned out, persuasive in the least to King and two colleagues who signed it. The Corps' ability to analyze environmental effects *after* a valley fill was approved, King wrote, did not at all relieve it of the responsibility of analyzing the effects *before* the destruction.

King's last paragraph was poignant. "Finally," he wrote,

this case is of exceptional importance to the nation and, in particular, to the states in the Appalachian region. The Appalachian mountains, the oldest mountain chain in the world,
are one of the nation's richest, most diverse, and most delicate
ecosystems, an ecosystem that the mountaintop coal mining
authorized by the Corps' general permit may irrevocably damage or destroy. In enacting the Clean Water Act, Congress
mandated the protection of our environment through strict
procedural requirements. The panel's decision, in authorizing
the Corps to skirt the CWA-mandated permitting process, un-
dermines the enactment's primary purpose and poses unnec-
essary risks to one of this nation's great places. In further
support of this dissent, I adopt Judge Goodwin's fine opinion
for the district court.

"I respectfully dissent from the denial of rehearing en banc," Judge
King concluded, "and I am pleased to state that Judge [M. Blane]
Michael and Judge [Diana Gribbon] Motz join in this opinion."

Joe felt his throat tighten as he read those paragraphs. They didn't
make a whit of legal difference, but it was gratifying to know that in the
judges' chambers of that august building in Richmond, he and Jim had
a few defenders.

Then, with characteristic brusqueness, Joe put the dissent aside.
Even before the Fourth Circuit had issued its ruling, Joe had filed a
new case against the Corps. He still felt Nationwide 21 was plainly illegal. But so, too, he felt, was the individual permit, the one the Corps
granted only after greater scrutiny.

He was going to court to stop it.

TEN

MASSEY'S UNWELCOME NEW FRIEND

The silo squabble was embarrassing, but for Don Blankenship it was just a diversion. It had no effect on Massey's bottom line. It didn't even slow the flow of coal from the mountains above the Marsh Fork Elementary School down to Goals. Coal that didn't fit into Goals's first silo could legally be stored in open stockpiles. If Joe Lovett, Judy Bonds, and a ragtag army of activists succeeded in keeping Massey from building that silo in the end, what, really, had they won?

Everything else seemed to be going Don Blankenship's way.

Up on the state supreme court, Brent Benjamin had sat in on his first year of appeals, and the genial neophyte had performed as well as his largest benefactor could have hoped. At first, tensions with at least two of Benjamin's fellow judges had run high. Larry Starcher, the court's most outspoken critic of the mining industry, had gone so far as to post a cartoon on his chambers door showing Benjamin arriving in a crate marked "courtesy of $3.5 million from Massey Coal and other coal interests." But in the stately courtroom, civility had soon ruled. When Benjamin's father died, Starcher had even joined the other judges in going to Columbus, Ohio, for the memorial service. Of the first forty-eight decisions the court issued, forty had been unanimous. Five of the balance had gone 4–1, with Benjamin in the majority.

Cases involving Massey, though, had yet to be heard. Several were appeals Massey was bringing of fines and suspension orders issued originally by Matt Crum in the DEP's short-lived golden era of vigilant mine inspection. Then there was the fifty-million-dollar verdict in the case of Harman Mining—Hugh Caperton's little coal company that Massey Energy had driven out of business. Whenever a reporter asked Benjamin if he would recuse himself from cases involving Massey, the rotund judge demurred. The question was speculative, he opined. He would have to wait until an attorney in a particular case actually asked him to recuse himself, then make a decision based on the motion filed. The idea of recusing himself *without* such a request, based merely on the fact that he would be hearing a case brought by the company whose chairman had been his largest campaign contributor by a multiple of perhaps one hundred, appeared not to have crossed his mind.

As for Benjamin's vanquished foe, his story, too, had ended just as Don might have wished. Still fuming from his loss, Warren McGraw had brought a libel suit against Don and local media owners, arguing that in its television commercials, Don's 527 group And for the Sake of the Kids had spread slanderous half-truths about him. The commercials had made viewers think that concerned parents had funded them, not coal executives. They had said McGraw endorsed sending a "convicted rapist" to work as a school janitor. McGraw's lawyer, Richard Neely, a longtime Charleston litigator with a healthy ego, felt his case was both strong and nationally important. It would decide just how loose with the truth these new 527 groups could be. If he won, Neely felt, the verdict would have a profound effect on the 2008 presidential campaign season.

Unfortunately, Neely lost.

In dismissing the case that July, a West Virginia circuit judge observed that the state supreme court *had* endorsed the idea of sending Tony Arbaugh to work as a janitor in a school, even if the plan called for Arbaugh to work under constant supervision and even if the plan was dropped in a later opinion. McGraw had gone along with that first opinion. So the commercials weren't libelous. Neely had a succinct reaction: "We're fucked."

In his own more modest law office along a highway outside Beckley, Warren McGraw tried to make sense of his last year. He'd still not met the man who spent at least $1.7 million to smear him and push him out of office. He knew him only by reputation. "What could I do?" he said sadly one day in a small conference room adjoining the offices he and his son shared, as traffic whooshed by his window. "I had only the money I was paid: as a supreme court judge, I was paid $95,000. I didn't have the money to buy television commercials."

The anti-McGraw campaign had been Don's first victory as a public figure. His second—defeating Governor Manchin's pension plan—had been his second. Emboldened, he embarked now on his third campaign—with an eye, perhaps, toward his fourth.

That summer, Don began barnstorming the state. The governor should abolish the state's food tax, he declared. West Virginia's working families could ill afford to pay an extra 6 percent for household groceries. Once again, he had made a smart choice of issues. Only a handful of states had any food tax at all, and of those only Tennessee had one as high as West Virginia's. In his speeches, Don liked to invoke his mother and the gas mart in Delorme. He knew how damaging a food tax could be to working families, especially in a border county: it drove shoppers right over the line to Kentucky, which had no food tax at all. Don wanted a ten-cent rollback in state gasoline taxes for the same reason. "There used to be thirteen gas stations between where I was reared in Delorme, West Virginia, and twenty miles down the road in Williamson," he declared in his talks. "Today there's not a single one— every one of them is across the Kentucky border." The chairman of Massey Energy said he was only doing his part to help West Virginia's working citizens, a part to which he was pledging, he said, at least $500,000 in issue advertising. "I have no political ambitions whatsoever," he declared. More and more, though, he looked like a man about to run for governor.

Don on the hustings was a curious sight: a budding Huey Long of West Virginia. Like Long, he called himself a radical populist. Long had won the governorship of Louisiana in 1928 by castigating the rich, and Don could hardly do that: aside from Don himself and a few other coal barons and their lawyers, the state was pretty thin on rich folk. But Don substituted politicians for plutocrats, and the effect was the same. Whether he would go on to as notorious a political run remained to be seen. Like Long, he enjoyed near-absolute power. But he may have been telling the truth when he said he had no political ambitions. After all, he was arguably the most powerful person in the state already. Why bother with an elected office?

If he did harbor hopes of running for governor, Don would need some elocution lessons. On a typical evening, he spoke at a Republican party buffet dinner in Parkersburg, a small city eighty miles north of Charleston. The local faithful had gathered at a country club on the outskirts of town, coming in from the day's last light over the golf greens to pile up their plates at the buffet table. Through the dinner, Don sat on a raised dais, flanked by eager-to-please worthies. Unlike a politician, he made no effort to look interested in their patter: he'd been Massey's chairman too long for that. Finally, a party official took the floor to introduce Don amid the clink of dessert forks, and the speaker of the evening pushed back his chair to vigorous applause.

In person, Don was taller than his roundish face suggested: well over six feet. He'd lost weight since his debut in public life and was now quite svelte in an expensive-looking suit, loosely cut in the European style. He spoke in a soft Appalachian accent, an odd blend of backcountry roughness and courtly Southern charm, but an odd mannerism occasionally belied his graceful demeanor. His tongue would dart out, then in, like a lizard's. Whether it was a grown-up's nervous tic or some vestige of childhood, it had a disconcerting effect, as if he were on a quite unconscious surveillance for tasty gnats.

In his opening remarks, Don referred to himself more than once in the third person. "One of the things you often hear about Don Blankenship is that he's from out of state," he said, in a jibe at the governor who'd charged his nemesis with having a Kentucky address. "I know I'm a true West Virginian because I know stores do not have bags, they have totes. I can pronounce words like 'Allegheny' and 'Monongahela.' I know that a traffic jam in West Virginia is being stuck behind a coal truck." As his audience laughed, Don struck a more somber note. "It's sad in a way, coal truck drivers have no chance. If they're going the other way, they're driving too fast; if they're going in the same direction they're going too slow. They're some of the most maligned people in the state, but they work very hard."

Declaring himself a conservative radical in the tradition of Teddy Roosevelt, Don said he didn't care much for party labels. But facts were facts. "How long have the Democrats been in control of the legislature? The answer is seventy-four years." Don believed that against all odds, the state could elect a conservative legislature within two election cycles. After all, he asked, how long had it been since a Republican sat on the West Virginia supreme court? Eighty-four years. But with Brent Benjamin, that record had been broken. "So it shows it can be done," Don said. And on the state supreme court, more could be done. Don put it candidly: "We have to replace Starcher."

The twelve-year term of Larry Starcher, the court's most outspoken and generally liberal judge, was to expire in 2008. If the judge was foolish enough to seek reelection, Don would be ready to do to him what he'd done to Warren McGraw. "Let me show you what the future will be like in terms of TV ads that go after Starcher," Don told his audience. On the screen across the stage, a video clip showed Starcher saying scornfully of Don, "What he says about McGraw applies to me, because I was one of the three votes that did whatever they say we did." Then came an ominous voice-over: "Judge Starcher let a child rapist out of prison. Court records show the plan called for the rapist to work at a local school."

The staunch Republicans of Parkersburg laughed, but a little nervously.

Why, Don Blankenship asked, was Don Blankenship doing all this? "We have a case that everyone thinks is the reason I got involved in the supreme court, in Boone County by the Lincoln County judge." Don was referring to the Harman ruling—the one he would almost certainly be asking the state supreme court to reverse within the next year. "We're at three years and seven months and don't have a transcript yet. We've seen the bond go from $50 million to soon to be $70 million. [The case] involves 300,000 tons of coal, which at gross value is probably $15 million. We're in a situation where the judicial system is broken and you can't get a transcript to file an appeal."

About the transcript, Don was right. The legal system in West Virginia did appear to suffer from some grievous ailments, because both sides of the Harman case had pleaded for a transcript, yet the wheels of justice had failed to turn. Finally, the state supreme court in disgust had ordered the work parceled out to various transcribers all over the state. Now, at last, the case appeared headed for court on appeal, where the judges, including the genial Brent Benjamin, would decide if the original fifty-million-dollar judgment, now up to seventy million dollars with interest, should be upheld.

The Harman case was one reason he'd started speaking out, Don said. But there were, he said, a hundred others. "One was that I've actually watched coal miners go out of their vehicles and be beaten with bats by masked men while the state police watched. I've been involved in situations where a coal miner was killed in the state of West Virginia, [people] knew who his murderer was and didn't even bring charges because they were so fearful of the mine workers [union]." Don paused to let the words sink in. "But I've been involved in so many things that could be the reason I'm involved in this, I'm not sure what the ultimate reason might be. I just think it's pretty obvious in West Virginia who needs help, and it's not the liberal side, it's the conservative side. And if we're going to have balance, someone's going to have to throw his weight to the conservative side."

The message was blunt. But as Don plunged on, his speech began to lose coherence, the memorized lines dealt randomly like playing cards. His hands stayed at his sides, his eyes seemed not to connect with anyone in the audience, and his soft drawl, charming at the outset, grew soporific, a monotone that after an hour had his listeners casting furtive looks at their watches. He had the same effect on his employees at those Massey Energy picnics and seemed just as oblivious to their growing discomfort—perhaps because as different as those Massey picnickers were from these Parkersburg Republicans, both were captive audiences.

"I've got about twenty or thirty minutes of slides which I think will show the truth of things," Don said. At that, his audience sagged. Most of his slides showed quotes from venerable politicians, from Abraham Lincoln to Ronald Reagan. The quotes were pithy and amusing, but they made his own remarks dreary by comparison. Finally the slides were done, and so, with no rousing crescendo, was the speaker. "I'll say this in closing," Don said, and his drooping audience looked up with relief. "Don't take life too seriously because you'll never get out of it alive."

The Republicans of Parkersburg raced for the doors, and Don was left standing almost alone in front. The Massey chairman confused his audience. He was rich enough and powerful enough to help get their candidates elected. But as he was the first to declare, he came from the wrong side of the tracks—from right *beside* the tracks—and still lived proudly in the southern coalfields. He wasn't of their social ilk at all. Like most political marriages, the one between this self-styled radical populist and his mainstream Republican audience was a somewhat awkward one: promising, but not without peril.

That September, the West Virginia legislature chose not to repeal the food tax but did reduce it from 6 percent to 5 percent—a sop to Don from lawmakers who hoped that would be enough to get the coal king off their backs. It wasn't. Don predicted that voters would "target" lawmakers who hadn't pushed to repeal the tax altogether. He would spend more of his own money, he vowed, to ensure that those lawmakers lost in the 2006 midterm elections. One reporter asked him if his hardball approach might backfire. "It doesn't matter what people think in that regard," Don said. "I don't need popularity."

At first look, Massey Energy's prospects appeared as rosy as its chairman's political future. For the second quarter of its fiscal year in 2005, the company reported a 194 percent increase in net income, to $37 million from $12.6 million in the second quarter of 2004. Coal prices had continued to rise, and with it rose Massey's share price, just over $50, nearly twice its low of the year before. But as its chairman duly reported, Massey was having trouble getting the rail service it needed to meet its market demand. Finding the labor it needed to meet that demand was a chronic problem now, too. Experienced workers were scarce—experienced workers, that is, who'd never been members of the UMWA—and for some reason Massey had trouble keeping the ones it hired. Yet Massey's rivals seemed to be coping just fine. In this boom market for coal, their profits exceeded Massey's across the board—which was why two new shareholders of Massey Energy were starting to ask pointed questions of its chairman and not liking the answers they got.

Beginning in mid-August, a New York hedge fund called Third Point LLC made twenty-seven purchases of Massey Energy stock. In mid-September, the fund submitted an SEC filing reporting its intentions. "The purpose of the acquisition of the shares by the [Third Point] funds is for investment," the filing blandly noted of Third Point's purchase of 5.9 percent of Massey Energy stock for $218.7 million. In a separate letter to Don, Third Point's founder and chairman, Daniel S. Loeb, expressed himself more directly. Massey stock, he wrote, was selling at a discount, which seemed "attributable to the company's many operating glitches, disappointments in earnings and recent failure to hedge its diesel costs." Loeb demanded that any available cash flow be returned to shareholders via a share repurchase. "Should you and the board remain like deer frozen in the headlights," Loeb concluded, "I am certain that, with the constitution of the company's shareholder base, we could rally support for new leadership to manage the company and its capital structure more effectively."

The same day, a second hedge fund, JANA Partners of San Francisco, announced that it, too, had made purchases of Massey stock over a period of weeks. It now owned 6.5 percent of the company—an investment of $225.9 million. In his own letter to Don, Barry Rosenstein noted that Massey's stock, which had been selling at about $51 per share, should be trading much higher. Rosenstein thought Massey should borrow $1.5 billion and use that money to buy back outstanding shares. That, he predicted, would boost the remaining stock up to about $80 per share.

Loeb and Rosenstein weren't working in concert, or so Loeb claimed. But as owners in sum now of 12.4 percent of the stock, they had just become Massey's largest shareholders. Over the next months, Rosenstein was to take a backseat role to Loeb, who would lead a proxy fight to get himself and a fellow executive at Third Point elected to Massey's board of directors at the next annual meeting. It was Loeb who had started looking into Massey some months before and concluded the company was undervalued enough and badly managed enough to be his next target as an activist investor. And it was Loeb who, on the midsummer days his company was buying Massey stock, was likely to be found on a surfboard off Montauk, Long Island, waiting for the next series of rollers to come in.

In person, Loeb was indistinguishable from the college students and twentysomething slackers who bobbed on boards beside him, waiting for the next perfect wave. Slim and boyishly handsome at forty-

four, with dark hair and a penetrating gaze, he emerged from the surf
to introduce himself with a gentle, almost deferential air, as if still an
adolescent in the company of grown-ups. But while most of his fellow surfers repaired to modest homes, Loeb headed down to his new
fifteen-million-dollar oceanfront house in East Hampton, a brutally
modern construction with a wavelike roof that reminded neighbors of
the old TWA terminal at New York's John F. Kennedy Airport. Then he
got on the phone to resume the business that would earn him, in 2005,
approximately $150 million.

A native of Santa Monica, Loeb had started Third Point in 1995
with $3.3 million from family, friends, and his own savings. The fund
was named after one of his favorite surf breaks at Malibu. In the
decade or so since he'd graduated from Columbia with a degree in eco-
nomics, Loeb had worked for various Wall Street firms—Warburg Pincus, Lafer Equity, Kent Capital, and others—learning a lot about the
financial world's trickiest and highest-risk games. But working for companies that merely aimed to outperform market indexes by a modest
amount exasperated him. "My eyes glaze over when people start talking about their performance relative to an index," Loeb told one financial writer. At Third Point, Loeb had gone for what he called "absolute
returns," investing in troubled, even bankrupt companies that had potential. By the fall of 2005, Loeb was managing three billion dollars, after posting an average 28.9 percent annual return for Third Point's first
decade. He used the clout of his large stock positions to oust greedy or
incompetent top managers, and he talked wryly of being in the "moral
indignation" business. But he readily admitted that the goal, in the
end, was to enrich his shareholders—and himself.

Along the way, Loeb had become mildly famous in financial circles
for the caustic letters he wrote to the chairmen and CEOs of his latest
targets. Perhaps it was his mother's influence: Clare L. Spark was a
Melville scholar and author of a study called *Hunting Captain Ahab*.
Loeb clearly enjoyed the rhetorical flourishes of his damning epistles.
"Do what you do best," Loeb advised one chairman. "Retreat to your
waterfront mansion in the Hamptons where you can play tennis and
hobnob with your fellow socialites." When Loeb saw another chairman
in choice seats at the U.S. Open—while his company presumably
sailed adrift and its shareholders suffered—he fired off another tart

epistle: "My bewilderment turned to anger when I saw the crowd seeking autographs from the Olsen twins just below the private box that seemed to be occupied by [the chairman] and others who were enjoying the match and summer sun while hobnobbing, snacking on shrimp cocktails and sipping chilled Gewürztraminer."

Not all of Loeb's investment picks had panned out. He'd lost sixty million dollars in October 2002, betting the high-tech market had one more bounce. It didn't. Once he'd lost twenty million dollars in an afternoon. To cope with the stress, he went to a yoga class every morning, avoided caffeine, and had a rabbi in to give him weekly Torah lessons. "Money's not everything," he told one reporter. But he was winning a lot more than he lost, as his recent acquisitions confirmed. With his thirty-three-year-old wife, Margaret, whom he'd married in the summer of 2004 at the East Hampton house, Loeb had bought an eight-bedroom town house in Greenwich Village for $11.2 million, then decided it wasn't quite right. Now he'd just broken the price record for a residence in Manhattan, paying $45 million for an apartment that didn't yet exist. For that money, he would be getting the 10,700-square-foot penthouse condominium of a building designed by Robert A. M. Stern, under construction on Central Park West on the site of the razed Mayflower Hotel. The apartment was said to include eight bedrooms, ten full bathrooms, a screening room, his-and-hers offices, a library, and wraparound terraces. It was to be ready by the end of 2007.

Massey, in its SEC filing of response to Loeb and Rosenstein, declared it might consider repurchasing some modest amount of stock—not with debt but with cash on hand. The company's newest shareholders were nonplussed. They were no more impressed by Massey's third-quarter net earnings of $22.5 million, up from $2 million the previous year. Again, Massey's rivals had done better, recording windfall profits in this banner year for coal. In the requisite conference call with analysts, Don had his first verbal exchange with Daniel Loeb, and it wasn't a pleasant one.

"How do you think you are doing relative to your peers?" Loeb asked, after Don had run through the numbers.

"I try to keep an even keel and not get depressed about the situation," Don said. "If you look at our position relative to our peers in Central Appalachia, we usually outperform our peers."

"Your stock is up 8 percent, and Consol's stock is up 40 percent," Loeb shot back. "So the market is speaking a little different than you are. Is the board satisfied with your performance as an executive?"

Don declined to answer the question. He could bring the conference call to an end, but he knew he hadn't heard the last of Daniel Loeb.

That fall, at least, Massey's lawyers managed to thwart a stockholder threat that had hung over the company for more than three years. Phillip R. Arlia, a Massey shareholder, had charged Don and various directors with insider trading. The complaint made for pretty dramatic reading. Don, it noted, had sold more than 100,000 shares of company stock in early 2002 at $22 per share, for a profit of $2.4 million. Yet just two months later, Massey had reported a steep drop in profits, due to flooding, geological problems in one mine, and financial setbacks, including a $6.9 million settlement with West Virginia for the millions of dollars in workers' compensation premiums unpaid for years by Massey's subsidiaries. The stock had dropped along with those profits, eventually down to $10 per share. Arlia charged that Don knew of the coming bad news and profited accordingly, as did several of his directors. Worse, the suit observed, Don had told analysts on December 10, 2001, that Massey would have a "really good year" in 2002, with earnings of more than $400 million. That prediction had sent the stock up, just before sales by Don and various officers.

Arlia was represented by Milberg, Weiss, Bershad, Hynes & Lerch, a San Diego firm that had made twenty billion dollars from bringing such shareholder derivative suits, as they were called, against companies ranging from Apple Computer to Aetna. The game plan was to gather so much dirt about a company that the company would settle out of court. So the suit against Massey didn't end with insider trading. It went on to chronicle the company's messy history of union busting and its almost innumerable environmental misdeeds, noting that the West Virginia DEP had branded Massey a "chronic violator." In the out-of-court settlement announced in November 2005, Massey agreed to several key changes in corporate governance. The board would be expanded from eight members to twelve, with an independently appointed director. Before, the company had required a supermajority of 80 percent of shareholders to amend any decisions the directors made. Just the previous year, 70 percent of the shareholders had voted to exercise approval of executive severance packages—starting with Don's own. The uprising had failed without the requisite 80 percent support. Now a mere 70 percent would constitute a voting majority. The move put Don on notice that the era of unquestioned pay packages might be over. The settlement also awarded $2.5 million in legal fees to Milberg, Weiss. In exchange, all charges of lawlessness and malfeasance were dropped.

For Milberg, Weiss, it was a modest victory—and probably one of its last. The following May, a federal grand jury in Los Angeles handed down a twenty-count indictment charging the firm with case shopping. The firm was accused of paying individuals kickbacks for buying shares and serving as plaintiffs. One former Milberg, Weiss client had served as a plaintiff in approximately forty suits for the firm. Two other clients had served as plaintiffs in seventy cases *each*. The charges in Milberg, Weiss's suit against Massey seemed plausible, but Massey may also have been a victim—a word not often used to describe it—in a nation-wide shakedown operation by opportunistic lawyers.

The insider-trading case had barely been dispatched when Massey's lawyers reached another settlement, this one with the West Virginia DEP. Bob McLusky and his legal colleagues were definitely earning their retainers. In a one-paragraph notice issued without fanfare on January 5, 2006, DEP Secretary Stephanie Timmermeyer announced that Massey would pay $1.5 million to resolve five lawsuits filed by the DEP against four Massey subsidiaries. These were the suits that had grown out of Matt Crum's campaign to make Massey accountable for chronic water violations.

Of the four offenders, Independence and Omar were the most egregious. Seemingly indifferent to the show-cause hearings that Matt Crum had forced them to attend, both had kept right on spilling black-water into local streams. Eventually, both had been found guilty of criminal charges for the spills. In March 2003, a federal magistrate had fined them two hundred thousand dollars each—an astonishingly large fine for coal country—and put them on probation for five years. Yet by October of that year, the two had racked up sixty-eight more citations for wastewater violations, including, for Independence, a 250,000-gallon spill in August and a fifty-thousand-gallon spill in September. More than two years after a court review of their conduct, both subsidiaries were still operating, their fines still unpaid.

Yet of the five suits, the one against Marfork was the most significant. It was the one in which the DEP, on Crum's order, had called for a thirteen-day suspension of the permit for Marfork's massive Brushy Fork impoundment after chronic violations. Massey had fought the ruling up and down the courts. The settlement had been reached just as the Marfork case was due to be heard a final time by the state supreme court. Along with its share of the $1.5 million penalty, Marfork was slapped, ever so lightly, with two three-day suspensions, to take effect early in 2006 and not to run concurrent with any downtime for the operation.

The settlement gave Massey far more than it took away. Those five suits had grown out of 234 water violations, all of which would be wiped off the books. Moreover, as the *Gazette's* Ken Ward Jr. discovered after a careful look at DEP records, the settlement would also curtail fourteen other *pending* enforcement cases in which the violations were so egregious that permit suspensions were also sought. In fact, it would wipe the slate clean of *all* Massey violations, large and small, dated right up to December 1, 2005. Pressed by Ward, the DEP reluctantly released a twenty-six-page list detailing 1,900 unresolved violations written up at all Massey subsidiaries operating in West Virginia. The settlement would resolve them all. As part of the settlement, the DEP would also release Massey from any *potential* fines or enforcement actions that might come out of any water-pollution or waste-management violations "up to and including November 30, 2005."

By law, the DEP had to hold a public hearing for anyone who objected to the settlement. On March 10, 2006, three Coal River valley residents came to the DEP's headquarters in Charleston to voice their concerns. One was Pauline Canterberry, one of the two Sylvester Dustbusters. Another was Janice Nease, who now played an active role at Coal River Mountain Watch. The third was Freda Williams, the politely persistent cofounder of CRMW who now lobbied against King Coal from her home in the shadow of the Brushy Fork impoundment. All were eloquent in their dismay, but Freda made perhaps the most salient point.

"Why is this proposal necessary?" she asked. The DEP's cases were strong, none more so than the one against Marfork. Why, she asked, back off now? Though she was too polite to say it, her inference was clear: the DEP had reached its settlement right before its scheduled state supreme court trial date in the Marfork suit precisely because it might have *won* and extracted far more than $1.5 million from Massey. Perhaps Massey had blinked; perhaps the DEP had felt pressure from somewhere above. Either way, Freda said, "with this settlement the DEP is abrogating its responsibility to the public's welfare."

For Don, the $1.5 million was small change, well worth the satisfaction of dispatching all those DEP violations. But pressures were still mounting. He could ignore the growing outcry about mountaintop mining. He could wave off the lawsuits—most of them, anyway. But his new dissident shareholders posed the first real threat in thirteen years to his absolute rule of Massey Energy. Already, they were poring over the company's financial statements, its 8-Ks and 10-Ks, following leads and digging up dirt. They had the money and time, it seemed, to dig more deeply than a daily newspaper reporter. He knew where this was going. The dissidents would try to get on the board. Three of Massey's directors were up for reelection in May 2006. If the dissidents won a proxy fight and snatched one or more of those seats, they might push for more; they might push Don Blankenship out.

In public, Don remained as laconic as ever. At home, he could sometimes erupt. The target of his anger, often as not, was his maid.

Deborah K. May had been hired on May 4, 2001, as Don's personal maid for his house in Sprigg. In the statement she filed in March 2006 to petition for judicial review of her unemployment-compensation benefits, May reported that all had gone well until December 2002. That was when Don moved from Sprigg to a cabin complex just across the state line in Kentucky. Don's son, John, now a professional dirt-track car racer in the World of Outlaws series, moved into the Sprigg house. May was asked to stay on there but also to drive over and clean the Kentucky cabin complex. All this work took more time, yet her pay remained $8.86 per hour.

Don chose to move back to the Sprigg house in June 2003, yet May was told to keep cleaning both residences. She asked for a raise, because of the travel time and extra responsibilities involved. Her request was denied. The next year, she reported, Don acquired a luxury bus with living room, kitchen, and bedroom. May was asked to clean this on a regular basis, too. Again, she asked for a raise. Again, she was denied. In early January 2005, Don added to her duties the regular cleaning of his four-story mountaintop house in Kentucky. Again, May requested a raise; again, she was denied. By now, her duties were overwhelming—she was cleaning, on her own, three homes and a bus. One week, she worked thirty-three overtime hours and still fell short of finishing all her duties. That made her boss mad.

"Once while trying to stock the coach bus after a last-minute notice to do so," May's lawyer reported, "Don grabbed her arm, pulled her toward him, and told her to leave the bus. Ms. May found that treatment to be embarrassing since many of Mr. Blankenship's guests were on the bus when the incident occurred. On another occasion, Mr. Blankenship sent her to McDonald's to purchase breakfast for him and his interior decorator. Ms. May placed the order, accepted the food, and returned to the Blankenship home. As she unpacked the food, Mr. Blankenship discovered that McDonald's filled the order incorrectly; Mr. Blankenship started slinging the food and he grabbed Ms. May's wrist and told her, 'Any time I want you to do exactly what I tell you to do and nothing more and nothing less.'"

Don's nerves definitely seemed to be fraying by midsummer 2005. One Friday night in July, he called May at home. He was frantic, May related in her suit, about a carpet stain. "It looks like someone was murdered up here," he told her.

May was dumbstruck. "Murdered?" she echoed. "What are you talking about?"

Don was adamant. "I need you to come, there's something red on the carpet up here, and it looks like someone has been murdered."

May duly drove over to her employer's house. Don showed her the stain. For a moment, they both looked down at it in silence. "I think that's from a roof leak," May said at last.

"Then why haven't you fixed the leak?" Don demanded, as May recalled. "I should take you and the other workers out and stone you to death."

One day that same month, May got word from Don's secretary, Sandra, that the chairman wanted an explanation, in writing, as to why there was no ice cream in the freezer of one of his homes. "Mr. B," May dutifully wrote,

> I don't feel that the offensive comments were necessary concerning the ice cream. . . . You don't seem to realize the magnitude and heavy volume of work that has been put in my lap since I began working here, with only one $.30 cent raise in the last 4 years. Today you have crushed me. As for what excuse I have about the ice cream, I don't have one, other than—it was a minor oversight on my part. I send my apologies for that and will try to do what you want. That has always been my goal from the very start. . . . I really love my job, as I have told you before. I have even put you and your requests "first," even before my husband and my children many times in the past.

Don liked to do business by writing his responses in longhand in the margins of a letter he'd just received and faxing it back to the recipient. He did that with May's letter. "I realize you are under a lot of stress, and that some of my comments add to that," he wrote in a cramped schoolboy scrawl. "At the same time, you'd be lucky to find one person in all of WV and KY that earn[s] more for the job you have than you earn. As to my reactions please consider that I pay 4 or five people to save me time and make my life comfortable."

The notes continued down the right-hand margin of May's letter: "Sometimes they decrease my comfort, more than increase it. . . . If for example I go on a low carb diet it'll take 4 weeks to get something low carb, then I'll get billions of low carb stuff, then I go off the diet and everything stays low carb for a year." Don had run out of margin space, so he kept writing on a second sheet of paper. "Debbie K—You have or will get a call on why I tore the rack down."

May hadn't even mentioned the rack in her letter. She hadn't realized that Don had torn his closet coatrack and tie rack out that day or the day before and left them on the floor because he was angry at her. She had forgotten, it seemed, to leave a coat hanger out for him. Don went on to explain, though not apologize for, his temper tantrum, still writing in his schoolboy scrawl: "I've had 3 dogs stolen in 9 days, mines robbed, people complain incessantly, all of them want more money. None of them do what their [*sic*] asked. I can't hang my coat on air or my hats on dreams."

May asked a final time for a raise that fall. She wanted twelve dollars per hour, along with the use of a company vehicle and medical insurance for her children. Don refused to raise her pay at all. The last straw, May reported, was when Don brought a German police dog into the house and ordered May to care for it.

Her spirits broken, her physical strength exhausted, May quit on November 18, 2005, and filed a grievance with the state for unemployment benefits. The request was denied because May was found to have left her job voluntarily. That was when she called a lawyer.

The pressure was growing. For Don, it was about to get much, much worse.

ELEVEN

DON'S TERRIBLE YEAR

The crisis hit in the evening hours of January 19, 2006. That was when two miners died in Alma No. 1, an underground mine operated by a Massey subsidiary called Aracoma in Logan County, just west of the Coal River valley.

Ordinarily, when miners' deaths came in ones and twos, they weren't news. They showed up as one-paragraph stories in the local papers, forgotten the next day by all but the family and friends of the deceased. Aracoma was different. It followed directly upon the heels of the worst mining disaster West Virginia had seen in thirty-five years: Sago.

Sago was an underground mine complex northeast of Charleston in Upshur County. It was owned by Wilbur Ross, the New York bankruptcy billionaire. Ross had touted the safety record of mines now owned by his International Coal Group, but the mine at Sago ruined that record for a long time to come.

The explosion in Sago on January 2, 2006, trapped thirteen men in a compartment of the mine that filled inexorably with carbon monoxide. The one survivor, Randal McCloy Jr., later recounted a harrowing scene of men writing last words to their loved ones and curling up to fall into final, gas-induced sleep. As the national press swarmed over the site, details emerged of Sago's long record of MSHA citations: 208 in 2005, up from sixty-eight in 2004. Why had the mine been allowed to operate with so many citations? the national reporters asked. And why had Sago executives sat on the news of the miners' plight for a crucial sixty-nine minutes? Once again, America was reminded that Appalachian coal mines operated amid a culture of often flagrant disregard for miners' lives.

Then came Aracoma.

At 5:36 p.m. on January 19, a fire flared up on one of the conveyor belts that carried coal out from the deep recesses of Alma No. 1. A group of miners jumped on an underground vehicle and gunned it in an effort to outrace the billowing smoke and flames. They were forced to abandon the vehicle and run for the exit. Only when they reached safety did they realize that two of their own weren't with them. Don I. Bragg, thirty-three, a father of two, and Ellery Hatfield, forty-seven, a father of four, remained somewhere back in the heavy black smoke. Search teams returned as soon as they could, but all efforts were in vain: the men were found dead two days later. They became the third and fourth deaths at Aracoma since the mine's opening in 1999.

Details of the Aracoma disaster seemed all too familiar. As at Sago, site managers had failed to alert higher authorities in time: in this case, the head of the state office of the MSHA wasn't contacted until more than an hour after the fire broke out. As reporters began sifting through state and federal inspection records, they found, as at Sago, an alarming number of citations and violations. Aracoma had incurred more than ninety safety violations in 2005, more than one hundred in 2004. Many pertained directly to circumstances that could have caused the fire.

These latest mining deaths prompted Governor Manchin to draw up an emergency bill of safety measures. Miners would be outfitted with electronic tracking devices, and underground mines would have looping wires that enabled trapped miners to communicate by text messaging. When a tragedy did occur, mine operators would face new, severe fines for failure to notify the proper authorities within fifteen minutes. The bill passed unanimously. Just three hours after Manchin signed it on the morning of February 1, two more miners died in separate accidents. One was an underground miner, crushed by a collapsing wall support at a mine not owned by Massey in Wharton, West Virginia. The other was a Massey miner at a mountaintop site.

That second victim was a bulldozer operator at Black Castle, part of Massey's Elk Run operation. The operator was killed when his dozer ran into a gas line that erupted in fire. Fatal accidents at mountaintop mines were almost unheard-of, but they did happen. On September 7, 2003, two men had died at the Massey-owned Twilight surface mine, not far from Whitesville, when one of the giant trucks used to dump overburden into the valley drove into their shuttle van and crushed it. The dump trucks were so huge and high off the ground—their tires alone were eleven feet tall—that the driver hadn't been able to see the van directly below and in front of him. In the Clinton administration, Davitt McAteer had pushed a proposal at the MSHA to provide miners in the high trucks with devices to give them better visibility. The Bush administration had killed the plan in 2001. Since then, sixteen mine employees had died in high-truck accidents.

Aghast at the twin tragedies, Governor Manchin declared a statewide "safety stand-down" at West Virginia's 229 operating surface mines and 315 underground mines. "We will not produce another lump of coal until we can be certain the mines are safe," Manchin announced. "We will go mine by mine, surface job by surface job, until every mine is inspected."

Standing beside Manchin at a hastily called press conference was Bill Raney, the black-mustached head of the West Virginia Coal Association. To more than one observer at the press conference, Raney seemed to wince at the governor's proclamation. Just how long would the "stand-down" take? Raney took the microphone to suggest that it might take an hour, maybe two. Also, it would be voluntary, as the governor later amended. When the stand-down occurred that next Monday morning, it was a brief interlude indeed. Even Senator Byrd found that disconcerting. "I must say that shutting down the mines for one hour is not a serious solution," he said soberly. "It may be a time-out for safety, but it is not time enough for meaningful safety."

If Don ordered more stringent measures at Massey's mines in the weeks following the deaths of three of his miners, they were not evident at Aracoma. As MSHA inspectors sifted through the Massey subsidiary's mines and records, they wrote up more than one hundred citations for violations found since the fire. Among them, they issued five "D Orders" for "unwarranted failure" on Massey's part to remedy very significant and life-threatening violations. Two were for accumulations of combustible materials, one was for inadequate fire-detection equipment, one for the lack of a fire hose on a conveyor belt, and one for improper preshift safety checks. Any and all of them might have caused the deadly January 19 fire—or the next fire. Rather than acknowledge the lapses, Don made a point of touting Massey's safety record at an annual banquet in early March. At the Charleston event, the chairman declared that Massey had achieved its best safety performance ever in 2005, with a nonfatal days-lost injury rate of 2.41 per hundred full-time employees, lower than the industry average of 3.36. "It was another record performance," Don declared, "and something we are extremely proud of."

To Massey's new dissident shareholders, the Aracoma fire, along with staggering losses of $101.6 million in the last quarter of 2005 (down from a net profit of $13.9 million the year before), went to demonstrate why the company needed new oversight, perhaps with a new chairman. On March 16, Daniel Loeb informed Don that he would be nominating himself for one of the three board seats up for a vote in May. A colleague, Todd Q. Swanson, would run for a second seat. Massey, Loeb wrote in his SEC filing to Don, had not performed well and had lost sight of the concerns and interests of stockholders. While Loeb's ultimate motive was personal profit, he could rightly cast himself as a white knight trying to shake up a board that did little or nothing for its shareholders. The now settled Arlia suit had disclosed that each Massey director was given a grant of Massey stock upon joining the board (4,056 shares in 2001, when the suit was filed, worth $52,116 at that time), an annual retainer of $34,000, and an annual stock grant (2,208 shares in 2001, worth $30,798). The main task each board member had to fulfill to earn these handsome stipends was to come to an annual board meeting—for which each was paid an additional $2,000—and approve the chairman's increasingly lavish pay and perks. The board members had little incentive to act otherwise: they were appointed by the chairman himself.

Don had one of his directors respond on his behalf to Loeb's attack. William Grant declared Massey was "very sensitive" to shareholder concerns. That was why it had authorized a five-hundred-million-dollar share-repurchase program, using available cash flow. Loeb retorted that the company had put forth that plan only at the dissidents' goading, and anyway it was a pale version of their own proposal.

On April 24, Loeb fired off one of his caustic letters. Despite the company's dismal performance, Loeb wrote to his fellow shareholders, Massey "has lavished compensation on its Chief Executive Officer, paying him a multiple of the CEO compensation paid by four publicly-traded competitors—Peabody Energy Corporation, Consol Energy, Arch Coal Inc. and Foundation Coal Holdings, Inc." For 2005, Loeb reported, Massey's CEO had been paid $33.7 million; the average compensation for the competitors' CEOs had been $8.1 million.

That was eye-popping news. Massey's annual 10-K financial statement had Don earning $1 million per year, with bonuses that might come to an additional $2 million and perhaps $6 or $8 million more in stock options. But Loeb had studied the fine print of corporate documents to determine that Don was benefiting from various other hefty allocations of company stock. Don had sold a lot of stock in 2005, but he'd done pretty well in each of the three previous years, too, Loeb found. The chairman's compensation had averaged $15.6 million per year, compared with the industry average of $5.3 million. More shocking, these figures represented, in 2004 and 2005, 40.9 percent and 52.1 percent, respectively, of the entire adjusted net income reported by the company.

For Don, Loeb found, the goodies didn't end there. They extended to generous use of "Massey's Air Force." In the last year, Loeb charged, Massey's chairman had flown the company's Challenger 601 jet to Nassau, Bahamas; Las Vegas; Scottsdale; Bar Harbor; and numerous locations in Florida and California, including West Palm Beach, Naples, Los Angeles, San Diego, and San Francisco. What, Loeb wondered, did any of these locales have to do with Massey's Appalachian mines? "If elected to the Board of Directors," Loeb wrote, "we will urge the Board to get rid of the Challenger 601 luxury jet and review the use of other aircraft. We think a good place to put the cost savings from the luxury jet would be a program to reward and retain the company's miners."

At least, Loeb found, Don had spread the wealth a bit—to his relatives. Massey annually purchased more than one million dollars' worth of automobile and light-truck parts from A-A Tire and Parts, a business in Matewan presided over by Don's brother Anthony. Apparently, Loeb found, five relatives of the CEO worked for A-A Tire.

And why, Loeb opined, had Massey Energy promised Don the company-owned house in Sprigg as a retirement gift? "No one else at the Company gets free housing," Loeb declared, "much less an entire home as a retirement gift. What kind of example does it set when a CEO who makes $33.7 million in a single year is given free housing while the Company is having difficulty retaining its mine workers?"

The Jefferson Hotel, where Massey Energy convened its annual shareholders' meeting on the morning of May 16, 2006, was one of the jewels of Richmond, Virginia. "The most magnificent hotel in the South," its owners had dubbed it a century ago, "and unsurpassed in the north." A San Simeon–like castle of a place with fanciful towers, a fountain out front, and vast, ornate public spaces within, the Jefferson had opened in 1895, burned to the ground six years later in the worst Richmond fire since the Civil War, and reopened two years later to a parade of celebrity guests that came to include everyone from Charlie Chaplin, Thomas Wolfe, and Scott and Zelda Fitzgerald to Elvis Presley. Down the carpeted steps of its rotunda, flanked by vast faux-marble columns and graced overhead by a motif of tobacco-leaf vines against the vaulted ceiling, shareholders and executives of Massey Energy passed like royalty into the Grand Ballroom for their annual meeting. As they went inside, they were handed notices about the rules of decorum. Anyone violating those rules would be asked—or forced—to leave. Clearly, the organizers feared that mountaintop-mining activists might somehow sneak in.

The activists, in fact, were outside the building: a plucky dozen of them, including Judy Bonds, holding signs and chanting slogans as the corporate owners gathered within. In a sense, the real interloper was Daniel Loeb, conservatively dressed and waiting quietly in the front row for his appropriate moment. But in the days before the meeting, Don had decided to end the proxy battle by supporting Loeb's nomination. Now it was basically a fait accompli.

Under a massive chandelier, a seemingly chastened Don Blankenship introduced Massey's directors one by one. A short, owl-like man with glasses was Admiral Bobby R. Inman, U.S. Navy retired, former director of the National Security Agency and deputy director of the

Central Intelligence Agency. A tall, white-thatched and well-fed fellow near him was Dan Moore, an owner of West Virginia car dealerships who had run for governor of the state in 2004 while serving on Massey's board. A professorial fellow with a bow tie turned out to be Gordon Gee, former president of Brown University and currently the chancellor of Vanderbilt University. The directors were getting a good deal from Massey, and the company was getting a lot of clout and connections from them.

After invoking the dead miners at Aracoma and making a case for the company's "hundreds of safety enhancements," Don turned to the environment. "I know we're criticized for our supposed lack of concern," he said. In fact, the lands and waters under Massey's stewardship were improving, due to improved practices in surface mining. "Only 2 percent of streams in central Appalachia have been impacted by surface mining, and the industry actually creates more streams and wetlands than are lost."

Following this statement—completely at odds with the scientific conclusions of the EIS on mountaintop mining and its effects—Don showed a number of slides of bucolic valleys: mountaintop-mining sites that had been reclaimed as grassy meadows. "The bird and animal habitat, as you can see from these pictures, is not destroyed forever, as some would have the public believe," Don said. "Instead, the lawsuits, hyperbole, and misrepresentation only serve to increase the cost of electricity for average Americans who often can't afford the extra expense." The scenes in the slides were indeed pastoral. What went unsaid was that the meadow had replaced a ridge of exquisitely diverse, midtemperate forest that had had a complex prehistoric ecosystem of flora and fauna.

"Coal, simply put, provides for a better *total* environment," Don concluded, "an improved environment that includes homeland security, a job, health care, educational opportunities—as well as clean air and clean water."

Now came the meeting's top item: voting on whether or not to extend the terms of three directors on the board. "As you are aware," Don said, "Third Point LLC gave notice to the company to propose an opposition slate [and] has put forth two nominees as directors. Is there a motion for those nominees?"

Loeb came over to the microphone set up in the center aisle in front of the stage. "Good morning, Mr. Chairman," he said pleasantly.

Don nodded, as if the most routine business in the world was being conducted and not a direct challenge to his thirteen-year chairmanship.

Loeb nominated himself, along with Todd Q. Swanson, and went back to sit down. Don had not gone so far as to support Swanson's nomination, too. He was doing all he could to block it. Still, Loeb felt cautiously optimistic that two seats, not one, would go to the dissidents. He needed to be: with Massey's stock down after the rocky first quarter to about $35 per share, the hedge-fund populist had lost, on paper, nearly $50 million of his $218 million investment. Weeks would pass before the results were announced.

With business concluded, the chairman opened the floor to questions—not one of his most favorite duties, but one that was, by order of the Securities and Exchange Commission, unavoidable for all public companies. As he'd suspected, a trio of shareholding environmental critics came one by one to the microphone for their allotted two minutes each. But the critics weren't angry activists, like Judy Bonds, or lawyers, like Joe Lovett. They were nuns.

The three were in ordinary clothes, not habits, and had round, cheerful faces. Each described visiting West Virginia towns in the vicinity of Massey mountaintop-mining operations and seeing water, air, and communities contaminated. "How is our company going to become accountable to the communities in which Massey Energy operates," asked Sister Joellen Sbrissa of the Sisters of St. Joseph, "so that our company can be true to its mission statement of being responsible citizens and responsive to the needs of the environment?"

Gordon Gee, the Vanderbilt chancellor, stood up in his capacity as head of Massey's environment and public-policy committee to answer Sister Sbrissa. "I will tell you that the company has taken very seriously the issue of environmental safety and concern," Gee said, his brow furrowed in earnestness, his bow tie slightly askew. Gee said his own wife talked to him all the time about Massey's environmental policies. "I assure you that we will be doing everything possible so that in a tough environment we do precisely what is right for West Virginians. . . . I would not serve unless I felt I could personally make a difference." Gee's sentiments seemed sincere, but with Massey running up violations each week even now at Aracoma, Sister Sbrissa was left to ponder just how they might translate into action.

When the questioners had finished, Don brought the meeting to an end and came down to mingle with some of the dozens of dark-suited Massey executives who had come in a show of corporate force. Without quite meaning to, he drifted over to Dan Loeb, and for a few minutes the two made conversation, as casually as if discussing where to dine together that night. Don gently touched Loeb's arm a few times, and the two shook hands warmly as they parted. "It's not personal," Loeb told an observer. "And Don understands that."

In the foyer outside the Grand Ballroom, Don repaired to a corner with a few of his colleagues. The high arched windows of the Jefferson Hotel were set off with white muslin curtains. Frowning, Don pushed a curtain aside enough to get a glimpse of the street below. For a long moment, he looked down at Judy Bonds and her ragtag group of chanting placard-holders across the street. He gazed down not with annoyance but curiosity, as if by looking long enough he might understand just why they would engage in an exercise so obviously futile.

Two weeks later came the initial results of the proxy vote: Daniel S. Loeb was now a director of the board of Massey Energy. The company issued a tight-lipped announcement that Todd Q. Swanson had fallen short of nomination, but the dissidents begged to differ. In fact, Swanson had won enough votes to gain his seat, but Massey claimed the votes had been counted incorrectly and turned to the independent election inspector it had hired to oversee the process. After some weeks of deliberation, the inspector declared the vote to be correct. Swanson *had* won. In response, Massey declared it would challenge the election in the Delaware Court of Chancery—Delaware being where Massey was incorporated. It also announced it was adding a seat to its board and appointing to that seat one of the two directors who had just lost.

Don Blankenship was losing his cool, perhaps along with the absolute power he'd wielded at Massey Energy for fourteen years. Even if he managed to bat down Swanson's bid for a seat, Don would now have to endure the humiliation of hearing Daniel Loeb urge the board to consider issues and strategies Don preferred not to address, starting with his own grossly inflated compensation. The board could outvote Loeb, of course, but Loeb and his fellow investor Barry Rosenstein had the power of their stock and the potential, if their suggestions weren't adopted, to get other activist investors elected to the board.

Change might not come overnight, but it was in the air.

TWELVE

TURNING A COURTROOM
LOSS AROUND

Something very curious had happened with Joe's suit against the U.S. Army Corps of Engineers over Nationwide 21.

True, the Fourth Circuit had batted it down, reversing Judge Goodwin's ruling. Strictly speaking, Joe and Jim had lost. But in a chess game where one side had all the powerful pieces and the other had only pawns, sacrificing a pawn or two could, on occasion, entrap a queen.

When Joe and Jim had filed the suit in the fall of 2003, they'd hoped they could keep the issue tied up in court for at least a year, maybe two. That had happened: the Fourth Circuit hadn't reversed them until Thanksgiving 2005. In the meantime, hedging their bets, coal operators had gone the individual-permit route instead. They didn't want to apply under Nationwide 21, only to have Joe and Jim prevail in court. So one small victory was that no more Nationwide 21 authorizations had been issued between the fall of 2003 and Thanksgiving 2005. Lots of fresh ridgetops had been razed in that time, but all under old permits. New Nationwide 21s would have meant much more destruction.

The curious thing was that no Nationwide 21s had been issued *after* the Fourth Circuit's reversal, either. Why hadn't the reversal brought a flurry of new applications? That was where the game got interesting.

Judge Goodwin had based his ruling on just *one* of Joe and Jim's arguments for why Nationwide 21 was illegal, and that was the argument the Fourth Circuit had quashed. The Fourth Circuit's ruling had freed the lawyers to go back to Judge Goodwin to argue the *other* reasons. And they were doing just that.

This was disconcerting to the lawyers for Massey Energy and other West Virginia coal companies. They had read the coolly reasoned complaints. Whether or not they sensed in their hearts the points were persuasive, they suspected Judge Goodwin would find them so. A summary judgment ruling on one or more of these remaining merits might again be swatted down by the Fourth Circuit, but that would take more time. In that extended period of uncertainty, a coal company would be ill-advised to apply for a Nationwide 21.

By law, as Joe knew, the Corps had to review the Nationwide 21 permit every five years. In 2002, they'd subjected the permit to as little scrutiny as possible and blithely renewed it. That wouldn't be so easy in 2007. Joe's suit had made clear just how many ways Nationwide 21 violated the Clean Water Act. The Army Corps might well have to do a whole EIS on it involving lots of scientists outside the Corps' crenellated battlements. That would take more time. With the greater attention being paid to mountaintop mining in the media—thanks to lawyers like Joe Lovett and activists like Judy Bonds—the results of that EIS would be very public. The Corps might have a very tough time renewing Nationwide 21, even in the current administration. Joe had a pretty good idea what any coal company lawyer would advise his client to do under the circumstances: steer clear of Nationwide 21 altogether.

As a result of the Goodwin ruling in July 2004, the Corps had begun issuing individual permits almost as cavalierly as it did Nationwide 21s. But Joe had foreseen that. That was what his new suit was about: showing that the way the Corps issued individual permits was just as illegal as the way it issued Nationwide 21s, perhaps *more* so. If he won, he would force the Corps to subject each individual permit application to an EIS, as the National Environmental Policy Act (NEPA) required. If it did that, Joe knew, the Corps would have a very hard time justifying *any* new large mountaintop-mining operation.

Joe and Jim's arguments against IPs were pretty much the same as those against Nationwide 21s, only stronger, because of the greater scrutiny required in granting them. The more studies the Corps did for each IP authorization—or, more accurately, failed to do well—the more glaring its violations of NEPA and the Clean Water Act in granting IPs at all. Joe pounced on an application from a Massey operation that had just been approved. Aracoma wanted to start a new mountaintop site, Camp Branch, which would bury 15,059 feet of valley streams under four valley fills and four sediment ponds. In all, 915.9 acres of biologically diverse forest would be disturbed. The proposed site lay just one-third of a mile from the community of Ethel. Yet the Corps had declared that "the proposed project does not significantly affect the quality of the human environment and an environmental impact statement need not be prepared."

In their complaint, Joe and Jim pointed out that Camp Branch would completely destroy the site's aquatic environment. As usual, the Corps endorsed the notion that this damage could be "mitigated" by creating a man-made channel somewhere else. But even now, no such new stream in Appalachia had been made to work. The Corps had also ignored the downstream effects of valley fills—the increased levels of coal-associated mineral elements such as selenium, which in large quantities could cause reproductive failure and other ills in a wide array of aquatic life. And as usual, the Corps had ignored the cumulative effect of adding these valley fills to a region already riddled with mountaintop-mining sites.

For all these reasons and more, this new suit demanded that the Corps rescind this permit and prepare a full-scale EIS.

The Corps was furious with Joe now. Only by submitting FOIA requests and threatening to sue for noncompliance could he and his tireless aide-de-camp, Margaret Janes, learn anything about new permits. Through FOIAs in the fall of 2005, they had forced the Corps to admit it had just granted Massey another individual permit for surface mining in the Coal River valley. This one, a new Black Castle operation, would affect more than five thousand feet of streams and 521 acres of land. In amending his suit to include Black Castle, Joe pointed out that valley fills already covered 6.7 percent of the watershed in which it would be placed.

By the time Joe embarked on a series of terse exchanges with Bob McLusky in March 2006, he'd added a third new Massey site to his

list, again after filing FOIA requests with the Corps. Massey was calling that one Republic No. 2. Just northeast of the Coal River valley,
this operation was newly permitted to bury 9,918 feet of streams and
affect 753 acres of forest.

Joe had brought his suit in Huntington, on the state's western border, because the planned mines lay within that district of the Corps.
The judge he'd drawn, Robert Charles Chambers, was a former Democratic Speaker of the state legislature and a Clinton appointee. So far,
most of Joe's dealings with McLusky and the judge had been by conference call and e-mail. McLusky had been vague when Joe asked him
exactly what work had commenced at each of the three sites. Either he
didn't know, or, perhaps, he didn't want to know. Now the judge insisted McLusky be specific.

At Camp Branch, McLusky reported, two valley fills were well under way. Same for Black Castle. Republic No. 2 was a newer operation.
One of its valley fills had been timbered and grubbed, meaning that
trees had been clear-cut, then yanked out by their roots. Overburden
from the mountaintop above would soon be blasted and shoved below.
A second fill, though, had just been timbered, not grubbed. McLusky
agreed on Massey's behalf that the company would stop on the second
fill and no more significant work would be done at any of the three
sites until November 2006. By then, Judge Chambers would presumably have held his trial on individual permits and issued his ruling.

On March 17, 2006, McLusky e-mailed Joe to confirm that no
more work would be done at Republic No. 2's second valley fill. In particular, no grubbing would be done. Five days later, he e-mailed Joe
again. This time he attached photos showing that grubbing *had* occurred at the second fill. The photos had been taken on March 17.

Once again, McLusky's assurances had turned out to be at odds
with the truth. It was the same old game, Joe felt. If Massey did
enough damage to its sites quickly enough, there wouldn't be enough
landscape to save. The balance of harms would tip to the coal company: the investment it stood to lose by stopping work on the site
would outweigh the environmental harm the plaintiffs would suffer,
since the valley was already destroyed.

Within twenty-four hours of receiving that e-mail and photo, Joe had
his motion for a temporary restraining order before Judge Chambers. He

wanted work stopped at all three sites. Judge Chambers granted the TRO the next day, but the lawyers kept negotiating until they agreed that no new work of any *significance* would start at any of the three sites.

Joe hadn't meant to single out Massey. His target was the Army Corps of Engineers; his goal was another programmatic ruling that would affect all new mountaintop operations. Massey just happened to have three new IPs in counties where Joe had plaintiffs. But for one of those plaintiffs—Coal River Mountain Watch—Joe did take time that March to fight specifically with Massey, once again over the second silo behind Marsh Fork Elementary. After months of delay, the Surface Mine Board finally convened its hearing on the issue. There, too, as if in a real-life version of Whack-a-Mole, was Bob McLusky.

The day before, a circuit judge had ruled on the wrangle that had delayed the hearing month after month. The judge declared that any communication between Governor Manchin and the DEP relevant to the silo squabble should be released to the public, as Massey had demanded. "The choice is clear," the judge declared, "and it is in favor of open government." The DEP would appeal, but let its Surface Mine Board hearing proceed in the meantime.

The hearing had more than a few elements of farce. McLusky declared that the seemingly migrating western boundary of Goals was defined not by those conflicting maps but by a marker set in the ground. The marker had been placed in the early 1980s, more than a decade before Massey took over the operation. Weeds had all but buried the marker, until Goals's workers went looking for it. "There is no question," McLusky declared, "that if that marker is used, as we think it must [be], as the boundary, that the coal silos, both of them, are clearly inside of the line."

Unfortunately, as Joe explained, the ground marker recently unearthed by Massey was nowhere near where it was indicated to be on a 1982 map of the site. Ever since, Massey had ignored the marker and submitted maps with that migrating western boundary line. "The [Surface Mining] Act doesn't say anything about markers," Joe said drily. "It talks about the maps. The company has an obligation . . . to submit an application that is complete, accurate and in compliance with the Act."

With little hesitation, the Surface Mine Board ruled that the DEP had been entirely within its rights to rescind its permit for the second silo at Goals. On the issue of the first silo and whether it, too, lay outside Goals's property boundaries, the board remained silent. Joe would have to pursue that issue in court. Massey did have the right to reapply for a silo permit, the board observed. If it did, though, it would have to be very sure its western boundary was properly placed—and that the second silo it wanted to build somehow fit inside that boundary.

Judge Chambers had set a Tuesday in June as the start of trial in Joe's individual-permit suit. A tall, athletic figure in his fifties with a wry, no-nonsense manner, the judge always started his trials on Tuesdays. That way no one had a Monday-morning excuse for not being in attendance. As the trial date approached, Joe attached yet another new Massey IP—a fourth one—to his suit. Since the Corps refused to inform him of new permits without an FOIA request, he'd struck a deal with the Department of Justice, whose lawyers were representing the Corps. *They* would send Margaret Janes copies of any new permits at the same time the Corps sent them to the coal companies that had applied for them. In late April, the Corps sent Massey an IP—and Justice duly sent Joe a copy—for a site bigger than any of the other recent ones sanctioned so far. Laxare East would be in Boone County, in the heart of the Coal River valley. It would bury several tributaries of the Coal River under seven valley fills and eight sediment ponds. It would bury 24,860 feet of valley streams—six miles in all. The Corps had approved this new project despite the fact that at least twenty-two mines covering nearly sixteen square miles in that same watershed had already received or applied for mountaintop-mining permits. "Within the Coal River Basin where the Laxare East Mine is located," the newly amended complaint observed, "the cumulative impacts of mountaintop removal and other surface mining operations are devastating."

The permits kept coming, but Joe felt more than ready for them. He couldn't wait for this trial to start. Of all the suits he'd brought in nearly a decade of fighting mountaintop removal, this one seemed the strongest. So specific were the Corps' duties in deciding whether to grant an IP, so flagrantly had it ignored them, that even the Fourth Circuit's most conservative judges would have a hard time conjuring fresh pretzels of logic to defend the Corps.

Perhaps that was why, just days before the trial, the Corps took an astonishing and unprecedented action: it suspended the permits.

In a telephone conference, one of the Corps' lawyers informed Judge Chambers that the Corps had decided to study the permits further in order "to consider issues raised in the complaint." With that, all new work sanctioned by those permits was halted. Until further notice, not one more tree at those four vast sites could be clear-cut, its trunk grubbed and discarded, not one more sediment pond built to nudge the operation that much closer to blasting. Mountaintop mining at those sites was no longer permitted.

Joe didn't know what to think. If his suit had produced a true change of heart in the Army Corps' engineers—or at least their lawyers—well, fine. But somehow, after battling the Corps for all these years and encountering resistance to his requests for public documents even a month before, Joe had his doubts that the Corps had undergone a spiritual conversion.

More likely, the Justice Department lawyers had realized that the Corps' record was indefensible. For months, the lawyers had pushed Judge Chambers to block outside experts from testifying. They wanted the suit to be defined entirely by what the Corps felt was appropriate action. If the Corps said in its permit for a mountaintop site that stream damage could and would be mitigated by creating new streams elsewhere, the judge would have only the Corps' declaration that this could be done—because that was all that was in the record. Joe had argued that in order to prove the Corps had acted in an "arbitrary and capricious" manner, he had to bring in outside experts to show, for example, that stream "mitigation" was a fantasy. The judge had sided with Joe. Outside experts and evidence would be part of the trial. The Corps' lawyers had realized that when the record was hit with the bright light of scientific fact, they would lose.

The lawyers might have gone ahead anyway, hoping for a reversal from the Fourth Circuit. But they couldn't just count on the Fourth Circuit anymore. J. Michael Luttig had just resigned from the bench to become senior vice president and chief counsel at the Boeing Corporation. Joe's en banc request had drawn that passionate dissent from three of the circuit's judges, any of whom might be chosen on the next appeal. Even a conservative trio would need to hear *some* semblance of a case from the government. And the fact was that the government had none.

Once again, Joe had done the near impossible: he'd forced a moratorium on all new permits for mountaintop mining in southern West Virginia, both Nationwide 21s and IPs. In all likelihood, the Corps would come back after tinkering with its IPs and proclaim it had now done all the scrutiny needed to grant them. The Corps' record would be fattened with documents from scientists hired by the coal industry—how they justified their skewed conclusions to themselves, Joe could only wonder. In the trial that unfolded after all, their phony findings might not impress Judge Chambers—Joe had to hope for that, at least. But they would provide a reed of logic to the Fourth Circuit Court of Appeals.

If Joe did beat the Corps in federal district court—for the fourth time in a row—he knew what he wouldn't do after that. He was older and wiser than when his Haden 1 suit had halted Arch's vast Spruce No. 1 out by Pigeonroost Hollow. Soon enough, he knew, the mining industry would say the freeze on permits was forcing it to lay off workers, just as it had done with Spruce No. 1. Miners would be bused to Charleston to march by the capitol steps. Senator Byrd would take to the Senate floor to cry, "Fie on this judge!" This time, Joe would move his pawns with more care. He would do what he could to be sure no workers were laid off as a result of the suspended permits—maybe strike a deal with the Corps that some work could proceed after all. To make a court victory stick, he now knew, he would have to win, or at least not lose, in the court of public opinion.

For the moment, Joe was back on top—or as close to the top as he could be. But he had a way to go before he could start worrying about what it might mean to stop mountaintop mining once and for all.

THIRTEEN

A WALK THROUGH
WEST VIRGINIA

J udy Bonds and her band at Coal River Mountain Watch had a way
to go, too, but they, like Joe, felt a shift in the winter and spring of
2006, a small shimmering sense of hope.

For starters, they had a new ally. In the summer of 2005, a New
Orleans lawyer named Kevin Thompson had breezed into the valley,
set on fighting mountaintop mining in a whole new way. Thompson
was a class-action lawyer who felt he could show that mountaintop
mining had damaged the health of local residents. He had grown up in
West Virginia, the grandson of state troopers on either side, both of
whom taught their children and grandchildren to hate King Coal. He'd
never met Joe Lovett, but Lovett's relentless campaign had inspired
him. So had Brian Glasser, the Charleston lawyer who'd won the Dustbusters case. Both, Thompson felt, had proved to the downtrodden
coalfield residents that they could take on coal companies and win.
That was crucial: without plaintiffs who thought they could win, a
lawyer set on social change couldn't bring a suit.

Thompson had caught the attention of Judy Bonds and CRMW
with a suit on behalf of Mingo County residents who lived near
Massey's Rawl Sales, where Don Blankenship had gotten his start.
Dates were hard to establish, since Rawl claimed its records were lost
or destroyed, but right about the time Don arrived at Rawl in 1982, the
company had begun injecting slurry into old underground mines as a

cost-saving measure: it was cheaper than building an impoundment. Slurry injection was the practice that Tony Sears had managed to fend off at Green Valley in the late 1990s. The residents around Rawl hadn't been so lucky. Billions of gallons of slurry had been injected into mined-out seams right above the aquifer they relied on for drinking water. A DEP inspector in 1994 had confirmed that their drinking water contained slurry and ordered Rawl to begin providing bottled water. More than a decade later, the residents of Rawl were still fighting to get that water.

Thompson had agreed to represent the residents on contingency, as Brian Glasser had done with the residents of Sylvester. Under West Virginia law, a citizen who had been exposed to a toxic substance that increased the risk of disease could ask the court to have the alleged polluter pay for medical monitoring. Getting a judge to invoke that law was another matter, but that was Thompson's goal. If medical monitoring disclosed a link between the slurry and any symptoms, Thompson could then sue Massey for damages.

While Thompson was teeing up that suit, Judy and Bo put him in touch with families whose children attended Marsh Fork Elementary and got sick a lot. After meeting with the parents and children, Thompson decided Marsh Fork Elementary warranted a class-action suit of its own, one that he would undertake, as in Mingo, on contingency. Thompson wanted medical monitoring for his plaintiffs' children. He wanted the Goals coal silo removed. He wanted a trust fund established that would pay for all of Marsh Fork's schoolchildren to be routinely tested for various cancers. And he wanted personal-injury damages to compensate the parents for medical expenses they'd incurred on behalf of their children.

Thompson was in the Coal River valley when Hurricane Katrina hit. He drove straight home to his wife in New Orleans, stopping only to buy a generator. In the midst of the storm, but before the levees broke, he boarded up his house and drove his wife to Memphis. Neither his house nor his office was badly damaged.

By October, Thompson was back in coal country, bringing yet another suit against King Coal, this one against Arch Coal for using a farmer's property as an industrial dump. When a jury awarded Thompson's client $2.5 million, Judy and Bo and their fellow activists began daring to hope that Thompson might wring some meaningful money out of Massey Energy, too.

That fall, at Thompson's instruction, Bo Webb watched trains for six weeks. He watched them rattle in empty to Goals's 168-foot silo and roll out heaped with coal. They left every Monday and Wednesday, with a third train departing either Thursday or Friday, sometimes both days. Bo counted at least sixty to seventy cars in each train. That meant Goals was moving two hundred or more coal-filled cars per week. If Thompson's suit got to court, experts would debate the amount of dust that might be released by so much loading and whether it might affect the health of the schoolchildren. But counting the cars was a start.

Next, Thompson got a court order to allow him to take dust samples both inside and outside the school. The judge let the school's administrators choose the day. They chose Martin Luther King Day 2006, when no children would be present. The preceding weekend, Bo saw a flurry of activity at the school, with lots of cars parked by the entrance each day. He felt sure a major cleanup was being conducted.

The holiday was bitterly cold, so cold that Bo's hands froze even stuffed in his jeans pockets. At the appointed hour, he went to the big tree by the school's front fence. Kevin Thompson was there. So was a science professor, Scott Simonton of Marshall University, vice chair of the state Environmental Quality Board, who was the plaintiffs' sample taker. Rounding out Thompson's group was Jack Spadaro, the former mining inspector and administrator. Massey was represented by a lawyer—one more junior than Bob McLusky—as well as a scientist and, for reasons not quite clear, a hulking security guard.

"The first thing we need to do," Thompson announced, "is take water samples from the Coal River both above and below the prep plant." The unlikely group fell into single file along Route 3. Thompson had noticed that his team was wearing work boots, while the Massey representatives were all in dress shoes. He leaned over to whisper to Bo, "Take us on a really nasty way to the river."

Bo led the group a quarter mile up the road, then cut down through a patch of briar bushes toward the river. The Massey lawyer and security goon hesitated, then chose to stay on the road while Scott Simonton and the reluctant Massey scientist climbed down the riverbank to take water samples. Solemnly, the group then walked single file back along Route 3 to the school. The scientists took water samples from behind the building, downstream from the prep plant. Then they went inside.

The school, as Bo had predicted, looked glistening clean. The scientists went first to the gymnasium, where each took swabs off the bleachers and walls. They took more swabs in different classrooms. At Bo's suggestion, they made a point of seeking out the classroom closest to the Goals silo. Its door was closed, but the janitor opened it, and the group filed in. Bo asked the janitor to take the front cover off the room's air conditioner. There was black dust all over it. Simonton took his sample and then turned to the Massey scientist. "I saved some for you," he joked.

"Looks like there's plenty for both of us," the Massey scientist replied drily.

Simonton sent his samples to Dewey Sanderson, a fellow professor at Marshall University, who put the samples under a microscope to see if they were coal dust. Sanderson, a geologist, analyzed seven swabs from different places in the school. All had coal dust on them. Sanderson made no effort to determine how much coal dust was on each swab, only that coal dust was there. He did note that the particulate sizes of the dust were very small. All were below ten microns. The federal government had never established standards for how much coal dust in the air constituted a danger to human health, or what size particulates would be cause for concern. Underground coal miners took their chances in the mines and filed for disability when they got black-lung disease or silicosis. No one had thought that standards were needed for coal dust aboveground, certainly not to protect children. But the EPA did say that generally, toxic particulates of fewer than ten microns posed a special threat to human health. The body's immune system could deal with larger invaders; it could coat them with phlegm and have the body cough them out. But smaller particles evaded those defenses, and settled more easily, and deeply, in the lungs, where they could induce asthma, respiratory illnesses, or even black-lung disease.

Simonton wasn't surprised by the findings. He'd read a British study of children with significant respiratory problems living three thousand meters from coal facilities. Marsh Fork Elementary was about three hundred meters from the Goals prep plant and no more than one hundred meters from the silo. He did find it curious that in the months after the school visit, the Massey scientist chose to remain silent about his own findings.

For Bo and Judy, the only question was how to announce Simonton's findings as loudly as possible. Once again, the steps of the state capitol seemed the perfect venue. One morning in late May 2006, Bo Webb and Ed Wiley, along with a contingent of Coal River residents, held a press conference. By now they were quite good at facing a bank of television cameras and reporters. They'd also learned the value of a good PR stunt. Their mentor in that regard was former state senator Ken Hechler, now in his late eighties but still as outspoken about surface mining as he'd been in the early 1970s, when he advocated banning the practice altogether and held a ten-pound bologna aloft while giving a speech to illustrate his point that the coal industry was talking baloney. Bo and Ed had brought several pillowcases full of pennies: eighty-six pounds in all. They declared this the start of their Pennies of Promise campaign. The governor had said the state had no money in its budget to build a new school on a safe site for the children of Marsh Fork Elementary. Fine, then: the residents would raise the money themselves. They wouldn't just take excuses from the governor while their children kept ingesting tiny particles of coal dust.

After the press conference, Bo and Ed carried the sacks up to Governor Manchin's outer office and asked to present them to him. Not surprisingly, the governor was running a bit late in his appointments, a spokesman said. The spokesman wasn't sure the governor would be able to greet his visitors in person.

Ed Wiley, taller than the spokesman by at least a foot, looked down and nodded. "That's all right," he said. "We'll wait."

By coincidence, a middle-school orchestra had set up on another set of the capitol's steps to perform for the governor. When the governor swept back to his office, he found the Coal Valley contingent waiting for him. Graceful and telegenic as ever in a dark suit, his dark hair perfectly coiffed, the governor did an excellent job of appearing pleased to see his visitors. But his visitors were no longer impressed by his presence or his perfect manners.

"We've tried to work with you for two years, and we've been ignored," Ed Wiley declared bluntly. "Now we're raising money ourselves to build a school."

The governor thanked him for the fund-raising effort.

"We need you to be the leader you are," Bo said, "and help these kids get a new school."

Not a trace of irritation passed across the governor's handsome face. "You do agree there's a procedure to go through," he asked, "don't you?"

"That procedure has failed," Bo replied.

"But our problem is we don't want to overstep the Board of Education," the governor said.

"You're a higher power than the Board of Education!" Ed boomed.

"You're going to go down in history as the governor who didn't get those kids out of that school," Bo said.

The governor nodded. "We're going to do everything we can," he said. "I have children and grandchildren. . . ."

Reporters had followed the governor to his reception area and recorded the awkward scene as it unfolded. They followed him now as he left the Coal River residents and passed through a corridor to his inner office. One reporter asked him if it was true that studies of the school had been ignored.

"I have to find the answer to that," Manchin said, still graceful under pressure. "If it wasn't done, why wasn't it done? And if the tests were done, did they just not like the results? I've been to the school, and anything I can do to help . . ."

The reporter nodded. "It *is* in a curious location," she suggested.

The governor seemed to nod, then turned, slipped into his inner office, and closed the door behind him. Since the Sago mine disaster of early January, he had pushed through a strong state bill requiring new safety measures in mines. That bill had led directly to a federal version that President Bush seemed ready to sign. A national survey had declared Manchin America's most popular and effective governor, in large part because of his Clintonian empathy in the wake of Sago. But with the residents of the Coal River valley, the governor couldn't seem to catch a break.

For the next two weeks, Bo did his best to keep up the pressure with e-mails and press releases about Pennies of Promise to state lawmakers, journalists, and neighbors. The flurry of updates seemed to come from a whole posse of activists at Coal River Mountain Watch, but mostly it was Bo on his own, waking up at 5:00 a.m. and turning on the computer in his streamside trailer. The trailer was set in a steep, curving hollow of peach trees called, sensibly enough, Peach Tree. Bo's forebears had bought this land and much, much more along headwaters of the Coal River for fifty cents per acre in the early nineteenth century. A lot of it had been parceled out over time: in the last generation alone, Bo's father had been one of fifteen children, his mother one of fourteen. Bo had settled his modest lot only a few years back. Like a lot of West Virginians, he had spent the decades between his military service and early retirement in a large Midwestern city—Cleveland, in his case— because that was where the jobs were. He'd planned to spend his retirement back in the coalfields, sitting with his wife, Joanne, on his homemade deck with stream-chilled beers, but mountaintop mining— and Massey—had made him angry and kept him that way. Once he'd started working with Judy at Coal River Mountain Watch, he'd grown so passionate on the subject that his grown daughter, Sarah, and her husband, Vernon Haltom, had been inspired to move back to work full-time for CRMW, too. They lived in another trailer on the property, set back from the stream. They didn't wake up as early as Bo, though.

Ed Wiley woke up early, too, down at his own streamside house in Rock Creek, a few miles south, so he was into his first cup of coffee when Bo called in a quiet panic. "I've been doing all I can," Bo said, "but we've got nothing new, and I can feel this campaign dying. We can't let it die." Presenting that sack of pennies to the governor had been a great press play, but where to go from there? So far, they'd raised about five hundred dollars. A new school would cost about five million dollars. They'd need a lot more pennies to make Pennies of Promise a story again. What fresh gambit could they dream up to keep the governor from ignoring the students and their plight?

Ed hung up and walked around outside for a while, thinking about it. He was planning a new garden beside his house, and he started pacing off its dimensions. That gave him an idea. He went back inside, past the mounted head of a buck with eleven-point antlers that he'd bagged in nearby Sandlick, and called Bo back.

"What if I walked from the Capitol building to Senator Byrd's house?" The press could follow along, and when he reached Byrd's house, Ed could knock on the door and ask to speak with him directly.

"Great idea," Bo said. "The only problem is that Senator Byrd is never in West Virginia. He's in Washington."

Ed paused. "So I'll walk *there*."

"But that's hundreds of miles." As the men would soon learn, the distance between Charleston's capitol building and the nation's capital on back roads was, in fact, 455 miles.

"So?" Ed said. "I mean, the farther, the better, right?"

Bo started poring over maps. West Virginia accounted for much of the distance, and most of that was rural. Almost immediately out of Charleston, Ed could take two-lane blacktops, passing through a lot of national forest with campgrounds along the way. A support vehicle could drive ahead with camping gear and meet Ed at each day's destination. The logistics were easy enough. But was Ed up to the challenge? Towering and sinewy, with not an ounce of fat on him, he could still clamber up a mountainside, gun in hand, in search of deer or wild turkey. But he did no regular exercise, he smoked a pack of cigarettes a day, he had acute stomach pain every morning—he thought it might have come from working around slurry impoundments—and, as the local news stories kept observing, he was, at forty-nine, a grandfather.

A small crowd of well-wishers gathered in the Charleston parking lot of the capitol—and the governor's mansion, beside it—to see Ed off on the morning of August 3, 2006. Along with Bo and Judy Bonds and the rest of Coal River Mountain Watch, as well as Vivian Stockman and other members of OVEC, a dozen reporters and television crews were there as Ed stood on the capitol steps with his wife, Debbie Jarrell, to explain why he was undertaking his walk. Ed, as usual, was in blue jeans and a T-shirt, with a camouflage-patterned cap bearing the logo of H. S. Strut, a vendor of turkey-shooting paraphernalia. Ed hadn't thought to ask the company for sponsorship money. It was just his hat.

As he set off, Ed shouldered a large aluminum flagpole with the deep blue, handmade flag he'd decided to carry the whole way. Made by students at Marsh Fork Elementary, it showed the school, overshadowed by the coal plant; a shining sun in the middle; and the U.S. Capitol. Below the flag were the words "Every child deserves a safe and healthy school in their community." Without the flag, Ed felt, he'd be just another guy walking. With it, he was like a one-man army, marching off to battle. Another flag on the pole, this one small and white, read simply: "All Talk and No Action = Gov. Joe Manchin."

A few of the well-wishers accompanied Ed for the first few miles, but then he was alone, a man with a flag on Route 119 North. When the pole began to chafe his shoulder, he put a towel under it. When the flag end kept pulling down behind him, he tied a good-sized rock to the base to balance it. But when a wind came up, there was nothing to keep it from buffeting the flag like a sail, tilting Ed one way or the other.

That first day, Ed walked about sixteen miles to reach a roadside park on the Elk River. The support vehicle was waiting for him. Ed felt good. He felt even better taking that flagpole off his shoulder. His only worry was his feet. A sporting-goods company had donated three pairs of expensive boots for the walk, but Ed had had only a week or so to break in the first pair. Already, they were pinching his toes. He'd felt awfully grateful for the gift, but when he looked at his reddened toes, he wasn't sure how much farther he could go in those boots.

By the next day, news stories generated by the start of Ed's walk had popped up all over the state. Drivers honked their horns as they sped by and gave him the thumbs-up sign. Ed had been right about the flag: it made all the difference. Almost everyone seemed to recognize him, and everyone who did seemed pleased to see him. Young men in pickups, mothers with their children in SUVs, truckers in their semis—all greeted him as they passed. Even policemen in their patrol cars gave him a smile and a wave. That night, after almost twenty miles, Ed rode back in the support vehicle to the Elk River campsite: it was the only place to stay in those first thirty-five miles. The next morning, the vehicle took Ed right back to where he'd left off.

After two days of fairly flat terrain, Ed passed through the town of Clay and encountered his first foothills of the Allegheny Plateau. From now on, he'd have hills most of the way. On the downhill slopes, his boots pinched badly. After confirming that evening that every one of his toes had grown blisters, he traded the boots for a pair of comfortable old sneakers. Even so, he was to walk in pain for days. His stomach hurt him, too. Often at home he felt bad for two hours after waking. Now he had some homeopathic remedy that eased the symptoms. But he worried it might not work for long.

In the Alleghenies, Ed passed through thick copses of walnut trees, cedars, peach trees, and pawpaws. Often hours passed without a car from either direction. Still, Ed kept carrying the flag. The sounds of the forest awed him. Even at his house in Rock Creek, plumb at the dead end of a dirt road, the outside world intruded: television, computer, the Jake Brakes of passing trucks half a mile away on Route 3. Here the only sounds of the outside world were his breath and his footsteps on the blacktop road. He did have a cell phone in the sack that hung from one shoulder, and occasionally it did ring. A dozen days and 180 miles into the walk, it rang with the welcome news that Massey's second appeal for a new silo behind the Marsh Fork school had been quashed by the DEP.

This time, Massey had submitted survey maps based on the overgrown boundary marker the company said it had found in the ground. Those maps showed that the second silo lay within Goals's western boundary line. The DEP agreed with that interpretation—it no longer had a problem with defining the western boundary by an old marker rather than the maps. But the DEP now disagreed with Massey's contention that the second silo was the expansion of a preexisting operation, namely coal storing. Massey said that coal storing had occurred on the property before the passage of SMCRA in 1977, and thus the silo was exempt from SMCRA's rule that no coal facilities be built within three hundred feet of a school. The DEP disagreed, noting that in photographs of the site taken in 1977 there was no silo or coal-storing operation of any kind. In this decision, the DEP simply ignored the first silo, but by its own logic, as Joe Lovett had observed, that silo was just as illegal as the second one.

Ed could enjoy this small bit of good news, but he knew it would soon be eclipsed by Massey's next move. Almost certainly, the coal company would appeal the decision to the Surface Mine Board. If the board backed the DEP, Massey would drag the fight into court, as far as the company's lawyers and Don Blankenship's money could take it. Meanwhile, the children of Marsh Fork Elementary would remain in the shadow of Goals's slurry impoundment and towering coal silo.

More than once in the dog days of August, Ed walked through steady rains. Even in the mountains, the heat was often stifling, the air heavy with humidity. But when his blisters healed and his stomach symptoms stabilized, he knew he'd make it. His only fear was that he'd get all the way to Washington and not be able to meet with Senator Byrd.

Three times now, Ed had called Byrd's office, to be told with growing firmness by a secretary that the senator would be gone until after
Labor Day. Congress was on vacation. Here Ed was walking to Washington because he'd thought Byrd would be there and not in West
Virginia. Now he might get to Washington and learn Byrd was still in
West Virginia. The one person he knew who could get him to Byrd
was Davitt McAteer, the Clinton-era MSHA director who was also conducting Governor Manchin's investigation of the Sago mine disaster.
But McAteer, Ed had learned to his dismay, was on vacation, too.

By the time he reached Shepherdstown, a university town in the
state's panhandle, Ed was three days ahead of schedule. He'd stopped
in other towns along the way, handing out pamphlets about Marsh
Fork Elementary and talking to anyone who would listen. But Shepherdstown was his best stop yet. The support vehicle had brought
along a large placard he'd made with pictures of Marsh Fork Elementary and the coal plant behind it. When Ed stood on the streets of
Shepherdstown with it and his flag, passersby gathered to hear him
speak. A professor who taught public speaking invited him to address
his class of fifty students, and Ed accepted. At one point, Ed went into
a barbershop to chat up the customers and barbers alike—a captive
audience if ever there was one, as any number of politicians had
learned before him. Many of his listeners made small donations; a
state trooper slipped him twenty bucks. Ed earned nine hundred dollars for the cause in Shepherdstown. In all, he would net more than
five thousand dollars. That was pretty impressive for a guy with a flag.
But he still needed his audience with Byrd.

It was in Shepherdstown that Ed had a small epiphany. McAteer
worked in Wheeling, but he also had a law practice in Shepherdstown.
When the thought hit him, Ed found the office listed in the Yellow
Pages and hurried over to knock on the door. A secretary informed him
that McAteer had just returned from his vacation. And yes, she confirmed after a moment, he would see Ed.

In truth, McAteer had probably felt a bit reluctant to call Byrd on
Ed's behalf. He knew all about the impoundment behind Marsh Fork.
He probably knew more about impoundments and their danger than
anyone in the state. McAteer knew Ed, too, as the guy who had stood up
at local gatherings McAteer held around the state to talk about coal im-

poundments. Ed had a way of asking questions that McAteer couldn't answer. McAteer had a lot of respect for Ed, exasperating as he could be, but his relationship with Byrd was a precious resource. McAteer had a lot of ideas for how mining might be made safer and less destructive, and Byrd had the power to put those ideas into practice. McAteer didn't want to jeopardize those ambitions by urging the senator to meet with a fellow in blue jeans and a T-shirt who might ask combative questions.

Sitting across from him, McAteer felt his fears recede. Ed was still a little rough around the edges—a Coal River character, for sure—but he spoke from the heart. "Okay," McAteer said at last. "I'll make the call." The next day, when Ed checked in again with Byrd's office, the secretary sounded warmer. "He knows all about your walk," she said, "and we've put you on the calendar. But please understand: that doesn't mean he'll see you. Things come up every day around here that force us to cancel appointments." Ed said he understood.

Every day for more than a month, Ed had gotten honks of approval as he walked. Now, as he crossed the narrow walkway of Harpers Ferry bridge over the Potomac River into Maryland, he felt the support fall away. No one here knew why he was walking. Commuters whizzed by, focused on nothing more than getting to work. Trucks roared just inches from him, stirring crosswinds that tore at his flag and spun him around. He might have been the reincarnation of John Brown for all anyone cared, re-creating his ill-fated arsenal raid to inspire a Southern slave rebellion. His own mission seemed just as quixotic.

On his last full day of walking, Ed covered nearly thirty miles, the last of it in gathering dusk on busy Route 50, to reach Washington and the motel where he was staying for his final night. The next morning—September 13, 2006—he headed over to the Arlington Memorial Bridge for the last hour's walk through downtown Washington to a press conference in front of the Cannon Building. A handful of well-wishers and documentary filmmakers were waiting for him. When the Lincoln Memorial appeared over a rise, most of the group marveled at it. Not Ed, though. The last time he'd been to Washington, he was eight years old, he told the others. He'd been excited then. No longer. "That monument means nothing to me," he said sadly. "The wars are all about money, and none of those lawmakers do what they say they will.

I have respect for what the monuments stand for, but not what they've come to mean."

Ed was still carrying his flag as the group marched up Independence Avenue. At the Cannon Building, half a hundred more people were waiting for him. They'd come from as far as Charleston and Richmond. After a short address, he walked over to the Hart Building, where Senator Byrd kept an office. Ed handed his flag off but went up to the entrance with his white poster-board display in hand, accompanied by his wife, Debbie, and the documentary filmmakers who hoped to follow him inside. Two big security guards looked without expression at the strange assemblage and at Ed in the forefront, still in his blue jeans, T-shirt, and H. S. Strut hat. They wouldn't even let Ed go through the security scanner.

A call to Byrd's office brought down three young, officious-looking staffers. After a few whispered words, the guards relaxed. Ed was ushered through the scanner and allowed to take his poster board with him. Debbie followed, along with the filmmakers. The staffers led the way upstairs to the senator's offices. "We want you to know that the senator is looking into this," one of the staffers said, indicating Ed's display when they settled themselves in the reception area. "But we won't have an answer for you today. This is a county and local problem, and the senator is federal. It's not as easy as you might think." The staffer sighed. "If you wanted five million dollars for a new road, we could give you that right now. You don't even need to meet the senator. We can do that."

Ed thanked the staffers for their kind offer of a new road but said a new school was what he needed. After calling ahead, the staffers led the group to the underground subway that linked the outlying office buildings to the Capitol. At the Capitol, the staffers led the way down long, red-carpeted hallways hung with oil portraits, and under the Capitol dome with its frescoes of Christopher Columbus' landing, the Wright Brothers at Kitty Hawk, and other key scenes from American history. Ed started to feel awed in spite of himself. Finally they ushered Ed and his entourage into a large, red-walled room hung with gilt-framed portraits and furnished with silk-covered sofas. Senator Byrd was waiting for them, standing in front of his desk and leaning on his two canes.

At eighty-eight, Byrd was a Washington monument himself: a Democratic congressman from 1953 until 1958, a senator ever since. If he won reelection to a ninth term in November, he would become the longest-serving senator in U.S. history. Perhaps inevitably with a record so long, he was a figure of contradictions. He remained haunted by his early association with the Ku Klux Klan and had nearly lost his first congressional race after it was revealed. Yet he'd apologized for it ever since, and in a recent autobiography of nearly one thousand pages, he had ruefully acknowledged the stain that his youthful mistake had left. Recently, Byrd had offset his late support of Vietnam with early eloquence on the folly of George W. Bush's war in Iraq. The first senator to denounce the imminent invasion, he had seemed to many a bit of a crackpot at the time. Now, more and more, he seemed the voice of hard-earned wisdom.

A proud figure of modest height, dapper with almost delicate features and still-thick white hair, Byrd fixed Ed with a keen eye and nodded a welcome. The staffer introduced Ed and Debbie and indicated the others behind them. The senator seemed a bit put off by the cameras at this private meeting but nodded for the whole group to come in.

"We've already been warned there's nothing you can do to solve this today," Ed said, "but we're grateful to have a chance to explain it all to you."

"I'm going to listen to what you have to say," the senator said in a gentle, courtly voice, "that's for sure."

Ed had assumed he'd get five minutes, ten at most, so he launched right into his speech about the school, holding his poster to show the senator as the cameras filmed him. The senator remained standing, leaning on his canes, and listened with interest. After a short time, however, he turned to one of his staffers and indicated he'd had enough of the cameras. Ed assumed the meeting was over. It wasn't. The senator turned to him and smiled. "Let's sit down and talk," he said.

The entourage was gently dismissed. The door shut softly. Only Ed and Debbie remained with the senator and his staffers.

"Tell me about your walk," Byrd said. "I've been on the Hill a long time, and I've never seen dedication like this." He laughed. "How many pairs of shoes did you go through?"

Ed talked about the people he'd met along the way and then about the students at Marsh Fork and how they kept getting sick. Byrd grew somber. More than once, in talking about the preciousness of children and family bonds, he mentioned his wife. Byrd had nearly set a record for marriage as well as public service: he had been married to Erma Ora James for nearly sixty-nine years. The two had met in grade school. Ora had died the previous March at eighty-eight, and the senator, a strong Baptist in later life, talked of how much he wanted to see her again. "I'll be joining her soon," he said.

Ed kept the focus on the Marsh Fork children, but he talked about the need to protect other children from mountaintop mining as well. Maybe a new bill was needed, but maybe not: three or four enforcement laws were already on the books, starting with SMCRA. The problem was that those laws were bent or ignored in West Virginia. Byrd listened quietly, nodding as Ed talked. The senator had always supported the coal industry—he could hardly do otherwise in a state where coal had all the money and most of the power. Both he and the state's other longtime Democratic senator, Jay Rockefeller, supported mountaintop mining. But both had lately acknowledged dismay at some of coal's cruelest costs. Rockefeller had been appalled by the bankruptcy-court decision that cut all health benefits for the miners of Horizon Natural Resources and was working to pass a bill that would keep that sorry scenario from ever occurring again. Byrd had found three million dollars for Davitt McAteer's statewide study of impoundments and seemed to appreciate the risks they posed. And here he was this morning, listening hard to Ed. Finally he held up his hands and turned to his staffers. "Give me something!" he said to them. "What can I do for these people?"

The staffers stammered about various possibilities, though none of them seemed a sure bet. Byrd let his hands fall and turned back to Ed. "We'll leave no stone unturned," he said. "That I promise."

There was a moment of silence. Then Byrd said, "I want us to pray."

In the meeting, Ed and Debbie had acknowledged that they, too, were Baptists. Ed's father, in fact, had been a Free Will Baptist preacher. Now they, along with the senator, bowed their heads. The staffers a bit uncomfortably followed. Byrd recited a prayer of faith.

In the elevator, one of the staffers turned to Ed and shook his head in amazement. "There were a lot of firsts today," he said. "First that you even got into the Hart Building dressed like that. Then that you got in to see the senator for a whole hour on a constituent matter. I've never seen that happen. And in ten years of working for him, I've never seen the senator end with a prayer. He really, really wants to help you." The staffer sighed. "We have to find something."

A week or so later, Ed opened his mailbox to find a two-page personal letter from Senator Byrd. The senator thanked Ed for his commitment and called Marsh Fork Elementary a "dangerous situation" that needed redress. He went on to echo a line from his prayer. "The Bible teaches us that if we have the faith of a mustard seed, we can move mountains. I believe you have that faith. I sympathize with the situation that these children and their teachers at the Marsh Fork Elementary School face, but I know that you do not want sympathy. You want help."

By chance that same week, the EPA announced it had tested for coal dust at Marsh Fork Elementary. No signs of excessive dust had been found, the agency said, either inside the school or on its property. The tests were begun before a coal train was loaded at the silo, with results monitored through the loading process and for hours afterward. The loading, EPA inspectors concluded, did nothing to increase particulates in the air.

No action was deemed necessary by the EPA.

Perhaps Senator Byrd would take note of the EPA's report and conclude that Ed Wiley and his fellow Coal River activists were well meaning but misguided. Or perhaps he'd find a way to help after November, assuming he won reelection to an almost certainly final term. After more than half a century in office, he would be free at last of coal-industry clout, able to act exactly as he wished. Perhaps then he would see his way not just to moving the school to placate his constituents but tightening enforcement throughout the coalfields. For now, though, Ed Wiley had only the senator's letter, with its stirring words and a big, bold signature in black, while just up the road, another school year had begun at Marsh Fork Elementary.

Kevin Thompson was finding, too, that change took time in the coalfields. While Ed had been on his walk, the New Orleans lawyer had battled Massey up and down the courts in his Rawl Sales class-action suit over drinking water contaminated with injected coal slurry. Over the summer, a judge had ruled that Massey must start providing water on a weekly basis—immediately—to Rawl's beleaguered residents. The judge had also ruled that Massey must stop—immediately—its twenty-year practice of injecting slurry into the ground. Massey had filed various appeals to stay those injunctions in state supreme court. All had been rejected without argument. Even Judge Maynard, the judge known to be personally close to Don Blankenship, had sided against Massey on those appeals. So the injunctions stuck, and that was progress. But a trial for Thompson's class-action suit would not begin, the judge declared, for more than a year: October 16, 2007.

Thompson had brought enough class-action suits to know that that was a reasonable date. Massey had indicated that it wanted to depose all the plaintiffs, up to six hundred of them, and that would take months. Thompson felt, though, that the underlying purpose of doing all those depositions was to intimidate the residents. Being deposed, especially for a backcountry West Virginian who'd never seen the inside of a courtroom, was a scary prospect. Thompson would have to hope that his clients were angrier than they were scared.

At least in that case he had a lot of plaintiffs from which to choose. On the class-action suit he was putting together at the same time against Massey for contamination of children at Marsh Fork Elementary, he now had to depend on just one. Of the three families he had hoped to enlist as plaintiffs, two had dropped out. That left just Sherry Pettry, single mother of Corey, who had graduated from Marsh Fork Elementary a few years before, and Tyler, who still attended it and stayed home from school on antibiotics dozens of days a year. Massey had challenged her fitness as a plaintiff because she'd acknowledged suffering recurrent anxiety as a result of her relationship with one of the boys' fathers. One day that September, Thompson put her on the stand to ask her, before a district judge, if her anxiety might prevent her from all the obligations a plaintiff had to assume, starting with the cross-examination that a Massey lawyer was about to conduct. "It does make me nervous," she said, "because I know he's going to hammer me. But I know I have to gut it out for my kid." When the Massey lawyer did try to rattle her, asking if she could really represent the suit's whole class of plaintiffs, she took a deep breath and said she could.

The judge seemed satisfied with Pettry's testimony, but months would pass before he issued a ruling on whether she was, in fact, fit to serve as a plaintiff and whether the case could proceed. If she was, and if it did, Thompson didn't expect a trial to start until the summer of 2008.

With its endless motions and appeals, delaying as long as it could the trials it didn't want to face, Massey was a formidable foe. Over in Huntington, though, the lawyer who was Thompson's role model for court battles in the coalfields had once again done the near impossible: he'd brought the enemy to trial.

FOURTEEN

BACK IN COURT
AGAINST THE CORPS

$\mathbf{A}$ ll rise."

Just after 9:00 a.m. on a Tuesday in October 2006, Judge Robert Charles Chambers swept into his high-vaulted courtroom in Huntington to greet an audience of some three dozen. Most of those who hastened to stand were lawyers and coal-industry representatives, with a smattering of curious others behind the rail. Among the defense lawyers was Bob McLusky, ever alert and spry—hardly a day older, it seemed, than when he stood to represent Massey Energy in Haden 1 more than seven years before. At a table that faced the judge, Joe Lovett stood for the plaintiffs, along with two new legal partners, Steve Roady and Jennifer Chavez of Earthjustice. Joe was still close to Jim Hecker, but Trial Lawyers for Public Justice was relieved to let another nonprofit pay the bills for a change. The fight against mountaintop mining was not only endless, it seemed, but endlessly expensive.

This was work that took a toll, and yet Joe seemed as chipper today as his old nemesis ten feet away. Neatly dressed in a dark gray suit, he launched into his opening statement with hardly a look at his notes, his hands on his hips like a young professor exuding a quiet but unmistakable confidence. For more than a year now, Joe had been yearning to get this case to court. The four mines whose freshly issued permits he was challenging were all Massey mountaintop sites—that was why McLusky was there, as a lawyer for the "intervenors"—and Joe would be lying if he said he didn't take a special pleasure in targeting the most offensive of

Appalachia's coal companies. But at last he had his chance again at the big black bear behind Massey: the U.S. Army Corps of Engineers.

For a few brief weeks in June and early July, Joe and Margaret Janes had wondered if the Corps would surprise them this time. Perhaps after yanking those permits to review them, its lawyers would see how flagrantly the Corps was violating the Clean Water Act, not to mention the National Environmental Policy Act. Instead, the Corps had merely reissued the permits with modest cutbacks: a valley fill at Laxare East and two at Black Castle were eliminated. Each of the four sites at issue had several more valley fills; their effect on the landscape would barely be diminished. Recently, Margaret had discovered a fifth new Massey permit application in the works. It, too, was now attached to the suit.

"We will show," Joe declared of the individual-permit process, "that the Corps issues these permits through a veil of half-truths and evasion and pseudo-science." Remarkably, he pointed out, the Corps had made the same conclusion from its in-depth IP review as it always did from its Nationwide 21 reviews: none of these sites would have a significant impact on the environment. In doing so, Joe argued, it had violated the Clean Water Act's 404(b)1 regulation, which clearly forbade valley fills that did cause significant impacts. Most egregiously, the Corps had declared that whatever damage occurred to U.S. waters would be offset by re-creating stream channels at the sites, creating new ones, or just "enhancing" other streams. Yet the Corps could point to no stream-creation plan in Appalachia that had worked. And enhancing other streams was hardly compensation for streams destroyed. "The Corps has actually taken the position that its permits, which allow the destruction of thousands of acres, will *benefit* the environment," Joe said. He asked the judge to strike down the five Massey permits at issue. What Joe didn't say was that he and his Earthjustice co-counsels hoped Judge Chambers would stop the Army Corps from granting IPs altogether in the way it did, at least within the Southern District of West Virginia. They wanted the judge to require the Corps to prepare a full-blown EIS for every IP application it considered, as the law required.

The Corps' chief government lawyer, Cynthia Morris, was a short, tough-looking, stocky woman with a surprisingly musical voice. "The Corps did determine that discharges would not cause undue effects on human population and the aquatic environment," she said sweetly. "We have boxes of records here in the courtroom." She pointed to them, lined up on a bench against one wall like so many coal-train cars. "The plaintiffs assume that all these permits are the same. But each has its own administrative record. Each decision is based on different data. These aren't rubber-stamp approaches. In each case, the Corps has approved a project considerably smaller than that proposed by the permittee."

Morris suggested that at any rate, little was at stake. "The court will see that the waters that are subject to the Corps' jurisdiction for these projects are not abundant, flowing streams teeming with fish," she said with her cheery lilt. "The impacted streams are ephemeral streams and intermittent streams, often dry, not supporting fish life.

"The Corps is entitled to deference," Morris concluded, "because it has reviewed the record."

There it was—that unmistakable Army Corps logic that popped up in all these trials. The Corps had reviewed the permits and chosen to grant them, so the Corps must be right.

Morris surrendered the podium to McLusky, who supplied the coal industry's own favorite rationale. "The coal these mines will provide will equal a quarter to a third of West Virginia's annual production of coal—forty million tons," he told the judge. "Six hundred jobs are also at stake, for five to fifteen years, at an average salary of sixty thousand dollars. Last year, the coal industry paid West Virginia two hundred and eighty million dollars in coal severance taxes. If these permits are denied, that will come down significantly." Joe could have closed his eyes and been back in Judge Haden's courtroom, listening to virtually the same words nearly a decade ago—the same words, he might have added, that had no basis in law. Nowhere in the Clean Water Act did it say that environmental standards should be waived to save jobs and boost tax revenues.

Along with the many cardboard boxes of supporting records, the Corps had provided thick white three-ring binders of information for each mine—the combined decision documents, as they were called. For Joe, just figuring out which aspects of the process to focus on had been a challenge. He'd decided to start with the big picture—an overview of the whole geographic area due to be affected, as if seen from above—then zoom in to the effects of surface mining on a particular watershed and, finally, even more closely, to its effects on a headwaters stream. Ultimately he wanted to show why the Corps' approach to stream mitigation—on which, as he put it in his opening statement, the Corps' whole house of cards rested—was so thoroughly flawed.

To be effective, Joe knew, he had to use his witnesses like chapters in an unfolding story. For his prologue, he called Vivian Stockman of the Ohio Valley Environmental Coalition, who talked about hiking through the watersheds Massey had targeted. Stockman and the other members of OVEC were Joe's plaintiffs, so he took care to establish that many of them, including Stockman, lived in West Virginia, near enough to the sites at issue that they had legal standing. On cross-examination, McLusky asked Stockman if her main purpose in traveling the coalfields was to document mountaintop mining, as if that was a less-than-legitimate reason to be there. But he was just going through the motions. He knew the case would hardly turn on plaintiffs' standing.

For his first chapter, Joe had a perfect witness in Doug Pflugh, a geologist and geographer who used state-of-the-art technology to make area maps for Earthjustice. Pflugh had plugged in all available data to see how much of the overall Coal River watershed was covered by surface-mine permits. The answer: 13 percent. Then he'd mapped Laurel Creek, a smaller watershed within Coal River where two of Massey's mines—Black Castle and Laxare East—were planned. No less than 29 percent of the Laurel Creek subwatershed was covered by permits. In that area, 18 percent of the first-order streams were gone or slated for destruction. On cross-examination, there wasn't much McLusky could do to dispute those numbers. He asked as few questions as he could and sat back down. Joe could tell he was biding his time. But for what?

With the overall picture set by those maps, Joe tightened his focus. Jennifer Chavez of Earthjustice called Dr. Keith Eshleman, a preeminent hydrologist from the University of Maryland. Eshleman seemed the perfect choice to tell chapter 2 of Joe's story: what surface mines actually did to Appalachian watersheds.

For starters, Eshleman explained, surface mines increased rainwater runoff. Instead of infiltrating the ground cover on top of a mountain and being somewhat contained by it, the water just sluiced down-hill—eroding soil, swelling streams, sometimes flooding the towns below.

Eshleman had read the binders the Corps had issued for each of the mines. He couldn't understand, he said, how the Corps had concluded that runoff would *decrease* during mining or during the "postmining" period when the company was obligated to reclaim the ravaged land. "The Corps has just plugged in arbitrary curve numbers for soil quality and runoff that produce the answers they want," Eshleman declared. "The curve numbers for post-mining are wholly unreasonable."

Eshleman was talking about numbers used on a graph to determine how much rainfall might be expected to run off a mountaintop site before mining, during mining, and after mining, when the land was reclaimed. A hydrologist started with a "curve number" between 1 and 100 for how much rainfall and runoff a particular mountaintop site might be expected to receive in its natural state. From that, he extrapolated estimates of rainfall and runoff for the mining and postmining stages. Of course, the lower the curve number at the start, the lower the estimates for the later stages would be. Massey's consultants had exercised, in Eshleman's view, a lot of leeway in the curve numbers they chose.

"Isn't that like choosing the answer to your question?" Chavez asked.

"I don't know if it's like choosing the answer to the question," Eshleman said, "but I think what you mean is, perhaps, is there the potential for bias to come into the process of selecting the curve number."

Eshleman had another problem with the Corps' "rosy scenario," as he put it. Massey said on its permit applications that it would reclaim its blasted sites with eighteen inches of topsoil. That, the Corps said, was enough to support new tree growth. But as Eshleman observed, research done by the leading expert on reforestation of Appalachian surface-mine sites, Dr. James A. Burger, had shown that four feet of topsoil were optimal. Burger also recommended using native topsoil. Massey said it would do so "as far as practicable." At one of its sites, it said it would use alkaline shale as a substitute. "I found that particularly odd," Eshleman said, "given the fact that Burger and his colleagues specifically noted that that was not the kind of material that would be most suitable for growing trees.'"

With a breezy smile, Bob McLusky came to the podium to cross-examine the eminent hydrologist. "I was a philosophy major," he started off, "so some of this stuff gets lost on me."

Massey's top lawyer was being too modest. He knew his curve numbers as well as Eshleman did, maybe better. Quickly he revealed that he'd found not one or even two but three experts in Eshleman's field whose articles suggested that the curve numbers Massey and the Corps had used were within a reasonable range—not ideal, perhaps, but reasonable. Eshleman himself had cited one of those experts. McLusky had found an article by that expert suggesting that runoff might actually decline after a site was transformed from forest to surface mine. "And the reason for that," McLusky held forth, sounding suddenly a lot more like a hydrologist than a philosophy major, "is because as we change the shape and the flow path of the water, the way in which it's distributed changes. Is that correct?"

"Sure," Eshleman blurted miserably.

At his plaintiffs' table, Joe resisted the temptation to put his head in his hands. Eshleman was toast. All McLusky needed to do was show that *some* experts—even one—endorsed or at least failed to reject the way Massey had set its curve numbers. With that, he could make the case that the Corps had given the thumbs-up to accepted methodology. No judge would stoop to parsing whether Massey or the Corps should have used one expert over the other. One was enough to establish the realm of deference that any judge would grant the government.

But McLusky wasn't finished. He knew all about the expert on reforestation that Eshleman had cited—the one who recommended four feet of native topsoil. "He's written articles that say you could do it with as little as eighteen inches, hasn't he?"

"I think he said that," Eshleman floundered, "but his recommendation is four feet."

"Right," McLusky nodded. "But the one that says eighteen inches, for example, says that would produce a highly productive forest with native hardwood vegetation, didn't it?"

How could the same expert who recommended four feet of topsoil say that eighteen inches were fine? There was a story behind that.

Burger, a researcher at Virginia Tech, had worked with Joe in helping rewrite West Virginia's rules on reforestation of mountaintop sites
as part of the Haden 1 settlement. As a result of those new rules, now
embedded in the Surface Mining Act, coal companies had to use native topsoil if they claimed they were going to reforest a mined site, and
they had to take other measures that might actually produce new tree
growth. Those measures cost money and time. The coal companies
didn't like that. They had grown much more annoyed in 2004 when Joe
went to the Surface Mine Board to argue that *all* strip mines in the
state ought to be bound by the Burger provisions. Arch Coal was Joe's
target in that hearing, since the company had just been granted a permit that allowed it to use a topsoil substitute not endorsed by Burger.
Just before the hearing, an Arch Coal official paid a visit to Burger's
dean at Virginia Tech and threatened to pull the company's funding of
the center that sponsored Burger's work. Burger was about to embark
on a new research project that might last for years. With one phone call,
Arch could kill it.

At the hearing, Burger was a no-show. Instead, none other than
Bob McLusky, representing Arch that day, stood up to read a letter
Burger had written to the board. Perhaps, Burger wrote meekly, the
soil Arch wanted to use instead would be fine after all. He added that
he was revising his latest research proposal to be sure it didn't run
"counter" to coal-company interests.

Suddenly, as far as Burger was concerned, whatever kind of soil
the industry wanted to use for reforestation was fine. And eighteen
inches of it instead of four feet? No problem. Almost certainly, Judge
Chambers knew nothing of this backstory. And there was no way Joe
could tell him, since it wasn't directly relevant to the case.

That evening, after a crestfallen Eshleman had driven home, his
testimony in tatters, Joe, Margaret, the Earthjustice co-counsels,
and the remaining expert witnesses gathered for dinner and a postmortem on the day. As penance, they ate at a very bad, brightly lit
Mexican fast-food restaurant around the corner from the Holiday Inn
where they were staying. "Tomorrow we're going to eat better," Joe said,
"but only if we do better."

———

Joe's confidence rose as his next witness, a white-bearded, potbellied professor with a more-than-passing resemblance to Burl Ives, took the stand. J. Bruce Wallace was a well-known entomologist and ecologist from the University of Georgia who spoke with a deep and beguiling Southern drawl. At sixty-seven, he'd made a life's work of studying headwater streams, their aquatic life, and what happened to that life when the canopy of trees above those streams was destroyed. The story of headwater streams was Joe's chapter 3. When Wallace talked, even the defense lawyers seemed to succumb to his sonorous descriptions.

What, Joe asked him, *was* a headwater, anyway?

"It's where the stream starts," Wallace said, "usually an intermittent or first-order stream." "First order" just meant the first tributary, like the farthest-out twig on a tree. "I'm thinking of three primary habitat types," Wallace suggested. "One would be sort of rock outcrops, where water flows over resistant bedrock." Usually a stream of that sort appeared from groundwater, high up in the mountains. "Another would be cobble riffles, areas of a somewhat lower gradient. And another thing I would expect are pools. A lot of those pools are the result of debris dams."

"Are these intermittent or dry streams of little value," Joe asked, "as Mr. McLusky said?"

Wallace shook his head. "Oh, no. They're rich with macro-invertebrates. You can see them with the naked eye. Insects especially. Stone flies and caddis flies, mayflies and dragonflies."

At Joe's prodding, the professor expounded on the whole complex food chain of headwater creatures. He talked about scrapers, which use algae as a food source, and shredders, which feed on intact leaves and woody debris, assimilating the microbes. "Collectors are another type," the professor went on. "They feed on the fine particles excreted by the shredders. Filterers find suspended materials in streams, filter them, take nutrients from them. Some even cast nets. And then you have predators. Dragonflies are an example."

When first-order streams were buried, Wallace said, this whole ecosystem was destroyed. But the damage was greater than that. "You bury the first-order streams, you've lost a big order of organic output to the overall basin." More than water flowed down the mountainside from headwater streams in an ever-broadening network of tributaries.

A whole aquatic ecosystem provided life for larger creatures below. All this, the Corps had appeared to ignore.

Now it was McLusky's turn. In his cross-examination, he could hardly dispute the professor's descriptions of stream ecology. Instead, he focused on a list of stream functions that Wallace had suggested would make better criteria for testing than the traits the Corps chose before deciding those headwaters were dispensable. "Are these *all* functions the Corps should have utilized?"

"I didn't say they should utilize all of them," Wallace said. "I said those are examples of functions."

"Okay," McLusky said. "I guess my question is, which ones should they have utilized?"

"Production would certainly be one that could be used," Wallace said. "Nutrient cycling could be used. Transport and retention could be used. Decomposition is fairly easy to measure. Organic-matter dynamics are certainly measurable without much difficulty."

"All right, that's fine," McLusky said impatiently. "What do you propose they do with all this stuff after it's measured?"

"Well, it will give me some idea of how that headwater stream is functioning before I bury it. And I will have some idea of what I'm losing."

McLusky pursued this line of inquiry for some time without rattling Wallace in the least. Finally he said in exasperation, "And how long would that take to do?"

"Maybe a year."

"What would the cost be?"

"Well," Wallace said in his best Burl Ives drawl, "compared to the cost of the coal, I think it would be very small."

The plaintiffs' next witness was Margaret Palmer. An angular and earnest woman in her late forties with decades of experience in her field, Palmer was director of the Chesapeake Biological Laboratory at the University of Maryland's Center for Environmental Science. She agreed with Wallace that simply measuring certain traits of a stream on one day, as the Corps had done, revealed virtually nothing. To understand a stream, you had to measure its functions over time and calculate their rate of change.

What did Palmer think, asked Joe's co-counsel Steve Roady, of the plan to "enhance and create" perennial streams in exchange for filling in intermittent and ephemeral streams?

"Enhancing another stream, or restoring a sediment pond to a stream—I don't see how that could replace a first-order stream," Palmer said.

"They also say they'll create streams," Roady asked. "What's your reaction?"

"It was very naïve and not credible scientifically," Palmer said. "There's no question that it's theoretically possible. But they didn't do even the most basic steps to think about how they would do that. Forget nitrogen uptake—they don't know the annual discharge and other basic criteria. Streams are not simply the movement of water downhill. Water, nutrients, and lots of chemicals are interacting in a complex way. How much water exchange is there? What are the water flow patterns? What is the impact from banks and groundwater?

"The Corps just says, 'We're going to re-create streams,'" Palmer added. "I don't have a single case of stream re-creation in my project overseeing streams around the U.S. I expected the Corps to cite peer-reviewed literature demonstrating that this is possible."

One of Bob McLusky's colleagues from JacksonKelly, red-bearded and petulant, strode up to the podium to cross-examine Palmer. Grimly, he slapped a paper on the overhead viewer. The paper was an academic study written by Palmer herself. "I call your attention to the summary," the lawyer declared. "In the summary, it indicates that little agreement exists on what constitutes a successful river restoration effort, is that correct?"

"That's correct."

"And it indicates that billions of dollars are spent annually on stream restorations, but there are no agreed-upon standards for what constitutes ecologically beneficial stream and river restoration."

"Uh-huh," Palmer said, nodding.

"And this article was authored in—what—2005?"

"Uh-huh."

"So am I to take it as of that date the practice of stream restoration was not standardized, that many different types of restoration were employed, many different measures of success were employed, and that there was no standardization?"

"There was no agreed-upon standardization," Palmer agreed coolly, "unlike the situation in what I've reviewed here where it was very clear at the very beginning what the standards of success were that were expected."

Irked, the JacksonKelly lawyer turned to Palmer's list of stream functions, which she felt the Corps should have examined. "It's different from the list that was provided by Dr. Wallace earlier," the lawyer said darkly.

"Not really."

"There aren't additions or deletions from his list?"

"No, because my title said this is a minimum list of potential functions that could be measured. In some cases we used a different word for exactly the same thing, such as respiration. Its measure is decomposition. That process is respiration. It's the burning up of organic matter, which uses oxygen. So no, they're not different."

The lawyer persevered. "Could another biologist come up with a different list?"

"Of basic functions?" Palmer paused. "I doubt it very seriously."

Another lawyer tried a different tack with Palmer. Just because stream restoration was a new and emerging concept that hadn't been studied to death in peer-reviewed articles, was that any reason to think it wouldn't work?

"No," Palmer said calmly. In fact, she thought it *would* work—eventually. But it hadn't even been tried yet. "What was surprising to me was that it was accepted as mitigation when it hasn't been shown it works, but more than that, that the basic things one would have to measure to see if it works weren't in there."

The lawyer went back to his table in a huff. He hadn't been able to lay a glove on her.

Joe stood up. "We're resting at this point," he told the judge. Joe had had more witnesses lined up, but he could see now they weren't needed. Together, Wallace and Palmer had told the third chapter of his story as clearly as anyone could.

That night, Joe celebrated with his team. The best restaurant in Huntington was said to be a place called Savannah's, so that was where, in the gathering dusk, he led a gang of about ten. Following him down the city's desolate sidewalks at dusk were his co-counsels and expert witnesses, as well as Margaret Janes and Cindy Rank, the activist whose opposition to mountaintop mining now spanned more than a quarter century. Rank had driven hours from her home to attend the trial.

The restaurant occupied a 1903 white clapboard house with a front porch and candlelit tables outside and in. The group sat inside at a long table in a cozy room, and Joe ordered the wine. Once, he recollected, he'd grown grapes on his farm for some local Italians starting a vineyard. Making wine in West Virginia was about as daunting a struggle as taking on the coal industry, but Joe had actually helped produce a vintage or two before the venture collapsed. Now his apple orchard was his pride and joy. He had his hopes set on having his three sons work the orchard as a going proposition in their high school summers, if he could keep the deer from destroying it first. They'd certainly need to do something, he mused, to defray the impending weight of all their college tuition fees.

Upon sensing a courtroom victory, another lawyer might have pondered the financial rewards: hundreds of billable hours at three or four hundred dollars per hour. But Joe was an environmental lawyer, and a small-town one at that. He would be paid at a far more modest rate. And as long as he stuck with his programmatic suits against the Army Corps, no verdict would bring him a financial windfall. His windfall would be the satisfaction of forcing a stubborn, monolithic government agency to change the way it issued its permits.

Behind that stubborn monolith, it turned out, was a very ordinary-looking man. As the first witness in the government's case, Dr. Mark Sudol identified himself as chief of the Army Corps regulatory program. He told the court he oversaw thirty-eight districts in the United States and 1,200 regulators. Sudol looked to be in his midforties, with a full head of short-cropped black hair, a steady, intelligent gaze, and a successful government bureaucrat's lack of any rough edges or quirks. But while he looked almost robotic, he spoke calmly and clearly, with an unexpected and rather winning directness. Sudol was a bureaucrat, but he wasn't evasive.

At his lawyer's prodding, Sudol spoke of the Corps' commitment to stream mitigation and of his own rule in improving its practices. As a junior officer based in Southern California, he had studied seventy sites of attempted mitigation around the state and seen that at least half of those projects had failed. He had made a lot of strong recommendations, and the Corps had embraced them all. More recently, the Corps had extended its bottom line of "no net loss of wetlands" to "no net loss of aquatic resources." Some streams *could* be sacrificed to mining and other necessities. But by mitigating those losses, the Corps could say at the end of each year that it had allowed no net loss overall. Mitigation might be a new science, Sudol allowed, but the Corps was doing all it could to meet that pledge.

Meanwhile, as Sudol observed, the Corps had to keep issuing permits. It couldn't hold off on permitting until the science of mitigation was perfected. In the last year under his leadership, the agency had issued ninety thousand permits nationally—not just for mining but for all activities that affected navigable waters. Specifically for surface mining, the Corps had received permit applications in the last year to affect thirty thousand stream-bearing acres in the Huntington district of West Virginia. The district had issued permits for twenty thousand of those acres, while prohibiting mining on the other ten thousand acres. For the twenty thousand acres it did permit to be affected, the Corps had required its applicants to mitigate fifty-six thousand other acres, mostly by enhancing other watersheds. To judge by those numbers, West Virginia's landscape wasn't being destroyed at all. It was *improving*.

As Joe went to the podium for cross-examination, he looked tightly coiled, his jaw set and his shoulders hunched, as if he needed all his self-control to keep indignation from getting the better of him. Crisply, he asked Sudol about an outing the bureaucrat had taken two days before—the first time Sudol had ever seen mountaintop-mining sites in West Virginia. On direct examination, Sudol had described viewing a "stream restoration site" at a valley fill. Joe was curious to know more about that project.

"What did it look like?" he asked.

"They put a—what we call a small channel anywhere from four to six feet wide," Sudol explained, "leading from near the top of the hill where there was some ephemeral runoff that went down the benches of the valley fill leading down into the valley."

"Can I inconvenience you to try to draw that?"

Sudol obligingly left the witness box to draw a semblance of the re-stored stream on a large artist's sketch pad propped up on an easel. What he drew was a series of zigzags down the page.

"Is that what it looks like?" Joe said wonderingly. "It's a zigzag like that?"

"Yes."

"Have you been in the Appalachian Mountains very much, Dr. Sudol?"

"No," Sudol replied. "This is my first two days down here."

"Have you ever seen a stream running down zigzag like that?"

"Down the face of a valley fill, no," Sudol conceded.

"In your limited experience looking at Appalachian streams, have you seen hollows where the streams sort of come down steeply and then flatten out like this one and then go steep again and another flat bench? Is that typical of a central Appalachian stream?"

"Not what I've seen."

"This really looks nothing like an Appalachian stream, does it?"

"Other streams I saw, no, it doesn't."

Sudol capped his black Magic Marker and went back to the wit-ness stand. He was so forthright that Joe felt almost sorry for him. Al-ready, Joe felt, Sudol was doing more for the plaintiffs than he was for the defense.

"Now, you said that this one didn't work," Joe said. On direct exam-ination, Sudol had readily acknowledged that while the stream seemed to function at the top of the fill, it then went "subsurface" and thus failed to meet the criteria of what a restored stream should be. "So what's happening now there? What's the Corps doing?"

Sudol explained that the project was two years into a five-year monitoring period. If the new stream fared no better at the end of that period, the Corps would either have to "fix the hydrology" or find a new site and start all over again.

Judge Chambers was curious about this, too. "This is an example of stream *creation*?" he asked.

"Yes, sir."

"Now," Joe continued, "is that the only example of stream creation in West Virginia that you know of that's been built so far?"

"That I have personally seen, yes."

Joe paused. "There's not a stream creation project in West Virginia on a strip mine that's working, is there?"

"I don't have any information on that," Sudol said.

Joe turned to another aspect of Sudol's direct examination that intrigued him. The government lawyers had submitted various documents, after reviewing them with Sudol, which underscored the strict standards the Corps applied to stream mitigation. More than one of the documents referred soberly to a "functional assessment" that the Corps should do, as part of the permitting process, of any watershed to be mined. A functional assessment was a detailed checklist of attributes in a particular environment that a Corps permittee should try to avoid harming. "This functional assessment," Joe asked. "It's not used in West Virginia, right?"

Unfortunately, Sudol acknowledged, the Huntington district did not have "an approved functional-assessment method."

"What do you mean?" Joe asked. "Who would have to approve it?"

Each region of the country, Sudol explained, had to go through its own functional-assessment process, involving various departments, other agencies including the EPA, and local academics to peer-review the results. The process took up to three years and cost between $200,000 and $1 million. "How far along are you in doing that in West Virginia?" Joe asked.

"We are getting ready to start that this year," Sudol replied.

Joe reminded Sudol that the Corps' history of obligation to do functional assessments dated at least to 1990. Joe held up a Corps document from 2002—Regulatory Guideline Letter 02-02—that reiterated that obligation. Didn't this guideline call for the functional assessment to be applied?

"Well, what it states," said Sudol, "is that it *should* be applied."

"And to this day," Joe said, "the Corps still hasn't started developing such a functional-assessment scheme for the state of West Virginia, is that correct?"

"Yes."

The reason, Sudol went on to explain, was that the Corps' budget had been flat or declining the last several years. Only recently had he found the funds to track how much watershed was being lost in West Virginia, much less to do the functional assessment.

What, Joe wanted to know, did Huntington's Corps officers do to assess stream impact *without* a functional assessment?

"If they don't have a functional assessment," Sudol said, "they can use best professional judgment, which is what they use to identify what is the value, the function of that habitat, and then does the mitigation appear to replace it."

What did "best professional judgment" really mean, Joe asked?

"Best professional judgment of functional assessment is you go out there as a trained biologist, bachelor's, master's, with on-the-job training, determine what you believe with your view, without measuring variables, without measuring attributes at all, measuring function, what you would perceive the value function of that wetland [or] that stream is."

So there *was* no standard for assessing streams or mitigating them, Joe persisted. Only what seemed right to a local Corps employee.

Only what seemed right, Sudol repeated.

The branch chief of those local Corps employees was the government's next witness. Lucile Virginia Mullins didn't need to explain why everyone called her Ginger: the curls that framed her round, soft-featured face made her look a lot like Little Orphan Annie. Earnestly, she described how her eighteen project managers went through applications. They might or might not make a site visit, but they waded through the paperwork, got all needed sign-offs from other agencies like the U.S. Fish and Wildlife Service, then brought the applications to Mullins for her approval. Because the district didn't yet have the functional assessment that Sudol had described, its managers went by a "one-to-one" standard. For every linear foot of stream destroyed, the applicant had to create, enhance, preserve, or restore a linear foot of stream.

Joe had heard enough about stream "creation" from Sudol. So when he had his chance to cross-examine Mullins, he asked how the "one-for-one" ratio worked if a coal company chose, instead of creating a stream, to enhance another one somewhere else. Putting boulders in a stream to change its water flow might be one enhancement, Mullins explained. Shoring up falling stream banks might be another.

"So a consultant comes to you and says. 'We found some streams somewhere in a much lower down watershed that usually has some bank problems, and we think that if we fix these banks, the Corps should give us credit for that and allow us to fill other streams.'"

"That could possibly be a scenario," Mullins agreed.

"And how does the Corps decide if those enhancement projects are equivalent to the fill?" Joe asked.

"They would be one-to-one."

Joe was amazed. "Surely you wouldn't suggest that because there's a bank that's unstable—and I'm not suggesting that those don't need to be enhanced, I mean, that's a fine thing, to stabilize a bank—but you're not suggesting that stabilizing a bank is equivalent to filling a stream forever, are you?"

"I'm saying that in terms of our requirements on a one-to-one, that enhancement is allowed," Mullins said. "And if they demonstrate enhancement is needed and it will benefit the reach of stream, then they are given credit for that."

Joe sighed. "You don't really have a method for making a decision about whether the aquatic functions lost in the streams buried are being replaced by the stream enhancement project, do you?"

"We do not have a proficient method at this time," Mullins replied.

Joe might have felt sorry for Ginger Mullins, too, as he watched her primly reclaim her seat, if not for the power she wielded to reshape Appalachia. Over the next ten years, Joe thought grimly, Ginger Mullins and her crew of uninformed bureaucrats would sit in their little Army Corps offices in Huntington and make decisions that literally determined the future of the central Appalachian region for thousands of years.

With Ginger Mullins's testimony, the Corps rested its case. Perhaps, Joe wondered aloud during a court break, the Corps' lawyers had assumed from the start that Judge Chambers would rule against them and were simply going through the motions in anticipation of a warmer reception from the Fourth Circuit Court of Appeals. But while the government was done, McLusky wasn't.

Rising again on behalf of Massey Energy, McLusky called Edwin Kirk, a biologist and mining consultant who had helped prepare Massey's permit applications for the mine sites named in the suit. Kirk was both smart and feisty. Throwing off scientific terms with aplomb, he talked of all the stream traits he tested for, using the EPA's rapid bioassessment habitat evaluation. "It's a ten-parameter habitat assessment that's widely used," Kirk explained. "And it rates things from riparian zone width, bank stability, to the type of substrate that's on the streambed." Kirk had used RBP-II, as he called the EPA's plan, to see exactly what was being lost in a stream about to be buried and to enhance other streams with some or all of those traits.

In the case of Republic No. 2, Kirk had found a nearby stream that was in truly terrible shape. "It is completely choked to death with a plant called Japanese knotweed, which is an invasive species," Kirk explained. It had erosion problems, it lacked pool habitats, and to top it off a road crisscrossed the stream at frequent intervals. Downstream, people had settled on either side, cutting the bankside trees down, mowing their yards to the water's edge. Kirk had made various fixes—putting in boulders, for example, to create pool habitats—and the result was a much-improved stream, one that had far more fish and macro-invertebrates in it than before.

On his cross-examination, Joe had a hard time pinning Kirk down. The biologist kept contradicting him and making a spirited case for RBP-II. Perhaps without meaning to, Judge Chambers was the one who dented the defense witness, merely by asking for one or two clarifications. Kirk readily admitted that his whole approach was about habitat: boulders and banks and soil and trees. "Other than habitat," the judge asked, "are you making up for anything that's been destroyed?"

"We have sampled . . . probably very close to a hundred existing valley-fill sites downstream of the fill," Kirk replied. "It's been my experience that you can, if the water quality is still fairly good, end up with a healthy benthic community below that valley fill in that pond." Some invertebrates, like mayflies, failed to make the transition. But usually, Kirk said, caddis flies tended to make up for the lack of mayflies. Since caddis flies were of the same functional feeding group as mayflies, nothing was really lost.

Chambers paused to take that in. "All right," he said. "Given your experience and training, what's your best estimate as to how long the enhancements would remain effective?"

"I would expect the life span on those to be easily twenty years," Kirk said.

Joe did his best to hide his amazement. In prepping for the trial, he'd asked Dr. Bruce Wallace how long this habitat-restoration stuff would last. Wallace had scratched his head and said maybe fifty years, but he also said not to rely on him; that was outside his range of expertise. Joe had decided not to raise the issue at all, for fear of learning from one of the Corps' witnesses that habitat restoration might last much longer than that. Now the judge had asked the question for him—and the answer was more damning than Joe could possibly have hoped. Was Kirk really suggesting that the burying of a mountain stream millions of years old could be offset by downstream habitat changes that lasted twenty years? He was.

McLusky's next witness, an aquatic ecologist named Donald Cherry from Virginia Tech, hastened to repair the damage Kirk had done. The bug population in stream waters directly below valley fills did change from those of the headwaters, he averred. But a bit farther downstream, the original bug populations reappeared. Partly that was because the tree canopy returned. McLusky handed Cherry a photograph of the biologist himself at a stream below a fill. "It's such a beautiful, breathtaking experience to walk in that area and see how natural it is below a holding pond," Cherry exclaimed.

McLusky turned his witness over to Joe with the hint of a grin.

"I went through your CV," Joe said briskly. "It looks to me like it's heavily funded by the industry. Would you agree with that?"

Cherry could not disagree.

On direct examination, McLusky had shown Cherry pictures of water-filled ditches below one of Massey's mountaintop sites. When the mountain was mined out, the ditches would be connected to mimic the valley's original stream. Yet already, as Cherry had marveled, the ditches had various bugs flitting about them. There were even cattails and grasses growing around them. Joe was curious about how that re-created stream would match the original. "It won't have the same functions, will it, because it's a much different kind of water body? Correct?"

"Correct," Cherry acknowledged.

"It's exposed, correct? It's not steep, correct?"

Cherry nodded.

"It's going to be sinuous, not straight, correct?"

"Correct."

"All those things make it not the functional equivalent of the stream that's being lost. Would you agree with that?"

Cherry sighed. "Yes, I would."

Joe was especially curious about the cattails in the picture that had pleased Cherry so much. "That's remarkable, that there are cattails in the mountains of West Virginia in the summertime," he observed.

"That's remarkable?"

"It's remarkable. I mean, you would never find that occurring naturally, would you?"

Cherry thought cattails might be found in the higher reaches of southern West Virginia, sure. But, he added, gesturing to the mine site in the picture, "I've only been to these type of sites, not to the natural ones."

"You've never been to a first- or second-order stream in the central Appalachians?"

"It's been a long time," Cherry managed.

Joe was astounded. Here was a West Virginia ecologist who couldn't remember the last time he'd seen a natural mountain stream in his home state. He'd never bothered to walk in the woods behind his house. And he had no idea that cattails grew in wetlands, not mountain streams.

The ponds that Cherry had admired so much, Joe asked, the ponds that would one day be linked up to form a stream: was it not true that they would be fed with fertilizer that provided nutrients for the macroinvertebrates?

Cherry did think that was in the plans, yes.

"And those fertilizer inputs are for a limited period of time, correct?"

"Uh-huh."

"But when the fertilizer goes away, that shot of nutrients will decrease, won't it?"

"Correct."

Joe paused. "If after fifteen years they're gone, all of this photosynthesis that you've based your whole theory on goes away, doesn't it?"

"Okay," Cherry replied.

"Now, are you aware that most of the ecological world tries to keep extreme nutrients out of water?" Joe asked. "There are all kinds of problems with farms and, you know, nitrogen and phosphorus and potassium and all those nutrients getting into streams because they degrade the streams, right?"

"Correct."

"And how do they degrade the streams?"

"In a process called eutrophication."

"And that's . . ."

"Overenrichment," Cherry said reluctantly.

"And that's exactly what's happening here, isn't it?"

"Right."

Even with all that nutrient pumping, Joe observed, ecological diversity below the valley fill would still be much lower than that above the valley fill, would it not?

Cherry agreed.

In particular, Joe said, salamanders from first- and second-order streams wouldn't make the leap over a valley fill to downstream waters, would they?

"I haven't seen any," Cherry acknowledged.

"So the salamanders are being buried by the fills, correct?"

Cherry looked a lot less sanguine than when he'd started. "Yes," he said.

With his last witness, McLusky came full circle to his one unassailable argument: big money would be lost if these mines weren't allowed to proceed. Michael Snelling, a Massey vice president, now attested to that.

Snelling ticked off the consequences mine by mine. At one, Massey planned to hire two hundred miners for five years to produce seven to eight million tons of coal. "If this lawsuit was not an impediment to mining, we would probably start that operation within the very short term, I would say within three to six months," he said. If the judge found for the plaintiffs, none of those miners would have jobs. The company, Snelling confirmed, had no other places for them. So it went with the other mines. In all, Snelling said, some 637 jobs hung in the balance, to produce fifty million tons of coal over the next decade or so.

If the mines were shut down, Snelling continued, Massey itself would lose more than the profits from mining all that coal. It would still have to pay royalties on land it had leased and pay for leased heavy equipment. As for the state, it would lose more than one hundred million dollars in severance taxes levied on the coal sold. Already, out-of-state investors were pulling back, mindful of how this suit could affect the West Virginia coal industry. They were putting their money instead into import terminals for coal from South America. "The other concern I have," said Snelling, "is that out west we're seeing new rail lines being put in to bring coal from the west to the east. So we're seeing an infiltration of western coal."

Joe needed only a minute or two on cross-examination to put all this into perspective. "Massey doesn't have the right to these permits, does it?" he asked. "They have to comply with the Clean Water Act and NEPA before the permits can be issued, correct?"

"We have to comply with all state and federal regulations," Snelling allowed.

"And your investors that you talked about, all these capital investors, they're very sophisticated investors, aren't they?"

"Some more than others, yes," Snelling replied.

"And they understand the risks associated with the permitting process, correct?"

"To some extent, I would say yes."

"When Mr. Blankenship, for instance, talks to shareholders at Massey Coal, he informs them about risk from litigation and permitting, doesn't he?"

This was, in fact, a standard disclaimer that Blankenship as CEO had to provide with every statement he gave analysts and shareholders. "At times we do," Snelling allowed.

Joe had no further questions.

Judge Chambers retired to wade through towering stacks of legal documents, starting with the suit's 1,200-page transcript. He said he hoped to issue a ruling by the end of December 2006, but New Year's Day came and went without a verdict. So did most of January, until a dramatic turn of events forced him to convene a courtroom session on a challenge that weighed directly on the suit.

Ever since Joe's landmark 1999 victory in blocking Arch Coal from starting work on Spruce No. 1, Arch had pushed to get individual permits. After all, Spruce No. 1 was reckoned to hold fifty-five million tons of coal. The company had waited as the federal government slogged through the long, dreary process of preparing the EIS. When a first draft had been peppered with scathing criticisms—Joe's prominent among them—Arch had endured more waiting as the EPA took it back for review. Finally, in the fall of 2006, the EPA had issued its new and improved draft. Joe had found this latest draft woefully deficient as well and commented accordingly. What had followed, from the federal government, was four months of silence.

By the terms of the settlement Joe had reached with the Clinton administration in December 1998, the Department of Justice was obligated to inform Joe of any new permits granted for mountaintop mining by the Corps. But the Bush administration had long since abandoned that pledge. So every week, Margaret Janes submitted FOIA requests to the Corps, demanding to know what mining permits the Corps had issued in the Huntington district. Even so, the Corps had said nothing about a forty-one-page record of decision issued privately on January 22, 2007, to Arch Coal. That document declared the EIS had been finished on Spruce No. 1, and that with certain modifications—only seven miles of streams would be buried, not ten—the largest mountaintop-mining project in the history of West Virginia could proceed under an individual permit.

The tip-off came, as usual, from a local resident. The resident—one of the last hold-outs of Blair, the town all but depopulated by Arch through the 1990s—had seen a nearby hollow being clear-cut and alerted Cindy Rank by e-mail. Margaret Janes, to whom Cindy passed on the report, was baffled at first. Then she looked at the West Virginia DEP's Web site and saw something strange: on January 24, the state had issued Arch a routine violation for work done on one part of the Spruce No. 1 site.

Pressed, the Corps admitted that yes, it had issued an IP on Spruce No. 1 two days before. And yes, the EIS had been finalized, too. Within hours of receiving its permit, Arch had cleared ninety acres. The DEP had written it up for doing that work without first constructing sediment-control ponds. This was a technical violation. The DEP had no quarrel with Arch for embarking on Spruce No. 1, and secretly at that, for it was in on the secret: another public agency hood-winking the public it served. Both the state and federal agencies had issued the permits in secret for one reason and one reason only: to keep Joe Lovett from blocking them again.

Once again, Joe rushed to court to plead for a temporary restrain-ing order to stop work in a stretch of mountainous West Virginia forest: not just ninety acres, he learned, but an additional seventy acres adja-cent to them. Tersely, he told Judge Chambers he needed time to show that the EIS for Spruce No. 1 was still inadequate. The EIS's conclu-sion that Spruce No. 1 would have a minimal adverse impact on its environment was based on the same mumbo jumbo about "stream mit-igation" that was at issue in the IP suit. At the same time, Joe asked the judge to attach the Spruce No. 1 permit to the larger IP case.

Suddenly, all that Joe had fought for these last nine years seemed to hang in the balance. His first days as a lawyer in court had been spent trying to stop Spruce No. 1. Judge Haden's decision in that case, despite its later reversal by the Fourth Circuit, had forced Arch to slog through the EIS process and saved, for the meantime, those six square miles of forest that Joe had first viewed from the top of Pigeonroost Hollow with Jim Weekley. Now that vast swath of verdant land was again on the verge of being destroyed. In the balance with it hung the Army Corps' whole method of permitting. If Judge Chambers ruled that the Corps wasn't being stringent enough in its IP reviews, that would certainly stop Massey and other coal companies until the fed-eral government finished a favorable EIS on each prospective site. It would likely stop Spruce No. 1, since the reasoning that Judge Cham-bers used to strike down the individual permit would probably invali-date the Spruce permit, even with its EIS. And it would certainly kill the looser Nationwide 21 permit, currently pinned down by Judge Goodwin's gavel while Goodwin awaited the IP ruling. On the other hand, if Chambers ruled that the Corps had done all it needed to do in granting these IPs, then for Joe all was lost. All the IPs would be granted, including the one for Spruce No. 1. And then Judge Goodwin might decide that Nationwide 21 was legitimate, too.

By the time Joe got to Chambers's courtroom to argue for a TRO on Spruce No. 1, the issue was—for the moment—moot. Joe had got-ten on the phone with McLusky, as hardworking for Arch as he was for

Massey, and reached his own out-of-court agreement on Spruce. Joe agreed to let minimal work continue on the 160 acres Arch had cleared. McLusky agreed that Arch would not start work on any other part of the site. That was what Joe and his plaintiffs cared most about.

On the question of whether to attach Spruce No. 1 to the IP suit, Judge Chambers chose to reserve judgment. Perhaps, Joe thought, this was a hopeful sign that Chambers's ruling would strike down the whole process of individual permits in southern West Virginia.

Now both sides sat back to wait some more for Chambers's ruling.

FIFTEEN

DON GOES FOR IT ALL

At about the time Joe Lovett had stood up to give his opening state-ment in that Huntington courtroom, Don Blankenship began put-ting the state of West Virginia through a trial of his own.

Two years before, his 527 group And for the Sake of the Kids had steered $1.7 million of his money to help elect Brent Benjamin to the state supreme court. In the glow of that victory, Don had vowed to start a foundation of the same name to "provide needed clothing and other necessities to the most needy children of West Virginia." To pursue these goals, he had said he'd help the foundation raise about the same amount as he'd plowed into the Benjamin race.

In all the intervening months, no such foundation had been formed, and no such money had materialized. But in the early fall of 2006, Don began pouring money into And for the Sake of the Kids for a new political cause. He had decided to mount a grapeshot campaign against virtually every Democrat up for election to the West Virginia House and Senate that November. He vowed to wrest at least one of the legislature's two chambers from the Democrats and said he'd spend "whatever it takes." Don Blankenship was going to change the state's political landscape all by himself.

Clearly, Don hadn't gotten the message the legislature had sent him in the aftermath of the Benjamin campaign. In September 2005, by a vote of 33–0 in the State Senate and 91–4 in the House of Delegates, West Virginia became the first state in the union to pass a bill to blunt the impact of 527s in state races—a move made expressly because of Don Blankenship. As a consequence of that bill, no 527 could accept more than two thousand dollars from any contributor during an election cycle: one thousand dollars during primary season, one thousand dollars during the general election season.

Unfortunately, the new bill came with a gaping loophole. Individuals could still pour unlimited sums of their own money into 527s of their own creation and engage in campaign advertising of any kind as long as neither they nor their 527s had any communication with the candidates they were backing. Restricting that freedom, lawmakers had reasoned, would have violated the First Amendment.

This was exactly what Don had done in the last election cycle, so the new law did nothing to slow him down. Guided by a baby-faced but shrewd political operator named Greg Thomas, he began writing serious checks to AFSK in mid-September. Eventually, he would spend, by his own reckoning, about three million dollars on this attempted putsch. The money bought billboards and print ads and television commercials; it launched door-to-door canvassing, push-poll surveys, and statewide robocalls. Some of the forty Republican candidates Don was supporting received checks for one thousand dollars; others did not. But all of his chosen candidates saw expensive advertising appear, as if by magic, on their behalf, stressing hot-button social issues such as parental notification of abortions for minors and opposition to same-sex marriage. The ads also pushed Don's favorite economic issue, elimination of the state's food tax.

At least the new bill on 527s required donors to be named in every advertisement. Within hours of the campaign's launch, Don Blankenship's name was being broadcast all over the state. Perhaps because there was no point in being coy now, Don appeared in many of the commercials himself, delivering his messages in his trademark monotone. By mid-October, the candidates of both parties began feeling dwarfed by the hulking silhouette behind them. Some Republicans wondered how wise it was for the party to be so identified with a coal baron, and a controversial one at that. Democrats were worried, too, but a few sensed that Don might get his comeuppance. Like the mortals in Greek myths who took on the gods, Don was taking on a pantheon of Democratic power unshaken since 1928.

In an ordinary year, Don might have prevailed. But 2006 was no ordinary year. Deep frustration with the Bush administration had spilled
from blue states into red. The foundering war in Iraq, with its rising
death toll of American soldiers and no end in sight, infuriated many
voters. After six years of George W. Bush, there was plenty else to be
fed up with, too: tax cuts skewed to the top 1 percent, Orwellian surveillance of American citizens in the cause of fighting terrorists, deten-
tion without charge or trial or legal representation for anyone the U.S.
government suspected of terrorism, torture of prisoners by the U.S.
military and CIA in Baghdad's Abu Ghraib prison and Cuba's Guantánamo, special cases whisked to secret prisons abroad for even more
brutal interrogation. Republican majorities in both houses of Congress
had given Bush almost absolute power these last six years; in the rare
instance when a bill reached his desk that he didn't like, he merely appended a "signing statement" granting himself the right to ignore the
bill when he chose. Now Americans were itching to vote a resounding
no—no to Bush's handling of the war in Iraq, no to the trampling of
civil rights, no to one-party power in Washington with all the corruption it bred.

Six days before that national referendum, Don Blankenship cried
foul. The state, he had learned, was about to issue its report on the
deadly fire of January 19 at Aracoma Coal's Alma No. 1 mine. Don believed the report's release date had been moved up from after the
election as a political dirty trick. "It's a terrible coordination of state
government monies and political monies to defame and, obviously, intentionally," he told a television interviewer. State mine officials denied
the charge, but perhaps Don was right: also in the week before the
election, Governor Joe Manchin just happened to announce his support for reducing West Virginia's food tax to 3 percent. No one had ever
suggested West Virginia politics were anything less than rough-and-
tumble.

The Aracoma report was devastating. Massey had failed to do virtually everything it could for safety there. Based on those findings, the
widows of the two fatally burned miners announced they were filing
wrongful-death suits against Massey corporately and its chairman personally. They cited a memo that Don had written in October 2005 and
forwarded to all Massey deep-mine superintendents: "If any of you
have been asked by your group presidents, your supervisors, engineers

or anyone else to do anything other than run coal (i.e., build overcasts, do construction jobs, or whatever) you need to ignore them and run coal. This memo is necessary only because we seem not to understand that coal pays the bills." When that memo first came to light, Massey had provided another one, written by Don a week later, declaring "safety is the company's first responsibility." If it was, Aracoma's record since the fire seemed to belie that. In just ten months, MSHA inspectors had issued five hundred citations and orders to Aracoma for chronic or new violations. In the spring of 2007, the MSHA would hit Massey with a $1.5 million fine for violations of "reckless disregard" at Aracoma that had contributed to the deaths of the two miners—the largest fine in the agency's history.

On November 7, a historical wave of voter unrest, larger even than most pundits had predicted, washed over the country. Democrats regained control of the House and then, by the slimmest of margins in two key races, inched to an effective 51–49 majority in the Senate as well. Bush would be in the White House for two more years. But at last a balance of power had been restored.

If Election Day was a tipping point for Democrats nationally, it was a rout in West Virginia. In the 100-member House, Democrats actually increased their majority from 68 to 72 seats. In the 34-seat Senate, they went from 21 to 23 members. The Democrats were so dominant that one of them, Senator Randy White, won even after nude pictures of him wearing body paint were aired on television.

Of the forty candidates Don had backed, thirty-nine lost. Carol Miller, Don's one successful Republican challenger, defeated a delegate who at seventy-nine years old had been forced to curtail her campaigning in order to check into an assisted-living center. For that victory, a chastened Don took no credit. "My advertising didn't have any success for the other candidates that we were promoting," he muttered to one interviewer, "so I don't see any argument that it helped Ms. Miller either."

Republicans agreed Don Blankenship had not merely failed to make any political gains with his three million dollars, but had hurt their party as well. "This election is one the like of which has never been seen," sighed Republican party chairman Doug McKinney. "Even if you called him up and said, 'I wish you'd back off,' that would be coordinating with him, and you can't do that." To a proud and independent citizenry, Don had looked like what he was: King Coal using his money and influence as a puppet master. Democrats and Republicans alike had voted no—not just to George W. Bush but to Don Blankenship telling them what to do.

This year had become Don Blankenship's *annus horribilis* for economic reasons as well as political ones. The Aracoma mine lay idle, pending repairs. While other Appalachian coal companies continued to earn windfall profits in the ongoing boom, Massey's net income for the first quarter of 2006 was a paltry $5.6 million, compared to $50.6 million in the first quarter of 2005. Arch Coal's net profits, by comparison, were $60.7 million for the first quarter of 2006. As for Consol, it trounced both of its longtime coalfield rivals with net income for the quarter of $124.4 million. And while it did its share of mountaintop mining, it managed those earnings with barely a whisper of controversy in the press.

Don had steered Massey to an even worse second quarter: $3.2 million in net earnings versus $37 million for the same period in 2005. He'd done that while pocketing more than twice the company's net earnings for the quarter in personal income and benefits. Surely there weren't many chairmen of public companies in America who took home more money than their companies did, at least not for long.

The second quarter had also brought the proxy battle that put dissident Daniel Loeb on Massey's board. Loeb's colleague Todd Q. Swanson had secured his seat as well: after a few months of sullen legal threats, Don had stopped contesting Swanson's victory. At least one interesting development had occurred as a result of those victories. Goldman Sachs, the New York investment bank, had been hired to study the company and suggest ways it might boost its stock. Given that Massey's stock price had dropped from about $51 per share a year or so before to a low of $19 per share, it wasn't hard to guess who had instigated the review. "There's four or five things they're looking at," a laconic Don told analysts about Goldman Sachs at a New York City conference in late November. "Everything from acquisitions of synergistic properties to more broad acquisitions to mergers and so forth."

As Don saw it, these options wouldn't solve the fundamental prob-

lem of state and federal agencies targeting Massey unfairly, writing up
endless citations for tiny violations because the company mined more
coal in the region than any of its rivals and irritated the locals. Nor
would they help solve another problem weighing on Massey Energy: a
25 percent turnover rate.

It was a curious thing, this turnover. Massey paid well, but local
men kept leaving, either to work for rivals or to find employment out of
state. A Goldman Sachs analyst might have wondered, from a pragmatic point of view, if the long and fluctuating hours at Massey mines,
the harsh attitudes of supervisors toward their men, and the evident
lapses in safety measures had anything to do with those departures.
Perhaps more humane working conditions might slow the flow of miners to the exits and boost the bottom line. But Don appeared to think
the answer was to force new workers to sign strict employment agreements—and punish them severely if they violated them.

The Redhat Training Program, as Massey called it, offered training
to new, inexperienced workers. Massey's trainees were paid, but they
had to agree to work at a Massey operation, upon completion of the
program, for thirty-six months. *Three years.* The consequences of quitting prematurely were made chillingly clear in a letter sent to an ex-
employee on Massey's behalf by a Charleston lawyer, Scott Caudill.

The employee had signed the Redhat Training Program agreement
letter on November 18, 2005, and appeared not to like the work conditions: he resigned on February 8, 2006. Massey had invested almost
three months of salary in training him and was understandably irked
when he left. Other companies might write off the loss and look for
workers it could rely on. Massey focused on seeking redress.

"First," Caudill wrote, "you agreed that if you voluntarily resigned
from the company within the 36-month period, you would 'pay back to
the Company the sum of $7,500, plus interest at a rate of prime plus 1
percent.'" That was the approximate cost of the training program.
"Second," the lawyer wrote, "you agreed that if you voluntarily resigned
from the Company, then for a one-year period thereafter you would not
'compete or attempt to compete with the Company within the geographic territory of the 90-mile radius of the Company's primary place
of business.'" Since the employee had taken another mining job in the
area, Caudill informed him, he "must not only repay the Company

$7,500 plus interest, but also cease and desist from engaging in employment with one of the Company's competitors."

The employee had ten days from receipt of the lawyer's letter to pay back the money owed and quit his new job. For most miners, that was a sentence of bankruptcy if not considerable debt, with the added punishment of being forbidden to work off that debt with the one kind of job in the valley that paid a living wage. It harked back to the days of scrip and company stores, with workers hardly better off than serfs.

At the other end of the pay scale at Massey Energy, Don's own employment contract began to stir keen curiosity among journalists and activists as the calendar year came to an end. After such a miserable performance in 2006—economically, politically, personally—would the chairman's one-year contract be renewed on January 1? Or would his record, along with the influence of Massey's two new board members, inspire the company to bid Don Blankenship goodbye?

The answer came in an 8-K company filing of December 27, 2006. Don was offered a new one-year contract on the same terms as his last one. "I am very pleased that you will continue your leadership of Massey and look forward to the productive year ahead," wrote Admiral Bobby R. Inman, head of Massey's compensation committee, who, like all but the two newest members of the company board, had been chosen to serve by Don Blankenship. Along with his $1 million base salary and $900,000 performance bonus, Don would receive all the perks that had led Daniel Loeb to wage his proxy battle. In a proxy statement filed in April 2007, Massey would acknowledge paying Don roughly $27 million in pay and perks for 2006—despite a 30 percent decline in the company's stock for the year.

Profits might tumble, mines catch fire, political campaigns misfire, but Don was a hard man to dislodge. As if to show that his terrible year had bothered him not at all, Don sent his lawyers to courtrooms and boardrooms around the state to file a blitzkrieg of motions.

One cause seemed irretrievably lost. Don's libel claim against the Charleston *Gazette* for the paper's coverage of the Cannelton mine closing had been dismissed twice, and a judge had barred him from resubmitting it. Don's lawyers declared they might refile it in a new way, however.

Don had sued the UMWA and a group called West Virginia Consumers for Justice for maligning him during the McGraw-Benjamin campaign. Against these other two parties, Don fared better. Perhaps that was because instead of filing in West Virginia, he had Massey bring suit in the company's hometown state of Virginia. His rationale was that television commercials produced during the campaign by West Virginia Consumers for Justice and paid for, in part, by the UMWA had reached eighteen thousand households in Virginia. A Fairfax County circuit judge was persuaded at least not to dismiss the case, in part because of a charge made in the commercials that Massey had contaminated West Virginia's waterways. With more courtroom time pending to prove or disprove that charge, the grassroots group, now bankrupt, found itself obliged to settle.

In his suit against Governor Joe Manchin, Don hadn't won, but he hadn't lost, either. A judge had just ruled that the governor was not by definition immune from a civil rights charge that he'd threatened Massey with heightened regulatory scrutiny. Don was a long way—a very, very long way—from winning a suit against a governor who had, after all, simply declared his intent to make Massey conform to the law. But he seemed certain to go as far down that road as the law would let him.

Of more immediate interest and consequence was the case of the contested silo beside Marsh Fork Elementary School. Back in July, during Ed Wiley's walk to Washington, the DEP, citing SMCRA, had quashed for a second time Massey's appeal to build the second silo. Massey hadn't accepted that adverse ruling. It never accepted adverse rulings; it just litigated on. In early January 2007, Bob McLusky appealed the DEP ruling to the Surface Mine Board, just as Ed Wiley had predicted. The DEP had ruled that the second silo was clearly a new operation; McLusky begged to differ. Surely over time, he said, a preestablished coal operation might be transformed as mining methods evolved. A coal company that had used horses to haul coal in the old days might now want to use trains. Yet SMCRA would seem to prohibit that. Or as McLusky quaintly put it: "If you were using blind ponies, you can't use modern haulage." He argued that coal had always been stored one way or another on the Goals site. Silos were just the latest way to do that.

Surely, Joe thought, the Surface Mine Board would see this argument as the thin reed it was. But in a mid-March week while Joe was down in Florida with two of his three sons, cheering on the Boston Red Sox in spring training, the board surprised him. In a split decision, it ruled in Massey's favor. The migrating boundary line was no longer at issue: the DEP had accepted Goals's discovery of an overgrown boundary marker as a legitimate border instead of its inconsistent maps, and so the Surface Mine Board did, too. But the board also agreed with McLusky that coal storing at the silo would carry on a preexisting operation, even if the coal storing had been done on another part of the property in the past and in another way. Certainly if the silo were to imperil the health of Marsh Fork's schoolchildren, that would outweigh all else. But the whole point of the silo was to *decrease* and minimize dust by containing it rather than storing it in an open stockpile.

Tom Michael, the pragmatic environmentalist who headed the Surface Mine Board, had noted that irony himself. But he voted with the minority against the silo. Perhaps he'd taken a closer look at Massey's air-quality permit application for the second silo. True, the point of a coal silo was to contain coal dust. But for Goals, the second silo was part of a plan to load much, much more coal into open train cars. The permit application acknowledged that a conveyor belt would be built to increase the "load out" of coal in the first silo from 1,600 tons per hour to 4,000. The second silo would load out 4,000 tons per hour, too. So the amount of coal coming into and going out of that area so close to the school would increase by more than 400 percent. Crisply, the permit application noted that the increased traffic might generate an additional 3.49 tons of coal dust per year around the two silos. Of that total, 1.66 tons would be particulates of fewer than 10 microns—the small ones that lodged most easily in the lungs and could lead to respiratory diseases. It was a plan, Tom Michael concluded soberly in his minority opinion, that would place "a significant burden on the public health and the environment of the local community."

The DEP promptly announced its intention to appeal the Surface Mine Board's decision in circuit court. Not since the Matt Crum golden era had the agency shown such grit. Upon his return from Florida, Joe declared he would file a separate appeal on behalf of Coal River Mountain Watch. Certainly he would persevere until every legal option was exhausted. As for Massey, it would defend this latest victory with all its usual legal firepower, spending whatever it took to prevail. And so the silo struggle would lurch on, up and down the courts, perhaps for another year, perhaps longer. That was how all too many stories went in the coalfields: on and on and on.

Not everyone was willing to wait that long. On a rain-swept Friday in mid-March, more than fifty protesters came to the capitol to fight the silo in their own way. Some were from OVEC and Coal River Mountain Watch: Judy Bonds, Bo Webb, Ed Wiley, and others. Some were neighbors. And many were college students from West Virginia and other Appalachian states.

For nearly two years now, Judy had gone from campus to campus around the country—a road warrior, as she put it—inspiring her young audiences to get involved. In some small part because of her initial efforts, some fifty campus groups had formed and joined a new grassroots organization called Campus Climate Challenge. By the end of her second year of touring, the number of those groups had grown to more than five hundred. Some students had signed up for the second and now the third Mountain Justice Summer. Others just came when called. Hillary Hosta led this latest batch of students into the capitol building like they were the forward line of an advancing brigade. Judy, Bo, Ed, and the others came right behind her.

"Marsh Fork is a very clear example of energy injustice that's happening locally," Hillary told her troops as an outer ring of newspaper reporters and television-news crews hung on to every word in the capitol's dark and echoing halls. "Though I live in the Coal River valley and there are children at Marsh Fork Elementary that are very important to me, what's more important to me is that I have the right to turn on my light switch and know that other people are not suffering so that I can live in relative comfort."

At that, a troupe of young fiddlers started playing, and the protesters fell into song. A strange mix of anger, exhilaration, and anxiety hung in the air as the group advanced toward Governor Joe Manchin's wing of the building. Near the governor's reception area, the musicians stopped, and Larry Gibson, the pint-sized symbol of mountaintop resistance who still lived under siege atop Kayford Mountain, spoke in his unexpectedly deep voice, pulling at the suspenders of his denim overalls: "We're going to go in and try to see the governor, and see if he will at least deal with the new silo, and get us a new school."

Ed Wiley, in his usual H. S. Strut turkey-hunting hat, T-shirt, and jeans, spoke up, too. Months had passed since his meeting with Senator Byrd, and nothing had come of it, even with Byrd's reelection. The senator's staffers told Ed that money was tight as a result of the Iraq war. They did think the Army Corps of Engineers might be able to spare a bit of federal funding already granted to it for floodplain projects, since Marsh Fork Elementary lay within a floodplain. The Corps also had a new pot of $191 million for new water-related projects that Senator Byrd had helped secure. That might be another angle to play. But the senator's staffers warned that Marsh Fork Elementary's county school board would have to request that the school be moved, and so far it hadn't. Ed had come to feel his time with Byrd had done no more good than his time with the governor. "It's time to stand up," Ed said, bristling with anger. "No one in this capitol is man enough or woman enough to stand up to this governor."

Perhaps two dozen of the protesters surged into the governor's reception area. A posse of state troopers in wide-brimmed hats was waiting for them. An officer calmly told the visitors to leave. "Until the governor signs a paper saying a new school will be built in our community," Hillary declared, "it's unlikely that any of us will leave."

With that, the troopers started handcuffing the protesters nearest the hallway that led to the governor's private office. The protesters had learned their civil disobedience well. They collapsed in heaps on the carpeted floor, forcing the exasperated troopers to haul them out one by one. "Shame! Shame! Shame!" others chanted as the newspaper photographers clicked away and the television cameras recorded the scene.

The troopers zeroed in on Hillary, cuffing her hands behind her back rather than in front, as they'd done with the others. Four troopers carried her out, face down, pulling her arms up high behind her. "Ouch, my arms hurt," she kept saying, with cries of genuine pain. "Then stand up!" one of the troopers told her. But Hillary refused to stand, and so the troopers carried her all the way, as she kept crying, to a police wagon outside where Larry Gibson, Ed Wiley, and ten handcuffed others were packed in already. All were charged with obstructing a police officer, then released.

Within an hour, the governor's reception area was cleared and quiet again. But immured in the confines of his private office down the hall, Governor Manchin had to know that this issue wasn't going away.

The union miners of now-defunct Cannelton Coal knew how relentless Massey Energy's lawyers were. Still, they'd decided to take them on. Don Blankenship might view this particular legal action as a mere nuisance, but the National Labor Relations Board saw serious issues at stake.

Usually, when Massey took over a union mine, shut it down, and reopened it as nonunion, the NLRB felt powerless to intervene. Massey could just say it preferred the experienced miners it was hiring over the ones it chose not to hire back. But something very telling had happened at Mammoth Coal. With workers so scarce in the coal boom, Massey had advertised for help and *still* not found experienced men. Instead, it had hired a lot of inexperienced red hats. How, the NLRB wondered, could Mammoth Coal claim that those red hats were better than the 230 experienced miners—some of the most productive miners in the industry—it had ignored?

The NLRB had found that Massey showed discrimination in its hiring at Mammoth Coal, a ruling that had legal heft. Massey had appealed to an administrative law judge. That judge, picked from a pool of judges who worked for the NLRB as an extra duty, convened his hearing in late January 2007, presiding from an auditorium on the campus of West Virginia Tech. For several weeks, he heard testimony from both sides, including testimony from Don Blankenship, who coolly affirmed that non-union operations had an economic advantage over union ones, in part because of the "legacy costs" like health insurance that union companies were forced to pay. "Those are not my sentiments," Don said. "Those are facts." For the 230 lost souls of Cannelton, summer came without a ruling. Even if they eventually won, none expected to get his job back any time soon. Detailed and definitive though the judge's ruling was predicted to be, Massey almost certainly would appeal. It would aim to wear down the opposition, perhaps even to keep the ruling tied up in court until the men it was meant to benefit were no longer just dead souls but truly dead.

Above all these smaller suits hung one whose final resolution all Massey watchers—a group that now included most residents of West Virginia—were awaiting.

More than four years had passed since a Boone County jury found that Massey and a subsidiary had forced tiny Harman Mining out of business and awarded the plaintiffs—Harman and its founder, Hugh Caperton—fifty million dollars. As that penalty rose with interest to seventy-two million dollars, Massey's lawyers had done all they could to forestall paying it, while Don spent $1.7 million getting the un-known Brent Benjamin elected to the state supreme court. Benjamin might yet prove a judge of Holmesian probity, but the betting in the corridors of the Robert C. Byrd Federal Courthouse was that Benjamin gave Massey a reliable, and determining, third vote out of five on the Harman appeal, should it ever reach that august body.

In 2005, Hugh Caperton's lawyers had gone to the court to ask that Brent Benjamin recuse himself from the case. Benjamin had de-clined to do that. Some months later, Massey's lawyers had gone to the court to make a recusal request of their own. Justice Larry Starcher, one of the two justices left who often ruled against Massey and other coal companies, could not possibly render an unbiased judgment, they declared. They noted that Starcher had issued stinging public remarks about their client. "I think he's a clown," Starcher had said of Don Blankership, "and he's an outsider, and he's running around this state trying to buy influence like buying candy for children. And I think it's disgusting. He's stupid. He doesn't know what he's talking about." Starcher, like Benjamin, declined to recuse himself. He also declined to say if he would run for reelection in 2008. At sixty-five, he was young enough to contemplate serving out another twelve-year term. But Don rarely missed a chance to say he was ready to spend millions more of his own money to see Starcher beaten. Did Starcher want to take on that fight, with all the slurs that Don's apparatus of robocalls and push polls and statewide advertising could fling his way? In the summer of 2007, he seemed—publicly at least—undecided.

Caperton's lawyers had resigned themselves to having Benjamin as one of the five justices hearing Massey's appeal. Don's lawyers weren't nearly so sanguine about Starcher. By August 2006, they'd filed a suit claiming their client's Fourteenth Amendment right to due process had been violated because he had no recourse after Starcher had declared he wouldn't recuse himself. This was an ambitious claim, given that judges in courts all over the land reserved the right to decide whether or not to recuse themselves from a trial without any oversight or review. No less than U.S. Supreme Court Justice Antonin Scalia had declined to recuse himself not long before in a case involving Vice President Dick Cheney, even though Scalia had gone duck hunting with Cheney—and that, for better or worse, was that. But Massey's lawyers thought their client had been unjustly treated and sought redress.

The motion went nowhere, yet it had some effect. By the state supreme court's rotation schedule, Starcher was due to be chief justice in 2007, the year the Harman appeal might finally be heard. Without comment, three of his colleagues voted to break precedent and deny him the honor. Instead, Robin Davis would extend her term another year. Davis was the justice who had written the unsigned majority opinion in the Tony Arbaugh case suggesting Arbaugh could work as a janitor at a Catholic school—only to turn around and write the minority dissent criticizing that suggestion. Warren McGraw, voting in the majority, had lost his seat because of that opinion. Davis still denied she'd set him up or colluded in any way with fellow justice Spike Maynard to provide grist for the campaign against McGraw.

Massey's lawyers tried one last stalling maneuver. No one denied that the court reporter in the case had done a terrible job. She'd failed to produce a transcript within one year of the 2001 case, then within another year, then another year after that. Apparently the transcriber had had trouble with her equipment. This was frustrating to all parties, particularly Hugh Caperton, because without a proper transcript Massey couldn't appeal, and until the coal company exhausted that last appeal, Hugh Caperton wouldn't receive his settlement—not to mention the sense of vindication that came with it. Massey sued the hapless transcriber, charging she "intentionally misrepresented her ability to produce a transcript." But the case was thrown out, and by December a county judge ruled that the transcript was now complete. With no other recourse, Massey's lawyers at last declared they would formally appeal the Harman verdict.

And there, oddly enough, the matter sat. The state supreme court convened in January 2007 for its winter session, the appeal hanging over it like a leftover Thanksgiving float, and yet somehow Chief Justice

Davis managed to avoid scheduling a date to hear it, month after month after month. Would it *ever* be heard? In West Virginia, this was not a frivolous question. Or would the case be kicked like a tin can down the road, past the 2008 elections, when the court might acquire a second new justice backed by the raw political clout of Don Blankenship?

In the summer of 2007, Hugh Caperton had no idea. Like Joe Lovett, all he could do was wait.

SIXTEEN

A RULING AT LAST

Joe spent the early evening of Thursday, March 22, 2007, playing baseball out by the apple orchard with his two older sons, David, now seven years old, and Ben, eleven. It delighted him that both were ardent Little Leaguers—David was just starting out at the "coach pitch" level, but already he could throw and catch with real swagger. Yet they picked up their violins with equal enthusiasm, as did John, the youngest at five. Joe's father had been proud of those boys; he would have been prouder now. On this early-spring evening, Joe kept David and Ben out until nearly dark: he desperately needed a break from the now almost unbearable suspense of waiting—and waiting and waiting—for Judge Chambers's ruling in the individual-permit suit.

On Monday, Joe had reminded the judge's clerks that a first stand-still agreement on work at one of the mine sites was due to expire at the end of the week. When Joe had made those agreements the previous spring with Bob McLusky, both lawyers had assumed a ruling would come long before the agreements expired. But then the Corps had rescinded its permits, delaying the start of trial, and Chambers had taken longer than even he expected. If this agreement—on Aracoma's Camp Branch mine—expired Friday at 11:59 p.m. without a ruling, Massey could go onto the site the next morning and start blasting away. Bob McLusky had told Joe that work wasn't due to begin for some time, but Joe had heard those assurances before. One had come almost exactly three years ago, when McLusky had said nothing would happen over the weekend at Green Valley.

Judge Chambers's clerk told Joe he thought the ruling would come by the end of the week, but on Wednesday, when Joe called him again, the clerk was more cautious. "You better file your motion Thursday after all," he said. So Joe and Earthjustice filed for a temporary restraining order on Camp Branch and went home wondering if Chambers would even rule by week's end on the TRO, let alone the case. That night, after Gretchen and the boys had gone to bed, Joe sat up listening to Miles Davis, the haunting, drawn-out trumpet riffs a perfect expression of his anxious mood. As always, he was pessimistic. And yet, on the eve of this signal ruling, Joe was also at peace with himself. There wasn't any other way he would have lived these last nine years, frustrating as his work so often was. He wanted to be as effective as he could, but his ultimate goal wasn't to change the world, it was just to do the right thing. One tried to live an ethical life—that was the point. Even if the consequences weren't what you hoped they would be.

Surely, Joe thought, Chambers would at least deal with the TRO by midday. But Friday noon came and went, dragging the afternoon hours behind it. Joe fielded calls from curious colleagues, keeping an eye on his e-mail in case the ruling came that way. And yet as frustrating as the wait was, Joe mused between calls, it in no way compared to the agonies of Haden 1. Thrown then as a newly licensed lawyer into writing his first briefs, making his first court appearance, examining and cross-examining his first witnesses, Joe had lived each day with dread. The nights before Judge Haden's ruling, he'd hardly slept at all. Now he knew what he was doing; and despite his ingrained pessimism, he'd felt good about this case from the start. He'd almost felt he couldn't lose. But now here it was 5:00 p.m. and still no word from Chambers. "He's not going to rule!" Joe exclaimed.

Fifteen minutes later, the judge's clerk called. "We've got it," he said. He meant the ruling in the case, not the TRO. "But the guy who has to post it just went to pick up his kids." The ruling came by e-mail at 5:45 p.m. Joe clicked it open and raced past the first paragraph to the all-important second. "For the reasons stated below," the judge wrote, "the Court GRANTS judgment in favor of Plaintiffs, RESCINDS the permits and decisions, ENJOINS Defendants and Intervenors from all activities authorized under those permits, and REMANDS the permits to the Corps for further proceedings consistent with this Memorandum Opinion and Order."

Joe and Earthjustice had won.

The eighty-nine-page ruling was somber, stately, and moderate—and all the more devastating for that. Judge Haden, in the earlier suits, had faced absolute, up-or-down decisions and not balked at making them. The sweeping nature of those rulings was doubtless partly why the Fourth Circuit Court of Appeals had found cause to strike them down. Mindful of that, Joe had asked Judge Chambers to rule merely on whether the Corps' *process* of analyzing permit applications met the standards set down for it by the Clean Water Act and the National Environmental Policy Act. Had the Corps followed its own rules?

Accordingly, Chambers had reached what seemed at first a mild decision. He didn't say that individual permits were illegal on their face. He said that with the four permits at issue—and the fifth that was attached to the suit—the Corps had failed to do what its own process required. So the judge in his ruling was politely handing those permits back to the Corps for the Corps to do with them as it saw fit. Perhaps the Corps would find that each of these permits required an EIS. Perhaps it wouldn't. That was up to the Corps. But then Chambers went on to explain exactly why, and how, the permits failed to meet the standards of the Clean Water Act and NEPA. How the Corps could meet those standards *without* doing an EIS for each site was hard to fathom after reading the ruling. And if it did do EISes—properly and scientifically, as the judge outlined—it was hard to imagine how the Corps would be able to grant those permits again.

At the heart of the Corps' case, Chambers observed, was the claim that Massey could offset the burying of mountain streams by mitigation. But there were two basic steps in that regard that the agency needed to take—figuring out exactly what would be lost, then seeing if mitigation could really replace those losses—and it had failed to do either. The Corps' regulatory chief said his staffers used their "best professional judgment" to assess losses and mitigation, but that could not be an excuse, the judge wrote, for the Corps to "exercise unbridled discretion" and "ignore its own regulations." In studying the headwaters to be lost, the Corps had taken a few onetime measurements but had "given no more than lip service," as the judge put it, "to the other attributes of headwaters that must be considered in assessing the structure and function of a stream." The Corps said that it couldn't analyze the impact that destroying headwaters would have on the broader watershed because the science was uncertain. Wasn't that "precisely the type of scenario," Chambers asked, that should be addressed by an EIS?

The Corps talked about stream enhancements as mitigation. But, as Chambers had determined from his own questioning of Massey expert Edwin Kirk, "the buried streams are lost forever while the enhancements may be effective for only a limited time." They wouldn't even be monitored for more than ten years, according to the permits. "The Corps offers no explanation," Chambers wrote, "for concluding the gains expected from enhancements with a limited life-span in perennial streams will make up for the permanent loss of headwaters."

As for stream "creation," Chambers noted, the Corps' own witnesses had offered no evidence that these strategies worked to create and sustain a flow of water, much less the complex functions of an intermittent stream. "The Corps asserts that the new stream will eventually provide the same structure and functions as a real stream," Chambers wrote, "but the record contains no scientific basis for this assumption." Indeed, Chambers added, echoing Joe, "the Corps' witnesses . . . conceded that the Corps does not know of any successful stream creation projects in the Appalachian region."

But the Corps' failings, Chambers explained in his calm, clear style, did not stop there. By the Clean Water Act and NEPA, the Corps was required to study more than just the streams a valley fill would bury. It was obligated to study the valleys themselves and their outlying hollows. "The Corps abused its discretion," the judge ruled, "by limiting its scope of analysis to just the stream and immediately adjacent riparian areas." Because the Corps had done that, the judge observed, it could in no way meet its obligation of studying *cumulative* losses, both of headwaters and their outlying forest lands. Instead, the Corps merely declared that cumulative losses would be insignificant. "The Court presumes that the Corps reached this conclusion," the judge wrote drily, "by assuming that mitigation entirely eliminates the adverse impacts of many additional miles of headwater streams, despite the alarming cumulative stream loss caused by valley fills in these watersheds. This assumption is a fallacy, which could allow the destruction of most of the headwaters in a watershed without the Corps ever considering any adverse impact it may cause."

The judge did throw the Corps a bone near the end of his ruling. He wrote that the plaintiffs had failed to make a persuasive case that mountaintop mining would increase surface runoff. Joe had expected that, after the floundering performance of Dr. Keith Eshleman and his-curve numbers under slice-and-dice cross-examination by Bob McLusky. The judge found that the government's experts had chosen curve numbers within the range of acceptability. "The Court cannot simply substitute its judgment or prefer one expert over another," he wrote, "where the Corps has a reasonable basis and did not act arbitrarily." But it was a small point. On appeal, it might even be helpful: a bit of added assurance to the Fourth Circuit that Chambers had reasoned with appropriate restraint.

The bottom line, Chambers concluded, was that the Court had found "fundamental deficiencies" in the Corps' approach. The Corps would have to take the "hard look" that Congress had told it to take at the environmental effects of all that surface mining, then decide if the permits could be issued or not.

When Joe got home that night with a printout of the ruling in hand, he was euphoric. Gretchen was happy, too, but pragmatic. "I cooked dinner the last three nights," she said. "It's your turn tonight."

With the ruling, there was no need for Chambers to issue a TRO on Camp Branch: the permit for that site was rescinded along with Massey's others. The fate of Arch's Spruce No. 1 was less clear. Chambers hadn't ruled on Joe's motion to stop Arch from acting on its own new permit, and that permit came with a formally issued EIS. But Joe felt sure he could block that mother of all surface mining sites, too. After all, its EIS suffered from the same defects Chambers had just ticked off. Its headwater studies were woefully inadequate, it relied on bogus stream mitigation, and its findings of no significant cumulative impacts were simply wishful thinking. If Chambers didn't rule to enjoin

Arch, Joe would file again as soon as Bob McLusky gave him thirty days' notice that work was about to begin. Joe doubted McLusky would find a way to wriggle out of *that* pledge: it had been given in front of a federal judge. However the site was enjoined, Joe felt, Arch would have no realistic hope of starting work on Spruce No. 1 until the Corps figured out how to fix the permits Chambers had just rescinded. And that time, Joe dared hope at last, might not ever come.

The broader implications of Chambers's ruling were staggering. Though he had ruled specifically on the mine sites at issue, the shortcomings in those permits were identical to those in thirty other prospective mountaintop sites in southern West Virginia. Those were just the ones for which permits had been, or were soon to be, granted. Massey, Arch, and other coal companies had planned to apply for roughly thirty *more* permits after that. Those mines, too, were now effectively stopped.

The total was greater than sixty mines stopped, though, because these were just the ones for which Don Blankenship and his fellow coal barons had sought individual permits. In an earlier, sweeter time, before Joe Lovett had made their lives so difficult, the barons would have sought and painlessly, quickly received Nationwide 21s for dozens of others—the more the better in these boom years. But Nationwide 21s were still gummed up over in Judge Goodwin's courtroom, and the barons hadn't even bothered to apply for them in the nearly three years since Joe, with Jim Hecker, had brought suit against the Corps for how it issued them.

A few days after Chambers's ruling, Judge Goodwin handed down an order asking Joe and Jim, as well as Bob McLusky, how they felt the ruling affected the Nationwide 21 case. He wanted to know, too, what they made of the Corps' decision to recertify Nationwide 21 as a legitimate permit process for five more years. To Joe, it was just more proof, if any were needed, that the Corps was a rogue agency. In order to reapprove the permit process, the agency had had to go through the motions of conducting another environmental analysis, or EA, then conclude, despite all the evidence in the pending Nationwide 21 suit, that the valley fills sanctioned by Nationwide 21s would have "no significant impact" on their environments. Just how rogue an agency the Corps was, Joe discovered only after the fact.

In early March 2007, with Judge Chambers poised to issue a ruling in the individual permit suit, the Army Corps had done a remarkable thing. It had secretly authorized a vast new mountaintop mining
site in southern West Virginia—not with an individual permit but under its recertified Nationwide 21 permit. The applicant, for once, was
not Massey Energy. Apogee Coal was a subsidiary of Magnum Coal.
But the subterfuge was no less glaring for that. When the maneuver
came to light, Apogee readily admitted it had applied first for an individual permit—after Judge Goodwin put a stop to Nationwide 21 in
July 2004. Now, with Judge Chambers almost certain to put the same
lock on individual permits, Apogee had simply resubmitted its application, this time for a Nationwide 21. The application had gone in to the
Corps on February 5, 2007. The Corps had complied in record time:
less than a month. Issuing a Nationwide 21 in the wake of Chambers's
ruling on more stringent individual permits could only be seen as a
flouting of the law. Here was a government agency actively circum-
venting the courts to collude with the coal industry. Within hours of
getting the permit, Apogee had started work on its valley fills. By the
time the Corps replied to Margaret Janes's latest FOIA—taking its full
twenty days to reply—significant damage had been done.

How much? Enough that Judge Goodwin was reluctant to issue a
temporary restraining order when Joe and Jim filed a motion for one.
This time, the issue really was moot. Goodwin was shown photos of the
site by Apogee's lawyer—none other than Bob McLusky. "There's no
stream there," McLusky said with satisfaction. Goodwin had to agree.
"The only thing that injunctive relief would accomplish at this point,"
the judge noted, "would be to keep it from being buried deeper." The
judge did note that Apogee's mining plans called for the stream to be
buried in the fifth of six phases. "I'm just wondering how they got to
phase five," he said. "This permit has been in place for a month."

Though he put aside Joe and Jim's TRO motion, Judge Goodwin
scheduled an injunction hearing, at their request, for late May. As a
compromise, Apogee agreed to cease work until then. More than sixty
miners were laid off as a result: more than sixty *union* miners. Many
more men had either lost or were about to lose their jobs over at
Massey, after Judge Chambers's decision in the five mines affected
by his individual-permit ruling. But Massey miners were nonunion

miners. They weren't organized to protest. Within days of the Apogee decision, the UMWA decried the environmental groups whose selfish lawsuits had put union miners out of work. A rally was staged at a local middle school. Governor Manchin showed up and spoke on the miners' behalf. "We're either going to hang together or hang separately," the governor declared. "Let me tell you one thing: they'll have to hang us as a bunch, because we're going to hang together."

This was exactly what Joe and Jim had feared. With enough political pressure, Judge Goodwin might back off from a bold decision quashing Nationwide 21 on the various grounds that they had resubmitted to him. And if Apogee's quick, secretive work at the North Rum mine in Logan had buried the streams they were trying to save, why push for a Pyrrhic victory? Instead, they suggested to Apogee that a company executive take two of their plaintiffs, Cindy Rank and Vivian Stockman, on a tour of the site. Don Blankenship had never agreed to such a request, but Magnum's president, Paul Vining, saw that the proposal might be to his advantage. He offered to drive the environmentalists himself.

In her years of advocacy for OVEC, Stockman had almost grown accustomed to the raw gash of earth that indicated a mountaintop mining site. This one, though, was more heartbreaking than most. It was so new that the ground cover on North Rum's ridgetop was still intact. The trees were felled, but the steep slopes were ablaze—for the last time—with orange azalea and mountain laurel. Below lay the streambed the women had come to inspect. It was indeed gone, obliterated by huge rocks. At Vining's signal, two backhoe operators halted their machines so that Stockman and Rank could take photographs in silence. Soon, Stockman knew, the streambed would be filled with many more tons of rubble, starting with the ground cover of the slope above it: the azalea and mountain laurel; herbs and shrubs; tree roots, seedbed, and soil. At the edge of the destruction, Stockman saw a proud and imposing barred owl on a high branch. That owl, Stockman thought, would have to seek new habitat. Was that proud symbol of wisdom headed for a place, she wondered, where human wisdom prevailed?

With that, Joe and Jim wrote a terse motion to Judge Goodwin withdrawing their request for the injunction hearing on May 31. The Corps' new terms of engagement were all too clear. Until Judge Goodwin blocked Nationwide 21 again as clearly as Judge Chambers had blocked its individual permit, the Corps would issue more Nationwide 21s in secret, avoiding public scrutiny and tacitly encouraging the coal operators to destroy streambeds in the brief window of time they had before the Corps was forced by law to respond to Margaret Janes's FOIA requests. With the Corps' blatantly illegal cooperation, those coal operators could hope, at least in the immediate future, to keep filling streambeds quickly enough to thwart those pesky environmental lawyers again and again.

That spring of 2007, presented with photographic proof that significant damage had already been done to the valleys of three of the mining operations he'd blocked, Judge Chambers declared that he was suspending parts of his ruling. The decision seemed like a reversal, but was just a matter of legal reality. "Most of the substantial harm plaintiffs complain about has already occurred," he said. "It cannot be undone."

His ruling came after a long, tense hearing in his Huntington courtroom attended by dozens of out-of-work Massey miners. The miners hadn't put on a rally and gotten the governor to speak, but they made their pain and frustration very clear. Somewhat to their surprise, Joe appeared to sympathize with them. "We're not here to take away anyone's jobs, particularly when it concerns areas that have already been disturbed," he said. So he had no objection to Chambers's stay of the ruling—pending its appeal to the Fourth Circuit Court of Appeals. The stay in no way undercut the cool, clear logic of Chambers's March ruling: it just recognized reality at three of those five mines and let the miners at those mines keep working until the Fourth Circuit reached a decision.

Then, in mid-June, Judge Chambers issued a ruling that seemed intended to tilt the balance back against the industry. It was a dangler from the March ruling—another reason, Joe and his co-counsels at Earthjustice had argued, why the Corps' permit-granting process violated the Clean Water Act. After mining companies created valley fills and buried the streams beneath them, it was standard practice to turn downstream segments into what they called settling ponds. Into those ponds they flushed water used to separate coal from rocks and dirt adhering to it. Theoretically, the solid materials fell to the bottom of the ponds, enabling the companies to send water from those ponds downstream as "clean." The industry had always claimed these ponds were waste treatment systems—not waters of the U.S. government protected by the Clean Water Act—and the U.S. Army Corps of Engineers had gone along with that. This was flatly illegal, Joe had argued—and Judge Chambers now agreed. The Corps, he wrote, "has no authority under the Clean Water Act to permit the discharge of pollutants into these stream segments." Bill Raney of the West Virginia Coal Association was furious. "It's absolutely astounding to me," he declared. "Here's a judge outlawing a practice that has been in place for almost four decades."

Raney could take comfort, however, in a Bush administration edict not long after. To almost no one's surprise, the Office of Surface Mining announced that its two-year EIS on whether or not to change the buffer-zone rule had concluded that yes, changing the rule was a fine idea. Mine operators would no longer face an absolute ban on placing mining waste within 100 feet of a valley stream—the 1983 rule they had all but ignored anyway. Instead, as the Bush administration had proposed in 2005, they could make their best effort to avoid filling in those streams. And if they failed—well, they'd tried. The change, of course, completely gutted the rule. The *New York Times* ran the story on its front page, and followed up with a lead editorial titled "Ravaging Appalachia," a welcome indication, at least, of growing national awareness of mountaintop mining and its consequences.

The change had come about for one reason, and one reason only: because Joe and Jim had targeted the buffer-zone rule in Haden 1. If they'd kept after the rule—in a state court, as the Fourth Circuit had directed they do—this new wording would have knocked the pins out from under them, just as the new definition of "fill" had KO'ed Haden 2. But they hadn't. They'd moved on. No point in challenging the buffer-zone rule before a state judge subject to reelection pressure from the coal industry. Fortunately, the rule change would have no effect whatsoever on either of the pending suits against the Corps. Why? Because the buffer-zone rule was part of SMCRA, while the Nationwide 21 and individual permit suits were based on the Corps's failures to follow the Clean Water Act. Different acts, different legal worlds.

Overall, Joe felt pretty good about the legal ground that he stood on in that summer of 2007. Judge Goodwin would have to rule again on Nationwide 21 eventually, and having found it flawed once, he was hardly likely to find that its cracks had disappeared. Judge Chambers's ruling in the individual permit case would go to the Fourth Circuit Court of Appeals. Assuming Judge Goodwin ruled again for the plaintiffs, the industry would drag that ruling back to the Fourth Circuit as well. Then what? More reversals? More pretzel-like logic from the conservative judges of the Fourth Circuit? Maybe—but maybe not. For the Fourth Circuit Court of Appeals was undergoing some very interesting changes.

Throughout the Bush years, the Fourth Circuit had lived up to its reputation as the most conservative court in the land. Among other decisions that had pulled the country toward the right, it had issued some of the judiciary's sternest rulings on national security. Most notably, it had approved the government's policy of denying al-Qaeda terrorist Zacarias Moussaoui the right, as his own defense attorney, to interview fellow prisoners who might corroborate his claim that he hadn't participated in the September 11 attacks. Despite such rulings, however, the court's conservative strength had been ebbing, slowly but surely, for more than a decade.

One conservative vacancy on the court's panel of fifteen members had lingered since 1994, when Judge J. Dickson Phillips Jr. took senior status before retiring in 1999. President Bush had nominated U.S. District Judge Terrence W. Boyle of North Carolina to replace him, but Democrats had found Boyle's views extreme even for the Fourth Circuit—civil rights was just one problem area for the former assistant to Senator Jesse Helms—and kept his nomination bottled up in committee ever since. To replace a conservative judge who died in 2000, Bush had nominated Claude A. Allen, a conservative from Virginia, only to see Allen arrested for shoplifting. (Allen initially denied the charge in strong terms, only to plead guilty later.) No one had been named in his stead. A third conservative seat had gone empty when J. Michael Luttig left the court for Boeing. The news was startling, since federal judges are nominated for life and tend to step down only in the event of debilitating illness or extreme old age. Luttig was blunt: he needed to earn more than his appeals-court salary of $150,000 to put his two growing children through college. Bush, a lame duck long before he'd ever imagined he would be, had named no one to fill that seat, either.

Paul Niemeyer remained, but two more conservative judges had announced their plans to move on as well. Chief Judge William W. Wilkins Jr., a reliable law-and-order vote since his appointment to the court in 1986, would take senior status in July 2007. H. Emory Widener Jr. longed at eighty-three to take senior status, too, and would, he said, as soon as his replacement was confirmed. Unfortunately for his plans of a well-earned rest, Bush's nomination for that seat was William J. Haynes II, whose role as a top lawyer at the Department of Defense put him at the center of the administration's legal justifications for torture of prisoners and denial of their legal rights as enemy combatants. Even Republican senators had spoken out about Haynes; finally, his name was withdrawn. In July 2007, Widener retired after all, his health too precarious for him to hold on for another term.

As of midsummer 2007, then, the score on the Fourth's remaining justices stood at 5–5: a perfect balance between conservatives and moderates. But the moderates might hold an edge. Judge Allyson K. Duncan, though counted in the conservative camp, was a frequent swing vote. On the issue of mountaintop mining, Duncan might even be joined by one or more of her conservative colleagues in taking a receptive view of Chambers's ruling—or Goodwin's next one. After all, three of the court's moderate judges had written that ardent dissent from the Fourth's majority opinion on Nationwide 21. Assuming the Fourth's judges engaged in *some* honest debate despite their ideological divisions, Chambers's eminently reasonable ruling just might be upheld, and Goodwin's after that. "Call me foolish," Joe told Steve Roady and Jennifer Chavez, his exuberant co-counsels from Earthjustice, "but I do think we might get a good hearing in the Fourth." With Democrats in control of Congress for two years, one or more of the Fourth's vacant seats might actually be filled by a moderate. If the Democrats retained their majority in 2008, the conservatives' long reign on the Fourth would be over for a generation to come. An underdog at the Fourth for a full decade now, Joe might find his next ten years as a lawyer a lot less frustrating.

Joe doubted that a decision on individual permits would come before early 2008. Whenever it did, a victory by the plaintiffs—Coal

River Mountain Watch, the West Virginia Highlands Conservancy, and the Ohio Valley Environmental Coalition—would have enormous repercussions. Then Judge Chambers's ruling would apply to the Fourth Circuit's whole realm. The relevant parts of that realm in regard to mountaintop mining were all of West Virginia and all of Virginia. The coalfields extended into Tennessee but just minimally. A somewhat larger piece of the coalfields extended into eastern Kentucky, which lay within the Sixth Circuit's domain. That was why Joe had filed a Nationwide 21 suit there, nearly identical to the one before Judge Goodwin, and why he planned now to file an individual-permit suit there as well. The judge in the Kentucky Nationwide 21 suit was holding off, just as Judge Goodwin was. But if the Fourth Circuit upheld Chambers's ruling, Kentucky would likely follow, and the Sixth Circuit would likely affirm. A Sixth Circuit knockdown of Nationwide 21 would start to seem inevitable. Then, until the U.S. Army Corps of Engineers found a way to re-create headwaters streams—to do God's job as well as God—there would be no more large valley fills in America. Mountaintop mining would hardly stop overnight, but the worst of the big new operations, the ones too big to do anything with their overburden but dump it into valley streams, would be stopped, perhaps for good.

As Joe settled in to wait for these two key rulings—the appeal of Chambers's individual-permit ruling to the Fourth Circuit and Goodwin's new ruling on Nationwide 21—another hint of better times to come rested in the unlikely form of a U.S. government complaint against Massey Energy. On May 10, 2007, the EPA had filed a whopper of a suit against Massey in the Southern District of West Virginia. The civil action charged that the company and most of its subsidiaries had "an extensive history of violating the Clean Water Act." It declared that "despite several prior enforcement actions, including two criminal plea agreements, settlement of suspension and debarment matters, civil actions by the State of West Virginia and the Commonwealth of Kentucky, and private suits by citizens in West Virginia and Kentucky, Massey Energy and its subsidiaries continue to violate the CWA."

The sheer number of violations was egregious, if unsurprising to longtime Massey watchers. The EPA noted that "from January of 2000 through March of 2006, Massey Energy subsidiaries violated the CWA

by discharging pollutants in excess of their average monthly or maxi-
mum daily permit limits approximately 4,100 times, resulting in approximately 60,534 days of violation." Remarkably, this careful total had
been compiled by Massey itself, in the self-monitoring reports its subsidiaries were required to file with the West Virginia DEP. The DEP
had filed most of these reports without taking action on them. The
small fraction it had pursued—mostly at Matt Crum's instigation—it
had abandoned in the end by reaching its pathetic $1.5 million settle-
ment with Massey in early 2006. In the months after that settlement—
from April 2006 through December 2006—the EPA noted that Massey's
subsidiaries had reported 8,537 *more* violations. In accordance with the
Clean Water Act, the EPA was demanding civil penalties of up to
$27,500 per day of violation for all violations occurring from January
2000 through March 15, 2004, and up to $32,500 per day of violation
for all violations since that time. Some violations might have been re-
dressed soon after they occurred; any that went unaddressed were liable for each successive day of violation. By one Wall Street coal
analyst's estimate, Massey might be liable for as much as $2 billion.

The final figure would almost certainly be far lower, since the
largest fine levied to date under the Clean Water Act was $34 million.
(The offender was Georgia-based Colonial Pipeline, which paid the
fine for spilling 1.45 million gallons of oil from its pipeline in five
states.) But a substantial penalty was all but inevitable, since Massey
could hardly argue in court that its own reports were wrong. And how
would Massey keep operating after that? By letting its subsidiaries
keep polluting, and paying heavy fines for every violation, as well as
for each day those violations continued? Or by doing what other Appalachian coal companies did—cleaning up their acts? If the latter,
there was nothing in Massey's record under Don Blankenship to
suggest the company had the inclination to do that. Massey's response
to the suit—which was to say, Don's response—showed no contrition,
or any intent to do better. "For the permits in question," Massey's press
release stated, "the Company believes it achieved a compliance rate of
99% or better." Randy Huffman, head of the DEP's mining division,
was asked how Massey might have reached that conclusion. Huffman
didn't know. Perhaps, he said, Massey was figuring that when the DEP
tested one of its mines for fifteen pollutants and found one in excess of

the parameter allowed for it, Massey's record at the mine that day was nearly 100 percent, since it was in compliance on the other fourteen pollutants. Unfortunately, that wasn't how the EPA saw it.

That the EPA had leveled the suit at all was amazing. This was, after all, still George W. Bush's EPA. Its lawyers were assistant U.S. attorneys from the U.S. Department of Justice, still under the leadership of scandal-plagued Attorney General Alberto Gonzales. They worked in the same building as the DOJ lawyers fighting, in effect, for Massey Energy by representing the U.S. Army Corps of Engineers in its appeal of the individual-permit suit to the Fourth Circuit Court of Appeals. Did the DOJ's right hand not know what its left was doing? Perhaps not.

Or perhaps, as occasionally happened in sprawling federal agencies, one resolute official could make a difference. Until recently, Perry McDaniel had headed the West Virginia DEP's Office of Legal Services in Charleston. He'd been involved in several enforcement actions against Massey. But perhaps he'd felt hindered from taking the action those thousands of self-monitoring reports deserved. In December 2006, McDaniel had joined the EPA as the agency's regional criminal enforcement attorney at the U.S. Attorney's office in Charleston. Soon after, the EPA had started preparing its suit against Massey.

Sometimes even now, it seemed, individuals could make a difference.

If Massey was to avoid the corporate calamity that a future of endless fines foretold, it might need to chart a new course, of working *with* the regulatory agencies rather then against them, of being a good corporate citizen rather than the bully of the industry. For starters, a new chairman would help. But change wouldn't come from the efforts of Massey's newest board members. In mid-June 2007, Daniel Loeb and Todd Q. Swanson announced their resignations. They had tried to steer Massey into a helpful merger with another coal company, they wrote in their resignation letter, but the merger had collapsed because of the board's "misguided insistence" on keeping Don Blankenship as Massey's chief executive. The dissidents noted the various lawsuits weighing down on Massey's reputation and depressing its stock. "These and other correctible deficiencies combine to maintain a 'Blankenship Discount' in the market price for Massey's shares, and do a grave disservice to our shareholders by masking the underlying strength of the company's business, assets, and workforce. We cannot stand by while the board fails to address these concerns."

Smart and slick as those New York hedge fund boys were, Don had quashed them with raw power. The rest of Massey's board would do his bidding, even as the company lurched from lawsuit to lawsuit, loss to loss, and virtually the entire electorate of West Virginia united in wanting Don Blankenship gone.

The Army Corps might keep pulling fast ones, but Joe Lovett felt the gathering pull of legal momentum. Change was coming to West Virginia—not enough, and not quickly enough, but it was coming. The bigger picture, though, still demoralized him. Joe saw his fight for what it was: one battle in the war against coal.

In the last two years, as the global coal boom led to hundreds of new proposed coal-fired electrical plants, Joe had become more outspoken on the subject of coal and the part it played in global warming. He put no stock in the burgeoning hopeful scenarios of "clean coal." He'd read about how coal would be heated, not burned, releasing gases that then could be used to heat water that powered a steam turbine, creating electricity. At the same time, its advocates enthused, clean coal's carbon dioxide could be separated and injected harmlessly into the ground, instead of released into the air. Coal gasification was, like the fuel-celled car, a wonderful notion in the abstract. But to Joe, it had three glaring problems. The first was obvious: the coal still had to come from the ground, and there was nothing clean about coal extraction. If every coal-fired power plant in the world switched overnight to coal gasification, Massey and other Appalachian coal companies would do just as much mountaintop mining as they'd done the day before. Indeed, the demand for coal would *rise* dramatically. Second, the process of converting coal to gas created about twice as much carbon dioxide as burning oil did. Injecting all that CO_2 into the ground might sound like the proverbial free lunch at last in energy production, but Joe was highly skeptical. Who knew how long the CO_2 would stay in the ground? Some, Joe felt, would seep out sooner or later. Third, even if injecting CO_2 did work—and Joe was adamant in his opinion that it wouldn't—hundreds of clean-coal plants would have to be built in order to have any effect on the levels of carbon dioxide annually spewed into the atmosphere. Just as many dirty-coal plants would have to be shuttered.

So far, the trend was not encouraging. In the decade or so that coal gasification had been an established technology, exactly one such plant had been built in the United States. Of the 154 new coal-fired plants proposed in the United States, more than ninety were to use fifty-year-old technology: burning pulverized coal. Together, the U.S. Energy Department estimated, they would increase the amount of carbon-dioxide emissions from U.S. power plants 50 percent by 2030. The reason so many new plants with old technology were on the books, Joe knew, was that power plant operators could see the future as easily as anyone else. They knew global warming was occurring. They knew that carbon dioxide was its greatest contributor, and that 40 percent of America's carbon dioxide came from coal-fired plants. Sooner or later, the U.S. government would have no choice but to regulate carbon-dioxide emissions. If industry got its new plants approved in advance of those standards, though, the plants might be exempt for much or all of their sixty-year lifetime, despite spewing tens of billions of tons of carbon dioxide into the atmosphere.

As Joe saw it, the world would have to stop burning coal, period. What choice, really, was there? More than two thousand leading climatologists and other scientific experts from around the world agreed that if and when the United States built those 154 plants, and if and when China built even more by 2025, the earth's temperature would rise 3.5 degrees Fahrenheit by 2050. That would cause significantly higher sea levels, more intense storms, widespread desertification, hundreds of millions of environmental refugees, and mass extinctions of species. Coal burning was the single greatest cause of that apocalyptic prospect. It had to be stopped.

Conservation, alternative energies, enlightened public policy—all would have to play a part. None would be easy. Doing them all at once would be more difficult still. But Joe could see one step that might be taken with surprising ease: an outright, across-the-board ban on mountaintop mining.

Coal operators threw up their hands at such "extremism" and repeated their mantra that mountaintop mining was more efficient than

underground mining. How would their companies compete and survive without it? But if all coal companies were covered by a ban, Joe
observed, the playing field would be level. All would simply go back to
competing on underground coal. Half of the state's mines were still underground; operators would just have to work those and expand them
as needed. West Virginia operators liked to invoke the market threat of
western states' open-pit mining, but most western coal was higher in
sulfur content and contained fewer BTUs than Appalachian coal.
Power plants strongly preferred low-sulfur coal—it helped them meet
Clean Air Act standards for sulfur. If anything, a short-term reduction
in Appalachian coal production from banning mountaintop mines
would put a higher premium on underground coal and help offset the
losses.

Whenever Joe sought to stop work at even one mountaintop site,
the industry played the jobs card. In Joe's experience, those fears were
always trumped up. Three years ago, Bob McLusky had declared to
Judge Goodwin that without its new permit to inject coal slurry into
the hillsides, Green Valley would have to close down. Dozens of workers would lose their jobs. Long after abandoning that scheme, Green
Valley was washing and shipping as much coal as ever. None of the
workers had lost their jobs. Apparently, the company had found some
other, less destructive way of disposing of waste.

A ban on mountaintop mining would mean job losses, but the sky
would not quite fall. West Virginia coal companies employed a tiny
fraction of the workers they had a generation ago. Most of those were
underground. A mere 3,500 workers in the state worked mountaintop
mines in 2007. An enlightened ban on mountaintop mining would al-
locate monies for retraining them. The transition would be hard for
some of those workers and the companies that employed them. But in
the balance of harms, who might be said to be harmed more? The coal
industry, if mountaintop mining was stopped? Or local residents and
the rest of America, so many of whose remaining Appalachian mountains and forests and streams would be obliterated if mountaintop mining went on?

No number of grassroots activists and environmental lawyers
could bring about such a ban. All of West Virginia's elected officials,
from the governor and U.S. senators on down, were insufficient for the

task. A federal government willing to follow and affirm the law was needed.

A moderate president from either party in 2008 would do. Democrats might seem the more environmentally conscious, Republicans the more business-minded. But as Joe put it, how likely would Teddy Roosevelt have been to sanction mountaintop mining? A new president, Democrat or Republican, would only have to read the Clean Water Act—the law that a Republican, Richard Nixon, had signed into law— to see the truth. Mountaintop mining was illegal.

For more than a decade, Joe had devoted himself to proving that obvious truth in court. Now, perhaps, he had only to hold on for a while longer until a new administration came into power and let the law prevail.

THE VIEW FROM
KAYFORD MOUNTAIN

For Larry Gibson, as for so many residents of the Coal River valley, Joe's courtroom victory had come as extraordinary, almost unbelievable news. Larry wasn't accustomed to good news. He wasn't accustomed to hope. It was a painful feeling, hope, so likely to be short-lived. If it was snuffed out, the feeling was worse than if he hadn't felt any hope at all. And in truth, even if Joe did win in the high court, that was good news too late for Larry's Kayford Mountain and the ridgetops that framed, or once had framed, the Coal River valley. Those mountains were being leveled by permits already granted—permits no judge's ruling could rescind.

Three years before, Larry had been able to walk from his mountaintop cabin through a copse of trees and look out at a forested ridgetop to the west, less than half a mile away. Now that mountain—the last one near Kayford Mountain—was gone. Month by month, section by section, Larry had watched it get blasted and bulldozed away. It stood five hundred feet lower now. It wasn't a mountain anymore.

From the top of Kayford, Larry could see the army advancing from north to south along the sides of the valley. Just below Whitesville on the west side, Massey was blasting new mountaintop sites through its subsidiaries Twilight and Independence. Farther south lay Massey's new 1,849-acre mountaintop complex at Edwight. Coal from there was getting belted down to the Goals Coal prep plant on Route 3. The plant, and its giant impoundment, still rose above Marsh Fork Elementary School, up into the blasted hollow once known as Shumate's Branch.

On the east side of the valley just down from Whitesville lay Marfork, at the top of the hollow where Judy Bonds had grown up. Marfork was the hub now for a dozen or more mines, some underground, some mountaintop, belting their coal to a prep plant dwarfed by the Brushy Fork impoundment. Just in the last year, the army had started in on vast new sites farther down that east side, well below Marfork, clearing ridgetops above Dry Creek and Horse Creek and Rock Creek, all hollows where Coal River families had lived for generations.

Dell Ray, a mine electrician who lived up one fork of Dry Creek, had known Massey was headed his way. Still, he was startled when his wife, Belinda, told him over dinner one night in the cozy kitchen of their wood-frame house that she'd seen a car driving up and down the hollow. Thinking the driver was lost, she'd gone out to help. The driver told her in a flat, unfriendly way that he was taking note of every house in the hollow. Massey needed to know who owned each house—if the current residents were the owners outright, or if the house was owned in heirship.

One day soon after, Dell had come home to find that a freelance timber cutter who did a lot of work for Massey was logging the hillsides at the top of Dry Creek. Dell had hunted deer and turkey and bear in those woods from childhood, learning how to shoot from his father. By the spring of 2007, those woods were timbered clear down to Clay's Branch and out by Dorothy. Massey had blocked off the top of Dry Creek altogether and posted guards and vehicles there. For generations, residents of the creek hollows had been accustomed to hike over the ridgetop from one hollow to another, to forage and to hunt and to visit one another. In recent decades, they'd taken their ATVs. A lot of backcountry residents in the hollows traveled more by ATV on the ridgetops than they did by car on Route 3 below. They couldn't do that anymore. They couldn't go on the ridgetop at all.

Dell kept a copy of the newspaper ad that Massey ran informing local residents that it was applying for a permit to dump mining debris into Sturgeon Fork. Sturgeon was the fork that ran down Dell and Belinda Ray's side of Dry Creek Hollow. It was where they lived. Rumor had it that Massey would buy up every house along Sturgeon Fork, de-populate that whole side of the hollow, and eventually put a refuse fill there. One of Dell's neighbors, Denny Christian, had said he would slow Massey down, all right. Thanks to a stubborn forebear, he owned the mineral rights for his property. Other Dry Creek families had sold those rights a century ago to the Rowland Land Company, which owned them even now and was apparently leasing them to Massey. But Denny was in his late sixties and not in good health. He wasn't sure how long he could hold out.

Dell had told his wife that if Massey forced them to sell their house, he'd take her and leave the state, maybe try Tennessee. He didn't want to move up the valley, the way Judy Bonds had done. He wouldn't want to be reminded, every day, of what Massey had done to him and the land that his family had loved and tended for nearly two hundred years. But the cemetery—that was different.

Dell's parents and grandparents, forebears and in-laws going back to the early nineteenth century were buried in the family cemetery across the hollow. So far the cemetery's hillside lay green and unspoiled, the first spring bulbs just coming up around it. But if Massey put debris in Sturgeon Fork, it might back up the hillside and reach those stones. A valley fill would cover them for sure. That was where Dell Ray drew the line. If Massey touched a teaspoon of that hallowed dirt, he told his wife, he would come to the cemetery with his shotgun, aim it at the intruders, and be prepared to fire. He said that almost every day now.

"If they could," Dell told Belinda about Massey, "they would put a gate across Route 3 at Glen Daniel, and another one thirty-five miles north at Racine. They would depopulate this whole valley. From Glen Daniel to Racine there's *beaucoup* coal in this country, and they're going to get it one way or the other. The poor man can't fight people like that."

From the top of Kayford Mountain, Larry Gibson took a stroll in the fading light of a summer day with the latest of his visitors. In the distance, floodlights cast a yellowish glare over active work sites as ant-sized bulldozers and trucks wheeled about, pushing overburden off the blast-flattened hilltops. At his feet, in the only grass that remained as far as the eye could see, rose a dozen or more small white headstones, most of them cracked or tilted with time. This was Larry's own family cemetery. These were forebears who, like Denny Christian's, had never sold their land and mineral rights. Larry would do whatever it took to protect their remains, as Dell would down in Dry Creek. He might lose, but he hadn't stopped fighting yet.

In the deepening dusk, Larry walked back to his mountain cabin, a small figure in overalls and wire-rimmed glasses. Inside, he lit his kerosene lamps. Then, like an early Appalachian pioneer, he went out to the porch and sat there, listening to the sounds of the night and keeping watch.

NOTES

This book is based principally on reporting done on frequent trips to southern West Virginia from early 2004 to early 2007—the period recounted in these pages. Interviews mentioned in the notes were held during this period. A full list of interview sources appears in the acknowledgments.

Among secondary sources, I relied most on the careful reporting of Ken Ward Jr., in the Charleston *Gazette*. I haven't made note below of daily news facts taken from his stories—they can be Googled easily enough—but I do reference quotes used. Other local publications that I relied on include the Charleston *Daily Mail*, the Charleston *State Journal*, the Beckley *Register-Herald*, and the Huntington *Herald-Dispatch*.

The great fun of writing about trials and other legal procedures is that they come with transcripts. All courtroom dialogue in *Coal River* is taken from transcripts, with their titles listed in the notes below. Otherwise, dialogue is used sparingly. All exchanges were recounted by at least one of the two people speaking; occasional statements in quotes are taken from secondary sources and credited as such.

To learn something of the history of the region, I read *The Appalachians: America's First and Last Frontier*, edited by Mari-Lynn Evans, Robert Santelli, and Holly George-Warren (Random House), as well as *Appalachia: A History*, by John Alexander Williams (University of North Carolina Press). To appreciate the harsh times mining brought to Coal River and its environs, I read with awe *Night Comes to the Cumberlands*, by Harry M. Caudill (Little, Brown), a great book that deserves to be as widely read as Upton Sinclair's *The Jungle* or Rachel Carson's *Silent Spring*. And for an elegaic account of mountaintop mining's consequences, I read *Lost Mountain: A Year in the Vanishing Wilderness*, by Erik Reece (Riverhead).

ONE: THE TIP-OFF FROM TONY

12 **"You-all are dealing"** The dialogue among Tony Sears and others at the West Virginia Surface Mine Board is taken from *Edward Rudd et al. v. Division of Environmental Protection,* appeal 98-21-SMB, September 15, 1998.

TWO: A BRUTE FORCE CALLED MASSEY

After several courteous exchanges, Don Blankenship chose not to grant me an interview or cooperate in any way with the reporting of this book. He also declined to have others at Massey Energy participate. Fortunately, his increased visibility beginning in the fall of 2004 led him to grant a number of other interviews for local newspaper profiles of him. Childhood friends and one of Blankenship's siblings, Anthony, helped round out the story of his early days.

19 **But Don had two houses** Details of Blankenship's homes were gleaned from reporting and from a thirty-minute portrait, *The Kingmaker,* produced by West Virginia Public Broadcasting and aired in November 2005. The documentary also recounts Blankenship's role in Massey's 1985 standoff with the United Mine Workers of America. Details of Blankenship's role in the strike appear in Bernard Condon, "Not King Coal," *Forbes,* May 26, 2003.

33 **It was he who** E. Morgan Massey's quote about the 1981 Elk Run strike occurring "on my watch" was said to me at the May 2006 shareholders meeting.

THREE: FIGHTING BACK

I accompanied Judy Bonds and other members of Coal River Mountain Watch to the West Virginia summer legislative session.

Some of the details of rural life in Appalachia come from "Tending the Commons," a marvelous oral-history project sponsored by the U.S. Library of Congress, available online at memory.loc.gov/ammem/collections/tending.

42 The Whitesville bridge calamity occurred July 24, 1926.

54 Details about the Sylvester "Dustbusters" suit are taken from interviews with Brian Glasser, Pauline Canterberry, and Mary Miller, as well as court transcripts from *Ralph Anderson et al. v. Elk Run Coal and Massey Energy.*

FOUR: A SHORT-LIVED LEGAL VICTORY

Dialogue in Judge Goodwin's chambers, and in the subsequent Nationwide 21 trial, is taken from court transcripts in *Ohio Valley Environmental Coalition et al. v. Colonel William Bulen et al.,* civil action 3:03-2281 in the U.S. District Court for the Southern District of West Virginia.

63 **Pointing to a framed picture** Bill Raney's sentiments about mountaintop mining and reclamation come from my interview with him in the summer of 2004.

74 **"While what constitutes the commencing of construction . . ."** "Judge's Mining Order Ignored?" Charleston *Gazette,* August 9, 2004.

75 **"I trust that the Corps will enforce my unambiguous orders . . ."**

"Goodwin Declines to Clarify Mountaintop Removal Ruling," Charleston *Gazette*, September 1, 2004.

75   **Judge Goodwin's ruling, he said**   "Corps to Appeal Federal Mining Ruling," Associated Press, September 2, 2004.

FIVE: STACKING THE STATE SUPREME COURT

76   **This summer**   Don Blankenship's summer-outing speech to his employees in 2004 was posted at the time on Massey Energy's corporate Web site.

78   **On August 7, 2004, Don wrote**   "Justice Says Ads Factually Wrong," Sunday Charleston *Gazette-Mail*, September 26, 2004.

78   **The chamber was no longer a little office**   Statistics on chamber political contributions from Robert Lenzer and Matthew Miller, "Buying Justice," *Forbes*, July 21, 2003. See also Jeffrey H. Birnbaum, "A Quiet Revolution in Business Lobbying: Chamber of Commerce Helps Bush Agenda," *Washington Post*, February 5, 2005.

79   **In five years of workman's comp cases**   *Forbes*, July 21, 2003.

80   **The case in question**   *State of West Virginia v. Tony Dean Arbaugh Jr.*, case 31326, Supreme Court of Appeals of West Virginia.

83   **Brent Benjamin didn't know that, either**   Interview by the author.

85   **By then, the campaign had become**   Carol Morello, "Political Ads Aired in D.C. Target W. Va. Audience," *Washington Post*, November 1, 2004.

85   **"Over the years," he declared**   "Coal Companies Provide Big Campaign Bucks," Charleston *Gazette*, October 15, 2004.

86   **"It will be worthwhile win or lose"**   "Big-bucks Backer Felt He Had to Try," Charleston *Daily Mail*, October 25, 2004.

94   **"I can tell you I am not bought by anybody"**   "Benjamin May Face Bias Questions," Charleston *Gazette*, November 4, 2004.

94   **Don Blankenship was also nearby**   Ibid.

SIX: THE WAR WITH WASHINGTON

96   **White-haired and in failing health**   Interview with Joe Lovett. See also Ken Ward's account of the meeting in the Charleston *Gazette*, August 19, 2001.

99   **Arch Coal was holding a public meeting**   Some details of this meeting are from "Strip-mining Battle Resurfaces in State," Charleston *Gazette*, March 22, 1998. This story became the first in a series titled "Mining the Mountains," which is available on the *Gazette*'s Web site. Other details are from interviews with Joe Lovett.

107   **"I might put you to your proof as early as tomorrow"**   All dialogue from the TRO hearing of February 3, 1999, and the subsequent preliminary-injunction hearing is taken from court transcripts for *Bragg v. Robertson*, civil action 2: 98-0636. U.S. District Court, Southern District of West Virginia. Dialogue outside of the court-room is from recollections by Joe Lovett, Jim Hecker, Ben Stout, and others.

116   **In his ruling of October 20, 1999**   Judge Haden's Memorandum and Or-

der, *Bragg v. Robertson,* civil action 2:98-0636, U.S. District Court, Southern District of West Virginia.

118   **On one of his many campaign trips**   Christopher Drew and Richard A. Oppel Jr., "Friends in the White House Come to Coal's Aid," *New York Times,* August 9, 2004.

120   **Less than a month after that blow**   Details of Griles's biography, his sale of Steven J. Griles and Associates, and his communications with former clients are from Griles's interview by the author and other reporting for the author's "Land for Sale," *Vanity Fair,* September 2003. See also Joby Warrick, "Appalachia Is Paying Price for White House Rule Change," *Washington Post,* August 17, 2004.

121   **In a memo of October 5, 2001**   "'It Appears the DOJ May Feel They Have a Loser in This Suit,'" Charleston *Gazette,* April 7, 2002.

122   **"Congress never permitted . . . fills"**   "Judge Blocks New Valley Fills," Charleston *Gazette,* May 9, 2002.

123   **Bill Raney spoke for the whole coal industry**   Ibid.

123   **The court, stressed Niemeyer**   *Kentuckians for the Commonwealth v. John Rivenburgh et al.,* case 02-1736, Fourth Circuit Court of Appeals.

124   **"All we have proposed," rued one government scientist**   Warrick, "Appalachia Is Paying Price for White House Rule Change," *Washington Post,* August 17, 2004.

SEVEN: A SCHOOL IN MASSEY'S SHADOW

131   **Rowland was said to be**   Clayton Coleman Hall, *Baltimore: Its History and Its People* (New York: Lewis Historical Publishing Company, 1912), p. 783.

137   **"What is a radical?"**   Blankenship said this in a variety of ways in different venues. This particular wording is from a speech given in Parkersburg, West Virginia, June 2006. Blankenship also cites himself as a radical in the Charleston *Gazette,* August 21, 2005, among other articles.

138   **"I grew up sleeping on a dirt floor,"**   "Blankenship Calls Pension Bonds a Crap Shoot," Charleston *State Journal,* June 8, 2005.

142   **"Which chemicals do you look for?"**   "Marsh Fork Air Quality Unknown," Charleston *Gazette,* August 27, 2005.

142   **"Over time," he said**   "Coalfield Residents Air Concern over Massey Site," Charleston *Daily Mail,* July 9, 2005.

143   **A spokesperson for the DEP**   "Work Started without Permit," Charleston *Gazette,* July 13, 2005.

145   **"It's a technicality"**   "Both Massey Silos off Permit, DEP Says Survey Shows," Charleston *Gazette,* July 28, 2005.

145   **"He shut my silo down"**   "Blankenship Sues, Gov. Manchin Responds," Charleston *Gazette,* July 27, 2005.

EIGHT: THE DEAD SOULS OF SMITHERS

148   **Ross could have shut them down**   Interview by the author.

149   **A company spokeswoman**   "Union Planning Strike over Closed Coal Mines," Charleston *Daily Mail,* October 7, 2004.

152 **Like a lot of Appalachians** Details of Don Blankenship's parents and childhood come from "Not King Coal," *Forbes*, May 26, 2003; "Blankenship Used to Controversy," Charleston *Gazette*, November 7, 2004; "Don Blankenship Tells What Makes Him Tick," Charleston *Daily Mail*, July 11, 2005; "Massey's Blankenship a Lightning Rod in West Virginia," Associated Press, November 26, 2005; and "A Coal CEO's Unusual Pastime: Firing Up West Virginia Politics," *Wall Street Journal*, February 13, 2006. Some details also come from author interviews with Anthony Blankenship and Eddie Croaff.

156 **"I was with her when she died"** "Don Blankenship Tells What Makes Him Tick," Charleston *Daily Mail*, July 11, 2005.

156 **"It doesn't matter whether you're hated or not"** "Massey's Blankenship a Lightning Rod in West Virginia," Associated Press, November 26, 2005.

157 **From 1995 through 2005, the MSHA** Statistics from the Mine Safety and Health Administration.

157 **An electrician unhooking a tester** *Jerry R. Cline and Glenda Cline v. Aracoma Coal Company, Inc.*, case 04-c-147, Logan County Circuit Court.

157 **An experienced supervisor** *Clifford Lee Goble and Wilma Jean Goble v. Spartan Mining Company, Rawl Sales & Processing Co., and Massey Coal Services, Inc.*, case 02-c-294, Logan County Circuit Court.

157 **One worker had slipped** *J. Bradley Wright v. Rawl Sales and Processing and Sprouse Creek Processing Co.*, case 94-c-301, Mingo County Circuit Court.

157 **A shuttle-car operator** *Buford Elkins v. Massey Coal Capital Corp. and Massey Coal Services, Inc.*, case 94-c-342, Mingo County Circuit Court.

157 **A miner had been pulled toward** *Wetzel Paris v. Rawl Sales & Processing Co.*, case 95-c-291, Mingo County Circuit Court.

157 **A miner had been directed to unhook** *Gary Reynolds and Mary Reynolds v. Massey Energy Company and A. T. Massey Coal Company, Inc.*, case 03-c-247, Mingo County Circuit Court.

157 **A "red hat" miner** *Jeffrey S. McKinney v. Elk Run Coal Company, Inc.*, case 03-c-84, Boone County Circuit Court.

158 **A worker alleged** *William O'Dell and Tenia P. O'Dell v. Elk Run Coal Company, et al. and Star Manufacturing Company, Inc.*, case 91-c-497, Boone County Circuit Court.

158 **A miner manning** *Joshua McNeely and Melissa McNeely v. Independence Coal Co., Inc. and Massey Coal Capital Corp.*, case 01-c-3, Boone County Circuit Court.

158 **A bulldozer operator had hit** *Ricky Adkins and Melinda Adkins v. Independence Coal Company and Massey Coal Services, Inc.*, case 02-c-31, Boone County Circuit Court.

158 **A miner had been pinned** *Charles Buckland, Jr. et al. v. Independence Coal Company, Inc. and A. T. Massey Coal Company, Inc.*, case 03-c-63, Boone County Circuit Court.

158 **A miner alleged that his managers** *John F. Dickens v. Independence Coal Co. and A. T. Massey Coal Co.*, case 04-c-119, Boone County Circuit Court.

158 **A shuttle-car operator had sustained** *Gary Hatfield and Sharon Hatfield v. Marfork Coal Company and Universal Coal Services, Inc.*, case 02-c-192, Boone County Circuit Court.

158 **Due to the failure of one worker's managers** *Terry Vilacha v. Eagle En-*

ergy Inc., Massey Coal Capital Corp., Massey Coal Services, Inc., case 01-c-23, Boone County Circuit Court.

158 **After one man was killed in a roof fall** *Lauretta Vance, Administratrix of the estate of Ricky D. Vance v. Massey Energy and A. T. Massey Coal Co., Massey Coal Services, Inc., Independence Coal Company, Inc., and Lightning Contract Services, Inc.,* case 02-c-224, Mingo County Circuit Court.

NINE: MARCHING IN THE VALLEY

169 **Heyman learned that the MSHA** West Virginia Public Radio, August 16, 2005.

170 **"It's primarily a quality control"** "Blankenship Downplays Coal Silo's Importance," Charleston *Gazette,* July 30, 2005.

170 **Bob McLusky, Massey's hardest-working lawyer** "Citizens Group Intervenes in Massey Silo Case," Charleston *Gazette,* August 4, 2005.

173 **Theodore Roosevelt IV** Theodore Roosevelt IV, "An Ecological Betrayal," Boston *Globe,* September 4, 2001.

178 **"This is the third time in five years"** Courtroom dialogue from author's reporting.

TEN: MASSEY'S UNWELCOME NEW FRIEND

185 **"There used to be thirteen gas stations"** From Don Blankenship's standard stump speech; this version was delivered to the Republican Club of Parkersburg, West Virginia, in April 2006.

189 **"It doesn't matter what people think"** "Blankenship Takes Notes," West Virginia *Metro News,* September 15, 2005.

190 **"Should you and the board remain like deer"** "Investment Groups Put Pressure on Massey," Charleston *Gazette,* September 21, 2005.

191 **"My eyes glaze over"** Steve Fishman, "Get Rich Quickest," *New York,* November 22, 2004. For more on Loeb, see "Hostile Takeover: Daniel Loeb and the Hedge Fund Cowboys," *Men's Vogue,* December 2006.

192 **"How do you think you are doing relative to your peers?"** "Massey Earnings Disappoint," Charleston *Gazette,* November 1, 2005.

193 **Phillip R. Arlia** *Phillip R. Arlia on behalf of Massey Energy v. Don Blankenship et al.,* case 02-c-139, Boone County Circuit Court.

196 **Deborah K. May had been hired** See *Deborah K. May v. Chair and Members, Board of Review; Commissioner, West Virginia Bureau of Employment Programs; and Matecreek Security, Inc., Employer, respondent,* case 06-aa-42, March 30, 2006, Kanawha County Circuit Court.

ELEVEN: DON'S TERRIBLE YEAR

202 **"I must say that shutting down the mines"** "Industry Reacts to Stand Down," Huntington *Herald-Dispatch,* February 3, 2006.

203 **"It was another record performance"** *International Mining Project News,* March 13, 2006.

203 **On March 16, Daniel Loeb**   Amendment 1 to Schedule 13-D, Massey Energy SEC filing by Third Point LLC and Daniel Loeb, March 16, 2006. See Massey Energy filing at www.sec.gov/edgar.html.

204 **On April 24, Loeb fired off**   Schedule 14-A, Massey Energy SEC filing by Daniel Loeb and Third Point LLC, April 24, 2006.

TWELVE: TURNING A COURTROOM LOSS AROUND

212 **In their complaint, Joe and Jim pointed out**   *Ohio Valley Environmental Coalition, Coal River Mountain Watch, and West Virginia Highlands Conservancy v. United States Army Corps of Engineers et al.,* civil action 3:05-0784, U.S. District Court, Southern District of West Virginia, Huntington Division.

214 **The day before, a circuit judge**   "Judge Says DEP Should Release Internal Discussion on Coal Silo," Associated Press, March 14, 2006.

214 **The hearing had more than a few**   *Goals Coal Company v. West Virginia Department of Environmental Protection and Coal River Mountain Watch and Honorable Joe Manchin III,* appeal 2005-23-SMB, West Virginia Surface Mine Board, March 15, 2006.

216 **In a telephone conference**   "Mining Trial Canceled While Permits Reviewed," Charleston *Gazette,* June 15, 2006.

THIRTEEN: A WALK THROUGH WEST VIRGINIA

219 **By October, Thompson was back in coal country**   *James B. Simpkins v. Arch Coal,* case 03-c-336, Mingo County Circuit Court. The $2.5 million jury verdict was subsequently reduced to an undisclosed sum in an out-of-court settlement.

FOURTEEN: BACK IN COURT AGAINST THE CORPS

All dialogue in this chapter is taken from trial transcripts in *Ohio Valley Environmental Coalition, Coal River Mountain Watch, and West Virginia Highlands Conservancy v. United States Army Corps of Engineers et al.,* civil action 3:05-0784, U.S. District Court, Southern District of West Virginia, Huntington Division.

FIFTEEN: DON GOES FOR IT ALL

261 **He vowed to wrest**   "Latest Don Blankenship Blitz Ambitious," Associated Press, July 17, 2006.

263 **"It's a terrible coordination"**   "Massey CEO Says Campaign Coordinated against Him," MetroNews Talkline television, November 1, 2006.

263 **"If any of you have been asked"**   "Massey CEO Memo Rankles Some Miners," Associated Press, February 25, 2006.

264 **"My advertising didn't have any success"**   "Blankenship: Campaign Met Defeat," Huntington *Herald-Dispatch,* November 9, 2006.

264 **"This election is one the like of which"**   "Blankenship Hurt GOP, Chairman Says," Charleston *Gazette,* November 9, 2006.

265 **"There's four or five things"** "Massey CEO Says Acquisitions, Mergers Among Possibilities," Associated Press, November 29, 2006.

266 **The consequences of quitting** Copy of letter sent by Scott Caudill, Caudill Law, March 13, 2006.

272 **"Those are not my sentiments"** "Blankenship: Unions Hurt Bottom Line," Charleston *Gazette*, February 14, 2007.

273 **"I think he's a clown"** "Massey Wants Starcher off Case," Charleston *Daily Mail*, November 1, 2005.

SIXTEEN: A RULING AT LAST

282 **"There's no stream there"** "Permit Switch, Secrecy Ended Mine Challenge," Charleston *Gazette*, May 27, 2007.

282 **"I'm just wondering how they got to phase five"** Ibid.

283 **"We're either going to hang together or"** "Logan County Miners Claim Environmental Group Is Out to Destroy Them," *West Virginia Media*, May 17, 2007.

284 **"We're not here to take away anyone's jobs"** "Parts of Mining Ruling Suspended," Charleston *Gazette*, April 18, 2007.

288 **The civil action charged** *United States of America v. Massey Energy et al.*, civil action 2:07-0299, May 20, 2007, U.S. District Court, Southern District of West Virginia.

289 **"For the permits in question"** "Massey Energy Addresses EPA Suit," *PR Newswire*, May 14, 2007.

ACKNOWLEDGMENTS

My principal debts are to Joe Lovett and Judy Bonds for many interviews and for the ongoing research and fact-checking help that they and their colleagues provided. At Joe's Appalachian Center for the Economy and the Environment, Margaret Janes was endlessly helpful; Joe's co-counsel, Jim Hecker of the Trial Lawyers for Public Justice in Washington, D.C., was also very gracious. At Coal River Mountain Watch, help was provided by, among others, Bo Webb, Patty Sebok, Vernon and Sarah Haltom, and Hillary Hosta. Vivian Stockman of the Ohio Valley Environmental Coalition was an amazing resource, tracking down answers and articles, putting me in touch with valuable sources while also keeping up OVEC's daily online compendium of news articles on mountaintop mining and related subjects. Susan Lapis of SouthWings generously volunteered to fly me over many mountaintop mining sites. Ken Ward Jr.'s stories in the Charleston *Gazette*, as noted elsewhere, are an invaluable chronicle of the ongoing calamity of mountaintop mining in central Appalachia.

For one or more interviews, I am also grateful to Connie Barnhart, Carolyn Beckner, Brent Benjamin, Anthony Blankenship, Rick Bradford, Sylvia Bradford, Trish Bragg, Daniel Branham, Jackie Browning, Mike Buckner, Michael Callaghan, Pauline Canterberry, Paula Cantley, Hugh Caperton, Libby Chatfield, Tom Clarke, Bob Cole, Grant Crandall, Dave Crawford, Eddie Croaff, Matt Crum, Herb Elkins,

Andy Gallagher, Larry Gibson, Brian Glasser, Steve Griles, Ken Hechler, Frances Hughes, Margaret Janes, Gina Jarrell, Carl and Carol Leake, Theresa Lewis, Davitt McAteer, Jeff McCormick, Darrell McGraw, Warren McGraw, Brian McNeil, Tom Michael, Leon and Lucille Miller, Mary Miller, John Morgan, Richard Neely, Corey Pettry, Kenny Pettry, Sherry Pettry, Dan Ramsay, Bill Raney, Cindy Rank, Dell Ray, Wilbur Ross, Loretta Scarborough, Tony Sears, Jerry Shelton, Scott Simonton, Jack Spadaro, Ben Stout, Lena Stover, Kevin Thompson, Rick Wagner, James Webb, Ed Wiley, Freda Williams, and Bolts Willis.

Thanks to Mary Bahr, who first suggested I write the environmental story for *Vanity Fair* from which this book emerged. Thanks to Joni Evans, my agent of many years at the William Morris Agency, for believing in the book and persuading Farrar, Straus and Giroux to take a chance on it; thanks also to Suzanne Gluck for taking over when Joni retired to start a new life. Eric Chinski, my editor at FSG, offered many wise suggestions on the book as it evolved, for which I am especially grateful.

INDEX

A-A Tire and Parts, 204
Abernathy, Gary, 83
abortion rights, narrowing of, 177, 262
Abramoff, Jack, 124
Abu Ghraib prison, 263
accidents: mining, 29, 76–77, 157,
  200–203, 206, 223, 263; impound-
  ment spills, 49–50, 130, 142–43, 169
acid rain, 66, 67
Addington brothers, 147
AEI Resources, 147
Aetna Insurance, 193
Afghanistan, 77
African-Americans, 42, 130
air pollution, 66
air-quality standards, 125
Allen, Claude A., 286
Alma No. 1 mine, 200, 201, 263
al-Qaeda, 286
Alt, Larry, 109
alternative energies, 292
American International Group (AIG),
  79
And for the Sake of the Kids (AFSK),
  83–86, 93, 184, 261–62
Apogee Coal, 282–82
Appalachian Center for the Economy
  and the Environment, 13–14, 103

Apple Computer, 193
approximate original contour (AOC),
  102, 107, 109, 114–15
aquifers, contamination of, 219
Aracoma Coal Company, 200, 201, 203,
  206, 212, 263–65
Arbaugh, Tony Dean, Jr., 80–82, 84, 94,
  184, 274
Arch Coal, Inc., 9, 97–100, 117, 242;
  compensation paid to CEO of, 204;
  profitability of, 265; Thompson's
  lawsuit against, 219; union and, 152;
  violations issued against, 34; see also
  Hobet Mining; Spruce Mine No. 1
Arctic National Wildlife Refuge,
  126
Arlia, Phillip R., 193, 203
Armstrong, Louis, 14
Army Corps of Engineers, U.S., 14, 38,
  291; approximate original contour
  variances granted by, 103; Freedom of
  Information Act requests filed with,
  68; funding of, 271; lawsuits against,
  15, 36, 60, 68–75, 96, 104–105, 112,
  122, 126, 177–82, 210, 236–60, 281;
  permits issued by, 15, 69–70, 102 (see
  also individual permits; Nationwide 21
  permits); Regulatory Guideline Letter

Army Corps of Engineers, U.S.
  (*continued*)
  02–02 of, 250; responsibilities under
  Clean Water Act of, 14–15, 61
Ashcroft, John, 165
A. T. Massey & Company, *see* Massey
  Energy

Baptists, 232
Beckner, Brittany, 129
Beckner, Carolyn, 129
Bellow, Saul, 14
Benjamin, Brent, 79–81, 183–84, 188,
  268; Blankenship's support for judicial
  candidacy of, 83, 84, 187, 261, 273;
  election victory of, 93–94
Big Branch impoundment, 50
Big Sandy federal penitentiary, 64
bituminous coal, 40
Black Castle mine, 201, 213, 237, 239
black lung disease, 221
blackwater spills, 45, 52–54, 56, 77–78,
  128, 194–95
Blair (West Virginia), 99, 258
Blair Mountain, Battle of, 33
Blankenship, Anthony, 152, 153, 156, 204
Blankenship, Beulah, 152, 153, 156
Blankenship, Don, 18–23, 36, 39, 53,
  74, 95, 160, 169, 183, 202, 234,
  261–68, 281, 283; background of,
  151–56; Cannelton mine complex
  acquired by, 146–49; at company
  picnics, 76–77, 188; compensation
  package of, 35, 137, 152, 194,
  204–205, 209, 265, 267; Department
  of Environmental Protection accused
  of bias by, 144–45; economic justification for mountaintop mining of, 8–9;
  and Environmental Protection Agency
  lawsuit against Massey Energy, 289;
  and Goals Coal Company's second
  silo, 127, 136, 143, 227; Harman
  Coal contract broken by, 87–92; hired
  by Massey, 32, 155–56, 218; houses
  of, 19–20, 138, 196–99, 205; Manchin sued by, 145, 146, 162, 164,

  268; McGraw's libel suit against, 184;
  political involvement of, 77–78,
  83–86, 94, 137–39, 145, 184–89,
  261–65, 273, 275; libel suits of,
  163–64, 267–68; mine safety claims
  of, 76–77, 203, 206; personality traits
  of, 21, 22; shareholder lawsuit
  against, 193, 203; standard risk disclaimer provided by, 257; stockholders' uprising against, 190, 192–94,
  196, 203–209, 265, 267, 290; Surface
  Mine Board appeals of, 170, 171,
  227; suspensions fought in courts by,
  53–54; union busting by, 23–31,
  33–34, 45, 146, 148–49, 152, 163,
  188, 272; wrongful death lawsuits
  against, 263–64
Blankenship, George, 152, 153, 156
Blankenship, Jennifer, 156
Blankenship, John, 156, 196
Blankenship, Nancy McCoy, 152–56,
  160
blasting, 128, 132–33; construction
  problems on land softened by, 64–65;
  impact on wildlife of, 132; regulation
  of, 49, 56
Bleak House (Dickens), 54
Boeing Corporation, 216, 286
Bonds, Judy, 36–37, 40, 45, 50–51,
  55–57, 137, 144, 218, 224, 225;
  background of, 41–44, 296; Goldman
  Environmental Prize awarded to, 56;
  and Lovett's Nationwide 21 lawsuit,
  36, 56, 211; Manchin meets with,
  139, 140; Marfork home sold by,
  47–48, 297; and Marsh Fork Elementary School, 57–58, 127, 142, 172,
  183, 219, 222; Massey Energy annual
  shareholders' meeting picketed by, 205,
  207, 208; protest marches led by, 135,
  136, 164, 168, 270; at West Virginia
  legislature summer session, 37, 38
Boone, Daniel, 8
Boyle, Terrence W., 286
Bradford, Rick, 136, 168
Bradford, Sylvia, 130–32, 136
Bragg, Don I., 201

Bragg, Patricia, 103–104
Brazil, illegal logging in, 165
Brown, John, 229
Browning, Daniel, 159
Browning, Jackie, 158–60
Browning, Scott, 159
Brown University, 206
Brushy Fork impoundment, 45–50, 56, 195, 296
Buffalo Creek disaster, 50, 142
buffer-zone rule, 103, 107, 116–17, 121; Office of Surface Mining "clarification" of, 125, 285
Bulen, William, 177–82
Burger, James A., 240–42
Burger, Warren, 177
Bush, George Herbert Walker, 126, 177
Bush, George W., 67, 122, 142, 165, 169, 258, 290; environmentally de-structive policies of, 125–26, 173–75; Goodwin's Nationwide 21 ruling opposed by, 75; Interior Department under, 119–21, 124; Iraq War of, 231, 263; judicial nominations of, 177, 284, 286–87; and mine safety, 202, 223; in 2000 presidential election, 117–19; 2004 reelection of, 93, 96, 121, 173; and 2006 midterm elec-tions, 263–65
Byrd, Erma Ora James, 232
Byrd, Robert C., 67, 82, 115, 141, 170, 224–25, 227–28; Haden's ruling denounced in Senate by, 117, 217; mine safety concerns of, 202; projects in West Virginia named after, 59; reelection campaigns of, 60; Wiley's meeting with, 230–33, 271

California: protests against clear-cutting of redwoods in, 135; stream mitiga-tion projects in, 248
Callaghan, Michael, 52–55
campaign financing reform, 83
Camp Branch Coal Corporation, 212, 213, 277, 280
Campus Climate Challenge, 270

Canada, preservation of old-growth forest in, 165
cannel coal, 147
Cannelton Coal, 146–51, 162–63, 272
Canterberry, Pauline, 54, 136, 167, 195
Cantley, Justin, 129
Capehart, Rob, 83
Caperton, Gaston, III, 86–87
Caperton, Hugh, 86–92, 184, 273–75
carbon dioxide (CO_2), 66, 119, 291
Cary, Bray, 84
Caudill, Scott, 266
cemeteries, family, 46, 296–97
Central Intelligence Agency (CIA), 206, 263
Chafee, Lincoln, 174
Chamber of Commerce, 79; of West Virginia, 78, 79, 84
Chambers, Robert Charles, 213, 215–17, 257, 259–60; individual permits trial before, 236–57; rulings issued by, 257, 260, 276–82, 284–87; temporary restraining order granted by, 213–14
Chaplin, Charlie, 205
Charleston Area Medical Center, 161
Charleston Daily Mail, 56, 86, 143
Charleston Gazette, 56, 74, 86, 99, 143, 163, 195, 267–68
Charleston Symphony Orchestra, 101
Chavez, Jennifer, 236, 239, 287
Cheney, Dick, 119, 274
Cherokees, 8, 37
Cherry, Donald, 254–56
Chesapeake and Ohio railway, 41
Chesapeake Biological Laboratory, 244
China, 77; coal mining in, 9; coal-fired power plants in, 292
Christian, Denny, 297, 298
civil disobedience, 165
Civil War, 131, 177
class-action suits, 218–20, 234–35
Clean Air Act (1963), 67, 100, 175, 293
Clean Water Act (1972), 17, 18, 68, 100, 238, 284–85, 294; Army Corps of Engineers responsibilities under, 14–15, 61; Goodwin's ruling on,

Clean Water Act (1972) (*continued*)
71–72, 126; Haden's ruling on, 122;
individual permits under, 212, 257,
278, 285; Massey Energy sued for
violations of, 288–89; Nationwide 21
permits under, 69, 178–82, 211, 285;
passage of, 15; Section 404, 101–102,
105, 117, 179–80, 237
clear-cutting, 49, 73
Clear Skies policy, 125, 174
Clinton, Bill, 67, 170, 202, 223, 228,
258; and Environmental Protection
Agency mercury emissions standards,
174; and Haden's rulings, 114, 117,
121; judicial appointments by, 177,
181, 213
coal gasification, 291
coal-preparation plants, *see* prep plants
Coal River Mountain Watch (CRMW),
36, 40, 55, 134, 218, 224, 225; found-
ing of, 48–50; Manchin's meeting
with, 138–39; Mountain Justice
Summer organized by, 135–36,
164–66, 172, 270; in Nationwide 21
lawsuit, 36, 56, 68, 287–88; in silo
appeal case, 144, 171, 214, 269–70;
West Virginia Department of Environmental Protection settlement with
Massey Energy opposed by, 195; at
West Virginia legislature summer
session, 37–39
Cole, Bob, 129
Cole, Davy, 129
Colonial Pipeline, 289
Columbia University, 191
commercial reclamation projects, 64–65
Congress, U.S., 115, 117, 228, 280;
Clean Air Act in, 67; Clean Water Act
in, 69, 72, 122, 182; Clear Skies
policy in, 174; Democratic control of,
287; Republican control of, 263; *see
also* House of Representatives, U.S.;
Senate, U.S.
Connaughton, James, 75
Conrad, Robert J., Jr., 177, 178
Consol Energy, 9, 34, 152, 157, 193,
204, 265

Consolidated Coal Company, *see* Consol
Energy
Constitution, U.S., 176; First Amend-
ment, 145, 146, 262; Fourteenth
Amendment, 273
"continuous miner" machines, 23–24
Court of Appeals, U.S., *see* Fourth Cir-
cuit, U.S. Court of Appeals; Six
Circuit, U.S. Court of Appeals
Crawford, Dave, 150, 160, 162
Croaff, Eddie, 153–55
Crum, Matt, 51–56, 135, 144, 269;
enforcement practices of, 52–54, 56,
86, 171, 184, 194, 195, 289; fired by
Timmermeyer, 55, 139
cumulative impacts, 212, 215

DaimlerChrysler, 79
Dal-Tex, 98, 109–11
Davis, Jefferson, 177
Davis, Miles, 100, 277
Davis, Robin, 81–82, 274–75
Dean, Howard, 83
Defense Department, U.S., 287
Delaware Court of Chancery, 208
Delorme (West Virginia), 153–56, 185
Democratic party, 55, 59, 60, 137, 175,
213, 231, 232, 265, 294; and appoint-
ment of federal judges, 286, 287; in
judicial elections, 78, 79, 83; in presi-
dential elections, 67, 82, 93, 118–19;
in West Virginia legislature, 187, 213,
261, 262, 264
Dickens, Charles, 54
draglines, 63, 66, 98, 111
drinking water, contamination of, 12–13,
219
Duncan, Allyson K., 287
Dustbusters, 54, 60, 136, 167, 195, 218

Eades, Rick, 49
Earth First!, 135
Earthjustice, 236, 237, 239, 242, 277,
278, 284
Edwards, John, 82

Edwight Mining Company, 295
Eisenhower, Dwight D., 118
electric plants, *see* power plants
Elkins, Herb, 129
Elk Run Coal Company, 5, 32–33, 55,
    130; fatal accident at, 201–202; im-
    pact on local community of, 54, 132;
    union protests at, 32, 48
Ellington, Duke, 100
en banc hearings, 181–82, 216
Endangered Species Act (1973),
    126
energy conservation, 292
Energy Department, U.S., 292
English immigrants, 41
environmental analysis (EA), 178–79,
    281
Environmental Impact Statement (EIS),
    102, 105, 115, 121, 178–79, 285; for
    individual permits, 211, 212, 237,
    258–59, 278–80; for mountaintop
    mining, 104, 122–25, 174, 206
Environmental Protection Agency, U.S.
    (EPA), 7–8, 77, 119, 123, 221, 250;
    Army Corps of Engineers Spruce No.
    1 permit and, 100, 105, 108, 121;
    Marsh Fork Elementary School in-
    spected by, 233; Massey Energy sued
    by, 288–90; mercury emission cuts
    proposed by, 174–75; rapid bioassess-
    ment habitat evaluation plan (RBP-II)
    of, 253
Eshleman, Keith, 239–42, 280
eutrophication, 256
Exxon Valdez oil spill, 49–50

Fawcett, Dave, 92
fill, legal definition of, 101–102, 117,
    121; Bush administration change in,
    122–23, 125
Fish and Wildlife Service, U.S., 77, 108,
    251
Fitzgerald, Scott and Zelda, 205
Flanagan, Paul, 81
flooding, 37–39, 44, 240
Flower Industries, 156

Fluor Corporation, 32, 35
Food and Drug Administration, 177
food tax, 185, 189, 262, 263
Forbes magazine, 79; 400 list of wealthi-
    est Americans, 148
force majeure, 87–88
forests, 41, 64; clear-cutting of, 49, 73,
    113, 213; destroyed by valley fills,
    124, 212; national, logging in, 125;
    old-growth, preservation of, 165; open
    canopy in, 111
Foundation Coal Holdings, Inc., 204
Fourth Circuit, U.S. Court of Appeals,
    71, 72, 75, 117, 126, 215–17, 252,
    280; Chambers's rulings appealed to,
    284–88, 290; en banc hearing denied
    by, 181–82; Goodwin's rulings re-
    versed by, 176–81, 210, 211; Haden's
    rulings reversed by, 119–23, 125, 127,
    177, 210, 259, 278
Freedom of Information Act (FOIA;
    1966), 68, 73, 168–69, 172, 212, 213,
    215, 258, 282, 284
Frost, Robert, 14

Gallagher, Andy, 78, 80–82, 84, 86,
    93–94
Gardner, Blair, 99
Gee, Gordon, 206–208
Georgia, University of, 243
Gibson, Larry, 6–7, 136, 270–71, 295,
    297–98
Glasser, Brian, 54, 61, 218, 219
global warming, 66, 67, 126, 291–92
Goals Coal Company, 57–58, 128–34,
    144–45, 158–59, 166, 295–96; im-
    poundment at, 57–58, 130, 133,
    140–42, 167–70, 227, 228, 295;
    inspections of, 142; protest march at,
    136, 138; silos at, 127, 133, 136–37,
    139–44, 164, 167, 168, 170–73, 183,
    213–15, 219–21, 227, 233, 268–71
Goldman Environmental Prize,
    56
Goldman Sachs, 265–66
Gonzales, Alberto, 290

Goodwin, Joseph R., 17, 69–75, 126, 259, 293; Fourth Circuit Court of Appeals reversal of, 176–81, 210, 211; Nationwide 21 case before, 69–71; rulings of, 71–75, 95, 182, 211, 281–88; temporary restraining order granted by, 59–62
Gore, Al, 67, 118–19
Grant, William, 203
greenhouse gases, 66, 119
Greenpeace, 165
Green Valley Coal Company, 11–18, 53, 59–62, 69, 219, 277, 293
Griles, J. Steven, 119, 120, 124–26, 142
Guantánamo, 263
Gunnoe, Maria, 38

Haddy, Loretta, 166
Haden, Charles H., II, 105–18, 174, 181, 217, 242, 277; death of, 127; and Fourth Circuit Court of Appeals reversals of rulings by, 119–23, 125, 127, 177, 210, 259, 278, 285; hearing for preliminary injunction against Spruce Mine No. 1 before, 107, 109, 111–13, 236, 238; rulings of, 113–18; temporary restraining order granted by, 105–108; viewing of Hobet Mining reclamation sites by, 109–11
Haltom, Sarah Webb, 224
Haltom, Vernon, 224
Hamilton, Chris, 82
Harding, Warren G., 33
Harman Mining, 86–93, 184, 187–88, 273–74
harms, balancing of, 112–13, 293
Hatfield, Ellery, 201
Hatfield clan, 152
Haynes, William J., II, 287
Healthy Forests initiative, 125
Hechler, Ken, 222
Hecker, Jim, 17, 96, 100, 103, 109–10, 120, 125, 212, 236, 285; Army Corps of Engineers lawsuit filed in Kentucky by, 122–23, 126; Environmental

Impact Statement for Spruce Mine criticized by, 121; and Fourth Circuit Court of Appeals, 176, 178–81, 210, 211; in Nationwide 21 case before Goodwin, 69, 95, 281–83; in settlement negotiations with mining industry, 114–15; at temporary restraining order hearing, 106, 107
Hedges, Dan, 97
heirship, property owned in, 47, 295
Helms, Jesse, 286
Heyman, Dan, 168–69
Hobet Mining, 97, 98, 106–107, 109, 111–13, 115
Hoke, Jay, 93
Home Depot, 79
Hominy Creek, 11–12, 14, 15–18, 59, 61, 114
Horizon Natural Resources, 146–48, 151, 163, 232
Hosta, Hillary, 165, 166, 172, 270, 271
House of Representatives, U.S., 264
houses, purchase and demolition of, 46–48, 99, 295–96
Howard, William S., 148
Huffman, Randy, 144
Hurricane Katrina, 219

IBR Number 9, 62
impoundments, 16, 45–46, 69, 132, 142–43, 225, 228–29, 232; at Brushy Fork, 45–50, 56, 195, 295; at Goals Coal Company, 57–58, 130, 133, 140–42, 167–70, 227, 228, 295; sediment ponds for, 73–74
Independence Coal Company, 130, 158, 194, 295
individual permits (IPs), 15, 75, 182, 210–17, 236–61, 287, 290; Chambers's ruling on, 276–82, 284–87; Environmental Impact Statements for, 211, 212, 237, 258–59, 278–80; for Green Valley Coal Company, 15–17; for Spruce Mine No. 1, 115, 257–60
Inman, Admiral Bobby R., 205–206, 267

Interior Department, U.S., 119, 124
International Coal Group, 200
Iraq War, 66, 96, 231, 263, 271; death toll of American soldiers in, 76–77, 263
Irish immigrants, 41, 169
Italian immigrants, 41

JacksonKelly law firm, 17, 245, 246
JANA Partners, 190
Janes, Margaret, 68–69, 73, 215, 237, 242, 247, 258, 284
Jarrell, Gina, 129
Jarrell, Josh, 129–30
Jefferson Hotel (Richmond, Virginia), 205, 207
Jews, 101, 176
Justice Department, U.S., 60, 104–106, 117, 215, 216, 258, 290

Kayford Mountain, 6–7, 136, 270, 295, 297
Keebler company, 155
Kennedy, John F., 14
Kenny, Katharine, 149
Kent Capital, 191
Kentuckians for the Commonwealth, 122
Kentucky, 7, 57, 124, 138; Nationwide 21 lawsuit in, 96, 122, 123, 126, 288; Martin County disaster in, 49–50; Massey Energy operations in, 19, 288; nonunion miners from, 34; penitentiary built on reclaimed mountaintop land in, 64
Kerry, John, 82, 93, 96
Kessler, Elizabeth, 178, 179
Kimbler, Dick, 118
King, Robert B., 181–82
Kirk, Edwin, 252–54
Kiss, Bob, 139
Korean War, 152
Ku Klux Klan, 231
Kyoto Protocol, 118, 119

Lafer Equity, 191
Lambert, Alison, 150, 151, 161–62
Lambert, Mike, 149–52, 160–62
Laxare East mine, 215, 237, 239
Lewis, Theresa, 134
Lincoln, Abraham, 188
Loeb, Daniel S., 190–93, 203–205, 207–209, 265, 267, 290
Loeb, Margaret, 192
Loeb, Penny, 97
logging, *see* timbering
Long, Huey, 185
longwall mining, 23–31
Lovett, Ben, 100, 101, 276, 277
Lovett, Chester, 101, 106–107, 175–76, 276
Lovett, David, 276, 277
Lovett, Gretchen, 100, 101, 107, 277, 280
Lovett, Joe, 13–14, 65, 67, 98–117, 207, 218, 275, 291–95; background of, 101, 106–107; and buffer-zone rule decision, 116–17, 119–20, 285; and Bush administration environmental policies, 125–26, 173–75; Coal River Mountain Watch and, 36, 56, 68, 127, 171, 269; Dustbusters and, 54, 60; family of, 100, 269, 276; and father's death, 175–76; first case taken on by, 96–100, 103–105; Green Valley temporary restraining order motion of, 13–18, 59–62, 69; individual permit lawsuit of, 182, 211–17, 236–61, 276–82, 284–88; jazz collection of, 100–101; and Marsh Fork Elementary School case, 127, 137, 143, 144, 164, 171–73, 183, 214–15, 227, 269–70; media contacts of, 99; Nationwide 21 lawsuit of, 36, 60, 68–75, 95–96, 122–23, 126, 176–82, 210–11, 217, 236, 281–87; programmatic rulings in cases brought by, 61; in settlement negotiations with mining industry, 114–15; Spruce Mine No. 1 case of, 96–100, 103–15, 121
low-sulfur coal, 67, 292
LTV Steel, 87, 89

Lundquist, Nethercutt & Griles, 124
Luttig, J. Michael, 119, 123, 177–81, 216, 286

Magnum Coal, 282–83
Mammoth Coal, 149, 151, 163, 272
Manchin, Joe, III, 137–38, 172, 185, 186, 214, 225, 263, 283, 284; Blankenship's lawsuit against, 145, 164, 268; Coal River Mountain Watch members and, 138–42, 222–23, 270–72; mine safety actions taken by, 201, 202
Marfork Coal Company, 31, 45–47, 196–97, 296
Marist Brothers, 81
Marsh Fork Elementary School, 57, 133–34, 139–43, 171–73, 183, 214, 219, 225, 228, 268–70, 296; boundary line between Goals Coal and, 143–44, 227; Byrd and, 232–33, 271; campaign to raise money to build replacement for, see Pennies of Promise campaign; chronic illnesses of children attending, 57–58, 129–30, 134, 166, 168, 232; inspections of, 142, 143, 164, 172, 220–22, 233; Manchin's promises about, 139–42; protest marches in front of, 136, 167, 168; Thompson's class action lawsuit on behalf of students at, 219–20
Marshall University, 155, 220, 221
Martin County disaster, 49–50
Maryland, University of, 239; Center for Environmental Science, 244
Massey, Antonio, 33
Massey, E. Morgan, 31, 33–34, 67, 154
"Massey Doctrine," 32–33
Massey Energy (originally A. T. Massey & Company), 19–22, 59, 94, 154, 178, 284, 291, 295–97; accidents at facilities of, 157–58, 200–203, 263–64; Army Corps of Engineers permit applications of, 16–18, 74, 114, 211–15, 236–37, 239–41,

252–57, 259, 276–81; Blankenship hired by, 32, 155–56; Blankenship's compensation package from, 35, 137, 152, 194, 204–205, 209, 265, 267; citations for violations issued against, 34, 51–56, 77–78, 86, 183–84, 195, 265–66; class action lawsuits against, 54, 219–22, 234–35; Coal River Mountain Watch and, 36–39, 50, 51, 135–37, 164–65, 167, 168, 224; company culture of, 21; company picnics of, 76–77, 188; corporate headquarters of, 17, 20; Department of Environmental Protection accused of bias against, 145; economic justification for mountaintop mining of, 8–9; employment practices of, 21–23, 29, 159–60, 189, 266–67; Environmental Protection Agency lawsuit against, 288–90; flooding caused by, 38–39; growth of, 20–21; Harman Mining breach-of-contract lawsuit against, 87–92, 184, 187–88, 273–75; houses bought and demolished by, 46–48, 295–96; impoundments built by, 45–46, 50; injection of slurry into abandoned mines proposed by, 12–13; libel suits filed by, 162–63, 268; low-sulfur coal reserves of, 67; net income of, 35, 189, 192, 265; personal injury lawsuits against, 157–59; Redhat Training Program of, 266–67; settlement of Department of Environmental Protection lawsuits against, 193–96; shareholder lawsuit against, 193–94, 203; stockholders' uprising against, 189–90, 192–93, 203–209, 265, 267, 290; Surface Mine Board appeals of, 170, 171, 227; subsidiaries of, 17, 20, 22, 32–33, 53, 57, 74, 195 (see also Elk Run Coal Company; Goals Coal Company; Independence Coal Company; Montcoal; Rawl Sales); tortious interference lawsuit against, 90, 92–93; union busting by, 23–34, 44–45, 146, 148–49, 152, 193, 272; workers' compensation

lawsuits against, 22, 85, 86; wrongful death lawsuits against, 263–64
Matewan (West Virginia), 33
May, Deborah K., 196–99
Maynard, Elliott E. "Spike," 94, 234, 274
McAteer, Davitt, 169–70, 202, 228–29, 232
McCain-Feingold Bipartisan Campaign Reform Act (2002), 83
McCloy, Randal, Jr., 200
McCoy clan, 152
McDaniel, Perry, 290
McGinley, Patrick, 100, 106, 109
McGraw, Dan, 83
McGraw, Darrell, 84, 93
McGraw, Warren, 77–86, 93–94, 137, 163, 184–85, 187, 268, 274
McKinney, Doug, 264–65
McLusky, Bob, 54, 74, 170, 259–60, 276–77, 282; communications between Manchin and Department of Environmental Protection requested by, 172; on defense team for Lovett's lawsuit against Army Corps, 212–13, 236, 238, 239, 241–45, 254, 256, 280; Department of Environmental Protection ruling on Goals Coal silo appealed by, 268–69; and Green Valley, 12–13, 17, 59–60, 62, 277, 293; Massey Energy defended against Thompson's lawsuit by, 220; and Spruce Mine No. 1, 259–60, 280–81; settlement of Department of Environmental Protection lawsuits against Massey Energy negotiated by, 194; at Surface Mine Board hearing, 214
Medicaid, 162
Melville, Herman, 191
mercury contamination, 174–75
metallurgical coal, high-grade, 87
Michael, M. Blane, 182
Michael, Tom, 171, 172, 269
Milberg, Weiss, Bershad, Hynes & Lerch, 193–94
Miller, Carol, 264
Miller, Mary, 54, 136

mineral rights, purchase of, 131, 297
Mine Safety and Health Administration (MSHA), 156–57, 168, 169, 200–202, 228, 264
minimal adverse impacts, determination of, 69–70, 72, 108, 179–81
mitigation, see stream mitigation
Monk, Thelonius, 100
Montcoal, 22–23, 44, 130, 132, 159
Moore, Dan, 206
Morgan, John, 110
Morris, Cynthia, 237–38
Motz, Diana Gribbon, 182
mountain culture, 8
Mountain Justice Summer, 135, 136, 164–66, 172, 270
Mountain State Justice, 97, 100, 103, 109
Mount Olive Correctional Facility, 64, 65
Moussaoui, Zacarias, 286
Mullins, Lucile Virginia, 251–52

Nader's Raiders, 169
Naoma (West Virginia), 164–66
National Environmental Policy Act (NEPA; 1969), 15, 102, 211–12, 237, 257, 278
National Labor Relations Board (NLRB), 272
National Mining Association (NMA), 121
National Parks Conservation Association, 173
National Public Radio, 99
National Resources Defense Council, 68
National Rifle Association, 93
National Security Agency, 205
nationwide permits, minimal adverse impact standard for, 69–70, 179
Nationwide 21 permits, 15, 36, 67–71, 95–96, 126, 176, 178–82, 210–11, 237, 285; for Apogee Coal, 282–84; Environmental Impact Statement for, 104, 107, 123, 178–79, 211; Goodwin's

Nationwide 21 permits (*continued*)
rulings on, 71–75, 95, 182, 211,
281–88; for Green Valley waste site,
15–18, 60–62, 69, 105; moratorium
on, 217; for Spruce Mine No. 1, 100,
107–108, 114, 115, 259
Native Americans, 8
natural gas, 66, 173
Navy, U.S., 205
Nease, Janice, 195
Neely, Richard, 184
New Source Review, 118, 119
New York Times, 285
New York University School of Law,
Brennan Center for Justice, 85
Niemeyer, Paul V., 119, 123, 177–81, 287
nitrogen oxides, 66
Nixon, Richard M., 118, 294
Norfolk and Western Railroad, 153–54
North Rum mine, 283
Norton, Gale, 119

O'Connor, Sandra Day, 177
Office of Surface Mining (OSM), U.S.,
120, 125, 143, 285
Ohio Valley Environmental Coalition
(OVEC), 49, 55, 177–82, 225, 237,
239, 270, 283, 288
oil, 173; carbon dioxide produced by
burning, 66; drilling for, on federal
lands, 126; price of, 44, 66
oil spills, 49–50, 288
Omar Mining Company, 194
open-pit mining, 9, 63, 292

Palmer, Margaret, 244–46
Parker, Charlie, 100
Peabody Energy Corporation, 9, 23, 34,
44, 132, 152, 204
Pennies of Promise campaign, 222–24
Pennsylvanian Period, 40
Performance Coal Company, 130
Petre, Absalom, 130–31
Petre, Burwell, 131
Pettry, Corey, 129, 234

Pettry, Jacob, 129
Pettry, Kenny, 129
Pettry, Sherry, 129, 234–35
Pettry, Tyler, 129, 234
Pflugh, Doug, 239
Phillips, J. Dickson, Jr., 286
Pleistocene Age, 41
Polish immigrants, 41
pollutants, discharge of, 285, 288–89
power plants, coal-fired, 44, 66, 67, 119,
147, 174, 291–92; mercury contamination from, 174–75
prep plants, 5, 11, 54, 130; conveyor
belts from mining sites to, 63; for
metallurgical steel, 87; transport of
coal from, 65; *see also* Elk Run Coal
Company; Goals Coal Company;
Montcoal
Presley, Elvis, 205
programmatic rulings, 61
public-interest law, 17, 97, 109

Quinn, Hal, 121

Raney, Bill, 63, 64, 72–73, 118, 123,
202, 285
Rank, Cindy, 103, 247, 258, 283
Rawl Sales, 32–34, 156, 218, 234
Ray, Belinda, 296, 297
Ray, Dell, 296–98
Reagan, Ronald, 119, 123, 142, 188
reclamation, 63–64, 206, 240; approximate original contour variances for,
102–103, 114–15; for commercial
development, 64–65, 115; of Dal-Tex
operation, 109–11; reforestation and,
240–42
Redhat Training Program, 266–67
Rehnquist, William, 177
Republic No. 2 mine, 213, 253
Republican party, 106, 113, 173–75,
186–88, 287, 294; Blankenship's
campaign contributions to, 262,
264–65; control of Congress by, 263;
in judicial elections, 78, 79, 83, 187;

in presidential elections, 67, 82, 93, 118–19
Republicans for Environmental Protection, 173
Roady, Steve, 236, 244–45, 287
Roberts, Cecil, 32, 151
Roberts, John, 177
Robertson, Dana, 104
Robinson & McElwee, 79
Rockefeller, Jay, 67, 82, 232
Roman Catholic Church, 81
Roosevelt, Franklin D., 33
Roosevelt, Theodore, 186, 294
Roosevelt, Theodore, IV, 173
Rosenstein, Barry, 190, 192, 209
Ross, Wilbur, 148, 163, 200
Rothschild Group, 148
Rowe, Jim, 78, 79, 81
Rowland, Samuel C., 131
Rowland Land Company, 131–32, 297

Sago mine disaster, 200–201, 223, 228
Salley, John Peter, 40
same-sex marriages, opposition to, 262
Sanderson, Dewey, 221
Sbrissa, Sister Joellen, 207–208
Scalia, Antonin, 177, 274
Schiffer, Lois, 104, 117
Scots immigrants, 41
scrubbers, 66, 67
Sears, Tony, 11–14, 16, 53, 114, 219
Securities and Exchange Commission (SEC), 189, 192, 203, 207
sediment ponds, 73–74, 98, 258; individual permits for, 212
segmentation, 18, 62, 114
Senate, U.S., 59, 117, 120, 175, 217, 264
September 11 terrorist attacks, 285
settling ponds, 284–85
Shawnees, 8
Shelton, Jerry, 22–27, 30, 44
Shumate's Branch (West Virginia), 130–33, 167, 295

silicosis, 221
silos, 127, 133, 136–37, 140–44, 164, 167, 171, 183, 213–15, 220, 221, 268–71
Simonton, Scott, 220–22
Sisters of St. Joseph, 207
Sixth Circuit, U.S. Court of Appeals, 126, 288
Slab Fork Coal, 87
slavery, 43, 57, 229
Smithers (West Virginia), 149–50, 161
"smokeless coal," 40
Snelling, Michael, 256–57
Southern District of West Virginia, U.S. District Court of, 105
Spadaro, Jack, 120, 142–43, 220
Spark, Clare L., 191
Sprouse, Randy, 48–50
Spruce Mine No. 1, 103–14, 217, 257–60, 280–81; Environmental Impact Statement for, 121, 258, 259, 280; Haden's ruling against, 111–12, 114; Nationwide 21 permit for, 100, 107–108, 115
Starcher, Larry, 77, 183, 187, 273–74
Starfire Coal Company, 148–49, 163
states' rights, 177
steel industry, 87, 148
Stern, Robert A. M., 192
Stockman, Vivian, 225, 239, 283
Stopover (Kentucky), 152–53
Stout, Ben, 110–11, 113
stream mitigation, 70–72, 216, 239, 252–56; Army Corps of Engineers standards for, 244–52, 279–80; for Camp Branch, 212; for Spruce Mine No. 1, 107–108
strip mining, 44–46, 97, 242
Sudol, Mark, 247–51
sulfur dioxide, 66, 119, 292
Superfund program, 125
Supreme Court, U.S., 72, 118, 126, 177, 274
Surface Mining Control and Reclamation Act (SMCRA; 1977), 102–103, 116, 120, 133, 214, 227, 232, 242, 268, 285

Swanson, Todd Q., 203, 207, 208, 265, 290
"Swift Boat" campaign, 82
Sylvester (West Virginia), 54, 132, 219

temporary restraining orders (TROs): against Camp Branch, 277, 280; against Green Valley Coal Company, 17, 18, 59–62, 69; against Spruce Mine No. 1, 105–108, 259; against Republic Mine No. 2, 213–14
Tennessee, 124, 185; mountaintop mining in, 7
Third Point LLC, 189–91, 206
Thomas, Clarence, 177
Thomas, Greg, 262
Thompson, Kevin, 218–20, 233–35
timbering, 38, 49, 131, 295; in national forests, 125, 173
Timmermeyer, Stephanie, 55, 139, 142–44, 164, 194
toxic waste, cleanups of, 125–26
Trial Lawyers for Public Justice, 17, 100, 103, 236
Twilight MTR Surface Mine, 202, 295
Twisted Gun Golf Course (Wharncliffe, West Virginia), 64, 65

U.S. News & World Report, 97
U.S. Open Tennis Tournament, 191–92
underground mines, 8, 21, 39, 40, 44, 97, 132; cost of surface mining versus, 9, 66–67, 293; beneath family cemeteries, 46; fatal accidents in, 200–201; health risks in, 221; impoundments built over, 50; injection of slurry into, 12–13, 218–19, 293; longwall, 23–31; history of, 40–43; shutting down of, 44–45
United Coal, 87–89, 92
United Mine Workers of America (UMWA), 23–33, 43–45, 132, 150, 152, 169, 188, 189; Blankenship's lawsuit against, 268; Coal River

Mountain Watch and former members of, 39, 48; environmental groups denounced by, 114, 283; Haden1 ruling opposed by, 117, 118; Harman Mining and, 87–89; Horizon Natural Resources and, 146–48, 151; National Labor Relations Board action against Massey brought by, 272; recruitment efforts of, 160
United Steelworkers, 148
Upper Big Branch mine, 23–31
USA Today, 163

valley fills, 15, 56, 63, 69, 96, 284, 287; Bush administration and, 122; Clean Water Act regulations on, 102; determination of minimal adverse impacts of, 179; Environmental Impact Statement on, 124; of Green Valley Coal Company, 15–16, 18; Goodwin's ruling on, 74–75; of Hobet Mining, 98, 113; individual permits for, 212–13, 237; mitigation of, see stream mitigation
Vanderbilt University, 206, 207
Vietnam War, 135, 149, 231
Virginia, 87, 124, 268; mountaintop mining in, 7, 288
Virginia, University of, 107
Virginia Polytechnic Institute and State University (Virginia Tech), 242, 254

Wagner, Rick, 22, 26–31
Wallace, J. Bruce, 243–44, 246, 254
Wal-Mart, mountaintop site for, 64
Warburg Pincus, 191
Ward, Ken, Jr., 99, 143–44, 195
Webb, Bo, 38, 39, 56, 142, 172, 225; Pennies of Promise campaign of, 222–24; protest marches led by, 135, 136, 164, 165, 168, 270; Manchin meets with, 139, 222–23; and Thompson's lawsuit against Massey Energy, 219–21

Webb, Joanne, 224

Weekley, Jim, 96–99, 103, 105, 109, 259

Weekley, Sibby, 98, 99, 103, 105, 109

Weise, Suzanne M., 106, 109

Welsh immigrants, 41

West Virginia Board of Education, 80, 223

West Virginia Coal Association, 63, 82, 118, 120, 202, 285

West Virginia Consumers for Justice, 268

West Virginia Department of Education, 172, 142

West Virginia Department of Environmental Protection (DEP), 50–51, 74, 139, 164, 219, 289; approximate original contour variances granted by, 109; Brushy Fork impoundment deemed safe by, 49; Crum as head of enforcement at, 51–56, 86, 135, 139, 171, 184; and Goals Coal silo and impoundment permits, 134, 140–45, 169, 170, 172, 214, 215, 227, 268–69; Green Valley waste site approved by, 18, 60; Office of Legal Services, 290; public meetings held by, 51; and Spruce No. 1 site clearing, 258–59; lawsuit brought by Lovett and Hecker against, 104, 106, 112, 116–17, 119, 125; violations issued against Massey by, 34, 86, 171, 193–96

West Virginia Environmental Quality Board, 220

West Virginia Health Safety and Training, 158

West Virginia Highlands Conservancy, 103, 288

West Virginia legislature, 37–39; blasting regulations passed by, 49; campaign contribution restrictions enacted by, 261–62; Democratic control of, 187, 264

West Virginia Organizing Project, 49

West Virginia Public Radio, 168

West Virginia Supreme Court of Appeals, 77–81, 86, 93, 94, 137, 183–84, 187, 195, 196, 273–75

West Virginia Surface Mine Board, 12–13, 53, 108, 170–72, 214–15, 227, 242, 268–69

West Virginia University, Institute of Technology (West Virginia Tech), 272

West Virginia Workers' Compensation Fund, 85

wetlands, loss of, 126, 173, 248

White, B. W., 40

White, Randy, 264

White House Council on Environmental Quality, 75

Whitesville (West Virginia), 5–6, 26, 39–40, 42, 56; closing of schools in, 128; Coal River Mountain Watch storefront in, 48, 135, 140

Whitman, Christine Todd, 119

Widener, H. Emory, Jr., 287

Wiley, Debbie, 230–32

Wiley, Ed, 133–34, 142, 172; Byrd meets with, 230–33, 271; Manchin meets with, 138–42, 164; Pennies of Promise campaign of, 222, 224; protest marches led by, 134–36, 270, 271; walks to Washington, 224–30, 234, 268

Wilkins, William W., Jr., 287

Williams, Freda, 48–50, 56, 195–96

Williams, Karen J., 119

Willis, Bolts, 150

Wise, Bob, 52

Wolfe, Roger, 108, 110, 112, 113

Wolfe, Thomas, 205

workers' compensation, 22, 29, 79–80, 85, 90, 96

World of Outlaws car racing series, 196

World War II, 42, 101, 176

Wyden, Ron, 120

Wyoming, open-pit mining in, 9

Youth Systems Services program, 81